THE MUSTANG ARCHIVES

SILK ROAD STUDIES XX

SILK ROAD STUDIES

XX

The Mustang Archives

Analysis of Handwritten Documents via the Study of Papermaking Traditions in Nepal

Agnieszka Helman-Ważny
and Charles Ramble

BREPOLS

Ancient Cultures Research Centre
Macquarie University
Sydney Nsw Australia

Silk Roads Studies (SRS)

SRS 1: *Uygur Buddhist Literature*, 1997
SRS 2: *Worlds of the Silk Roads: Ancient and Modern*, 1998
SRS 3: *Das nestorianische Christentum an den Handelswegen durch Kyrgystan bis zum 14. Jh*, 2000
SRS 4: *Realms of the Silk Roads: Ancient and Modern*, 2000
SRS 5: *De Dunhuang à Istanbul*, 2000
SRS 6: *Walls and Frontiers in Inner-Asian History*, 2003
SRS 7: *Nomads, Traders and Holy Men Along China's Silk Road*, 2003
SRS 8: *Iranica Selecta. Studies in Honour of Professor Wojciech Skalmowski on the Occasion of his Seventieth Birthday*, 2003
SRS 9: *Calling the Soul of the Dead*, 2005
SRS 10: *From Palmyra to Zayton: Epigraphy and Iconography*, 2005
SRS 12: *Art, Architecture and Religion Along the Silk Roads*, 2009
SRS 13: *Peace and Peril. Sima Qian's Portrayal of Han-Xiongnu Relations*, 2016
SRS 14: *The Yuezhi. Origin, Migration and the Conquest of Northern Bactria*, 2007
SRS 15: *The Old Uyghur Āgama fragments preserved in the Sven Hedin collection, Stockholm*, 2017
SRS 16: *Aspects of Research into Central Asian Buddhism*, 2008
SRS 17: *Die Erforschung des Tocharischen und die alttürkische Maitrisimit*, 2013
SRS 18: *Between Rome and China*, 2016
SRS 19: *Language, Society, and Religion in the World of the Turks. Festschrift for Larry Clark at Seventy-Five*, 2019

D/2021/0095/231
ISBN 978-2-503-58534-5

Printed in the E.U. on acid-free paper.

Contents

Acknowledgements

This book is a product of the project "The Mustang Archives: Analysis of Handwritten Documents via the Ethnographic Study of Papermaking Traditions in Nepal" directed by Agnieszka Helman-Ważny in the years 2015–19. The research was funded by the Deutsche Forschungsgemeinschaft (DFG, German Research Foundation, project no. HE 7116/2–1 and HE 7116/2–2). The research was conducted within the scope of the Centre for the Study of Manuscript Cultures (CSMC) at the University of Hamburg. This task was combined with research carried out within the ANR/DFG programme "The Social History of Tibetan Societies 17th to 20th centuries" (SHTS) directed by Charles Ramble and Peter Schwieger, from 2012 to 2016, and subsequently continuing in the framework of a follow-on project, "Social Status in the Tibetan World" (TIBSTAT, 2016–20).

The authors would like to thank and acknowledge the work and help of our field assistants Nyima Drandul, Kemi Tsewang, and Rinchen Loden Lama. We also thank Mengling Cai for her work on the laboratory fibre analyses, as well as Bob France for reading sections of the book and offering useful advice on English-language matters. We are grateful for the support of the Centre for the Study of Manuscript Cultures (CSMC) at the University of Hamburg. Unless stated otherwise, copyright for all images used in this work belong to the authors and the Mustang Archives Project.

List of Illustrations

INTRODUCTION

The physical aspects of Tibetan books have received some attention in recent years, but documents from Tibetan archives have yet to be scrutinised. Since the study of dated Tibetan documents of known provenance offers a rare opportunity to create solid references for further study of unidentified books and documents from the same region, this study is the first to focus on a selection of locally-produced documents from certain private and community archives in Mustang, mostly dated to a specific year within the last two centuries. Mustang is located in the northern highlands of west-central Nepal at the edge of the Tibetan Plateau. Many private houses and communities there possess substantial archives which became the source material for the project "The Mustang Archives: Analysis of Handwritten Documents via the Ethnographic Study of Papermaking Traditions in Nepal" (2015–19) funded by the Deutsche Forschungsgemeinschaft (DFG) and led by Agnieszka Helman-Ważny in collaboration with Charles Ramble, the authors of this book. The project was the first study to seek to characterise the material make-up of the documents studied together with other codicological aspects of these collections, with a view to enhancing our knowledge of the rich and diverse repository of paper in the form of local documents and manuscripts.

Although a number of researchers, including Alexander Macdonald, Tadeusz Skorupski and Michael Vinding, had previously photographed or transcribed selected archives in Mustang, notably in the villages of Panchgaon, extensive photographic documentation of such materials began only in 1986 with a project dedicated to the history of Mustang conducted by the Centre for Nepal and Asian Studies of Nepal's Tribhuvan University. Only a small proportion of the documents collected was published, but the project did lead to at least one book, Ramesh Dhungel's *The History of Lo (Mustang)*.[1] While this work made use mainly of Nepali-language materials, the photographic collection and study of Tibetan-language archives received a significant stimulus from Dieter Schuh and Christoph Cüppers, who made several visits to the area in the 1980s and photographed a number of collections in the Muktinath Valley and adjacent areas. The photographing of the archives was further intensified under the Deutsche Forschungsgemeinschaft (DFG)-funded Nepal-German Project on High Mountain Archaeology (NGPHMA), which ran from 1992 to 1997 under the leadership of Dieter Schuh (Fig. 1). During this period more than twenty community archives were photographed (over 3000 local documents), leading to several book-length publications and numerous articles. In spite of the large volume of material thus collected, the researchers were concerned exclusively with the content of the documents that were photographed. 35 mm monochrome film was used; very little attention was given to codicological aspects of the documents, and none at all to the paper on which they were written. The study of these features required revisiting a selection of these archives, photographing them again, this time digitally, and subjecting them to the detailed examination described in Chapter 5 of this book. The first publication to combine the study of content and material was a lengthy article based on a study of the archives of Tshognam.[2] Not all the documents on which this study was based were previously known. Several hundred items had been photographed in Geling in 1993, but in the course of a visit to the village in 2016 we were given access to a trunk, kept in the same house, containing a further 172 documents previously unseen by researchers.

Fig. 1. Photographing the folded documents in the community archives of Te, South Mustang, in 1993. Photograph by Charles Ramble.

Work on the manuscript collections in Mustang was also carried out under the aegis of the Franco-German project "The Social History of Tibetan Societies, 17th to the 20th Centuries" (henceforth SHTS) led by Charles Ramble and Peter Schwieger, between 2012 and 2016. Research on these archives later continued within the framework of a follow-on project, "Social Status in Tibetan Societies" (TIBSTAT, 2016–2020). The aim of these two projects was to carry out research on the social history of Tibetan societies over a period corresponding to the duration of the Ganden Phodrang government in Tibet (1642–1959). In both phases the members of the research teams addressed issues such as the nature of legal, fiscal and administrative relations among the various centres and peripheries in the region; whether it was correct to characterise Tibet as a feudal society; the social rôle of clerics and nobles, farmers, nomads, craftsmen and traders; the organisation of civil society; strategies of dispute resolution and the numerous legal systems that prevailed in different areas.

During the course of the present project, the most recent of such projects, four expeditions to Lower and Upper Mustang were conducted between 2015 and 2018. While the first expedition was interrupted by an earthquake on 25 April 2015, the later trips were exceptionally fruitful in gaining access to selected documents in targeted archives in Mustang. The authors, together with three local assistants, Nyima Drandul, Kemi Tsewang and Rinchen Loden Lama, visited Tshognam, Geling, Dzar, and Lubrak. Each place was mapped with GPS, and the locations are given on the map below (Fig. 2). The documents we saw were preserved in wooden or metal boxes, baskets or bags as loose assemblages of folded sheets of paper (Figs 3–7). To gain access to previously selected documents in the archives visited we needed to seek the permission of the village community, and these boxes had to be opened in the presence of community representatives.

As well as being an important source of information regarding the reconstruction of Mustang's social history, documents are an extremely valuable source of knowledge concerning

Fig. 2. Location of the collections studied in the course of the Mustang Archives project. Map drawn by Dorota Helman.

Fig. 3. Metal boxes used for storing the archival documents in Lubrak village. Photograph by Agnieszka Helman-Ważny.

Fig. 4. Lubrak community opening the boxes in which documents are kept. Photograph by Agnieszka Helman-Ważny.

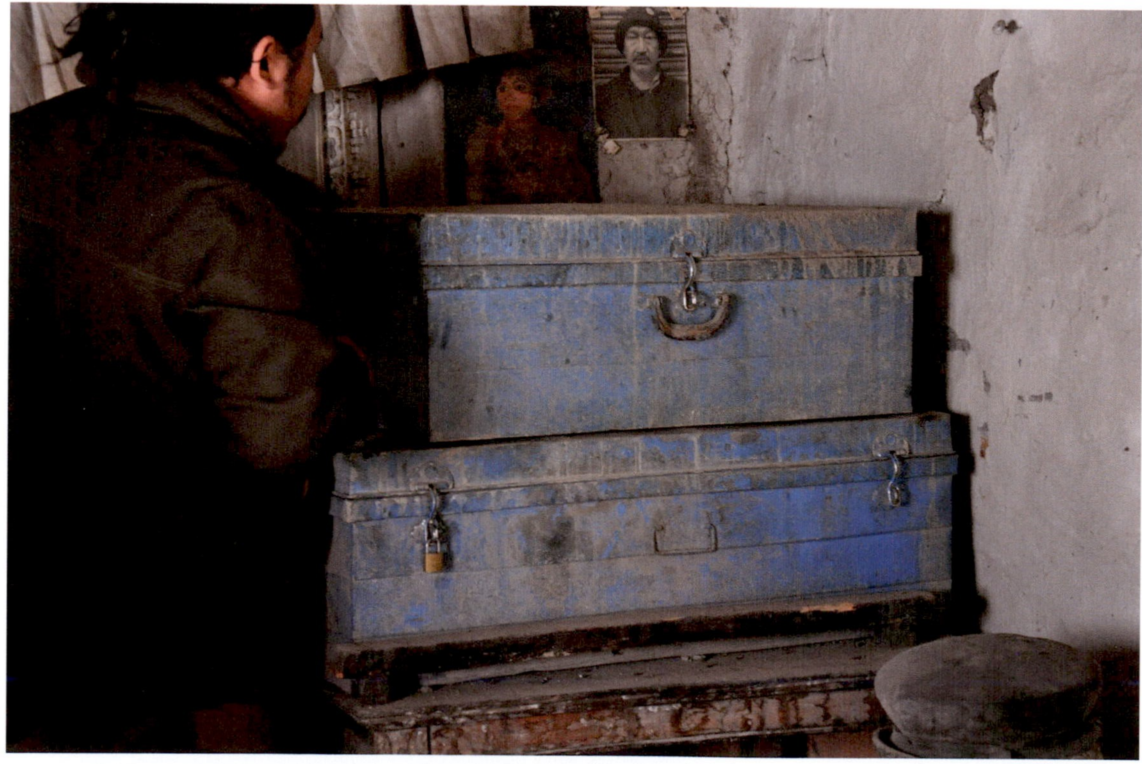

Fig. 5. The boxes in which the Lower Tshognam documents are kept. Photograph by Agnieszka Helman-Ważny.

Fig. 6. The community of Tshug opening boxes of documents at a meeting during which they gave the authors permission to study the collection. Photograph by Agnieszka Helman-Ważny.

Fig. 7. Documents from the Lower Tshognam archive taken out of the basket where they were kept by their owner. Photograph by Agnieszka Helman-Ważny.

local papermaking and book-production. It is their physical material together with their content that provide information essential in tracing the past and clarifying, among other things, the economic factors that shaped their production. The fact that the archival component of the material to be examined was also produced within the last two centuries makes it possible to link data from the material study of documents with ethnographic findings. The latter were obtained by interviewing people who know about the craftsmanship of bookmaking and the tradition of papermaking. Most of the documents also contained exact dates of when they were written. This helped to give a chronological context to our observations on paper and other material features.

In the case of the analyses of paper from unidentified books or documents, the core problem is that we lack chronological references for the materials used in particular regions that might enable us to interpret the results of analyses of materials in a wider context. For this reason, the corpus of documents studied was catalogued and translated. By identifying the fibre composition and studying variations in production methods, raw materials, and treatment of the paper surface in dated documents, it was possible to better understand the technologies involved. The identification and classification of varieties of old Tibetan paper became much easier thanks to knowledge about papermaking tools and terminology.

Thus, besides textual content and social history, this book deals with the physical aspects of the production, use and preservation of the documents. The unique characteristics of the documents examined have allowed us to present a new methodology that may be applied to studies and conservation of Tibetan archival documents and manuscripts. Fibre analysis of papers unleashes the potential to understand the history of papermaking in Mustang, and the history of the trade and distribution of books and documents along the Silk Roads.

The task of cataloguing, photographing, protecting and publishing these documents enhances our understanding of local history and archaeology, and the significance of this region in the wider context of the ancient world. The texts may also reflect ideas that underpin current religious and cultural traditions in this region and enhance regional pride and respect for the indigenous archaeological heritage. At the same time, the information derived from documents creates a primary source of knowledge that is entirely independent of social and political considerations.

Chapter 1 (*Methods: A cross-disciplinary approach*) proposes an interdisciplinary model for the study of documents that combines the analysis of materials that make up these objects with a study of the methods of their production. The model brings together different disciplines of science, history and Tibetan studies, shedding light on the wide range of information contained in these documents. The chapter addresses the specificity of materials and the region, and merges codicological, textual and ethnographic methods for the documentation of papermaking traditions. This section concludes with practical guidelines, such as the template for the description of documents, the selection of relevant features and those most useful for the typology, and a comprehensive compendium of methods for material and codicological research, making it possible to establish connections between various documents. The chapter concludes with a detailed methodology for the study of paper, discussing approaches and paper typology, including the variety of raw materials used and their microscopic features.

Chapter 2 (*The archives in a regional and historical context*) provides a general overview of the history of Mustang and its status in the nation of Nepal. The early history of the Kingdom of Lo, which was founded in the fourteenth century, is reasonably well known thanks to a number of studies based on biographical and other historical sources. Since the earliest document considered in this work dates from the seventeenth century, however, rather than retrace this ground we shall concentrate instead on the local history of the area and the period in which they were produced. Whereas the existing historical accounts of Mustang have tended to focus on the lives and activities of major religious figures and on political events, for the sake of consistency with the content of the documents considered here the emphasis will rather be on local economic issues and inter-community relations. The chapter also provides a brief outline of the system of social stratification in Mustang, since this is reflected in the structure and content of the archives.

Chapter 3 (*Archival documents as a part of the tangible cultural heritage of Mustang*) provides a context for Tibetan archival documents as objects of the tangible cultural heritage of Mustang. The discipline of paper conservation has not yet been developed in Mustang, or even in Nepal or Tibet. Over the last twenty years, conservation of Tibetan thangka paintings, sculptures, and elements of architecture has developed. Various projects on the restoration of architecture and paintings in Tibetan monasteries have been conducted by Westerners. In some of these projects, conflicts have arisen between the Western code of conservation and the expectations and ambitions of local communities, who simply wished to have copies of old objects made. Like Tibetans, the people of Mustang have no tradition of preserving their material heritage in a way that includes all the material components. In practice they understand conservation as the replacement of an old object with a new one. In effect, then, the number of original objects is constantly dwindling. With the replacement of original books and documents and the copying of wall paintings, a great deal of historical and scholarly information is lost forever. In the case of archival documents there is often little sense of their historical and cultural value, or even any kind of initiative to preserve these documents. Despite the dry climate of Mustang which favours their survival, many documents are in a poor condition. This chapter offers an insight into the full range of problems related to the preservation of archival documents in their natural environment. It presents the status and condition of particular archival collections and describes a range of the typical kinds of damage they might suffer, as exemplified by the half-burned documents from Gyaga resulting from a fire in the building where they were kept, or discarded parts of the collection from Geling. Possible approaches to the preservation and protection of these documents are discussed, with the aim of building awareness and support for the local communities who are the owners of these documents.

Chapter 4 (*The Mustang Archives: where they are kept and what they are about*) provides a general overview of the content of the archives examined here in the context of the places they are stored. Private households and most communities in Mustang, especially in the south, possess archives of documents dealing with a wide range of mainly secular affairs. Where religion features in these documents, it is usually in relation to the financial or organisational aspects of religious ceremonies.

One of the collections – that of Lubrak – is a community archive in a strict sense, to the extent that it is kept in a public building in the care of village officials and may be opened only in the presence of representatives from each household. The other four are kept in private households, but many of the documents in these collections deal with public matters. In addition to their ritual functions, the lamas of Tshognam were the scribes and clerics for the adjacent communities, and retained copies of transactions between their clients. The Dzar collection is kept in a house belong to an important noble family, and is a similar mixture of private and public items. Geling, located between Baragaon and the Kingdom of Lo, was a political entity in its own right. From the early nineteenth century, however, the hereditary headmanship lay with a family originally from Lubrak that was appointed to this position by the king. This archive, too, contains both public and private documents, but exhibits much closer links to the royal court of Lo Monthang than do the others.

Chapter 5 (A *codicological study of the documents*) focuses on the codicological features of the documents. Most documents in the Mustang archives belong to the category known as *gan rgya*, a term that may be translated as "contract", "covenant" or "written obligation" according to the context. In view of the wide-ranging application of the *gan rgya* genre, the documents under consideration are classified in ad hoc categories based on their actual function and the identities of the parties involved. Private archives typically consist of documents such as contracts for loans of grain or cash, sales of land, wills, disputes over ownership and inheritance of property. Community archives may be classified according to various criteria, but broadly fall into two categories: documents relating to internal affairs and those concerned with dealings with outsiders. The former includes records of community gatherings, rules for local natural resource management, such as forests, water and grazing, disputes between fellow-villagers that were mediated by the community, and annual grain taxes to the communal fund. The latter may include pasture boundary agreements with neighbours, and directives or other correspondence from political authorities such as the King of Lo or the Government of Nepal. This chapter presents our general typology of documents arranged according to particular codicological features such as format and layout, script and scribal hands (grouping documents written by the same person), seals, fingerprints and paper. Through their codicological features and the materials they consist of, the preserved documents illuminate the meaning and the use of the written word in past societies.

Chapter 6 (*Papermaking traditions in Nepal: the spread of technological knowledge in Central Asia*) presents a wider view of the history of the Tibetan papermaking technology adopted in Nepal, together with the innovation and dissemination of papermaking knowledge throughout the Himalayas. It aims to integrate an understanding of technologies with the historical development and spread of social and cultural practices, and the potential for mapping the papermaking workshops and areas known for paper production in Nepal. The high altitude of the Himalaya, combined with its climatic extremes, makes the local vegetation distinctive in comparison with all other areas of Asia. The specificity of Tibetan papermaking lies in the properties of the native plants, the living conditions of those dwelling on the world's highest plateau, and aspects of their culture that combine to create a distinctive craft. The connections between Tibet and other Himalayan regions through corridors such as the Mustang-Kali Gandaki Valley and the Kyirong-Rasuwa Valley have facilitated the development of distinctive paper- and bookmaking craftsmanship in the region. In this chapter, we look especially at possible pathways through which the papermaking technology could have been brought to Mustang. We explore history, trade, modes of production, and the transfer of papermaking technologies across the Himalayas, and the way tradition interacts with natural resources, climatic conditions and how the spread of paper is connected to trade in the region.

Chapter 7 (*Mustang paper: A glimpse into the economic history of paper production in Western Nepal*) presents the first attempt at a reconstruction of the history of paper in Mustang between the eighteenth and twentieth centuries from two main bodies of information that support each other in the face of a complete lack of written sources on this subject: first, the documents themselves, dated by examining fragments, identifying the paper and fibre components, and reconstructing the history of papermaking from the findings; and secondly, the living traditions of papermaking that persists in various areas of Nepal, and that are potentially related to traditions in Mustang. We attempt to relate the results of the examination of the paper features to the living tradition of papermaking in Mustang and neighbouring areas, and support this study with information collected from interviews. The questions that arise from the recorded raw materials described in the previous chapter concern the provenance of particular types of paper: the type of paper locally produced in villages where archives were established, and the kinds traded from greater distances. The best way of differentiating among papers in books and artworks is by the systematic study of the plants used in their production, along with other features useful for typology. We thus describe properties, distribution and the usage of papermaking plants in Nepal. Since documents were in constant circulation, in relation to the complex networks of their producers and users, we address questions concerning trade routes, trading posts and the possible location of papermaking workshops.

A note on transcription

As a general rule, Tibetan words will be italicised and presented in Wylie orthographic transliteration. In certain cases, notably to avoid ambiguity, Tibetan words will be preceded by "Tib.", while terms in Nepali will be preceded by "Nep." Names of people and places will be given in roughly phonetic form, though in certain cases the Wylie orthography will also be provided.

Chapter 1
Methods:
A Cross-Disciplinary Approach

Codicological examination of the documents studied

Despite the previous assumption that many northern settlements in Mustang appear to have no significant collections of documents, we were able to gain access to 330 new documents.[1] In the past, political authority was concentrated in the figure of the King of Mustang, and it is certain that many documents concerning the different communities in the former kingdom are kept in the royal palace of Lo Monthang, the capital. At the time of writing, no study of this collection has yet been published. As well as the palace's own archival collection, many private and community archives still exist in Upper Mustang. During our fieldwork we also gained access to some of the collections of documents that had not been photographed in the 1990s. We were allowed to study altogether 330 documents, including 50 documents from Upper Tshognam, 20 from Lower Tshognam, 172 from Geling, 82 from Lubrak, and 40 from Dzar. Nearly all these documents are dated: while the majority are from between the mid-nineteenth and the mid-twentieth centuries, a few are from the early eighteenth century.

The fact that the original documents were not clearly numbered during the photographing process in the 1990s complicated our present work; documents pre-identified from the catalogues or the photographs taken by Charles Ramble in the 1990s had to be sought out again among the hundreds of loosely-stored papers (Fig. 8). Furthermore, despite the help of Nyima Drandul, Kemi Tsewang and local authorities, some catalogued documents were no longer to be found 20 years after they had been photographed. It is impossible to verify whether these are damaged, permanently lost, or just temporarily misplaced.

Fig. 8. Nyima Drandul and Charles Ramble examining documents from Geling in April 2016. Photograph by Agnieszka Helman-Ważny.

[1] Ramble 2018: 112.

Of the 330 documents, only those from Tshognam had been previously catalogued, but the rest of the material had to be identified and translated during this project. Documents were organised into categories according to function and codicological features, then read, summarised and checked for dates, names of places, scribes and other parties concerned. A methodology for identifying scribal hands, imaging seals and matching fingerprints developed gradually. Grouping documents on the basis of these codicological features has enabled us to create some typologies and allowed us to look at those archives in various combinations.

As the documents were studied in the specific environment of Mustang, the methods of analysis had to be carefully considered. The most important work was thus completed *in situ*, so that documents were never moved from their original location. Working in a region where solar generated electricity is available only in a few places and the interiors are unheated, we were often left with only our creativity, a clear idea of what we wanted to do, and a good sense of humour to help us overcome all these difficulties. The effectiveness of our work was often dependent on the light, temperature, solar energy, and wind which made our work impossible when it precluded the opening of packages with loose sheets of paper, which would very easily blow away. It was also often too dark to work inside even in the middle of the day, challenging us to use Mustang's natural high-contrast light for adequate photographing of the documents.

Approximately 30 images were taken of each document. These included images of full recto and verso, Dino-Lite digital microscopic documentation of paper texture, microscopic images of the fibres that made up the paper and close-ups of authentication marks and fragments of text showing particular letters for comparative studies of script. Between 10 and 15 images were then selected for each document and recorded in three different formats: tiff, jpeg and png. In order to achieve a visual overview, posters with all those images for each archive separately were prepared using InDesign (Appendix 1). All data were also entered into the repository of the Centre for the Study of Manuscript Cultures (CSMC) and are accessible via the CSMC website.

Data derived from each document were recorded according to the codicological template developed by Agnieszka Helman-Ważny and organised in tables to facilitate comparative examination.[2] The template (Appendix 2) is explained below. It has been organised into six sections: general information, writing, format and layout, authentication marks, paper and ink. Each section is described below. Tables 1–4 are in Appendix 3.

General information

Collection/Accession N°: In general, this is the number under which a document is catalogued within an archive and is the designation by which the document is known. Some of the documents from Mustang in our sample were photographed in black and white in the context of the Nepal-German Project on High Mountain Archaeology (NGPHMA). Studies of these archives that have been published identify the documents using the prefixed abbreviation HMA, followed by the location of the collection (for example UTshognam for Upper Tshognam), then Tib for Tibetan, and finally the number of the document. Since some of these archives were photographed again – digitally – in the context of the present project, the numbers have been retained but the prefix has been changed from HMA to MA (for the "Mustang Archives" project). In the case of documents from Geling, Lubrak and Dzar which have not previously been photographed, we used the same scheme. For example, in MA/Geling/Tib/1, MA (Mustang Archives) is followed by Geling, the location of the Archive, then Tib, signifying the language of the document, but here 1 denotes that it was the first to be photographed. In other cases Lubrak denotes the Lubrak archive, and Dzar the Dzar archive; the principle of numbering in these two cases is the same as that for Geling insofar as the numbers represent the order of documentation, not chronological sequence. A number of other documents used here were photographed in colour within the framework of the Franco-German project "Social History of Tibetan Societies, 17th to 20th Centuries," which ran from 2011 to 2016. These documents bear the prefix SH, for "Social History."

[2] Helman-Ważny 2014; Dotson and Helman-Ważny 2016.

Date of access: This indicates the date the document was accessed and photographed *in situ* in Mustang.

Archive location (village): This indicates the place in which the evidence of the document is preserved. In this case it is usually the name of the village in which the document was found at the time it was described. We thus have Upper Tshognam, Lower Tshognam, Geling, Lubrak, and Dzar.

Category of the text: This consists of a short description of the type of text. Possible categories of text in private archives will be, for example, contracts for loans of grain or cash, sales of land, wills, letters or disputes over ownership and the inheritance of property. In community archives these will broadly fall into two categories: documents relating to internal affairs and those concerned with dealings with outsiders.

Title: Here we may note the title if the document has one, or furnish a title for future reference.

Date based on the text: Archival documents often include a date written in the body of a document, which denotes when the document was created (a legal requirement when the date validates the contract, or a customary indication of when the letter was written). This date is usually given, however, according to the Tibetan calendar, which still does not allow for precise dating. The basis for the Tibetan calendar is the Kālacakra Tantra, an Indian system that was translated from Sanskrit into Tibetan in the eleventh century. The calendar became standard in Tibet during the second half of the thirteenth century. The Tibetan calendar and dating system are based on a cycle of 60 Tibetan years, each of which generally has 354 days (12 cycles of the phases of the Moon).[3] Adjustment to the solar year of about 365 days is made by intercalation of an extra month every three years. A Tibetan year is properly identified by three things: the first two, the animal and element and the third the particular 60-year cycle (Tib. *rab byung*), the first of which began in 1027 CE. We are currently in the 17th cycle which began on 28 February 1987. Unfortunately, the date given in a document does not always include all three of these designations. Often only the animal and element are explicitly mentioned, and sometimes the element is omitted. If it is possible to ascertain the author's dates to within a century on the basis of other sources, then it is possible to know the cycle. This should give us an exact date. Otherwise, we have several dates each 60 years apart.[4]

Date based on analyses of materials: At present, the potential for finding "fingerprints" suggesting the provenance of materials is promising, but depending on type of object and the period this is not always straightforward. From the point of view of scholarship, knowledge of materials and technology helps in the dating of manuscripts, since some of the materials and some of the technologies were used only in particular regions and during specific periods. In the case of Mustang documents, however, which were locally produced and for the most part dated to the year in the text, there is no urgent need to confirm dates by material analyses. We decided nonetheless to carry out paper analyses to learn more about documents produced in Mustang and to reconstruct the history of papermaking in the region. It also helps to build references for future work. We also performed ^{14}C dating for a small group of documents that were undated or in which the date was unclear. Radiocarbon dating is applicable to documents and manuscripts composed of organic materials using milligram-size samples. It is an independent, objective, and the only truly quantitative method for dating organic materials. As many scholars have pointed out, however, this technique alone is rarely able to resolve issues of authenticity or provide precise dating. Depending on the time period, the degree of accuracy can vary between as much as 50 and 300 years. Typically, there may be an error of $\pm$ 30 years on an uncalibrated date, which is then usually calibrated to obtain a date in calendar years with a similar error. Additionally, ^{14}C analysis provides the date when the plant cellulose molecules in the paper's fibres were formed rather than when the paper was made, and the paper-making process will sometimes entail blending fibres from a wide variety

[3] For information on the calculations of the Tibetan calendar using modern mathematical notations instead of the traditional methods, see: Janson 2014.

[4] For information on the Tibetan calendar and astrology see especially Schuh 1973; Cornu 1997: 49–77.

of original sources and possibly different times. Furthermore, other substances such as dyes or fillers may have been added during the paper-making process, and these may contaminate samples with the stable C12 isotope ("dead carbon"). This makes results of radiocarbon dating moot in the case of single samples. And from a conservationist viewpoint, large scale sampling from old manuscripts or documents is questionable and should be avoided if possible. For this study, radiocarbon analysis was used only as a control method. ^{14}C dates compared to dates from the text show the way the dating of material corresponds with the date of the written text. This may shed some light on the habits of scribes and the usage and storage of newly made paper for archival purposes in Mustang.

Writing

Language: This refers to the main language in which the text of the document is written. In our sample most documents were written in Tibetan, but a few documents in Nepali were included in special cases.

Script: Most Tibetan scripts fall into one of two main categories: "headed" (Tib. *dbu can*) and "headless" (Tib. *dbu med*) (Fig. 9). The headless category includes a wide variety of styles, ranging from clearly formed, unconnected letters to a fluid hand, called 'khyug, that can properly be described as cursive. Tibetan has names to describe numerous sub-categories of headless script, depending on features such as the length of the descenders, the form of the vowels and so forth. In the majority of cases the headless scripts in the documents under consideration may be classified as *'khyug*, *tshugs*, or *'khyug ma tshugs* (a script that exhibits features of both, and abbreviated here as *kmt*), though a few examples of other scripts, such as *'bru tsha*, do appear (see chapter 5).

dbu can	dbu med	Latin	dbu can	dbu med	Latin	dbu can	dbu med	Latin
ཀ		ka	ཨ		a	གྷ		gha
ཅ		ca	ག		ga	ཌ		ḍa
ཏ		ta	ཇ		ja	དྷ		dha
པ		pa	ད		da	བྷ		bha
ཙ		tsa	བ		ba	ཇྷ		jha
ཞ		zha	ཛ		dza	ཥ		ṣa
ར		ra	འ		'a	ཀྵ		kṣa
ཧ		ha	ཤ		sha	ཊ		ṭa
ཁ		kha	ང		nga	ཋ		ṭha
ཆ		cha	ཉ		nya	ཎ		ṇa
ཐ		tha	ན		na			
ཕ		pha	མ		ma			
ཚ		tsha	ཝ		wa			
ཟ		za	ཡ		ya			
ལ		la	ས		sa			

Fig. 9. Tibetan "headed" *dbu can* with horizontal lines along the tops of many letters and "headless" *dbu med* scripts without these lines. Image by Goran tek-en, CC BY-SA 4.0, https://commons.wikimedia.org/w/index.php?curid = 66153789

Number of scribal hands: In recent years scholars have made some attempts at analysing handwriting styles in Tibetan manuscripts.[5] Handwriting, understood as the extension of the scribe's personality defined by extraordinarily detailed individual features, can help us to attribute manuscripts to specific scribes and consequently group them in ways that would otherwise have been unjustifiable or even unimaginable. The average person may recognise the handwriting of an individual and differentiate between individuals to some degree, but only the broader features of the handwriting, such as letter-formation, letter-size and slope of the handwriting are observed in such cases.[6] Such an approach fails, however, to take into account the subtleties in the writing that may distinguish one hand from other very similar hands. More advanced forensic identification may follow in cases of historical importance.

The Mustang archives afford a rare opportunity to test the extent to which we can or cannot identify the same scribal hands. Most of these documents were produced by a small community of local scribes using a very narrow selection of materials and tools and unrestricted by dogmatic script standards, as would have been the case with official documents produced in Central Tibet. In our sample we therefore dealt with personal handwriting rather than any standardised script. The documents were examined with a view to identifying the names of scribes and other parties concerned, developing a methodology for identifying scribal hands.

First, we take selected graphemes for comparison; for example, the *yig mgo mdun ma* (the opening flourish that begins the first line), and the consonants *z* and *l*; and examined them in documents written by the same hand (Figs 10, 11 and 12).

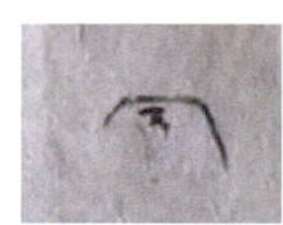
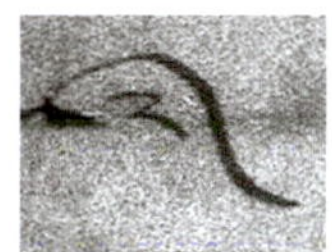

Figs 10 a–c. The *yig mgo mdun ma* (the opening flourish that begins the first line) from the documents MA/UTshognam/Tib/10, MA/UTshognam/Tib/11 and MA/UTshognam/Tib/19.

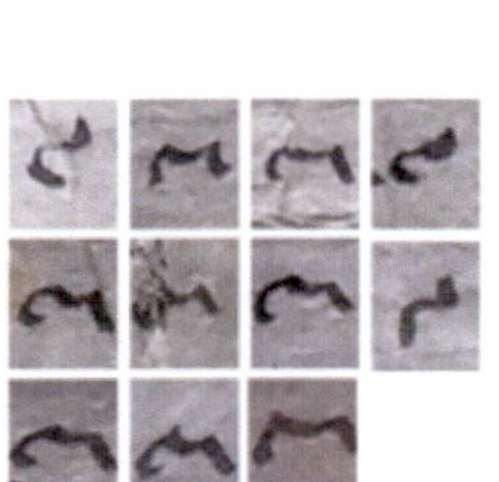
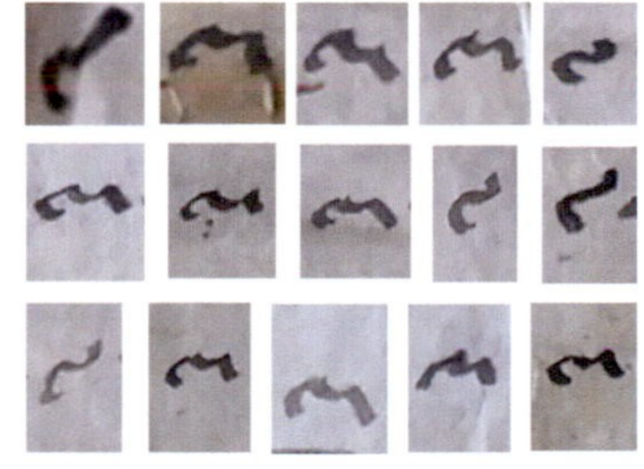
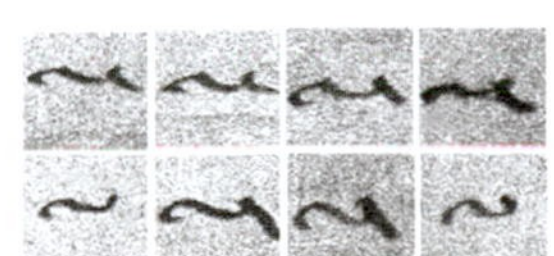

Figs 11 a–c. Examples of the consonant *l*, showing the occurrence of both cursive and *tshugs* forms in the same documents.

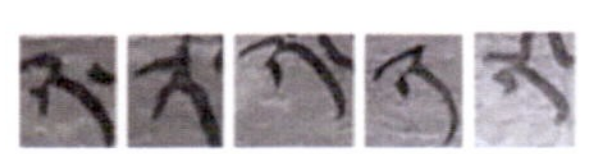

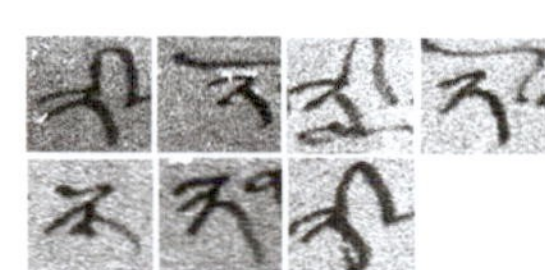

Figs 12 a–c. Forms of the consonant *ny* by Ösal Dorje (MA/UTshognam/Tib/10, MA/UTshognam/Tib/11); and c, by a different scribe (MA/UTshognam/Tib/19).

[5] Dalton et al. 2007; Van Schaik 2014; Helman-Ważny and Ramble 2017: 270–72.

[6] On methods for analysing handwriting, see Morris 2000 or Purdy 2006: 47–74.

Considering the facts that very few of the Tibetan documents include the signature of the scribe and that these documents are usually in poor condition, identifying the scribal hands is a difficult and laborious task that therefore costs handwriting analysts and experts in the Tibetan language significant time and energy. We therefore decided to explore how computer-based methods developed by Artificial Intelligence can help in our work, since the main challenge was to make comparative analyses within the large amount of data. We first collaborated with Boris Radovanovic and Andrei Sebastian Krauss to test whether the Tibetan Scribe Identification Software could be used for Mustang archival documents.[7]

The intention of applying the Tibetan Scribe Identification Software was to guide the experts by determining which documents were likely to have been written by the same scribe, beginning with a small sample written by scribes who are known. This was planned in the following steps: the selected documents written by identified hands formed our database, along with their pre-calculated features, and were grouped according to the individual scribes. Our sample was, however, insufficient to train the neural network to a desirable degree and to complete the software test. We did, however, collect data that are essential to test new pattern recognition tools, and thefore continued our work in collaboration with the project RFA05: *Pattern Recognition in 2D Data from Digitised Images and Advanced Acquisition Techniques* at the University of Hamburg, Cluster of Excellence: Understanding Written Artefacts, and with Hussein Adnan Mohammed, who published the Handwriting Analysis Tool v3.0 (HAT 3) in 2020.[8] Thus we tested our Mustang documents with the HAT 3, which aimed to measure the similarities between different handwriting styles, and offered the possibility of quantitative similarity measurements.

Text execution: This involves identifying the technology used to produce a text; whether it is handwritten or printed. It may be possible to identify the implement that was used to write a handwritten text. It is not always evident, though in some cases the difference between a wooden pen, a brush, a fountain pen or a modern gel-pen can be detected.

Format and layout

Form: Documents such as contracts and letters tended to be written on single sheets and folded into thin, rectangular packages. This format is distinctive for Tibet and is usually associated with official documents, the publication of binding legal acts, contracts and letters. Such portable format is highly functional, as documents were easily transported and also practically stored in chancelleries and homes. Such formats were often stored in larger textile rolls, which when unrolled were hung on a wall making all its separate documents visible. An example of such storage can be seen in the collection of the Berlin State Library where each roll might hold up to 60 documents, just as they were originally kept and displayed. The documents of central Tibetan administration were usually written on a composite background consisting of a one-layered sheet of paper lined with a layer of dyed silk or other fabric (Fig. 13). Fabric tape was attached to the folded document to hold it tightly together in a fashion similar to that of loose-leaf books held wrapped in protective cloth and held together tightly with a tape. Such double-layer construction of paper and fabric makes a paper more resistant to breaks on creases when documents are multi-folded into little rectangular packages, and it also makes a surface more suitable for writing due to its sizing (paste in the structure). The silk cloths used to reinforce the paper is usually prepared with various techniques. They were dyed with one colour or hand-stamped with colourful dots or other patterns (Fig. 14). Found among the Dunhuang

[7] On the technical side, the software currently enhances, and then binarises an input manuscript image, followed by feature extraction. This process consists of two steps: first, the manuscript image is enhanced using a pre-trained neural network. This enhancement attempts to remove any stains, paper creases, or other marks on the manuscript. The goal of this step is to remove anything that is not handwriting from the image. After this, Otsu's algorithm is applied in order to binarise the enhanced image. The optimal output will be a black-and-white manuscript image which contains nothing but handwriting. The neural network used in this step is adapted from this source code developed by Schomaker (Schomaker and He 2019: 379–90).

[8] Mohammed 2020: DOI: 10.25592/uhhfdm.900; Mohammed et al. 2018.

Figs 13 a–b. The typical form of the Tibetan document (no. 796) from the André Alexander collection. Silk fabric on the verso side of the document. Photographs by Agnieszka Helman-Ważny.

Fig. 14 a–b. Tibetan document no. 788 from the André Alexander collection. a. Recto side of the document; b. Silk fabric on the verso side of the document. Photograph by Agnieszka Helman-Ważny.

manuscripts and constantly used in Tibet, this popular format resembles a flattened scroll or, more rarely, a concertina, folded first from bottom to top in one direction, then horizontally into a short rectangle. In the Dunhuang documents this format was reserved for government documents, but here we find it widely used for various administrative purposes throughout Mustang's villages (Fig. 15). The horizontal or vertical method of folding such documents was identified when compared to direction of lines of text. Other formats, such as sewn booklets (Tib. *mgo tshem* or *mgo lteb ma*)[9] or scrolls (Tib. *shog dril*), were also occasionally recorded (Fig. 16).

Fig. 15. "Legal petition against Ösal Dorje et al. for various charges," archived as MA/UTshognam/Tib/25, comprising a single rectangular sheet folded into a little package. Photograph by Agnieszka Helman-Ważny.

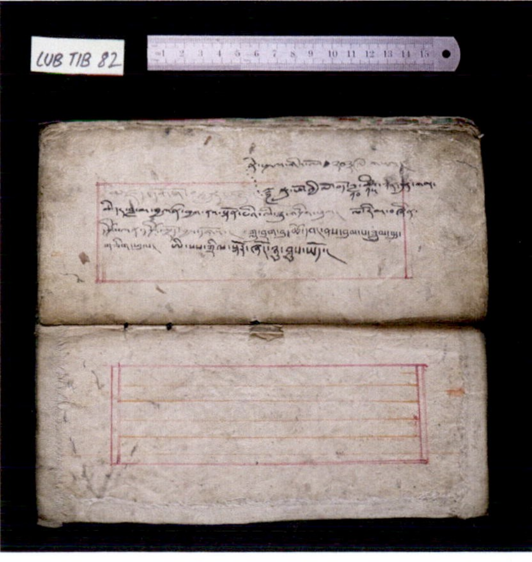

Figs 16 a–b. A registry of temple contributions in the form of a *mgo tshem* booklet. Archival document from Lubrak in Mustang, Nepal (archived as MA/Lubrak/Tib/81). Photographs by Kemi Tsewang.

[9] In using these terms we follow David Jackson, who mentions them in his *The Mollas of Mustang* (1984: 26), with an attribution to Tashi Tsering. He adds that "such 'bound' books were common in Lo" (ibid.: 34, fn. 26).

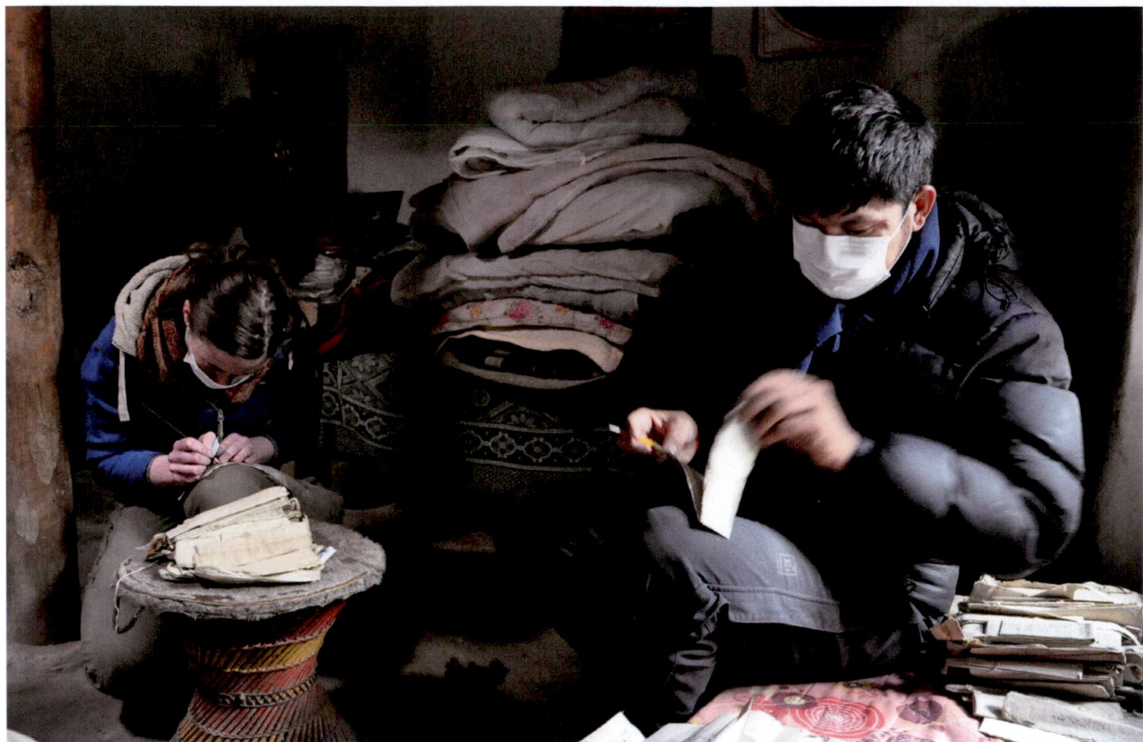

Fig. 17. Describing the format and measuring a document size in the Geling archive. Photograph by Agnieszka Helman-Ważny.

Size (h × w) cm: When measuring a document, its height is given first, then its width.

N° of folds: The number of folds usually follows the size of the document. The number of folds is also given here.

Overall N° of pages: In the case of a document in booklet format or consisting of more than one sheet of paper one should give the overall number of existing leaves or pages in the document.

No of text lines: The number of lines of text per page and the presence or absence of margins was documented *in situ* (Fig. 17).

Authentication marks

Seals: The use of seals was largely confined to certain social categories: Government offices, local rulers (including the King of Lo), religious institutions, village communities, aristocrats, *subbā*s, and hereditary lamas, although, as we shall see below, individual commoners also sometimes used seals, suggesting that there may have been no regulation prohibiting the use of seals by commoners, but simply that most commoners simply did not possess them. In Mustang itself, the King of Lo alone used a red seal. We photographed the legible seals and made close-up images, and preserved them in the CSMC data repository together with other data related to relevant documents. Then we grouped them, identified those that were legible, and summarised this information in a table (see Appendix 4).

Fingerprints: We recorded digital prints (finger- and thumbprints) and worked on adapting fingerprint-recognition software to ascertain whether the same prints may be identified on different documents. The software uses the classic minutiae matching algorithm whose main steps are: 1) to remove as much noise from the input fingerprint image as possible, 2) to identify the *arch* or *whorl* at the centre of the prints, 3) to identify minutiae points and their relative positions on the prints; 4) to account for rotation, translation, or stretching of the impressions; 5) to count the number of minutiae points that match between the two prints.

The fingerprint image is first denoised using the method developed by Mansar.[10] This method also attempts to remove the paper background from the image, as well as to reconstruct missing portions of the fingerprint, which greatly improves the quality and usability of the image. Afterwards, the image is further enhanced through unsharp masking. The ridge orientation field is then extracted using differentiation of the enhanced image. The image is then thinned using Zhang's algorithm[11] and then binarized using Otsu's method.[12] The ridge ending and splitting minutiae are then extracted. The minutiae extracted from 2 fingerprints are compared using the minutiae cylinder code algorithm.[13]

The main difficulty encountered in matching fingerprints was the poor quality of the fingerprints on manuscripts resulting from the specific interaction of the paper and inks used in the documents. The classical minutiae matching algorithm proved not to be robust enough to identify the same fingerprints on the Mustang documents. Features that make identification impossible for time being are shown in the picture below (Fig. 18). At this point the quality of the fingerprints impressed on paper was insufficient to obtain clear results (Fig. 19). Other approaches which are less sensitive to the quality of the fingerprint impression need to be considered.

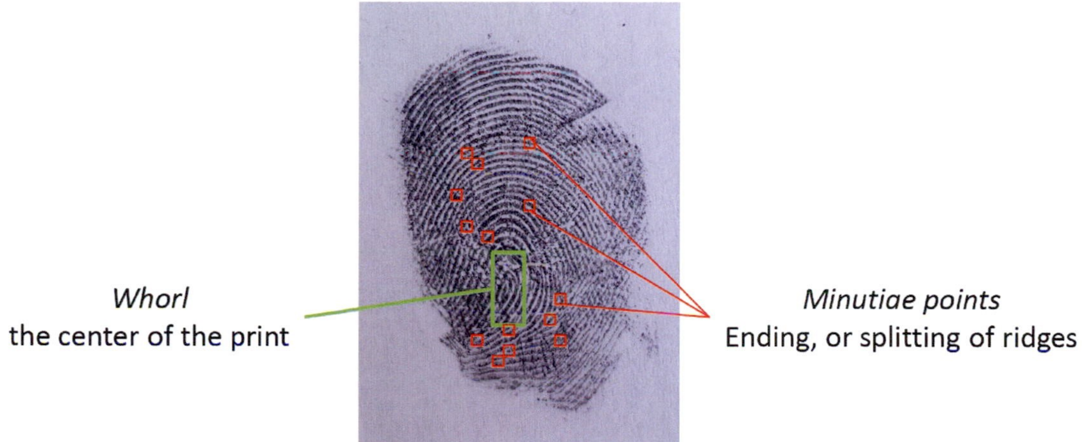

Fig. 18. The main features used to match fingerprints using classical minutiae matching algorithms. Illustration by Boris Radovanovic.

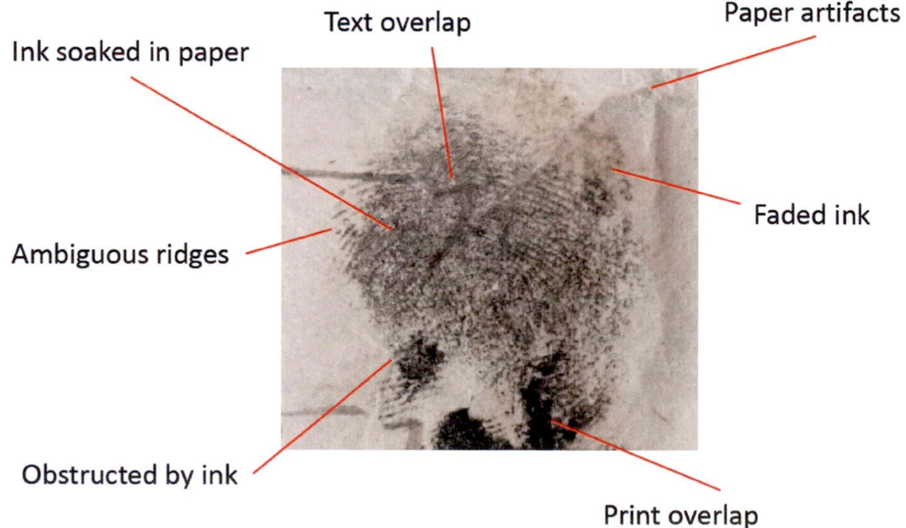

Fig. 19. The example of fingerprint in Mustang documents illustrating the problems raising from the quality of the fingerprints impressed on paper. Illustration by Boris Radovanovic.

10 Mansar 2018: 1–5.

11 Zhang and Suen 1984: 236–39.

12 Otsu 1979: 62–66.

13 Cappelli et al. 2010: 2128–41.

Crosses: Before the use of thumbprints became widespread, documents were commonly validated by means of crosses. In certain cases, signatories would pass the document or the stylus from hand to hand as a gesture of endorsement, and the scribe would place an "X" on the document to indicate that it had been approved. If there were several signatories, the scribe might add a single cross to represent the approval of the whole group, or, more often, one cross for each member of the group.

Paper

Type of paper: Here outlines of the features of paper described below are given in detail, but mainly those that may be read with the naked eye; for example, whether paper is handmade or machine-made, and what type of papermaking mould and sieve were used.[14]

Fibre composition: One further aim of the procedure is identification of the fibre in collected specimens of paper, using an Olympus BX51 Transmitted-Reflected light microscope with polarised light with camera attached for photographic documentation.[15] Olympus Stream Software is used for image analysis in identification. A varying magnification between 50× and 400× with both plain and polarised light is employed. For study, a sample is placed in a small beaker, immersed in distilled water, and boiled for about 20 minutes. The water is then decanted and the sample is drained, de-fibred into a fine suspension of individual fibres, and placed on the slide. Fibres are observed and then selectively treated with Herzberg stain. Attention is paid to stain colouring, morphology of fibres, and other cells and elements of pulp (Figs 20, 21 and 22). Fibre analysis informs us regarding of the composition of plants, since the primary feature of paper is the type of raw material used in its production. Fibre analysis, if applicable, may therefore be helpful in pinpointing regional origin and sometimes in dating, when using a method that entails overlapping typologies. When comparing the results of the fibre analyses of paper with the distribution of the same plant, we may acquire information about a document's possible region of origin. The area suggested by plant distribution may be critically evaluated against other sources of information, such as those features recorded in our table. In this way, we can ascertain whether all features originate from the same area (understood as a cultural context, country, or region). These results may help in answering some questions about the history of paper in the region, as well as the trade and import of paper and other writing materials in the Himalayas and Central Asia, even though much more research needs to be done in order to achieve higher precision in attribution of provenance.[16]

In this case the main aim is to produce reliable references for further work in the region, since almost all documents studied are dated and of known origin. The results of identification of the composition of fibre and other technological features of paper are put into the database established at the Centre for the Study of Manuscript Cultures.

[14] For information on paper examination, see: Tschudin 2002: 29–52, Rischel 2001: 179–88, and Tschudin 2004: 135–41.

[15] The laboratory fibre analyses were conducted by Agnieszka Helman-Ważny and her student Mengling Cai at the University of Hamburg.

[16] For other studies of paper in Tibetan manuscripts, see: Helman-Ważny and van Schaik 2013; Helman-Ważny 2016a; Helman-Ważny 2016c.

Fig. 20. *Daphne* fibres in magnification 100× collected in Ghandruk. Photograph by Agnieszka Helman-Ważny.

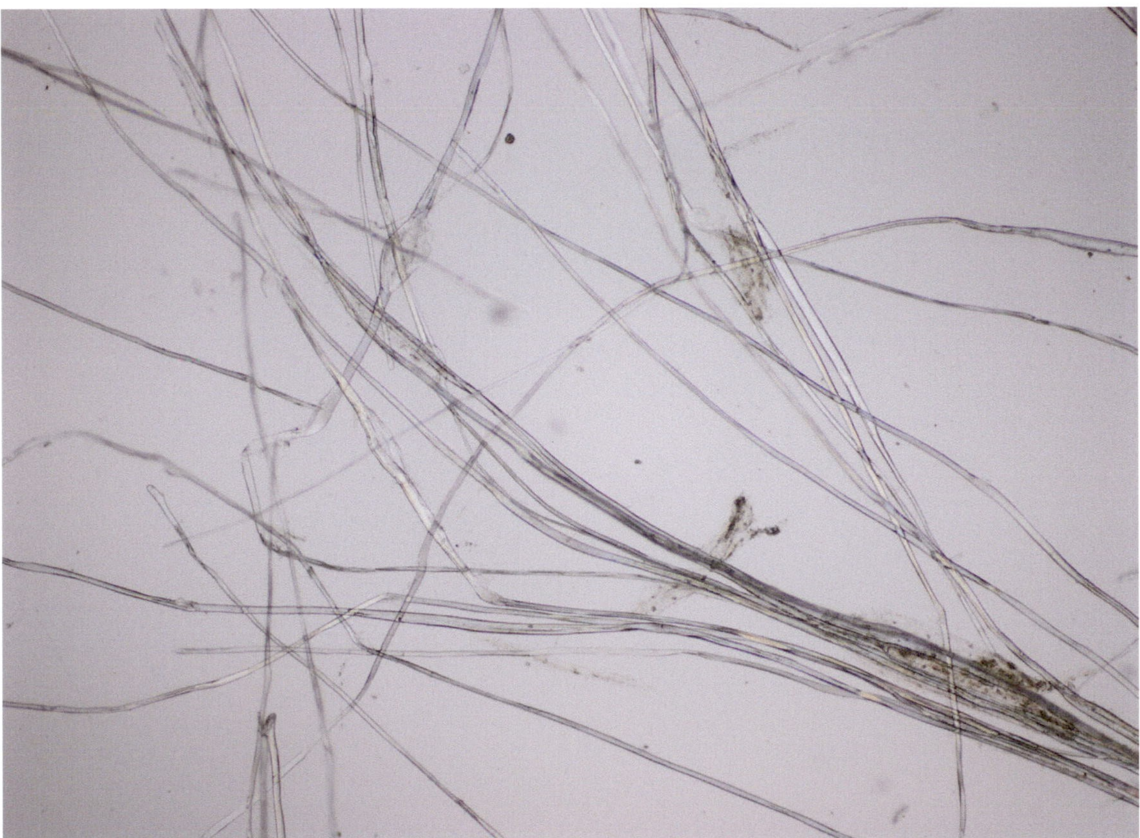

Fig. 21. *Edgeworthia gardneri* fibres collected in Nangi and observed under microscope in magnification 50×. Photograph by Agnieszka Helman-Ważny.

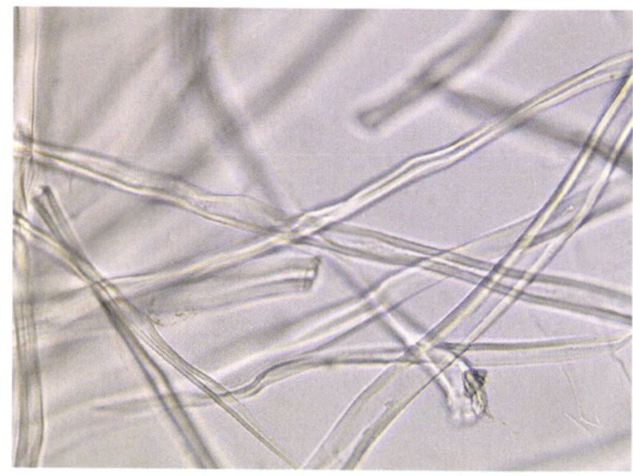

Fig. 22. *Stellera* sp. fibres in magnification 600×. Photograph by Agnieszka Helman-Ważny.

Sieve print: Technological features of paper in Mustang archival documents were documented via examination of sheets of paper against the light in order to identify the type of papermaking sieve used from its print. Due to shortage of electricity (only solar power was available) as may be seen on the figure 23 below, we had to use natural light to make such images (Fig. 23).

The print of a textile sieve (Fig. 24) clearly differs from one made of bamboo (laid, regular), reed, or other grasses (laid, irregular) (Fig. 25). When sealed in the paper structure, this allows us to distinguish handmade woven paper and handmade laid paper by the number of laid lines within a distance of 3cm. These may be categorised as laid, regular where there is unequivocal clear evidence; laid, irregular where the pattern is not regular; and, finally, laid, patchy where the pattern can be seen only in patches of the paper, but could not have been made by anything else. This effect comes from using a doubled sieve, when there is cloth over an attached bamboo, reed or grass sieve (Fig. 26). The laid type of mould or sieve is also sometimes characterised by chain lines, which are vertical lines from the screen on which the paper was manufactured. The sequence of measurements of the interval between two (or more) chain lines is given where chain lines are clearly visible. These intervals often vary within one sheet of paper, and in this case, the sequences of span values should be given.

Fig. 23. Photographing documents against light in Geling in 2016. Photograph by Agnieszka Helman-Ważny.

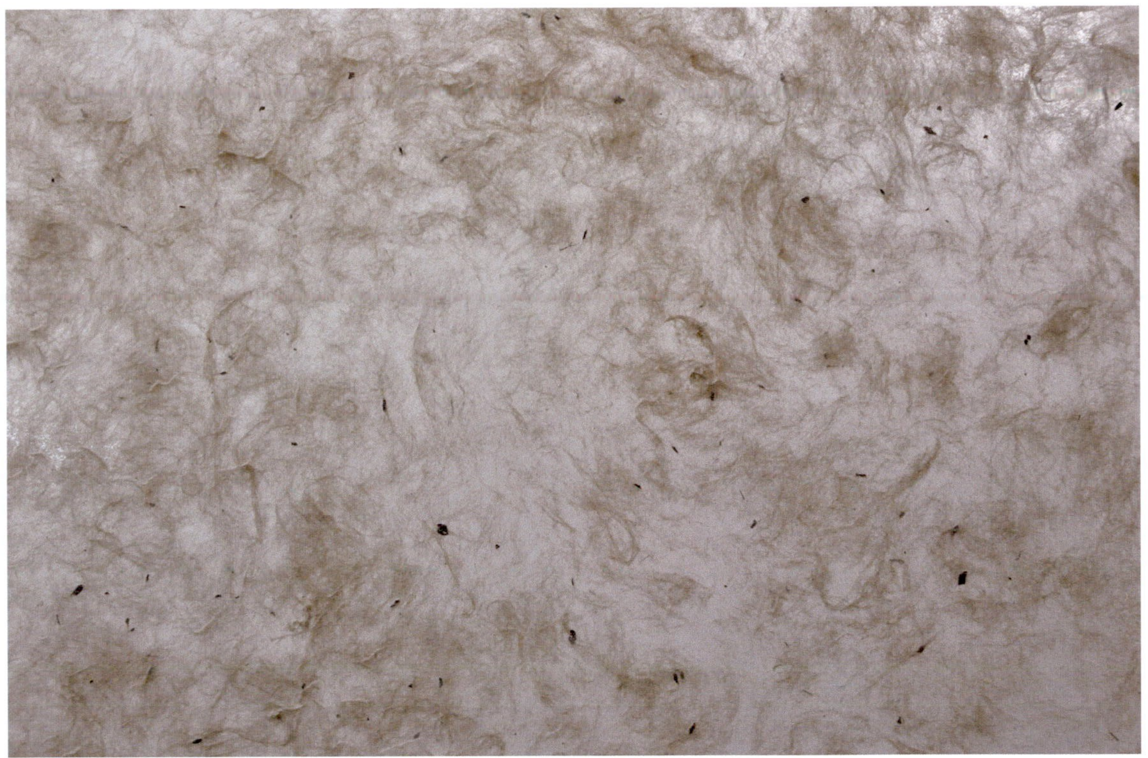

Fig. 24. The woven type of paper with a fibre distribution typical of a floating type of papermaking mould. Photograph by Agnieszka Helman-Ważny.

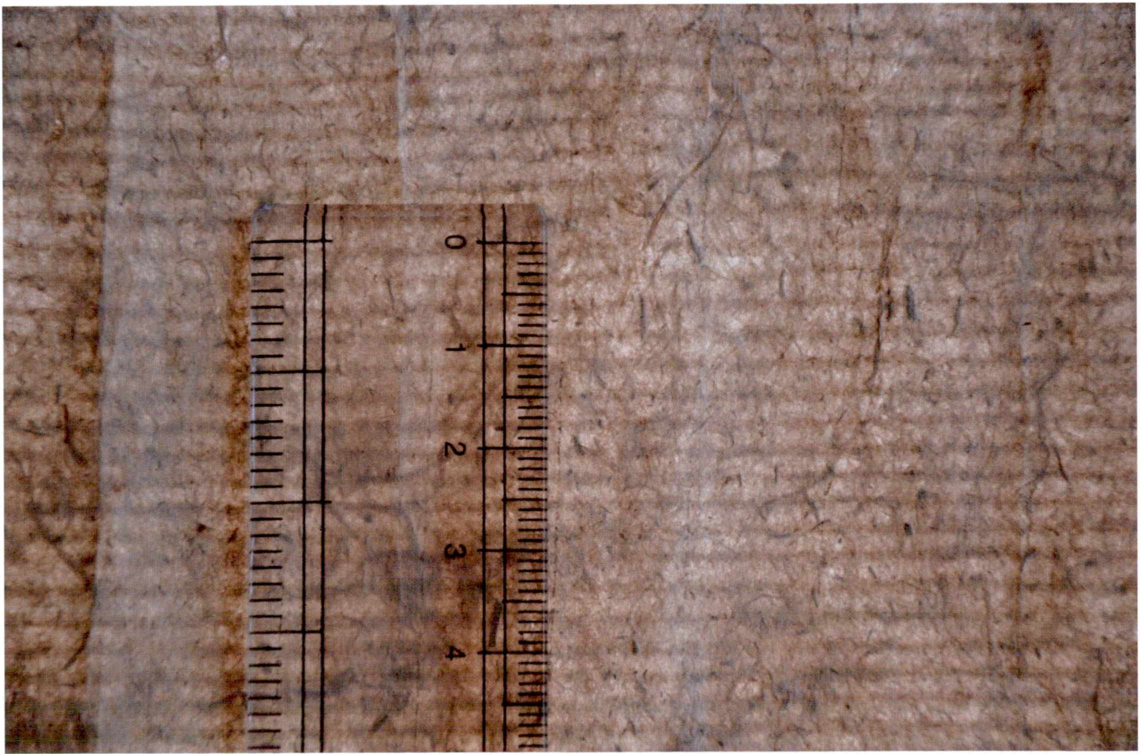

Fig. 25. Laid paper characterised by 12 laid lines in 3 cm. Photograph by Agnieszka Helman-Ważny.

Fig. 26. Various types of papermaking sieves. Photographs by Agnieszka Helman-Ważny.

Number of layers: One may note here whether a paper leaf is made up of one, two or more sheets of paper that have been glued together.

Thickness: This is a parameter that makes it possible to classify types and quality of paper. Using a caliper, one measures the paper in at least five different places and gives a span value (from lower to higher number measured). The presence of uneven pulp thickness distribution visible within a sheet of paper also helps with the identification of the type of raw materials used and the methods by which they were pulped. This feature is reflected in the thickness of paper which is usually lower in better quality paper, with an even distribution of fibre, rather than an uneven distribution of fibre in the rougher papers where raw material has not been beaten sufficiently during pulping. Good quality paper, for example, that made from mulberry fibres on a very fine bamboo sieve, usually has a very uniform thickness, in contrast with rougher paper made in remote, mountainous areas with a simple mould of textiles on a frame. This uniform thickness comes from extremely even distribution of fibres in the papermaking mould that was lifted when shaping the paper. Much Tibetan and Nepalese paper is of variable thickness, and this measurement may therefore have limited value here.

Texture (e.g., smooth, rough, polished): This is qualitative, but it may be an important indicator of the "natural recto," that is, the side of the paper that is smoother as a result of the manufacturing process and which is therefore the more desirable surface for writing. The paper surface was observed by Dino-Lite digital microscope (Fig. 27). This tool helped us to record the interaction of paper and ink and observe the degree of sizing and quality of paper.

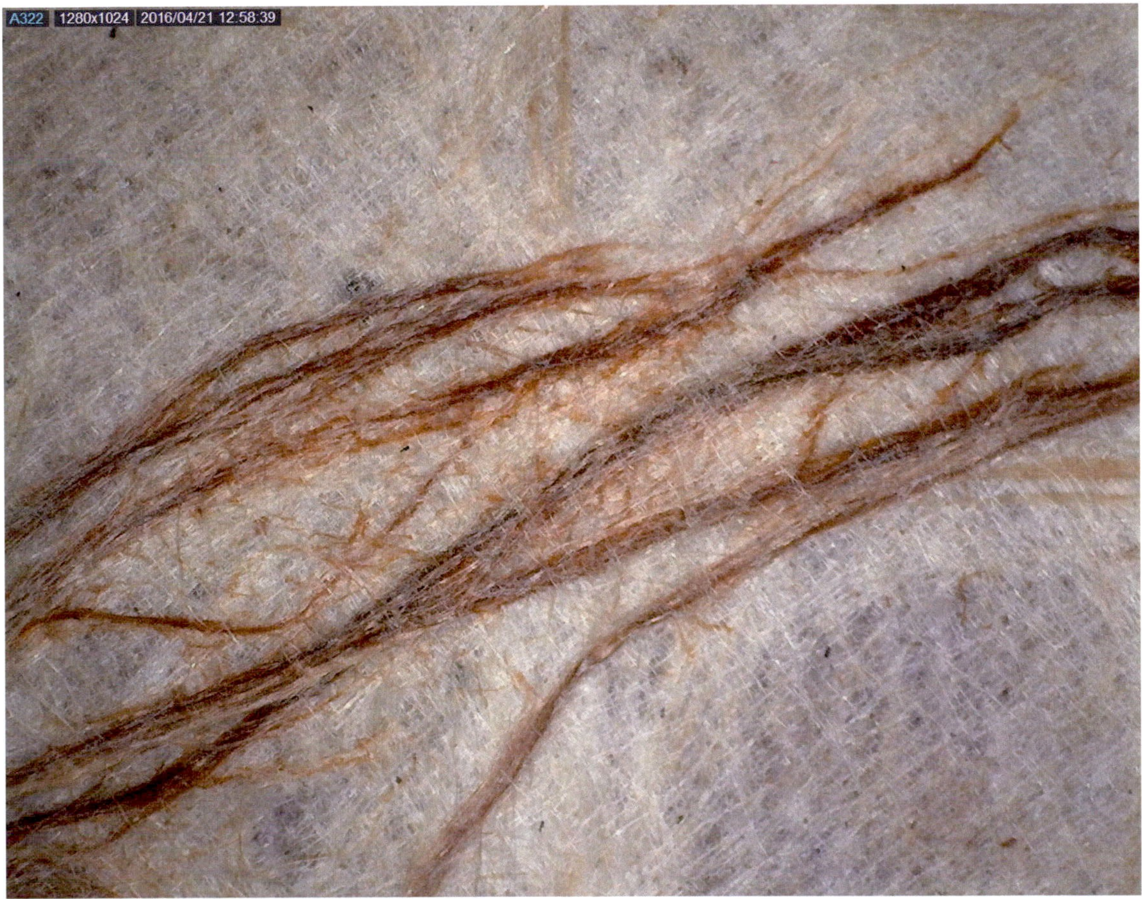

Fig. 27. The texture of paper in the document archived as MA/Geling/Tib/3 from the Geling archive observed under Dino-Lite digital microscope. Photograph by Agnieszka Helman-Ważny.

Fibre distribution: From the varying evenness of the distribution of the fibres, it is possible to determine whether the fibres were poured into the floating mould and spread by hand or scooped by the mould from a vat, and the speed with which drainage of the pulp took place. The presence of uneven pulp thickness distribution visible in a sheet of paper, sometimes along the chain and laid lines, sometimes evenly along one edge, also makes it possible to describe the type of raw material and pulping methods.

Ink

The black ink is usually made from main components of carbonised plants or soot, other colour pigments or metal with a possible admixture of gum, honey, borax or, for special occasions, other unusual materials. The inks and paints were manufactured in accordance with different recipes at different times and places.[17] The difficulties regarding the use of the necessary scientific equipment in the field, however, prevents precise determination of the composition of inks. Still, even basic descriptions of ink colour are useful for classifying documents. Most ink is black, but we also find red and occasionally other colours.

Most pigments used in Tibetan books for illustrations are of natural mineral origin. Many are found in Tibet, while others are imported.[18] Analyses of this compared to pigment analyses on mural paintings gives us an idea of whether the same paints were used, and at what period.[19] For identifying the provenance of the pigments there are also possible clues as to when they were made. A wide variety of analytical techniques may be employed, preferably more than one to obtain unambiguous results. In our case, however, we were unable to transport more advanced equipment to Upper Mustang, and we decided to avoid taking samples of the ink, since this would have damaged the texts.

Methods for the documentation of papermaking traditions

In this part of our project we have two main sources of information that support each other: 1) the documents themselves, by looking at fragments of which we were able to reconstruct a history of papermaking via fibre analysis; and 2) from the living tradition of papermaking that persists in various areas of Nepal and which could potentially be related to traditions in Mustang. When merged, these allowed us to put together, for the first time, certain facts concerning the history and technology of paper production in Mustang, Nepal.

[17] Cüppers 1989: 1–7, which contains a translation of the chapter from Mi pham rNam rgyal rgya mtsho's (1846–1912) *bZo gnas nyer mkho'i za ma tog* (Craftsmanship: A Basket of Necessities), where instructions for the manufacturing of nine different kinds of carbon-based black ink are provided.

[18] Ernst 2001: 900–14.

[19] For historical information on techniques of painting and materials used, see: Jackson and Jackson 1994; for results of pigments analyses on *thang ka* see: Duffy and Elgar 1996: 78–84; Ernst 2001: 900–14, 2010; comparative study of traditional and modern pigments: Mass et al. 2009: 108–17; for pigments on wall paintings see: Li et al. 2014: 1–6.

Chapter 2
The Archives in a Regional and Historical Context

The enclaves and villages of Mustang

Present-day Mustang District comprises a number of enclaves that are recognised either as the residues of former polities or the territories of ethnically distinct groups. The northernmost part is referred to as Lo. Upper Lo, Lotö (Glo stod), is the territory that was ruled by the king of Mustang at the time of the unification of Nepal by the Gorkhas in the eighteenth century, and recognised by them as his domain. The area is often referred to as Lotö Tshodün (Tib. Glo bo stod tsho bdun), "the Seven Counties of Upper Lo." Each of the seven counties (*tsho*) contains one or more settlements. Larger communities, like the city of Monthang and the village of Te, constitute an entire county, while other counties consist of several smaller villages. The counties may have been primarily tax-paying units, with all counties being required to pay roughly the same amount in terms of cash or other commodities. This sort of county-based organisation was not confined to Upper Lo and Baragaon; Dolpo, to the west, was traditionally divided into ten-and-a-half counties,[1] and Manang, to the east, into three, while areas of Tibet adjoining Mustang are also referred to in local documents in terms of counties.

Below Gemi, the southernmost village in Upper Lo, is the large community of Geling, which (with the help of Jumla) broke away from the kingdom in 1754 (Fig. 28).[2] Immediately to the south of Geling is Baragaon, corresponding to Lower Lo. Since the latter name is sometimes used in Tibetan works to include areas even further south, we shall use the unambiguous name Baragaon to refer to this enclave. Baragaon (Nep. Bāhragāũ) now is made up of nineteen settlements that, with the exception of five villages, are all populated by Tibetan-speaking people.

Fig. 28. Geling village. Photograph by Agnieszka Helman-Ważny.

[1] Jest 1975: 286.

[2] Schuh 1994: 85.

South of Baragaon is a group of settlements known as Panchgaon (Nep. Pāncgāũ), a Nepali name that has its Tibetan equivalent Yulkhanga (Yul kha lnga). Both terms mean "the Five Villages." Although the inhabitants of these villages speak Thakali, Tibetan was the main language for their administrative organisation, and all have archives of Tibetan documents (Fig. 29). The archives of Marpha in particular have been the subject of a substantial study by Dieter Schuh.[3] The region between Panchgaon and the southern boundary of Mustang District, made up of thirteen settlements, is known as Thak, and the people who inhabit it as Thakalis, an ethnonym that is also sometimes extended to include the inhabitants of Panchgaon.

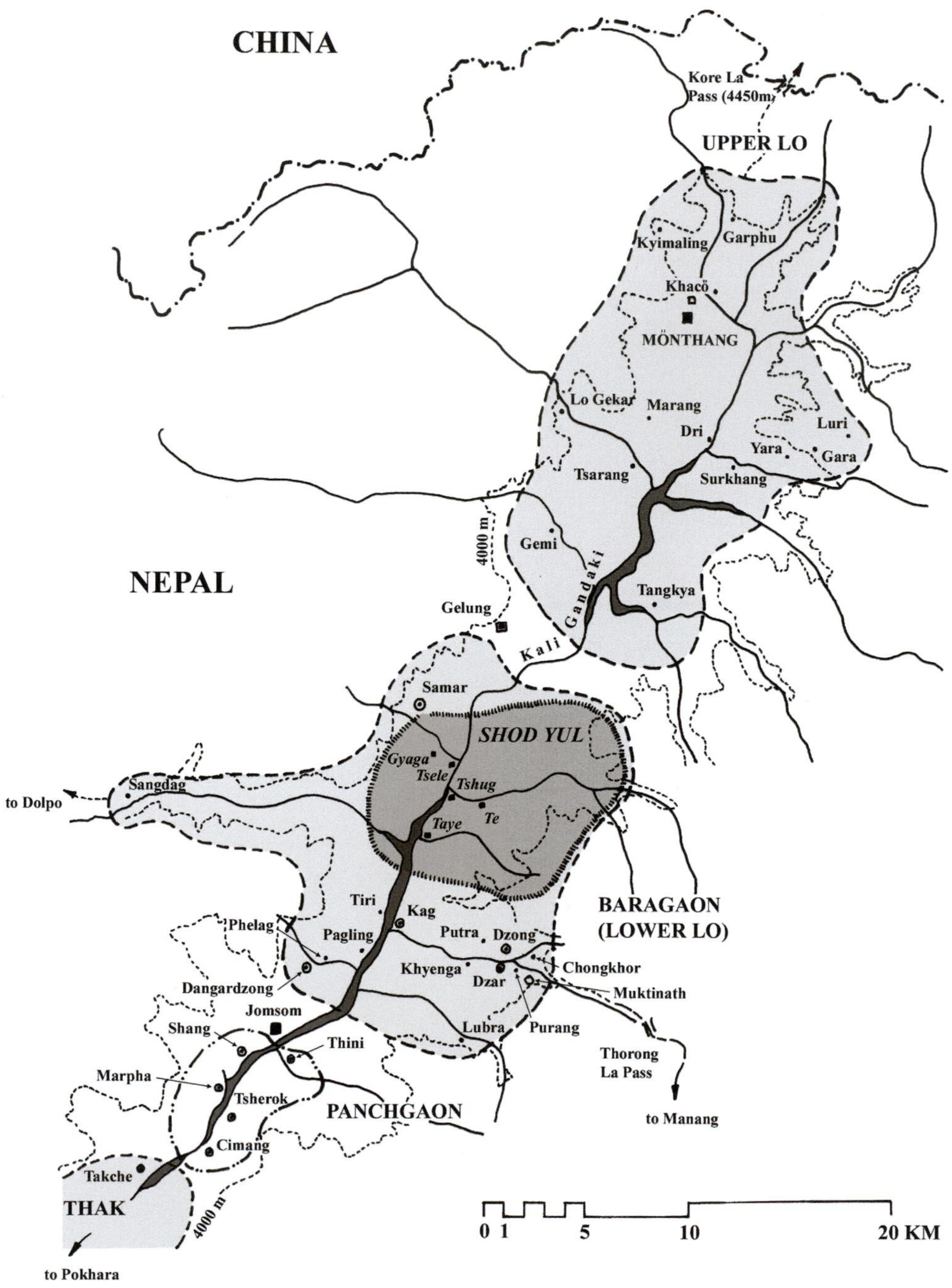

Fig. 29. Mustang District. Map by Niels Gutschow.

[3] Schuh 2015.

To return to Baragaon: an hour's walk north of Jomsom, the Kali Gandaki river is joined from the east by the Panda Khola, a small river that traditionally marks the boundary between Panchgaon and Baragaon. The village of Lubrak, whose houses and fields stand on its southern side, is also considered to be a part of Baragaon, though the land on which the settlement was founded in the thirteenth century originally belonged to Thini, the political centre of Panchgaon (Fig. 30). On the opposite side of the Kali Gandaki are two other villages, Dangardzong and Phelag. A short way to the north of these, and closer to the river itself, is Pagling. The village is said to be the most recent in Baragaon, having been settled by one family from each of the other villages. This collective undertaking may be at the origin of a variant of the name: Pigling, which may mean "the Common (or Shared) Place" (Tib. sPyi gling). There are references to a temple having been built at Pagling in the thirteenth century;[4] ruins near the present village support the suggestion that this is the site, and it is therefore possible that the place was abandoned for a period before being resettled.

North of Pagling, on the left bank of the river, where the valley converges to a narrow gorge, is the village of Kag, which has expanded from its now-ruined palace and its tightly built cluster of early houses to a large settlement with many modern buildings. The history of the development of Kag has been examined in detail by Niels Gutschow.[5] Kag appears on most maps as Kagbeni, a name that refers to its location at the confluence (Nep. *beni*) of the Kali Gandaki and the Dzong Chu, the stream of the Muktinath Valley that runs parallel to and north of the Panda Khola. At the head of this valley stands the temple of Muktinath, a site of importance to Hindu pilgrims, although the complex also contains natural features and temples that are revered by Buddhists and Bonpos. The villages on the south side of the valley, from west to east, are Khyenga, Dzar, Purang, and Chongkhor (Fig. 31). To the north of the Dzong Chu are two others: Putra and Dzong. The communities of the Muktinath Valley are sometimes referred to collectively as Dzardzong Yuldrug, "the Six Villages [including] Dzar and Dzong," or more briefly, Dzardzong. The dialect of Tibetan spoken in Baragaon, described by linguists as South Mustang Tibetan, is known throughout Mustang as Dzardzongke (*dzar rdzong skad*), the "language of Dzardzong".

Kag, Dzar and Dzong are the site of now-derelict castles. Noble families from the north, the most important of which was the Kyekya Gangba clan, who came to Baragaon in the sixteenth century on behalf of Lo, established themselves in these two settlements and in Kag, as well as in Dangardzong, and ruled the area from castles that (in the case of Dzar, Kag, and Dangardzong) they either built themselves or (in the case of Dzong) inherited from an earlier political era. Dzar, Dzong, Kag, and Dangardzong are accordingly referred to as "capitals" (Tib. *rgyal sa*), since they contained populations of aristocracy. There is a fifth capital, Samar, which is now a small village at the northern end of Baragaon. In addition to their castles, the villages of Dzar, Dzong, and Kag each has a monastery (Tib. *chos sde*) affiliated with one branch or another of the Sakyapa school of Tibetan Buddhism, with monks being recruited from a number of surrounding villages. Chongkhor, which stands on land donated to the founder lama by the village of Purang, is a community of householder priests (Tib. *dbon po*) of the Nyingmapa school. The inhabitants of Lubrak, to the south of the Muktinath valley, are also of priestly class (Tib. *bla mchod*) but are followers of the Bon religion.

Immediately to the north of Kag and on the opposite side of the Kali Gandaki is Tiri, the site of a former convent that features in one of the documents from Dzar. A long day's walk to the west of it, on the way to Dolpo, is Sangdag, the most isolated of the nineteen settlements that make up Baragaon.

Between Tiri and Samar is a subsidiary enclave of five villages: Tsele, Gyaga, Tshug, Taye, and Te, whose inhabitants speak a Tibeto-Burman language that is closely related to Thakali, a fact that led the anthropologist Christoph von Fürer-Haimendorf to describe them as "Ur-Thakalis".[6] The five villages are collectively referred to as the Shöyul (Tib. Shod yul) "the Low-Lying Communities," suggesting that the name was bestowed by Tibetan-speaking inhabitants of

[4] See Jackson 1978: 207.

[5] Gutschow 1994: 23–50.

[6] Fürer-Haimendorf 1966: 157.

Fig. 30. Lubrak village. Photograph by Agnieszka Helman-Ważny.

Fig. 31. Dzong village, a view from Muktinath temple. Photograph by Agnieszka Helman-Ważny.

Fig. 32. Te village. Photograph by Agnieszka Helman-Ważny.

the northern uplands. Upper and Lower Tshognam, the sites of priestly households whose archives form a component of this study, stand respectively on the territory of Te and Tshug (Fig. 32).

Baragaon is the anglicised form of a Nepali name meaning "the Twelve Villages" (Bāhragāũ), but documentary evidence suggests that this is the translation of an older Tibetan name, Yulkha Cunyi (Yul kha bcu gnyis), meaning the same thing.[7] In Tibetan documents of the nineteenth and twentieth centuries, at least, the term Yulkha Cunyi is habitually replaced by a Tibetanised rendering of "Baragaon" (*bha ra gung, ba ra ga'ung*, etc.), often in conjunction with the epithet "Lower Lo" (Tib. Glo smad). Another name for the area that appears commonly in local texts, either by itself or preceding the term Baragaon, is Ngazhab (Tib. mNga' zhabs), "the Subject [region or people]." The name – like Baragaon/Yulkha Cunyi – may date from the period when the region was under the rule of the Kyekya Gangba family. When it appears in documents, the name refers to the population or representative assembly of Baragaon without its aristocracy. The original justification for the name Baragaon/Yulkha Cunyi remains uncertain, since the region is made up of not twelve but nineteen settlements.

In spite of its linguistic heterogeneity, Baragaon has existed as some sort of corporate entity for at least as long as the period covered by available documents, although its boundaries may have changed over the course of time. Issues that concerned Baragaon as a whole – whether internal matters or questions of policy regarding the enclave's dealings with external agencies, such as Upper Lo or the Government of Nepal – were debated at general assemblies, when representatives of all the villagers were required to be present. The local nobility originally shouldered the task of representing Baragaon in dealings with Kathmandu, but after the rise of the *subbās*, the customs-brokers from Thak, a Thakali warden, called the *cikhyab* (Tib. *spyi khyab*), assumed this mediatory role. The people of Baragaon are said to have requested the intervention of the powerful Serchan family some time in the 1930s. Baragaon was duly apportioned out between prominent brothers. Mohanman took over the wardenship of southern Baragaon, while the five Shöyul and two villages

[7] Schuh 1994: 43.

of Panchgaon fell to Hitman. The two parts of Baragaon were united under a single warden in the next generation. For part of his long career, the last warden of Baragaon, Sankarman Serchan, combined this unofficial role with the official one of tax collector (Nep. *tālukdār*). The warden advised the villagers of Baragaon about developments in government policy, intervened in local disputes, and when occasion demanded, summoned general assemblies of the enclave. He was assisted by a team of eight supervisors (Tib. *spyan btsug*) who were appointed on the basis of their personal competence, and these in turn would liaise with villages through their headmen.

The historical background

The great majority of documents in the archives considered in this book date from the Rana period (1846–1951), while a few are earlier and a score or so – mostly from Lubrak – are from subsequent decades. The few historical accounts of Mustang by Western researchers have tended to concentrate on the mediaeval period,[8] while the centuries up to the absorption of the kingdom into the Gorkha state in 1788/89 have been addressed particularly by Dhungel and Schuh,[9] the latter especially with respect to southern Mustang. The history of the region during the Rana era has been tackled mainly by anthropologists, beginning with the pioneering work of Christoph von Fürer-Haimendorf.[10] These early studies formed the point of departure for work by later writers, notably Dor Bahadur Bista,[11] Andrew Manzardo[12] and Michael Vinding.[13] Most of these scholars derived their information from interviews with the key actors. More than any of the other authors, perhaps, Michael Vinding has made good use of the official documents available in the *Regmi Research Series*.[14] The period under consideration here is treated in the third chapter of his monograph *The Thakali*;[15] much of this chapter draws on his earlier publications and the work of other authors – especially Fürer-Haimendorf's *Himalayan Traders*.[16]

In the first half of the seventeenth century, the Kingdom of Lo was brought under the direct rule of Jumla, with an obligation to pay a substantial annual tribute and to provide military assistance in times of need.[17] Jumla seems to have adopted a policy of "divide-and-rule" by exploiting regional tensions and fragmenting the kingdom. An important instance of this policy in action was the secession by Lower Lo from the ruler of Monthang in the seventeenth century. Since the sixteenth century, Lower Lo had been governed by the noble Kyekya Gangba family, but when the local ruler sought the aid of Jumla in a conflict with the north, Jumla readily sent troops to help him. In the ensuing conflict, the political independence of Lower Lo from Monthang was assured. The archives of Geling contain a document with the text of the song that the soldiers of Lo used to sing on their way to the wars with Jumla. The origins of the Kyekya Gangba lineage are recounted in the autobiography of one of its most celebrated members, Tenzin Repa (bsTan 'dzin ras pa), who lived from around 1640 to 1723. According to this work, the founder of the lineage was a certain Jampa Thobgyal, a minister of the semi-mythical founder of the Tibetan dynasty, Nyatri Tsenpo. A more authoritative source has it that the first member of the family to come to Lo – at the instigation of the king – was a certain Trowobum (Tib. Khro bo'bum), who settled in a place called Kyekyagang, a short distance to the east of Monthang. It was Trowobum's son, Trowo Kyabpa (Tib. Khro bo skyabs pa), who was sent to the Muktinath Valley to rule southern Lo on behalf of the king in the first half of the sixteenth century.[18] Although the family may have adopted the name of its residence in Lo, it is now more commonly referred to in Baragaon as Jampa Thobgyal, after its legendary founder. The different branches of clan are identified by the names of their noble houses. The house of the main branch in Dzar is called Zimkhang Nya, and it is also

[8] Notably Jackson 1978, Vitali 2012.

[9] Dhungel 2002 and Schuh 1994, 1995.

[10] Fürer-Haimendorf 1966, 1967, 1975.

[11] Bista 1971.

[12] Manzardo 1978, 1982.

[13] Vinding 1998.

[14] The *Regmi Research Series* is a twenty-one-volume collection of English-language translations or summaries of Nepali archives. The full collection may be found online at: http://www.digitalhimalaya.com/collections/journals/regmi/.

[15] Vinding 1998: 75–92.

[16] Fürer-Haimendorf 1975; Fisher 1987.

[17] Schuh 1994: 77.

[18] Schuh 1995: 42–43; 52–53.

Fig. 33. The Zimkhang Nya house where the Dzar archive is kept. Photograph by Agnieszka Helman-Ważny.

the location of the Dzar archive that is considered in this book (Fig. 33). Following their secession from Lo, the Kyekya Gangba retained their power in the vicinity of the Muktinath Valley, but were thenceforth under the direct authority of Jumla, whose representative, the O-ompa, would reside in the area for several months each year.[19]

When the Gorkha forces passed through Lo on their way to make war with Jumla in 1789, they were offered no resistance. In recognition of this cooperative attitude, the Gorkhas permitted the rulers of Upper and Lower Lo to retain their customary power, and the tribute previously levied by Jumla was now simply paid to the new sovereign power.[20]

The earliest available Gorkhali document concerning Baragaon, dating from 1790 and addressed to the lord of Dzar, begins with the following reminder.

> [We] issued, be it recalled, a [lal]mohar in the past [lit. yesterday] to the effect that you should enjoy the birtto [of] Bāhragāũ (Baragaon), Nar, and Manaṅ (Manang) along with the jagat of Kak, which you have enjoyed since olden times.[21]

The date of the *mohar* in question is not given, but it may be noted that the nearest Monkey year to 1790 was the Wood Monkey year of 1788, just two years earlier.

From 1846, the Government of Nepal effectively shifted from the hands of the Shah dynasty to a succession of hereditary prime ministers, the Ranas, initiating a period that lasted until 1951. As far as Lo was concerned, the most immediate consequence of this change of national government was the creation of a monopoly on the salt trade along the Kali Gandaki. Since the late eighteenth century, the collection of trade duties had been carried out by entrepreneurs who held government contracts (obtained by auction), but from this time on traders from the north were obliged to sell all their salt to the contractor. The contractors in question – none of whom, as it turned out, was from Lo – were also entitled to exercise a considerable degree of legal authority in

[19] Schuh 1995: 23.

[20] Regmi 1970: 99.

[21] Pant and Pierce 1989: 21.

the area, a state of affairs that critically undermined the power of the ruling families. The practice of auctioning off customs contracts was abolished in 1927, but the old nobility never recovered its earlier dominance. It is true that the nobles of Upper Lo continue to enjoy certain material privileges in respect of their hereditary status, but the benefits of aristocracy in the southern part are now almost entirely ceremonial.

In short, until the era of the contractors, Upper and Lower Lo enjoyed a degree of autonomy as long as they continued to pay their tribute and to offer no political opposition to their sovereign or suzerain power. As we have seen, the ruling family of Lower Lo established its authority in the region in the sixteenth century. They built elaborate fortifications, established or confirmed local territorial boundaries, levied taxes, and promulgated certain laws; it is unlikely, however, that they entered a political vacuum or a region of political anarchy. No local documents concerning the political and administrative situation immediately before the arrival of the Kyekya Gangba have yet come to light, but there are good grounds for supposing that a system quite different from that imposed by these rulers prevailed before their arrival. This system survived the era of the contractors and probably remained largely unaffected up to the end of the Rana government in 1951. Ironically, it was probably the democratic reforms following the implementation of the Partyless Panchayat System in the 1960s that precipitated the decline of this system. By the same logic, this disintegration appears to be accelerating since the advent of multiparty democracy in Nepal in 1990. This being said, the archaic system of government survives with varying degrees of vitality in a number of communities.

In the accounts cited above, the vantage point of the authors has been the Thak Khola, the southernmost enclave of Mustang, and there are barely any accounts that address the history of the period from the perspective of Baragaon and Geling, the area where the archives considered in this volume are located. In the absence of any secondary literature, in order to get an idea of the relationship of this enclave with its northern and southern neighbours – and also with the national government in Kathmandu – during the period in question, we have to make use of the testimony of local archives. General overviews of the contents of the archives considered here are given in chapter 3. However, the dominant theme in local documents that are concerned with interaction between the different enclaves is that of north-south trade along the Kali Gandaki, which affected all the communities along the route. Since the archives that form the focus of this volume offer only a partial picture of relations among the various trading partners during and after the Rana period, we shall also have recourse to other private and community collections that were photographed during the 1990s.

The following section of the chapter is based on two sets of local documents.[22] The first is a collection of Nepalese archives that were in the possession of the late Sankarman Serchan, a member of the Thakali family that is associated with the salt monopoly more than any other. These were photographed by Charles Ramble and Nyima Drandul in 1995. Summaries of the contents of this archive were made by Harischandra Lal Singh. The other sources are Tibetan documents from the collective archive of Baragaon, which was photographed in 1993.[23] The Nepali documents record many of the discussions that took place and decisions that were made concerning the administration of the commerce, whereas the Tibetan documents offer insights into some of the tensions between the stakeholders.

Until 1857, the main figure of authority in Baragaon was the duke, *khri thog pa*. In conformity with a policy that had been applied in many parts of Nepal following the country's unification, the dukes were native rulers who, since 1789, had governed on behalf of the Gorkhalis in Kathmandu. In 1857, the Rana government introduced a system of contractual revenue-collection known as *ijāra*. Power at this time shifted to another local aristocrat who had the title of *sku zhabs* ("venerable one"), a common Tibetan term of address or reference for prominent laymen and clerics. It is

[22] The section is abridged and modified from a more extensive account given in Ramble 2018.

[23] Documents from Sankarman Serchan's archive are referenced here as "SS", followed by the document and page number (for example, SS/2.3). Documents from the Baragaon archive are cited as "Bar." followed by the number allocated to them in *Tibetan Sources 4*.

not clear whether the latter had the full jural rights of a contractor (*ijāradar*) or if he was the local representative of a southerner who held the contract. The title of *sku zhabs* was held by more than one individual at any given time, suggesting that the title was extended to a family rather than confined to a single person. The seals of these *sku zhabs* appear on several documents. The judicial power of the *sku zhabs* came to an end in the late nineteenth century when a family from the Thak area, in southern Mustang, secured the monopoly over the salt trade; the new contractors, who were given the title of *subbā*, thenceforth exercised direct control over the entirety of Baragaon and Geling and, to a lesser extent, over Upper Lo as well.

The fluidity of trade was periodically interrupted by disputes between groups, and its resumption was not enforced by governmental authority but through local reconciliation. As described above, Mustang is composed of small political units that were often in conflict with one another. The particular complexity of the situation was this: that the groups with which an enclave exchanged commodities were not neighbours, but entities that lay much father afield; however, the entities with which there was the highest incidence of conflict were, precisely, one's neighbours. The easiest way to hurt the neighbours was to damage their trading profits by imposing arbitrary transit duties and tariffs, or confiscating their merchandise. But there was nothing easier for a group that had been punished in this way than to impose reciprocal penalties. Furthermore, local conflicts that entailed such punitive measures hurt everyone in the chain, and saw prompt mediation by other parties to ensure that matters were resolved and trade could get moving again.

Trading patterns

For most of the period under consideration, Tibetans could bring salt down as far as Monthang, but were not permitted to travel any further south. The main northern entrepôt, however, was Tradum, situated some 80 kilometres north of the border as the crow flies. Tradum has an important place in the sacred history of Tibet insofar as the temple that stands there is considered to date from the time of Songtsen Gampo (d. 649/50), and belongs to the complex of edifices that he is believed to have commissioned in order to pin down the autochthonous demoness that was impeding the introduction of Buddhism to his empire. The temple was destroyed during the Cultural Revolution, and the only description of its images and murals may be a document from 1898 contained in the Tshognam archive that gives an account of a visit to the site by a pilgrim from Mustang (MA/LTshognam/Tib/15).[24] Tradum was the northern limit for traders from Nepal. Here the Lopas and Baragaonles (respectively, the inhabitants of Lo and Baragaon) would meet the nomads who had brought salt from the Northern Plateau. The Baragaonles could convey the salt to the main customs office at Dana, in Myagdi District to the south of Mustang, whereas the Lopas were permitted to go only as far down as Tukche. The southbound salt could be exchanged for grain at various points along the way, and the rate was fixed by the authorities, whether the government of Nepal or the contractors who held the monopoly. The rate of exchange varied along the way, the highest ratio of grain being in Lo Monthang, and the lowest at Dana.

Until 1862, the aristocracy of Baragaon were collecting revenues on commercial goods passing through Kag; both Lopas and Baragaonles could transport their salt south as far as Dana and, after payment of further duty, convey it down to the lowland markets. However, in this year the Government of Nepal introduced a policy whereby exclusive rights to collect revenue was auctioned to the highest bidder. Holders of this monopoly could acquire all the salt that came down the Kali Gandaki, and then exchange it for grain. The monopoly was highly unpopular with everyone who did not directly benefit from it – that is to say, the government and the contractors. Prior to the monopoly the customs office had been at Dana, but the *subbās*, the holders of the monopoly, moved it north to Tukche, a Thakali town on the main trade route. When the

[24] See Ramble 2015b.

monopoly finally ended in 1927 the office moved to Jomsom for much of the next three decades, though discussions about where it should be located continued for many years. Revenues on incoming salt were therefore being paid several days' walk south of the border between Tibet and Nepal. For fiscal purposes, then, the population north of Jomsom (who are ethnically Tibetan) were being treated as foreigners.

Baragaon's resentment at the Thakalis' tenure of the monopoly seems to have become especially acute in 1912. From 1905 to 1910 the contract had been held by two non-Thakalis in succession (Manilal Gurung and his son, Nar Jang), but in 1911 it returned to the Serchan family, and it may be the case that Baragaon, or at least the local aristocracy, had somehow benefited from the previous arrangement. In any event, in 1912, traders from Manang who had crossed the Thorang La pass into Mustang to follow the Kali Gandaki route up to the border found themselves blocked at Samar, the northernmost town in Baragaon. Representatives of the "Three Counties of Nyeshang" – that is, Manang – sent an impeccably polite letter to Baragaon. The text of the letter is as follows:

> To all the people of Baragaon who are led by their masters, foremost among them being the lords of Lower Lo *sku zhabs* Jamyang and *sku zhabs* Takla Wangyal, the source of benefits and peace and who know the Two Traditions, from the Three Counties of Manang, who are led by their headmen and officials. The subject is as follows: Baragaon in Lower Lo and the so-called Three Counties of Nyeshang, have from the past down to the present shared common interests. Helping each other without either side harming the other benefits both, since harming one would be damaging to the other. Now we have heard it said that we shall not be allowed to go towards Upper Lo beyond Samar. We, the Three Counties, have accordingly sent two people to present this petition, with sincere thanks in advance for your reply. It would be very desirable to preserve the status quo of previous generations. Sunday the first day of the 5th month in a Water Rat year, from the Three Counties of Nyeshang. (Bar. 19)

The implication in this letter that the restriction was imposed by the Baragaon aristocracy is supported by another letter, preserved in the enclave's archives, that followed five months later. This document was issued by "the lordly precious tax office in the town of Dana, Thak", and addressed to "The headmen (*rgan pa*), constables (*rol po*) and ordinary people (*mi ser*) of the eighteen communities of Lower Lo" (Bar. 20). The letter implies that Thak's monopoly of the salt-trade has been threatened by four men "carrying guns": *sku zhabs* Zangdor, *sku zhabs* Khamsum, Jamyang and Takla Wangyal, who all feature in other documents as prominent lords of Baragaon. The villagers should treat the customs post as if it were "a second government depot". The salt trade should not be interrupted but should continue regularly with the involvement of as many people as possible up and down the valley. If the salt trade is broken, the customs post will suffer a financial loss. As a result of this a request will have to be sent to the palace (*rgyal khang*) (in Kathmandu?). The villagers should decide what they ought to do about it. The letter is apparently a thinly-veiled threat. It states emphatically that only the four named people are responsible for the interruption in the flow of trade. Perhaps the people of Baragaon were using some other trade route or forcing their way past the customs? It is unlikely that the entire trade itself had stopped. Whatever the case, the letter seems to be offering the villagers a face-saving device to return to normal practice by simultaneously identifying four individuals as the guilty parties and suggesting that there may be government reprisals if they do not comply.

The rights of Manang, Baragaon and the more southerly enclaves to trade grain are described in an important document from the Geling archive (MA/Geling/Tib/101). The document – which is unfortunately undated – specifies that traders from Thak, Panchgaon, Baragaon and Manang may carry grain only as far north as the Dzeti Pass, which marks the northern territorial boundary of Geling. Some traders, the document states, have been violating this rule, and such transgressions must stop on pain of payment of a fine: 100 rupees for all the enclaves except Manang, which should pay a fine of 500 rupees. In any event, it is clear that Manang was authorised to take grain north of Samar at least as far as Geling.

Impediments to free trade

Smuggling seems to have been a perennial problem for the contractors, who in 1917 vented their irritation in an exasperated letter to the people of Baragaon (Bar. 21). The holder of the monopoly at this time was Ganesh Bahadur – a member of the Serchan clan – and the letter is issued by him and his two nephews, Hitman and Mohanman, who would themselves be the last two holders of the monopoly. Ganesh Bahadur reminded the Baragaonles that the *subbā*s were not only contractors but also the guarantors of the tax of 825 rupees that the enclave paid annually to the government. This relationship was fixed by a mutual agreement of which Baragaon had a written copy, an agreement – so the letter seems to say – that also committed the Baragaonles to paying duty on salt at the Tukche checkpost. Ganesh Bahadur accused the northern traders of "leaping over their taxes" (Tib. *khral mchong*) – that is to say, skirting around the customs office – but the difficulty of policing the trail is apparent in his rather plaintive insistence that the legal commitment has the character of a sacred bond that the smugglers are violating at the risk of divine reprisals: "If any officials acting on your behalf break the promise may the gods listed above [although in fact no gods are listed] punish them, since this is inauspicious."[25]

As mentioned earlier, the available documents are generally concerned with processes for damage limitation in times of conflict, and their preoccupation with immediate circumstances means that we often have no information about the background to the crisis. In 1932 (or so we may assume – the relevant document dates from March 1933) Baragaon imposed a ban on Lopas carrying salt and grain through its territory. On this occasion, at least, it appears that the *subbā* and the Baragaonles were on the same side. The latter confiscated several donkey-loads of northbound grain from a group of Lopas, and impounded it at a depot in Thak. The dispute was settled and the blockade lifted, but the Lopas then claimed (on what grounds we do not know) that the confiscated grain had been purloined. Later, however, they conceded that this claim had been a malicious one, and once they had gone to Thak to collect their goods from the depot, they sent Baragaon a letter to confirm that they had recovered their property, and the normal flow of trade was resumed (Bar. 22).

Tensions between Lo and Baragaon would flare up periodically. Apart from blocking the route or confiscating merchandise, enclaves would periodically impose transit duties on traders crossing their territory. In 1955, a trader called Jigme Chöphel was told that he would have to pay a tariff to transport his goods through Baragaon. Baragaon falsely claimed that this was normal practice, but Jigme Chöphel refused to pay, on the grounds that there was no precedent for such a tariff; that he had never in his life paid so much as a quarter of a rupee in transit fees, and that if anyone in Lo could be found who could attest to having paid such a fee he would willingly pay Baragaon a sum of 500 rupees (Bar. 30). The insistence that he pay transit tax was clearly a gesture of harassment by Baragaon against their northern neighbour for reasons that are not disclosed.

The village of Marpha is the only one of the five communities of Panchgaon that lies directly on the trade route, and northern traders would often use the settlement as an overnight halt. In the first half of 1933 Marpha imposed a ban on the sale of food and animal fodder to Baragaonle traders for reasons that are not specified. The nobility of Baragaon duly retaliated by imposing a similar ban on Marpha traders travelling through their territory, and for good measure forabade Baragaonles to sell salt or purchase alcohol in Marpha. Anyone who broke this rule was to be penalised with a fine of 5 rupees (Bar. 24). The stand-off is unlikely to have persisted for long: the damage to the common interests of these trading communities would have been too great to make any such reciprocal boycott worth anyone's while.

[25] Tib. *khyed rnams ... phyogs pa su phyogs nas dam tshig btangs na dgong khod gi lha srung ma rnams nas tshar spyad skra mi shi ba* (Bar. 21, lines 9–11).

Thieves and brigands

Impediments to the flow of trade were not always the result of conflicts between the main groups. In 1940 Sankarman travelled to Tibet on official business. His father, the *subbā* Mohanman, sent him a letter, but the bearer of the letter was robbed on the way. The letter and various other items were recovered, and the incident led to Mohanman's coordination of an agreement among all the enclaves to the effect that stolen goods that had been brought into their territory should be returned to their owner (SS/5.1).

By the mid-1940s, major political changes were taking place in the Sino-Tibetan borderlands, and it was not long before Mustang began to feel the effects of the unrest. In 1946 a large group of Tibetans – men, women and children – from Kham arrived as far south as Kag, armed with guns and swords. They robbed travellers and terrified the locals by firing into the air, but retreated north again when they sensed that the local communities were planning an attack on them (SS/11.3).

These fugitives from the war in eastern Tibet were not always anonymous: at least one of them made his way into Mustang folklore. In 1956 Sankarman received a letter from the small community of Chötsong, on the border of Tibet. The letter contained three points, of which the third was a plaintive cry for help:

> The one called Dobdob Yeshe Zangpo has stolen property from within Nepal: 800 yakloads of salt, and from seven households with [a population of] approximately 30 people with Nepal (or: with his retinue of thirty men [living in seven tents]) [he has taken] 2,000 sheep, 800 goats, nearly 1,000 yaks and thirty mules and horses. Dobdob Yeshe has already stolen (*zas*) this much property and livestock from within Nepal. After a potentially mortal engagement with a soldier at Nyichung [a location on the Nepal-Tibet border], Dobdob Yeshe would have killed him had he [the Dobdob?] not been restrained by the [people?] of Chötsong. There is no conflict between anyone in the four northern mountain communities and the people living within Nepal. In Nepal and Tibet the only person who causes trouble is Dobdob Yeshe. (Bar. 32)

Dobdob Yeshe Zangpo was a well-known borderland bandit of Tibetan origin whose main rival was another bandit called Amdo Godra. During the 1960s Dobdob Yeshe Zangpo managed to have him killed by friends he had made in the Tibetan guerrilla movement, the Chushi Gangdruk (Chu bzhi sgang drug). In his old age, Yeshe Zangpo became devoutly religious, gave away his property to good causes and died in the Tibetan refugee camp in Dhorpatan, in Nepal. He is reported to have passed into the post-mortem meditative state known as *thugs dam*, an indication of spiritual achievement that caused his enemies great annoyance. He is now remembered in Mustang as a kind of folk hero, and there are even songs about his adventures. Sankarman claimed that Dobdob Yeshe Zangpo respected him because he had once got the better of the brigand in a contest of marksmanship with rifles during an encounter in northern Lo.

Fixing the border

Following the end of the salt monopoly in 1927, there was a great deal of discussion about the future location of the checkposts and customs offices. The different interest groups had their own preferences about where it should be placed, but a site near Jomsom, the present headquarters of Mustang, was eventually decided upon, and the rights to the collection of revenue were contracted out to members of the Serchan family. According to Vinding,

> the government established, in 1928, a customs office in Jomsom and entrusted the collection of customs duties to government officials. This system did not function satisfactorily, and in 1930 the government appointed some members of Balbir's lineage as customs collectors in Jomsom against an annual payment of Rs 12,000. This contract was only of minor importance to the Thakali subba and the management of the customs office was entrusted to some relatives from Jomsom.

A footnote at this point adds the following information:

> In 1954 the government closed down the Jomsom customs office and the collection of customs duties on salt entering Nepal was done only at the customs office at Nechung in Lo near the Tibetan border. It is not known when the customs office at Nechung was established.[26]

Vinding mentions Fürer-Haimendorf's assertion that the office was operational in the 1930s. This claim, made in *Himalayan Traders*, states: "In the 1930s when the customs post was situated at Netsung [i.e. Nyichung] in Lo, Thakali traders would go there in the months of May and June to meet regular trade partners coming from nearby villages as well as from Tibet".[27] I have seen no documents to suggest that the customs office was anywhere other than in the Thak area at this time. Unless the Nyichung office was a short-lived experiment (that was to be revived in the 1950s), we should consider the possibility that this border post was not a customs office but simply a trade mart.

The decision to open the office in Jomsom had actually been taken before the end of the salt monopoly. On 28 Kartik 1984 BS (13 November 1927) an order was issued to the effect that a main customs office should be opened here (SS/18), whereas the monopoly was officially terminated on the last day of that year (corresponding to 13 April 1928) (SS/25.3). According to a document in Sankarman's archive, the contract on the office lapsed on 13 April 1955 (the last day of Caitra 2011 BS; SS/1.3). It is certain at least that by June 1955, in spite of lingering doubts, there was no need for the Baragaonles to pay revenues at Jomsom. They had probably heard that the customs office was going to be moved, but waited to take their merchandise up to Baragaon until they were sure that the post had been closed. They received confirmation of its closure in a letter from Sankarman in 1955:

> To the wise and blessed leaders of wide Ngazhab. The subject is as follows: I spoke to the government office in Baglung and it appears that you need not pay taxes at the Jomsom customs office. They said that you can take up whatever grain and merchandise you have in the Thak area. It appears that you will not need to arrange a time for [an emergency] meeting of Ngazhab [that had been planned]. (Bar. 31)

The date of 1954 given by Vinding for its closure is nevertheless supported by other documents suggesting that, even if the contract still had some months to run, it may have been abandoned prematurely in favour of a new site. The Jomsom office was highly unpopular with all the northerners, and in this year a group of Lopas who resented having to pay duties at this location attacked the office and threw all the weights and measures into the river (SS/1.3, Oct/Nov 1954). It is possible that the office was moved from Jomsom to Dana for the remaining six months or so of the contract, since we know that the Dana office had been contracted to Nagendraman (Sankarman's elder brother) from 1954 to 1955 (SS/4.3). If there was indeed such a move, it may have been precipitated by the Lopas' attack. The communities of Lo and Geling were strongly in favour of the customs office being moved south to Tatopani, and they expressed this view in an open letter sent in May 1954.

> [C]oncerning the revenues to be paid at the tax office in Jomsom, Baragaon and the Seven Counties of Lo have been enduring great suffering, and therefore Baragaon Ngazhab, the commonly-appointed headmen of the Seven Counties of Lo and the wardens of each region held a meeting. They reached an agreement to the effect that, henceforth, the customs office in Jomsom should be completely removed. The second point is that the Jomsom tax office be moved to Tatopani (in Myagdi District). The third point is that the people living above Tatopani and below the Kore La pass, the border between the Gorkha [Kingdom] and Tibet, should all pay whatever tax obligations might be imposed on them for their ruler, the great king of Gorkha and that, henceforth, there should be no customs office at Jomsom. This is the decision that we took and from which we shall not deviate. (Bar. 28)

[26] Vinding 1998: 88.

[27] Fürer-Haimendorf 1975: 191.

The gist of this document is that the participants in the meeting to which it refers – representatives of Baragaon, Geling and Lo – all agreed that the customs office be moved to Tatopani – well below the southern border of Mustang District, a measure that would (it is implied) ensure fiscal equality among all those who lived between there and the Tibetan border. The claim that "they reached an agreement" notwithstanding, the list of signatories makes it clear that not all the participants at the meeting were party to the accord: Baragaon is absent. The document is an agreement between Lo and Geling, but as an agreement among trading partner enclaves it is little more than an expression of wishful thinking.

The Lopas' claim that it was in the common interest of all those living between the Kore La pass and Tatopani to shift the office to the latter location is disingenuous. Few Lopas, if any, traded south of Tatopani, whereas groups living further downstream on the Kali Gandaki would have been seriously affected by such a move. Contrary to the Lopas' assertion, Baragaon actually favoured the small village of Nyichung – the northernmost settlement in Mustang before the Tibetan border – as the site of the office. At some point in 1954 the zonal administration in Baglung issued an order that the office should be established in Nyichung, and after some hesitation about whether Baglung had the authority to do this, the order was confirmed by the Finance Ministry in Kathmandu on 31 August 1954 (SS/22.3). The Nyichung post must have been established shortly after this, since the zonal revenue office in Baglung wrote to the Dana office to enquire how it was working. However, the Nyichung post was apparently not yet in operation. This is implied in a letter sent by Sankarman to his elder brother Nagendraman, the holder of the Dana contract, reminding him that his contract had expired and that he should hand over the weights and measures to be taken up to Nyichung (SS/4.3). Four years later the weights and measures had still not been moved to Nyichung. Moreover, matters were further complicated by a dispute between certain communities of the Shöyul of Baragaon, and a growing rift between powerful members of the Serchan family. Matters came to a head in late 1959, and eleven of the villages of Baragaon held a meeting to decide how best to proceed. They decided to ask Sankarman to request the Baglung office to move it up to Nyichung, on the Tibetan border, so that only international trade be taxed. This move was strongly opposed by the Lopas, most of whose trading activities took place north of the border. The task of carrying out the move was allocated to the village of Kag, one of the communities in Baragaon. Following Kag's refusal, on grounds of the danger of violent resistance from Lo, to convey the scales north, Tanka Prasad, a relative of Sankarman Serchan, undertook to carry out the task himself. He succeeded in delivering the weights and measures to the newly-established Nyichung customs office, but on his return journey was pursued south by a party of hostile Lopas. His pursuers caught up with him at the sacred caves of Congshi Ranjung, on Geling's territory. Tanka Prasad took the rifle from one of the soldiers who was accompanying him and shot one of the attackers dead. He escaped with his life, but the incident is said to have destroyed his political career.

The end of the trade route

The Kali Gandaki's days as a conduit for the salt trade were by now nearly over. The construction of a motorable road in southern Nepal had already opened the way to imports of inexpensive Indian salt, but developments on the northern border were a more decisive factor. The Nepal-Tibet border was redrawn – and officially closed by the Chinese – in 1962, though there is evidence to suggest that measures to bring an end to commerce between Tibet and Nepal across the Mustang border were taken two years earlier. At the time of writing, a new road through Mustang linking the Chinese and Nepalese transport networks is undergoing reinforcement that will enable it to carry a considerable volume of commercial traffic, while a major trade entrepôt is in the process of being built on the Chinese side of the border. While these measures will certainly revitalise the historical role of the Kali Gandaki as a historical conduit for trade, there is little doubt that they will contribute significantly to the ongoing demographic and social transformation of Mustang.

Chapter 3
Archival Documents as a Part of the Tangible Cultural Heritage of Mustang

Archives are both collections of documents providing information about a place, an institution, or group of people and the spaces where these collections are stored. According to Foucault in *The Archaeology of Knowledge*, the word "archive" can mean "the general system of the formation and transformation of memory," which designates the collection of all material traces left behind by a particular historical period and culture.[1] The Tibetan archival heritage, as with Tibetan culture, has developed in specific circumstances which have strongly influenced how this archival heritage is preserved.

The destruction of archives that took place in Tibet during the 1950s and again during the Cultural Revolution may have been very extensive, but it was not complete. It is estimated that there are some two to three million documents in the National Archives in Lhasa. Selections from the archive occasionally appear in officially-sanctioned academic publications, but the fact that each selection is made only after a careful vetting of its contents compromises the value of such material for research on any aspect of social history: this sort of selectiveness gives us a very partial view of what was surely a complex overall picture.

The abovementioned archive of the Tibetan written heritage is nowadays named the Historical Archive of the Tibet Autonomous Region (TAR) in Lhasa. This archive contains a complex collection of both government, political and administrative records on the one hand, and on the other, Buddhist religious and secular texts and records of monastery and temple management.[2] Perhaps the most important thing about the documents in this archive is precisely that – they are an archive, something that is qualitatively more than merely the sum of the parts that make it up. As interesting as an individual document may be, the availability of the context in which it was produced might make it possible for us to see the event to which it relates unfolding over the course of time, or perhaps to realise that it is an aberration that is at odds with the evidence of the other records. Access to a large number of documents that span an extended period is essential if we are ever to begin to address the questions that underlie certain political, social and economic institutions – the matter of whether Tibet was a feudal society or not being just one of these.

Some archival collections from Central Tibetan dependencies and semi-autonomous enclaves were brought into exile by groups of refugees who fled Tibet in 1959. A catalogue of one such collection from the south-western part of Central Tibet, notably the principality of Porong (Tib. sPong rong) and nearby areas, has been published by Hanna Schneider.[3] The importance of such archives is that they significantly modify the image of the Tibetan polity as a homogeneous entity under a monumental centralised bureaucracy. Although principalities such as Porong were within the political orbit of the Dalai Lamas, they enjoyed considerable autonomy under hereditary rulers, and sometimes with their own system of priesthood.

Although some Western archival thought has been incorporated into archival practice in the Tibetan Autonomous Region (TAR), the area's complex history, geography and political situation contribute tremendously to the backlogs in arrangement, description, and preservation of archival documents there. All these factors limit access to Tibetan archives for historical research. Because of this, all initiatives to preserve Tibetan archival documents are enormously valuable. The study of Tibetan history is still mainly based on literary and rarely on official sources, due to the severe limits on access to original documents. For this reason, the study of Tibetan archival documents is a primary goal of scholarly research.

[1] For discussion on archives and terminology see: Foucault 1972: 129–31.

[2] Moss 1996: 351.

[3] Schneider 2012.

The other important institution dedicated to the preservation and dissemination of Tibetan material culture is the Library of Tibetan Works and Archives in Dharamsala, founded in 1970 by the XIV Dalai Lama. There are more than 70,000 Tibetan manuscripts and documents in this library, and the collection is still growing. Beyond the Himalayan region, significant collections of Tibetan documents found in Dunhuang and Turfan are now preserved in the British Library, the Berlin Brandenburg Academy of Sciences (BBAW), the Berlin State Library (BSL), the Pelliot collection in the Bibliothèque Nationale de France in Paris, the Oldenburg collection in the Institute of Oriental Manuscripts in St Petersburg, and in the Otani Collection in Ryūkoku University in Kyoto.

The extensive use of digital technologies has allowed for broad dissemination of textual heritage. Thus, the task of cataloguing, photographing, protecting and publishing Tibetan archival documents has been undertaken for those collections that it was possible to access. A database called Old Tibetan Documents Online (OTDO) is an important resource for studying the Tibetan archival tradition with online images of texts dated to the seventh up to twelfth centuries, which also include transliterations that enable online searches.[4] The OTDO is an ongoing database project established in 1969 by Yoshiro Imaeda and is presently coordinated by Hoshi Izumi at the Research Institute for Languages and Cultures of Asia and Africa (ILCAA), University of Foreign Studies, Tokyo, Japan, and also supported by Kobe City University of Foreign Studies, Centre National de la Recherche Scientifique (CNRS), and the International Dunhuang Project (IDP). Tsuguhito Takeuchi, who was a chief editor of the OTDO, studied a large number of Old Tibetan contracts found in Tarim Basin, including Dunhuang, Miran, Mazar Tagh, Old Domoko, Khadalik, and the Turfan area. Besides translation, he discussed their formal characteristics and the social and socio-linguistic circumstances in which they were produced.[5] Another resource for early Tibetan documents is the International Dunhuang Project (IDP) at the British Library, whose corpus includes Dunhuang manuscripts, documents, inscriptions and related materials.[6]

Roughly at the same time as the OTDO project Dieter Schuh in Bonn set the stage for the study of Tibetan archival documents in Germany. He established the project for the study of Tibetan history called the Monumenta Tibetica Historica (MTH).[7] His aim was to create a scientific corpus (which includes historical material) from an area whose sources are underestimated by the professional world.[8] This core work was followed by a project carried out by Peter Schwieger of the Department of Mongolian and Tibetan Studies at Bonn University. The project aimed to lay the foundation of electronic resources for the study of Tibetan archival documents not accessible to Western scholars. In 1998, the University of Bonn initiated a DFG-funded collaborative project with the Archives of the Tibet Autonomous Region to digitise a part of the collection. The corpus was the archive of the monastery of Kundeling, near Lhasa. 2,620 documents covering the fourteenth to the twentieth centuries were digitised, and may now be consulted online on the website *Digital Tibetan Archives Bonn* (DTAB) within the *CrossAsia* Portal hosted by the Berlin State Library.[9] The other digitised texts concern diplomatic sources and administrative papers which are of critical importance to historical research in Tibet. An additional 1700 documents from the collections of the Berlin State Library, the Library of Tibetan Works and Archives (LTWA),

[4] Old Tibetan Documents Online (OTDO) http://otdo.aa-ken.jp/ (last accessed 06 June 2017).

[5] Takeuchi's work, besides translation, involves examination of the original items in order to check formal characteristics such as paper size and quality, to read faint letters and seals, to measure the finger seals, etc. See: Takeuchi 1995: 5–6, 1998; Imaeda and Takeuchi 2007.

[6] The International Dunhuang Project: The Silk Road Online http://idp.bl.uk/. Together with Sam van Schaik I had a chance to study material features of selected documents from this collection. See: Helman-Ważny and van Schaik 2013: 707–41.

[7] The scientific corpus and publication series was established by Dieter Schuh (Andiast, Switzerland), Luciano Petech (Rome), Wang Yao (Beijing, China), R. A. Stein (Paris), Geza Uray (Budapest), H.-R. Kämpfe (Bonn) und R. O. Meisezahl (Bonn). See: Monumenta Tibetica Historica http://www.tibetinstitut.de/monumenta-tibetica.html (last accessed 06 June 2017).

[8] Schuh 1994, 1995, 2015.

[9] See: https://crossasia.org/en/service/crossasia-lab/dtab/ at CrossAsia Portal hosted by the Berlin State Library (https://dtab.crossasia.org/).

Dharamsala, India, and private collections of Kurt H. Dahnke and André Alexander have also been digitally recorded.[10]

Digitisation and access to original documents enhance our understanding of Tibetan history and archaeology and mark the significance of this region in the wider context of the ancient world. Furthermore, they form an important part of preservation protocol, which allows these documents to be seen as part of material and cultural heritage of this region. At the same time, the information derived from documents creates a primary source of knowledge, which is entirely independent of social and political considerations. However, another face of such development is that while the above projects are mostly involved in translations of specific collections of individual texts as well as transliterations and their electronic record, most material aspects are still not addressed.

The rapid development of internet resources together with the almost total lack of research on Tibetan archival materials as *de facto* material objects has resulted in a field of scholars who associate both books and historical documents – indeed all texts – as virtual objects in digital or microform formats. This virtual awareness has created a narrowing focus in the research of Tibetan written heritage that has led to an accompanying diminution of the value of these same documents in their real, material form. As a consequence, research on Tibetan archival documents is now split in two with virtual texts and their physical forms separated and their collective meaning much harder to retrieve. It is vital to remember that Tibetan archival documents are objects of tangible Cultural Heritage.[11] These objects must be studied in the same way as all other archaeological objects because preserved documents validate memories; the actuality of the object, as opposed to a reproduction or surrogate, provides the living with a link to the past. Preservation of these documents demonstrates recognition of the past and of the things that tell its story. In a longer perspective, it can aid in the reconstruction of many still unknown fragments of history in Tibet and shed light on the materiality of these documents. Thus, the next logical stage of research is the preservation and revealing of documents' materiality. This also contributes to a better understanding of the role of physical objects in archival practices and also the socio-historical aspect of producing and archiving these objects.[12]

The awareness of documents' materiality can be increased in two ways, by the study and record of all possible information on the objects physicality, and then by applying various conservation-restoration procedures *in situ* to preserve these objects of cultural heritage for future generations. Accordingly, an important part of our research was the creation of the records of material features which are usually not documented during standard digitisation. Thus, as described above in chapter 1, besides photographing whole documents we made images of paper against light, images of texture with a Dino-Lite microscope, and a variety of close-ups showing techniques of writing and painting. All these images complete the standard images of text, and in this sense reveal the materiality of photographed objects much better. We created templates, database and started systematic data collection. Such a protocol allows for better understanding of documents at the material level. We were able to document the places and facilities where documents were stored and to inform the owners of documents about safe ways of keeping and handling these artefacts. However, implementation of any conservation treatment *in situ* was not performed, since this would have required another project and much more time. Indeed, there are no artefacts written on paper that have yet had a chance to be treated in Mustang by professional conservators.

[10] The site mentioned above used to offer high-resolution images of 1648 handwritten papers, mainly files and legal documents, from the following collections:
364 documents of the Berlin State Library;
179 documents of the private collection of Kurt H. Dahnke;
264 documents of the private collection of André Alexander;
841 documents of the Library of Tibetan Works and Archives (LTWA), Dharamsala, India.

[11] Tangible heritage includes buildings and historic places, monuments, artefacts, and objects significant for the archaeology, architecture, science or technology of a specific culture. Objects are important to the study of human history because they provide a concrete basis for ideas, and can validate them.

[12] Neate and Howell 2011: 9–14.

[13] For information about preservation of cultural her-

The concept of the preservation of the objects' materiality has not been understood in Mustang. The conservation of cultural heritage improved significantly when Nepal joined UNESCO in 1953, but activities that were undertaken were mostly conducted in the Kathmandu Valley and not in Mustang, which has not received any significant support largely due to its remote location. The territory of Mustang was not easily accessible to foreigners (Upper Mustang was opened to foreigners only in 1992), and local people have slowly become aware that their cultural heritage is under threat. Thus, it is only very recently that the people of Mustang were introduced to the Western idea of heritage preservation.[13] Although local communities are proud of their heritage, they lack both the resources and knowledge to safeguard their material culture. The situation became even more evident after the devastating impact of the 2015 earthquake on Mustang's unique cultural heritage. The continuing, albeit still rare, conservation projects funded by Western foundations and conducted by professional conservators deal with architecture and wall painting, but never with movable paper objects such as books or documents. These projects are thus unable at all to address needs that are obvious for the care of archival collections.

Also at the cultural level there is a significant gap between Western codes and practices in paper conservation and the reality of what can be implemented in Mustang due to the economic situation, hard climatic conditions, and prevailing cultural attitudes. The materiality of written artefacts is secondary for local people, and often neglected when it comes to the preservation of cultural heritage. In practice, conservation is understood as the replacement of an old object with a new one. In effect, then, the number of original objects is constantly dwindling. With the replacement of original books and the restoration of wall paintings, a great deal of historical and scholarly information is lost forever. Secondly, in the case of specifically archival documents there is often little sense of their historical and cultural value, or even any kind of initiative to preserve these documents. The documents, which are often legal acts, were not produced as religious books for use in generating spiritual merit. This explains why we were often unable to find the same documents when we visited the same places at different times, because they had been misplaced or discarded. Thus, despite the dry climate of Mustang, which favours the survival of documents, many documents are not to be found anymore or are in a poor condition. The collection of metadata on the material objects was thus especially important for cataloging archival collections, since many of those documents may not be available for future research anymore or may be destroyed.

An important aspect of our work was to carry out the documentation of the state of preservation of these documents and the storage facilities (furniture and architecture). In Mustang, the places where documents were preserved greatly varied from one location to the other. The documents examined were usually preserved in people's houses, sometimes close to home altars, and sometimes in randomly selected places with no specific features. There was no particular shelving system or special furniture, as it is usually the case for large collections of religious books. Interiors of such houses were usually poorly lit, as well as being full of dust and smoke, especially if the documents were kept in the kitchen. As can be seen on the photograph from Tshognam, light usually enters through an open hole in the roof (Fig. 34). Houses in Mustang are usually built from mud or rammed earth using a wooden framework.[14] Rammed earth is a construction technique where soil is taken from the ground and compacted to form structures.[15] Such houses are not well protected from either water or fire.

Documents were usually covered with dust and sometimes mud. In some places they were stored in wooden or metal boxes, as seen in the photographs from Lubrak, Lower Tshognam and Geling (Figs 3–7 and 35). In some other cases they were wrapped in cloth, placed in straw baskets, hemp or plastic bags (Figs 36 and 37). Occasionally we found individual documents being kept in small leather bags, such as one contained in the archive of Lower Tshognam (Fig. 38). In the case of larger collections of documents, these were sometimes bound into tight bundles as is done with the most valuable documents from the Geling archive (Fig. 39).

itage in Mustang see: Bista and von der Heide 1997: 168–73; Darnal 2001; Selter 2007; Fieni 2011: 138–40 and 2017: 5–20.

[14] Harrison and Ramble 1998: 23–37.

[15] For other examples of this construction in other parts of the world see: Jaquin 2008.

Fig. 34. Interior of the room in Tshognam where the archive is kept. Photograph by Agnieszka Helman-Ważny.

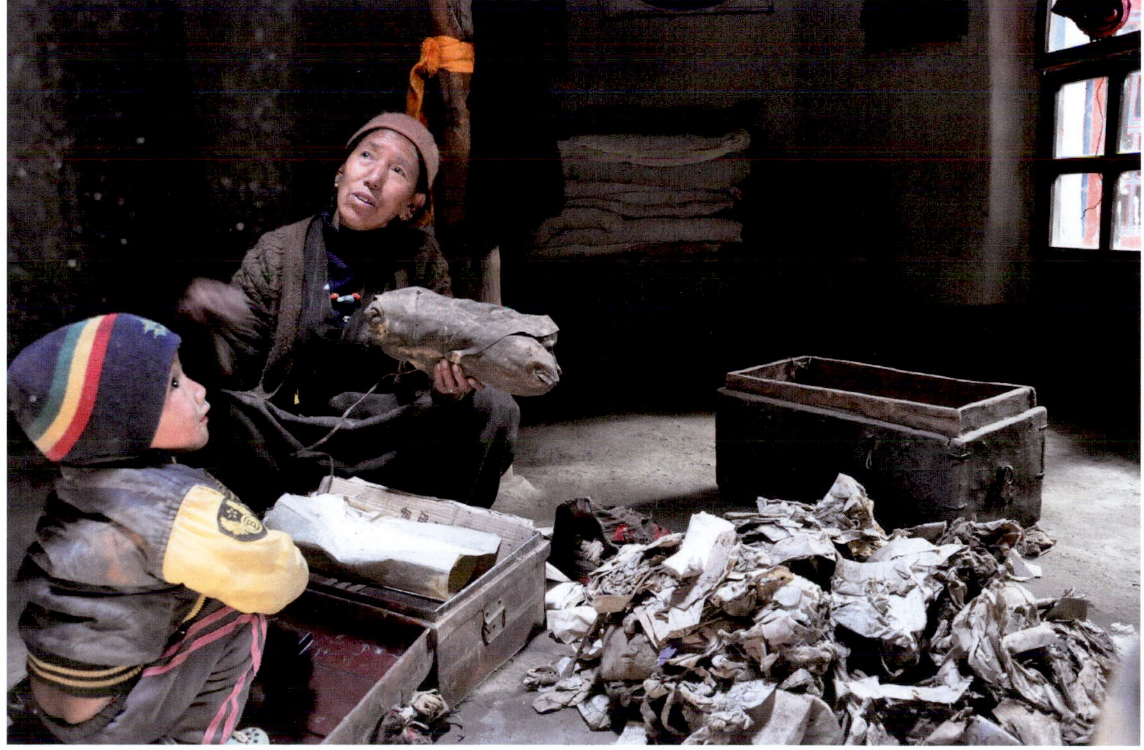

Fig. 35. Documents kept in wooden boxes from the Geling archive. Photograph by Agnieszka Helman-Ważny.

Fig. 36. Documents kept in a basket in the Lower Tshognam archive. Photograph by Agnieszka Helman-Ważny.

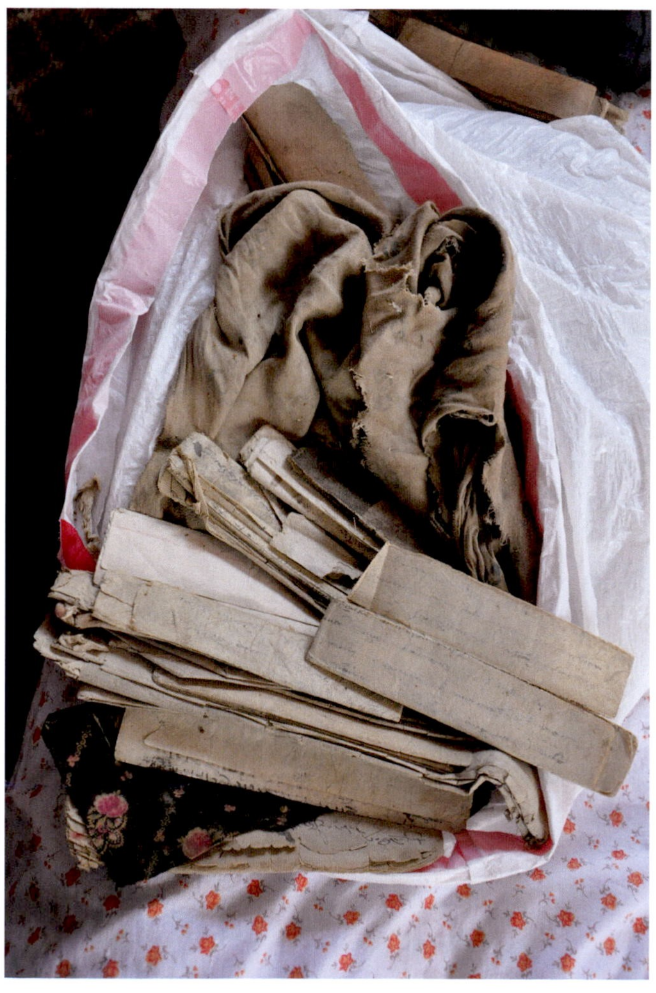

Fig. 37. Documents from Upper Tshognam kept in a plastic bag. Photograph by Agnieszka Helman-Ważny.

Fig. 38. The leather bag used for archival documents from Lower Tshognam. Photograph by Agnieszka Helman-Ważny.

Fig. 39. Bundles of folded documents in the Geling archive. Photograph by Agnieszka Helman-Ważny.

The status and storage environment of particular archival collections determined the state of the preservation of the documents. However, conditions may differ within the same archive, as for example in Geling where the most valuable documents are kept in a different place from the discarded part, which is loosely stored in a separate wooden box (Fig. 40). This part was in an exceptionally poor condition. We looked through this large collection and checked each document which we were able to open. It took us hours to select a small group of documents which were still legible (Fig. 41).

Fig. 40. Discarded documents kept in wooden boxes from the Geling archive. Photograph by Agnieszka Helman-Ważny.

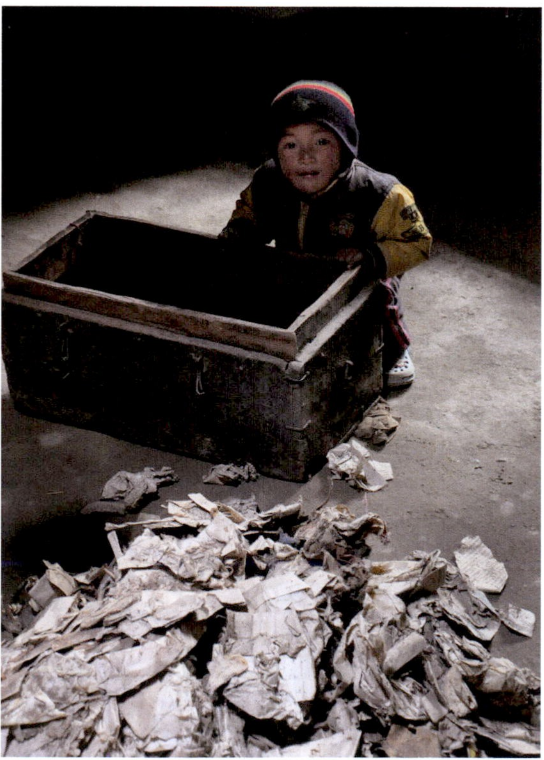

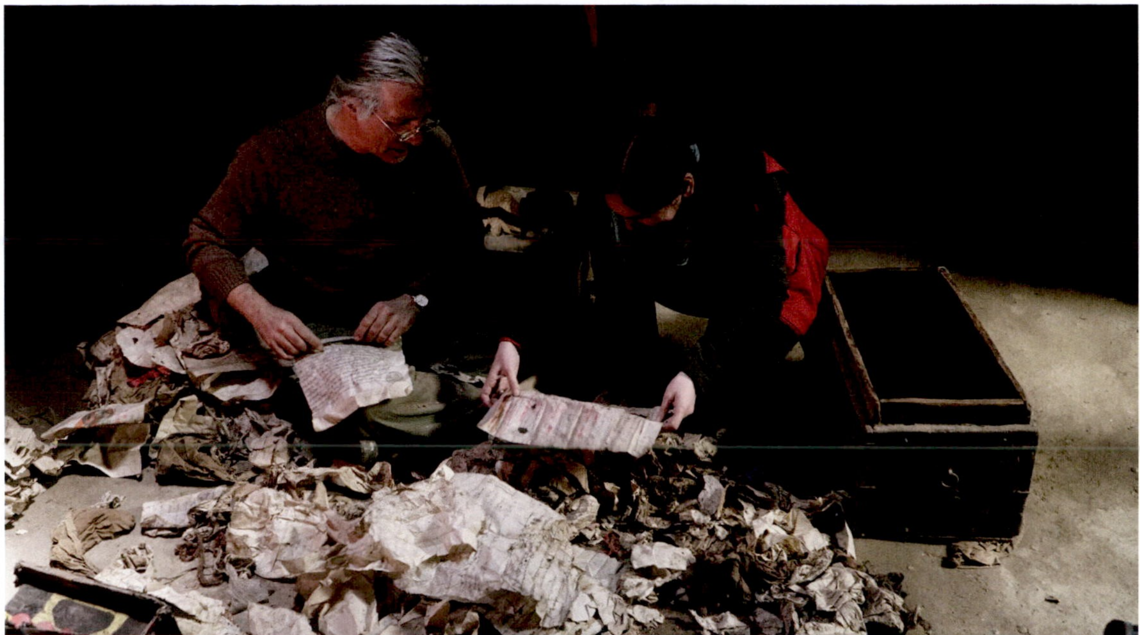

Fig. 41. Selection of legible documents from discarded items in the Geling archives. Photograph by Kemi Tsewang.

Fig. 42 a. Brown areas probably caused by fire (from high heat) observed in document MA/Geling/Tib/40 from the Geling archive. Photograph by Kemi Tsewang.

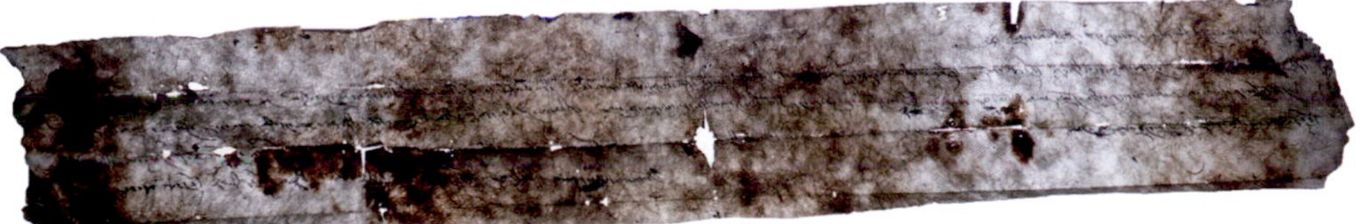

Fig. 42 b. Document MA/Geling/Tib/40 from the Geling archive when backlit. Photograph by Kemi Tsewang.

From our Mustang sample, after looking at many different kinds of documents in various places we were able to observe a range of the typical kinds of damage these documents might suffer, as exemplified by the half-burned documents from Gyaga resulting from a fire in the building where they were kept, or discarded parts of the collection from Geling (Figs 40 and 41). The brown areas resulting from high heat probably caused by fire were visible in some documents, as for example the document MA/Geling/Tib/40 from the Geling archive (Figs 42 a, b). Despite the lack of rain and low humidity we observed many examples of damage from water or other liquids appearing as yellow stained fragments of paper, sometimes together with cavities created by insects. This type of damage can be observed in documents MA/Geling/Tib/70 and MA/Geling/Tib/104 from the Geling archive (Figs 43 a, b and 44).

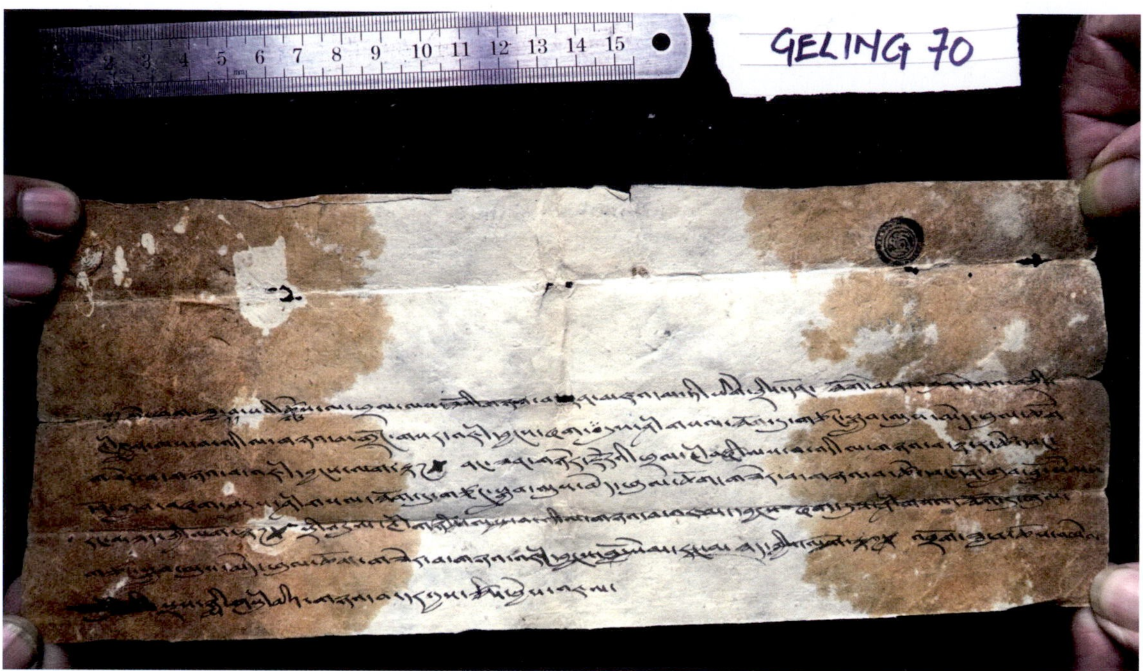

Fig. 43a. Document MA/Geling/Tib/70 from the Geling archive. Photograph by Kemi Tsewang.

Fig. 43b. Document MA/Geling/Tib/70 from the Geling archive when observed backlit. Photograph by Kemi Tsewang.

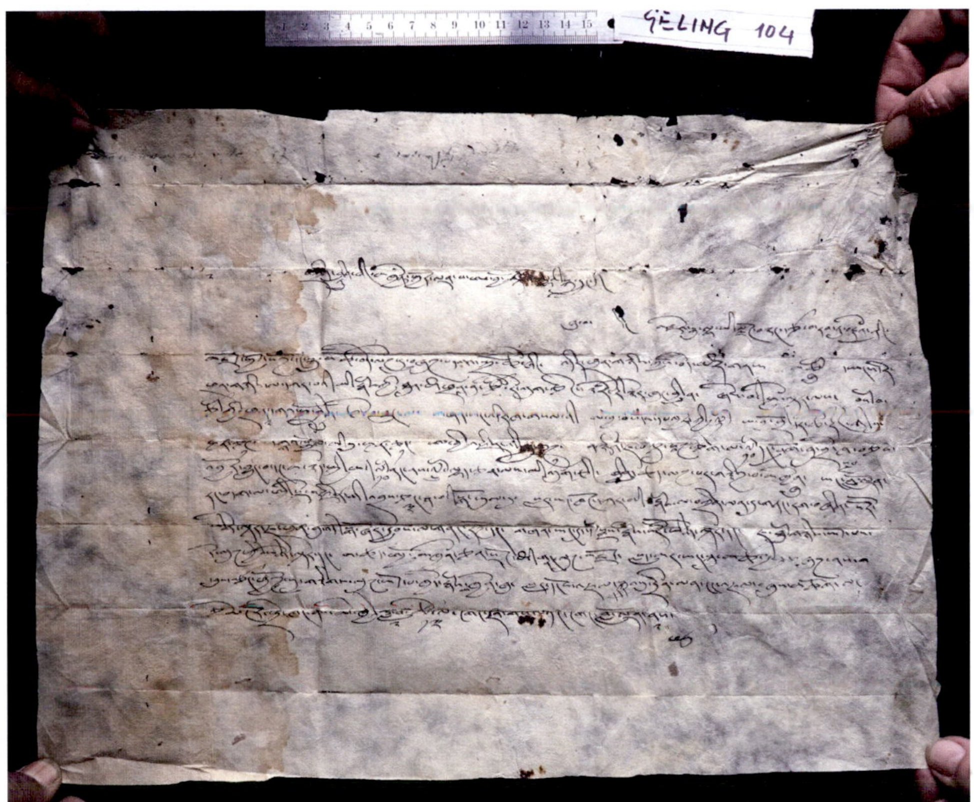

Fig. 44 a. Document MA/Geling/Tib/104 from the Geling archive with damage from water appearing as yellow stained fragments of paper. Photograph by Kemi Tsewang.

Fig. 44 b. Document MA/Geling/Tib/104 from the Geling archive when observed backlit. Photograph by Kemi Tsewang.

Many documents, especially from this discarded part, were entirely crumpled. Typical creases and wrinkles can be seen on document MA/Geling/Tib/168 and MA/Dzar/Tib/7 (Fig. 45 and 46). Documents MA/Geling/Tib/82, MA/Geling/Tib/142 and MA/UTshognam/Tib/24 show breaks along the folding marks, a typical form of damage in many other documents caused by its usage (Fig. 47, 48 and 49). Some documents, for example MA/Geling/Tib/141, had an unusual format, making it difficult to fold in the traditional way and therefore more vulnerable to damage (Fig. 50). Also, the upper part of documents is usually more damaged, as illustrated by document MA/Geling/Tib/124, since that part is usually in the last fold and therefore on the outside (Fig. 51). The unusual or exceptionally large size of documents make them especially vulnerable to various damages.

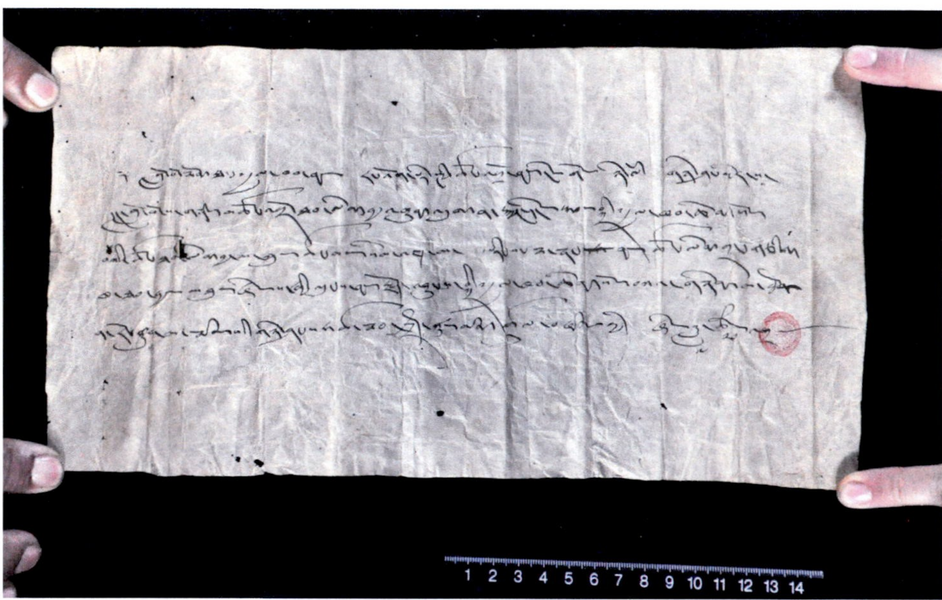

Fig. 45. Document MA/Geling/Tib/168 from the Geling archive with wrinkled surface. Photograph by Kemi Tsewang.

Fig. 46. Document MA/Dzar/Tib/7 from the Dzar archive with wrinkled surface and dirt spots. Photograph by Kemi Tsewang.

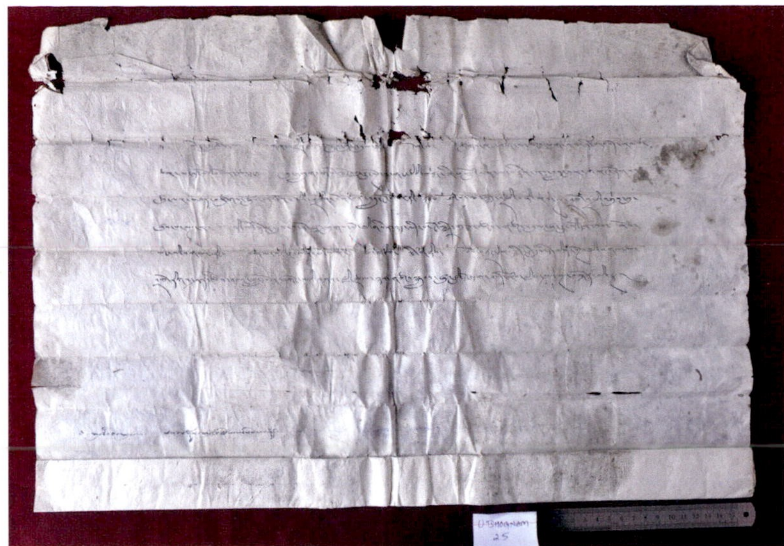

Fig. 47. Document MA/UTshognam/Tib/24 from the Upper Tshognam archive showing breaks along the folds, as well as deformation from the way in which it was folded. Photograph by Agnieszka Helman-Ważny.

Fig. 48. How large format documents are generally read. Document from the archive of Lower Tshognam. Photograph by Agnieszka Helman-Ważny.

Fig. 49. Typical damage, such as tears and cavities in a document from the Dzar archive. Photograph by Kemi Tsewang.

Fig. 50. Document MA/Geling/Tib/141, an unusual format from the Geling archive. Photograph by Kemi Tsewang.

Fig. 51. A large-size document, MA/Geling/Tib/124, from the Geling archive. Photograph by Kemi Tsewang.

Because conservation treatment is very laborious and difficult work and requires highly qualified experts, as well as both time and proper infrastructure, it was not possible to perform any treatment directly on documents within our project. Also, the idea of conservation was not really supported by owners, who did not feel a need to improve the state of preservation of their documents. In such circumstances we aimed at building awareness and support for the local communities who are the owners of these documents, by explaining the basic procedures for the storage, preservation and protection of these materials. Despite the difficulties, it would be possible to take some basic small-scale measures, for example cleaning (gentle removal of dirt and dust); disinfection and pest control; basic repair of paper support; improvement of the storage conditions (keeping documents in dry and safe places); periodic checks of the collection.

Chapter 4
The Mustang Archives:
Where They Are Kept and What They Are About

As an area of Tibetan culture, Mustang is the site of numerous monasteries and other religious communities of Buddhism and Bon, and possesses an abundance of religious literature of either local or Tibetan provenance. In addition to this religious heritage, however, many private households and most communities (especially in the south) have archives of documents dealing with a wide range of mainly secular affairs. (Where religion does feature in these, it is usually in relation to the financial or organisational aspects of ceremonies.) This chapter will offer an overview of the contents of the archives under consideration in this volume, and will cite excerpts from selected items in order to convey an idea of their subject-matter and style.

Tibetan archives in the Himalayan region

The examples discussed above are the archives of monasteries or else political centres of one sort or another, and the type of documents they contain are to a great extent concerned with "vertical" communication between authorities and ordinary people. Even if there was a certain amount of "upward" correspondence in the form of petitions to the ruler or higher authorities, much of the material in these collections consists of edicts and other orders to social inferiors, records of ceremonies and other official events, lists of gifts, financial matters and suchlike. There is little information about dealings between villagers; the overwhelming majority of the documents consist of different categories of communication from institutions or individuals in positions of authority to lower-ranking members of the population.

The archives of Mustang differ significantly in this regard. As we have seen in the previous chapter, Baragaon seceded from Upper Lo quite early on in the history of the kingdom, and was ruled by a succession of dukes who belonged to a local noble family. After the Gorkhas' annexation of the entire territory during their unification of Nepal, the king in the north and the duke in the south became the representatives of the Kathmandu-based government of the new country, and retained a high degree of autonomy. There is evidence that, prior to the arrival of the ancestors of those local rulers, many of the communities in the territory operated as something akin to miniature democratic city states, with elected or rotating leaders and a strong sense of integrity (several of them were even endogamous), and this system survived both monarchic rule and modern government structures in the form of a vibrant civil society down to the present day. Consequently, with the exception of a few missives from the King of Mustang, local dignitaries and monasteries in Tibet, much the greater part of the archives concern dealings *inter pares*.

Community archives are usually kept in a public building; responsibility for their care lies with the annually-rotating headmen, and they may be opened only in the presence of the village assembly. Alternatively, the box of documents may be kept in the house of one headmen, and the key with the other. In the case of certain private archives, the status of certain households is such that the archives contain a certain proportion of items of a public character. Private archives typically consist of documents such as contracts for loans of grain or cash, sales of land, wills, disputes over ownership and inheritance of property. Community archives may be classified according to various criteria, but broadly fall into two categories: documents relating to internal affairs and those concerned with dealings with outsiders. The former includes records of community gatherings, rules for local natural resource management (such as forests, water and grazing), disputes between fellow-villagers that were mediated by the community, and annual grain taxes to the communal fund. Those dealing with outsiders may include pasture boundary agreements with neighbours, and directives or other correspondence from political authorities such as the King of Mustang or the Government of Nepal.

What can we learn from archives?

Archives are the only source we have for the actual operation of institutions for which there is an abundance of prescriptive literature. This is the case with Tibetan law, for example. Although there are numerous law codes from different periods of Tibetan history, we should be careful about taking them at face value, or assuming that they were actually applied in practice. James Scott has alerted us to the existence of "hidden transcripts" – the oral or written strategies adopted by "subaltern" groups to express collective dissent, and their refusal to subscribe in anything other than a superficial way to the ideology of the dominant powers.[1] This is illustrated by a document from the late nineteenth century that presents the regulations for the management of disputes in Shang, one of the villages of Panchgaon:

> There should be no legal disputes within the community. But if there are, should [the disputants] go down to the government court without paying money to the community they shall be fined 8 rupees. After paying one flask of beer and 1 anna [one-sixteenth of a rupee] to the headmen, one rupee shall be taken from each of the disputants, and the headmen shall sit and pass judgment. One rupee shall be given to the community, and one rupee shall be for the headmen. If someone rejects [the judgment], he may not go [to the courthouse] before paying 1 anna [to the community]. If the dispute is settled internally, one part [of the deposited sum] shall be taken from the winner, and two parts from the loser, and the council ... shall take it.[2]

The document explicitly states that members of the village could, if they wished, take their disputes to be heard in the government court. However, in order to do so they first had to pay a fee to the community, and failure to pay this fee would have been punishable by a fine. There was an obvious preference for dealing with legal issues within the community, without having recourse to government structures. Is it possible that a similar reluctance to turn to official legal channels prevailed in villages in Central Tibet? We do not know; if villages ever did have archives that contained the answer, they have either been lost or destroyed.

Archives as a window onto everyday life

While there is little in the archives of Mustang that might tell us about its political or economic relations with the rest of Nepal or Tibet, the documents do offer a rare insight into the day-to-day concerns of local communities: the regulation of taxes and the use of natural resources, counts of livestock, and conflicts with neighbouring settlements over territorial boundaries, among other things. But beyond what they might tell us about local institutions and social organisation, the archives shine a patchy but nevertheless precious light onto the lives of ordinary people. As in the case of Europe or America, historians of Tibet have understandably focused on the bigger picture relating to the nation of Tibet and its affairs with its neighbours, with the vicissitudes of the religious schools, and the fortunes of great men. Until very recently, the perspective of "history from below" was largely neglected in historical writing on Tibetan societies.

Family documents, such as those that we find in the archives of Tshognam and Geling, are a particularly valuable source. Individually, such documents may not be particularly inspiring – contracts for sale of fields, inheritance disputes, arguments over fiscal payments, loan receipts and so forth – but taken together they can tell us a great deal about the life and character of a person. Biographical writing is a very abundant and popular genre in Tibet. However, since the purpose of Tibetan life-writing is to present an exemplary spiritual life, much of this literature is hagiographic, and tells us little about the mundane day-to-day life of the subjects. At the opposite

[1] Scott 1990.

[2] Undated Tibetan document from the village of Shang, southern Mustang, photographed by Charles Ramble and Nyima Drandul in 1993.

extreme to such accounts of saintly lives we have the archive of the lamas of Tshognam. The last member of the line died, heirless, in 1992, but the archives remained in a wicker basket in the abandoned family house. This archive made it possible to reconstruct the history of the family over six generations, and although some of this information is rather skeletal, there are enough documents pertaining to certain individuals that we can obtain a reasonably substantial picture of their lives. If classical Tibetan biography focuses on primarily on the subject's saintliness, documents are likely to emphasise the contrary characteristics. If a person generates a large volume of such material, that is likely to be because he (or she) was embroiled in disputes, or was litigious, or the target of lawsuits – or, in the case of one of the lamas in the family, Ösal Dorje, all the above.

The picture that emerges from the archives is not the beatific face that we would have seen from this lama's biography, had he or anyone else thought to write one. Ösal Dorje, who probably died some time in the second decade of the twentieth century, emerges from the archives as acquisitive, ruthless, and probably violent. In 1907, for example, he was accused of brutally beating a personal enemy and of practising destructive black magic. But of course, this portrait is no more rounded a picture of the man than we would have had from that unwritten hagiography: while it may be true that Tibetan biographies tend to inflate the spiritual qualities of the protagonist, the very nature of archival documents casts the subject in an unfavourable light and underrepresents his spiritual qualities. Given the circumstances of Ösal Dorje's birth and childhood, it is obvious that he had to fight to make his way in the world. He was the illegitimate son of a feckless trader, and his mother had forfeited her inheritance rights by virtue of this brief liaison. Before her death she bequeathed to him the house she had been grudgingly allocated by her brother, but was later evicted from it on the grounds that the main estate (*grong pa*) to which it belonged was impartible. He inherited absolutely nothing. There is little in such a childhood to foster open-handed generosity or financial recklessness.

We may return here to a point made earlier, about the value of an archive as opposed to an individual document. An archive provides documents with a context without which they might be completely misleading. Two examples will serve to illustrate this point. One is a claim by Ösal Dorje's son, Tenpa Gyaltsen, that he is the rightful heir to the house that his father had inhabited (Fig. 52). Ösal Dorje had inherited the house from his mother, Phurba Angmo, who had two brothers. To support his claim, Tenpa Gyaltsen cites the will of his great-grandmother – Phurba Angmo's mother – to the effect that "this house of ours, from its topmost point to its foundations, shall be the exclusive possession of our daughter Phurba Angmo, who gave us the filial service that ought to have been provided by all three of our children, and not in the possession of her two brothers." Tenpa Gyaltsen won the case against the cousin who wanted to evict him. If this document were all we had to go on, we might have no reason to doubt the veracity of the argument, and would probably derive a sense of satisfaction from the thought that justice had been done, and that the disadvantaged Tenpa Gyaltsen and his father Ösal Dorje had been allowed to retain the property. In fact, the situation was more complicated than this. Phurpa Angmo had got on well with her older brother, Rigden, but not the younger, Rangdrol. The two brothers allowed her to live in a small house belonging to the main estate, but in 1866, after the death of Rigden, who had protected her, Rangdrol wanted to evict her – and he would have been legally entitled to do so because her welfare was technically not his responsibility but that of her common-law husband. Thanks to the intercession of intermediaries, however, she was allowed to remain in the house until her death, after which it would not be inherited by her son, Ösal Dorje, but should revert to the main estate. The will that Tenpa Gyaltsen cited forty-six years later, in which Phurba Angmo's mother is reported to have bequeathed the house to her, obviously never existed. He simply made it up. In the event, the court's decision was later reversed, and Tenpa Gyaltsen had to move to another village.

Fig. 52. Document MA/UTshognam/Tib/32, a false claim by Lama Tenpa Gyaltsen to ownership of a house in Tshognam that he occupied. Photograph by Agnieszka Helman-Ważny.

Overview of the five archival collections

Since the project on which the present book is based entailed a more meticulous examination of the documents than simply photographing them in order to record the content, a selection of the numerous archives in Mustang had to be made. The five collections were chosen with a view to obtaining the greatest diversity of material, from the southern- and northern-most communities in the area under consideration (respectively Lubrak and Geling), and both community and private archives.

One of the five collections selected in this volume is a community archive in a strict sense: it is kept in a public building, responsibility for its care lies with the annually-rotating headmen, and it may be opened only in the presence of representatives of the village council. This is the archive of Lubrak, a village of hereditary lamas. The remaining four are kept in private households, but the status of the households is such that the archives contain a certain proportion of items of a public character: the lamas of Upper and Lower Tshognam were an important family who mediated in dealings between communities that lay in their parish, and were the trusted repository of the documents concerned; the archive of Dzar, in the Muktinath Valley, is kept in the house of a former ducal family, and is a similar – though smaller - mixture of private and public items. Geling was a semi-autonomous entity between Baragaon and the Kingdom of Lo, and the house of the hereditary headman contains both public and private documents.

In the following section, the contents of each of the collections will be presented before going on to make some more general observations concerning the nature of archival documents in Mustang. Tibetan has a well-established lexicon to describe different categories of legal and administrative documents. In the presentation of each of the archives given below the documents will be grouped not in terms of these formal designations but rather according to their subject-matter, since this will give the reader a clearer idea of the content of the archives. For example, many documents in the archives belong to the category known as *gan rgya*, a term that may be translated as "contract", "covenant"

Fig. 53. Copies of documents (archived as MA/LTshognam/Tib/8) from 1876 and 1866 confirming land and property rights enjoyed by Lama Ösal Dorje. Photograph by Kemi Tsewang.

or "written obligation" according to the context. In view of the wide-ranging application of the *gan rgya* genre, it is more useful here to group the documents into ad hoc categories based on their actual function and the identities of the parties involved. *Gan rgya* might denote loan contracts, community resolutions, marriage agreements and so forth; conversely, a single boundary dispute between neighbouring communities may generate a number of documents belonging to several different categories, such as letters, petitions, rejoinders and so forth. It should also be noted – and this is a subject that will be developed later in the present chapter – that the legal lexicon in Mustang often eschews Tibetan vocabulary in favour of Nepali terms.

Before turning to the five archives, however, we may give some illustrations of the terms that are found to designate different categories of documents. The following examples are all taken from the archives of Upper and Lower Tshognam.

What may be one of the earliest items in the collection (MA/LTshognam/Tib/23, possibly from 1854 or 1842) concerns the inheritance by Yeshe Angmo, the wife of the first lama in the lineage, of a house in her natal village of Tshug, in the face of opposition from rival claimants. This document is referred to simply as *'chod 'tshig* (<*chod tshig*). Disputes over the priestly estate in Tshognam itself arose in the following generation, between Yeshe Angmo's two sons and, subsequently, between her younger son and her daughter. In or around 1860 the two brothers, Lamas Rigden and Rangdrol, came to terms over the matter of who should inherit the estate in the generation below them, and recorded their agreement in a document described as a *'dum khra*, a "dispute resolution" (MA/LTshognam/Tib/4). In 1871 there was a disagreement over the ownership of a house by two people in Tshognam whose relationship to the main family is unclear. The matter was investigated by the Duke of Baragaon, who declared that he was "giving the mark of his seal" (*phyags [phyag] rtags gnang*) to the party in whose favour he had found. Here, as elsewhere, the honorific term *phyag rtags* – "seal mark" – is being used as a metonym for the certificate itself.

MA/LTshognam/Tib/8 is a valuable document for our understanding of the tensions in the family since it contains copies of two earlier documents, from 1876 and from 1866 (in that order), of which the originals have been lost (Fig. 53). Both sections are agreements, the first part concerning the terms of Ösal Dorje's usufruct of a field given to him by his uncle, and the second detailing the terms of his mother's occupancy of a house on the estate. The first part refers to itself as a *cham yi ge* – a document of accord or resolution – and the second section as a *chod rgya*, a term mentioned above as a probable abbreviation of *chod tshig gan rgya*.

MA/UTshognam/Tib/5, another confirmation of Ösal Dorje's usufruct of the same field, opens with the declaration that it is "a document that accomplishes a reconciliation" (*cham' thun bsgrubs gyis yi ge*) between two previously antagonistic parties (Fig. 54).

Fig. 54. Document MA/UTshognam/Tib/5, "Document that accomplishes a reconciliation," confirming Lama Ösal Dorje's right to usufruct of a shared field. Photograph by Agnieszka Helman-Ważny.

As we have seen earlier, in 1890 the elderly Phurba Angmo transferred the ownership of her house to her son, Lama Ösal Dorje. Interestingly, the declaration of the transfer does not use the term *kha chems*, the usual term for a will, perhaps in tacit acknowledgement of the fact that legal ownership lay with the main estate to which it was meant to revert following her death (although this was later disputed by her grandson). The term that is used is the vaguer *phog sprod*, which may be glossed as "transfer" or "bestowal". In contrast to this "transfer", the archive contains the will of a nun, who may or may not be a member of the priestly family. This document does use the term *kha chem* (<*kha chems*), but in fact it is only the moveable goods of two households of which she is the sole heir that are at issue. The heirs to the estates themselves are not specified, and it therefore probable that they were simply to be inherited by her closest relatives.

When the ownership of Phurba Angmo's house in Lower Tshognam was contested by the two main branches of the family in the next generation, Ösal Dorje's son, Tenpa Gyaltsen, submitted a legal petition to the government court (MA/UTshognam/Tib/31). As one might expect, Nepali legal terms become increasingly frequent as time passes, and this document, which dates from around 1912, is introduced as a *ba ti i sar* (Nep. *bādi ijhar*), denoting a legal petition. Similarly, a reaction to a petition in what may be the same case (MA/LTshognam/Tib/19; since the dates of these documents are uncertain, we do not know if this is a direct riposte to MA/UTshognam/Tib/32) is identified as a *phirād patra*, a formal rejoinder.

However, the adoption of Nepali terms is by no means ubiquitous, and a legal petition submitted at the same time and in the same case by someone who is either the plaintiff's brother or the plaintiff himself under a different name, contains no generic designation in either Tibetan or Nepali (MA/UTshognam/Tib/33).

One of the documents related to this dispute (MA/UTshognam/Tib/32) is particularly difficult to read because of the many deletions and interlineal insertions, but it is a valuable piece since it tells us something about how the author, Tshewang Angyal (who, it will be remembered, bore the same name as his great-grandfather), constructed his argument. The rough draft – which is what we suppose this to be – shows that his claims for ownership initially included numerous daring assertions that he omitted in the version that was later submitted to the court, presumably because he decided that they would not stand up under legal scrutiny.

Lubrak

The village of Lubrak is a little settlement of just seventeen houses beside the Panda Khola, an eastern tributary of the Kali Gandaki located between Jomsom and Kagbeni (see map, Fig. 2). The name of the village, meaning "the cliff (*brak*) of the serpent-spirits (*lu*)", derives from the pale striations on the rock cliff opposite the settlement. The main cultural importance of Lubrak lies in the fact that it is the earliest surviving community of the Bon religion in Nepal, and the only village of this faith in Mustang District. Lubrak had been an ancient cave complex, but after the arrival of an eminent lama named Trashi Gyaltsen (b. 1131) it came under the influence of Tibetan culture and became a centre of the Bon religion.

There are now no monks in the community, but only married householder-lamas. The eldest son in each household becomes a lama, and inherits religious responsibilities along with his secular status as head of a family. The culture of the village is a complex affair in which the Bon religion is intricately interwoven with folk ceremony. The community represents a vital cultural heritage in which, contrary to monastic usage, liturgical ritual is studied in meditative retreat but intimately reintegrated into daily life. Most of the religious activity is focused on the village temple, Yungdrung Phuntshokling, located in the middle of the settlement, which was built in 1846 by the Tibetan master Karu Druwang Tenzin Rinchen.

Lubrak's dual character as a community of lamas who marry and engage in similar economic activities is reflected in the archive, which we may conveniently divide into two parts: documents concerning the temple on the one hand, and items related to village life on the other. In the latter category we would also include documents dealing with the management of "secular" ceremonies, such as the annual spring archery festival, as well as the now-obsolete community of nuns, who had no temple of their own but would organise regular meetings in private households according to a roster. While this temple *versus* village categorisation would not be relevant in the case of the other collections considered here, a helpful distinction that might be made in the case of all the communities is the opposition between internal and external affairs.

Internal affairs

As a community of householder-lamas, Lubrak has a ritual cycle comprising some twenty ceremonies that are performed over the course of the year in the village temple. Each ceremony is perpetuated by its own endowment fund, known as *sbyor 'jags*. Put simply, contributions for a new ceremony are collected from donors from inside and outside the community, and distributed among the lamas. The lamas use this cash as capital in their trading ventures. They must give goods (flour, grain, oil and so forth) to the value of 10 per cent per annum of this capital for the performance of the ceremony, and any profit they make above that figure they are entitled to keep for themselves. Since the capital is never returned to the investor, it is understood that he or she will receive annual merit corresponding to the value of this interest in perpetuity, either for him- or herself or for a designated beneficiary.

These investments and the interest that must be paid by each of the estates are recorded in a register of temple contributions referred to as *ma yig*, the "mother document," which constitutes the basis on which memoranda for current use are drawn up. The *ma yig* documents are in the form of sheets of coarse paper sewn together along the centre and folded horizontally to make a booklet. The booklets are not, however, the original documents, but were copied from an earlier scroll by an educated lama from Mustang who lived in Lubrak for a short time at the request of the villagers. Most of the temple documents consist of records of endowments for these ceremonies as well as memoranda containing details of the annual performances of each. Nowadays this information is logged in commercially-produced exercise books or writing pads.

Depending on the size of the endowment, the performance of some ceremonies may require substantial quantities of comestible goods, especially barley, which is roasted and ground into the tsampa from which the tormas (*gtor ma*, altar effigies) are manufactured, as well as to produce beer; butter for altar decorations, and rice and oil for the lamas' meals. Several documents deal with the provision of these items, and also with the duties of the stewards who are responsible for organising the ceremonies.

An example of such an endowment record is a document from 1903 (MA/Lubrak/Tib/35) related to the establishment of a ceremony to commemorate the death of an eminent lama of the village (Fig. 55).

> [Homage to the lama, the yidam, and the dakini.] Water Hare year, tenth day. For the material base (*rgyu rkyen*) for the lama offering ceremony to mark the anniversary of the passing away of Kuzhab Tenzin Nyima there were 50 rupees. To this, the lama of Narukhung has added 5 rupees as an endowment for 108 votive lamps, and there is therefore a total of 55 rupees. This is now with the monks and nuns, who each have 5 *ṭam* in their own possession.
> The fund (*rgyu*) for the beer is 25 rupees.
> For food: 15 rupees
> For the flour [for tormas]: 5 rupees
> The barley for the base shall be taken from [the grain for] this flour.
> For butter and for the votive lamps: 4 rupees
> For the 108 butter lamps: 5 rupees
> For the interest on the cash, if two-row barley is given, 3.5 *zo ba* shall be given.
> The interest on the cash for the food shall be the same as in the case of the new ceremonies.
> From the monks and the nuns, each shall give one *zo ba* and one *bru brag*. If this does not make up a full *se khal*,[3] the two stewards shall make up [the difference].

[3] Note: 1 *se khal* = 30 *zo ba*; 1 *'bo khal* = 20 *zo ba*; 1 *zo ba* = 4 *bru drag* (variously spelled).

Each of the beer-dispensers shall receive an allocation of *yalung martshag* beer made from one *zo ba* of grain. The two beer-dispensers and the *sku tshab* shall receive an additional amount [of beer] from one *zo ba* of grain.

The stewards' share shall be half a *zo ba* of beer. The two stewards shall each receive eight full cakes made from the remaining *tshogs*, and four pieces of deep-fried bread. They should have all the *tshogs* that is [left over], as well as tea and beer.

The lama shall receive one vessel, a ceremonial container, of beer (*zhal phud*).

If a nun or a monk dies, his/her 5 *ṭam* shall be taken.

The two beer-dispensers shall be given a double portion of lunch. The sauce shall be provided from the interest from the half-rupee of each of the two beer-dispensers.

This section of the archive also contains documents concerned with disciplinary matters. Village rituals throughout the Himalayan region and much of Tibet are accompanied by *chang* (barley beer) as an indespensible ceremonial component, but excessive consumption sometimes leads to disorderly behaviour, as in the case of the incident described in this document from 1939 archived as MA/Lubrak/Tib/78 (Fig. 56).

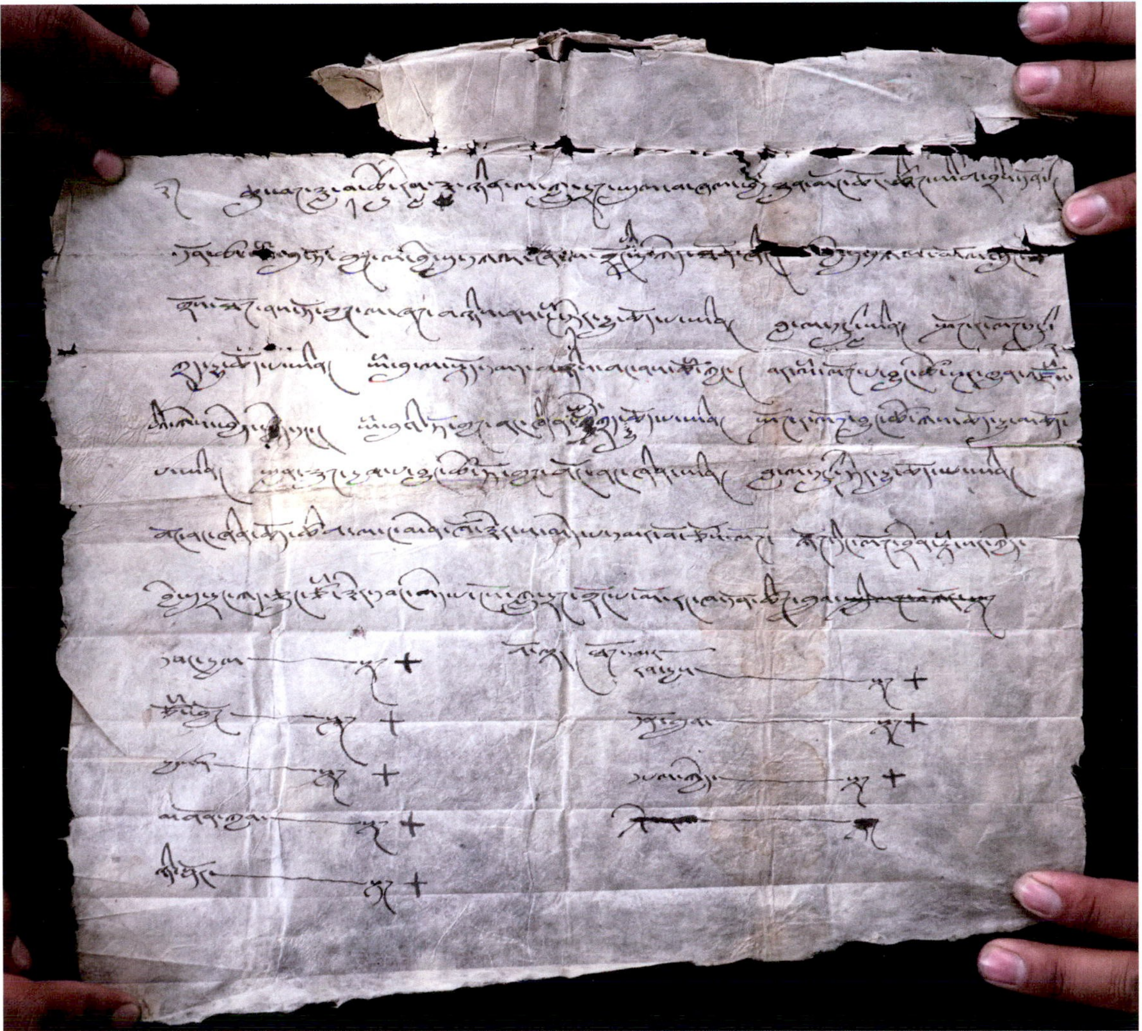

Fig. 55. Document MA/Lubrak/Tib/35. Record of investments and procedures for the performance of a ritual commemorating the death of an eminent lama, 1903. Photograph by Kemi Tsewang.

Earth Hare year (1939), twelfth month, eighteenth day, Saturday. The purpose of writing this *a dkar* document is as follows:

At the time the religious community was seated in its row, Tshering – because he was drunk – seized a knife and an axe and caused a great deal of disturbance, and brandished a stick on the roof while the monastic dancing was taking place outside. It was accordingly considered that it would be appropriate to apprehend him. However, when we came for him he climbed the hill (lit. seized the head of the hill) and brandished stones and threw them down. Religious-legal proceedings were implemented to find a solution. The anchorite Tshampa Pön, as well as the two people headman Takla of Kag palace and the chant-leader Gara, those three, acted as mediators and pleaded on his behalf, saying that, apart from the fault of being drunk, he had not erred from the monastery's rules in any other respect, and to support their plea gave beer, a ceremonial scarf and two rupees. Following monastery law, he should not behave badly in this way, and he should desist from drinking chang for one year. Having then given it up, he paid a fine of 50 rupees, and saying that in the future he would not act in this way, he paid his fine. Tshering freely and willingly sets his thumbprint to confirm that he will not act this way in the future, and that he is paying the fine.

In accordance with the above, in future no one in the community of monks should hold knives, staves, rocks and so forth during any religious assembly, and that if it happens that anyone should hold any [of these things], brandish them and strike anyone and so forth, since the matter is as set out above all the members of the monastic body have circulated the document and placed their marks.

The witnesses are listed in the margin. We whose names are set out below, above the door that is down below, and below the gods on high, wooden beer flasks, flagpoles, all ritual objects, copper and brass items, chang strainers, tables, book-wrappings and so forth – whatever monastic property there may be; if there is any disagreement or physical fight about these, or any breaking or throwing things, in accordance with the above document there shall be a fine of 50 rupees; and furthermore anyone who fails to obey because he is drunk and reckless shall only be bound to a pillar with waistbands and ropes with his hands behind his back, but not beaten with hostile intent; and if he listens, he should be released, whereas if he does not he should be bound to the pillar. On the basis of a discussion among the assembled monastic community, the members place their marks to attest that this document was drawn up after the text was written with their willing support. The witnesses and the document are indeed as above: Gyaltsen Dondrub; Palsekyab; the scribe was Lawang (Lama Wangyal).

The part of the archive that is concerned with the village (as opposed to the temple) may be grouped into a number of subsidiary categories. One of these would be what we may refer to as seasonal festivals or secular ceremonies. There are two of these: the spring archery festival (Dachang, *mda' chang*), which was established in 1935, and the horse-racing festival (Yartung, *dbyar ston*) that is held in summer in association with a number of other villages. There is also a single document concerning the management of the periodic (mainly monthly) ceremonies formerly held by the small community of nuns. Most of the documents concerning the nuns are not in fact included in the archive but are kept in the private collection of one of the lamas who was in charge of leading the nuns' ceremonies.

Most of the documents related in the village deal with civic affairs. These may be divided broadly into three groups: disputes and their resolution, natural resource management, and village taxes and other dues. The first of these is often the largest component of any community archive, but apart from a small number of high-profile conflicts there are relatively few recorded disputes in Lubrak, compared with (for example) the archive of Geling, which contains numerous examples.

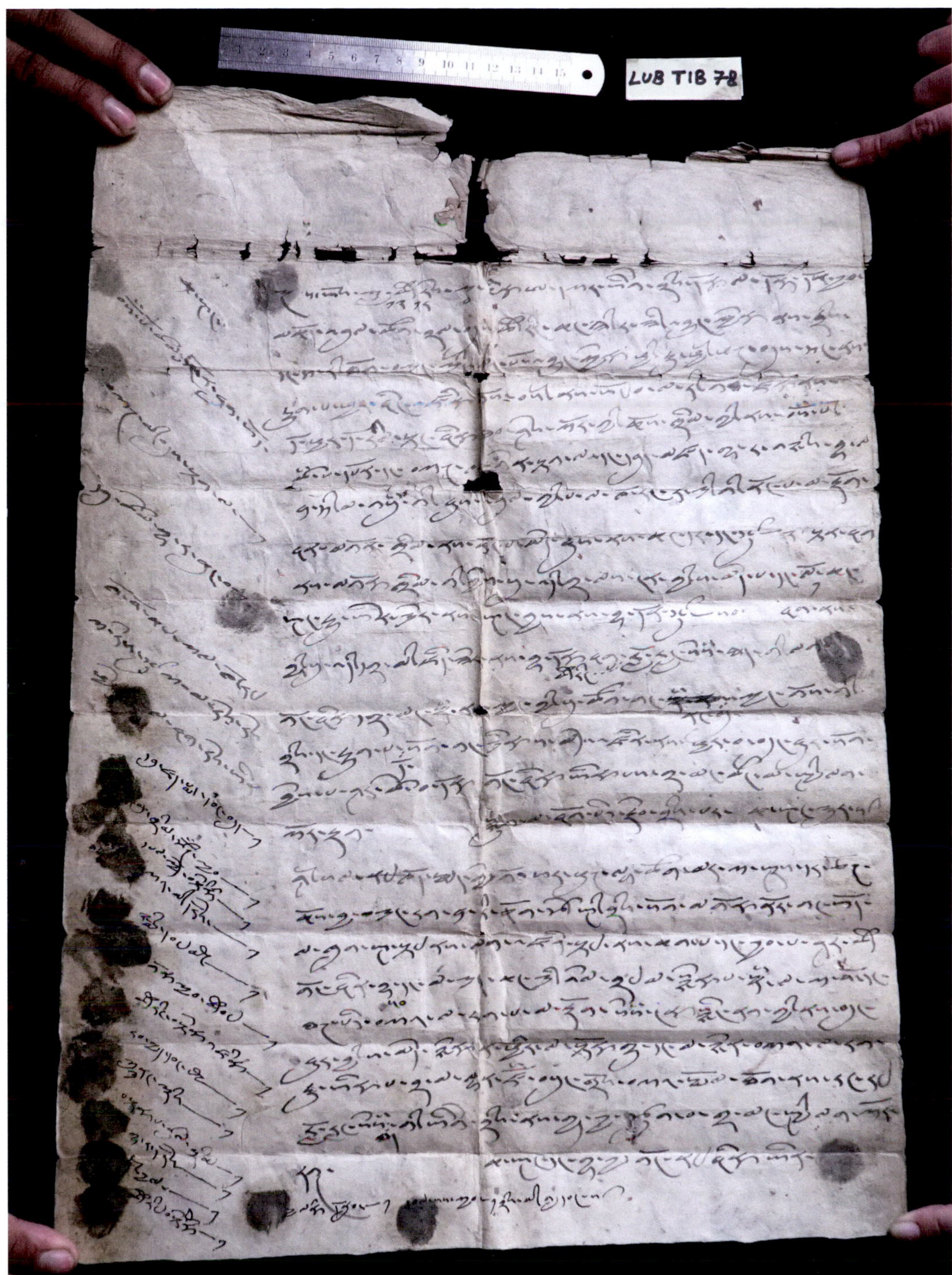

Fig. 56. Document MA/Lubrak/Tib/78. Memorandum of legal proceedings against a lama for alcohol-induced violence, 1939. Photograph by Kemi Tsewang.

While the main natural resources are water, forests and pastureland, the category may also include fields, water mills and livestock: the last three are not of course "natural", but their management consists primarily of the regulation of resources that *are* natural, notably water and grazing. The category also includes restrictions on the use of a source of red ochre located above the village of Lubrak (SH/Lub/Tib/3959).

Finally, in the "internal" section, there are several documents that deal with the regulations for the payment of grain taxes to the village fund, as well as certain other dues.

External affairs

Documents about external affairs fall into two main categories: first, disputes and other engagements with non-Lubrakpas, and secondly, government taxes and other financial interactions with outsiders. The documents in the first category do not concern so much Lubrak's disputes with its neighbours as its collaborations with its neighbours in the context of disputes with more distant entities. However, in recent times there have been some serious clashes between the village and others in the Muktinath Valley over the usufruct of an area of forest that Lubrak considered to be its own.

Regarding the second category, as a respected priestly community, Lubrak paid only nominal taxes until the late nineteenth century, when representatives of the Rana government abolished this privileged status. Most of the documents in this category deal with the imposition of the "Great Government Tax" and annual receipts for its payment.

Tshognam

Like Lubrak, Tshognam is a settlement of hereditary lamas, although with certain notable differences. To begin with, it is not a distinct village with its own territory. It has no land of its own, but straddles the territorial boundary of two major settlements: Te, upstream to the east, and Tshug, downstream to the west. Lower and Middle Tshognam stand on Tshug's territory, and Upper Tshognam on Te's. The Middle Tshognam estate, which is now empty, was never home to a priestly family, and possesses no archive.

Internal affairs: religious matters

The Tshognam archives enable us to reconstruct the lives of five generations of the family that occupied the two households (Upper and Lower Tshognam) in which they are preserved. The name by which the family is referred to nowadays is Drenjong Gyalpö Gyupa (Tib.'Bras ljongs rgyal po'i brgyud pa), the Clan of the Kings of Sikkim, but no documentary or oral elaboration of this suggestive title has yet come to light. The first member of the clan to settle in Tshognam was a certain Lama Chöying (or Chönyi – the name varies in the documents) Rangdrol. It is not known when he arrived, but he is named in three later accounts that review the family's activities in Tshognam. One of them refers to a gift of two female yaks that was made to him by an unidentified king of Lo (MA/LTshognam/Tib/16).

It may seem surprising that, in spite of the fact that these archives belong to a priestly family, religious affairs do not feature prominently. This difference from Lubrak is explained by the fact that whereas the latter is a village of several households and lamas, the owners of the two Tshognam archives were individual families whose religious activities were not based on a complex system of endowments and that did not require the mobilisation of officials and significant material resources. There are, however, a few items of relevance to religious matters, although they are almost all concerned with organisational aspects. One of these concerns the *Na rag* ritual. This is an important ceremony for the guidance of the dead in many Nyingmapa Buddhist communities, and in 1887 it was either established or augmented in Tshognam. The endowments received, and the various duties of the patrons and their families, are recorded in a document.

The lamas of Tshognam were Nyingmapas, but the dominant school of Buddhism in Mustang for many centuries were the Sakyapas, and particularly the Ngorpa branch of this school. The parent monastery in Tibet, Ngor Ewam Chöden (E wam chos ldan), was divided into four colleges, and it was from one of these, Ngor Khangsar, that the Tshognam family commissioned rituals for the transfer of merit to one of the lamas following his death around the turn of the century. The archives contain two receipts, one for cash and the other for an item of jewelry, as the fee for the transference of merit (*bsngo rten*) for the deceased lama. As we shall see presently, the connection between Geling and Ngor Ewam Chöden was even more significant, insofar as the archive contains private letters from several of this monastery's monks who were natives of the village.

Four other documents in the archive of Upper Tshognam concern the community of nuns. On the west bank of the Kali Gandaki, directly opposite Tshug, stands the now-abandoned nunnery of Kunzang Chöling, popularly known as Gönpa Gang, "the convent ridge". The convent seems originally to have served all five of the Shöyul. In 1906, apparently at the instigation of the lama of Upper Tshognam, the Te nuns withdrew from the convent, and signed a document to the effect that, thenceforth, they agreed to be under his tutelage. In 1915 the nuns of Tshug agreed that they would take collective responsibility for a theft that had occurred. The following year, the community of Te agreed to offer the second of any three daughters born in a family to be a nun under the authority of the Lama of Tshognam. The last document, probably from 1927, records an attempt by the declining body of nuns in Tshognam – there were only three at this stage – to preserve their ceremonial activities by redistributing the financial responsibility.

Two other documents are concerned with specifically religious matters. The first is a short account of the sacred imagery in Traduntse (Pra dun rtse), a famous temple located in Tibet to the north of Mustang. This document may be the only existing description of the temple to have been written before it was destroyed during the Cultural Revolution. The other is a *thob yig*, a list of spiritual teachings and initiations received by one of the Tshognam lamas from a hierarch of the Sakyapa school in Tibet.

Internal affairs: inheritance disputes

The primary cause of tension in Tshognam's priestly family in every generation was the question of inheritance. The protracted conflicts generated a wide range of documents, and the variety of terms for these will be examined later in this chapter. Depending on the context in which they were drawn up – notably, whether for addressing the issues within Tshognam itself, or else in an official court of law, the documents are identified by either Tibetan or Nepali terms.

External affairs: land acquisitions

Sixteen documents are related to the acquisition of land in the village of Tshug by the priestly house of Lower Tshognam. It is interesting to note that, without exception, these acquisitions were made by a certain Lama Ösal Dorje. As the natural son of sister of two of the lamas of Lower Tshognam, Ösal Dorje received no inheritance, and clearly felt it necessary to have an agrarian economic base to supplement the income he received from performing rituals and from lending money and grain. There are nine contracts for the outright purchase of fields, the first in exchange for grain and all the others for cash. The lama may also have acquired a certain amount of land by claiming the security on loans from defaulting debtors: there are five loan receipts, one of which incudes a confirmation that the borrower is also ceding a field to the lama in lieu of the repayment of 10 rupees.

Relations with neighbours

Like village lamas throughout the Himalayan region, the priests of Tshognam not only had a religious function but acted as physicians, astrologers and scribes for the communities – Te and Tshug – on whose territories their residences stood. Although other communities in the five Shöyul also had priestly families, those of Tshognam seem to have had parishes that extended beyond their immediate communities to embrace neighbouring villages. Two documents, written sixteen years apart (in 1816 and 1832) are records of plenary gatherings of the five communities, and deal with the integrity and security of the enclave. A later document from 1892 also records a plenary meeting of the five Shöyul in Tshognam for the purpose of appointing officials from each of the communities. Tshognam was also clearly regarded as neutral ground for contracts drawn up between individuals from other villages, notably Te and Tshug, and a number of documents in both archives are contracts that do not directly concern the priestly family.

Where contracts are concluded between individuals of the same community, it is considered sufficient for each of the two parties to have a copy of the document. (In the case of loan contracts, only the creditor need have a copy bearing the signature, or some other endorsement, of the debtor.) With dealings between members of these two different villages, however, it was apparently considered necessary to involve a third party. Most of these documents concern sales of land and loan contracts between villagers of Tshug and Te. In one case a Tepa and a Tshugpa agree to exchange two designated fields for a period of ten years, probably because of their relative proximity to the houses of the respective parties. In a few cases we cannot be sure whether both parties to a contract are members of the priestly family of Tshognam or not. As mentioned earlier, certain individuals who evidently do belong to the priestly family make a single appearance in the archives, but the documents in question give us insufficient information to be able to situate them in the genealogy. The two borrowers are from the priestly village of Chongkhor, in the Muktinath Valley to the south, but we do not know whether the lender was a nun from Tshognam or another community.

Relations between the lamas and their neighbours

Disputes with parties other than close relatives were more varied in character. Lama Ösal Dorje was the defendant in an interesting case (mentioned above) that was brought against him in 1907, when a man called Trogyal from Dzar, in the Muktinath Valley, accused him and several others of beating him up, robbing him and threatening to kill him and destroy his household by means of black magic (Fig. 57). In a formal response the lama vigorously defended himself against the charges, and issued a counter-accusation against Trogyal and others for making an unprovoked attack on him and his son. The case was examined at the government court in Lower Lo – probably in Kag – but since neither of the documents is signed, it is likely that the versions used in court were in Nepali; both the documents that are available to us are probably copies of the Tibetan originals that were submitted for translation for official use.

Another contentious case involved an accusation by a blacksmith against Lama Ösal Dorje and his son, claiming that they had refused to return some valuable jewelry that he had given them as a deposit against a loan. The lamas never did return the items, but paid the blacksmith a cash settlement.

Fig. 57. Document MA/UTshognam/Tib/25. Accusation against Lama Ösal Dorje of practising black magic. Photograph by Kemi Tsewang.

Taxes

The fiscal status of the lamas of Tshognam is the subject of several documents. In one case, Lama Tshewang Bumpa claimed that he and his brother Döyön were not liable for the payment of trade tariffs when travelling through Lo on the grounds that they, and not the king, were the owners of their priestly estate. However, the king rejected the assertion that they were the owners, citing the restoration sponsored by an earlier queen as the basis of royal ownership. He nevertheless acquiesced to the Tshognam lamas' exemption from tariffs, not on the basis of their ownership of the estate but on the grounds of their priestly status and activities. The other documents deal – sometimes in considerable detail – with the question of whether the lamas were liable for the payment of taxes to the village and the provision of conscripted labour to the local aristocracy.

The Shari Pöngyuta family

In 1938, some time after the death of the last member of the Clan of the Kings of Sikkim to inhabit the house, the priestly estate in Upper Tshognam came to be occupied by another Nyingmapa family, the Shari Pöngyuta (Sha ri dpon rgyud pa), from the Muktinath Valley. The family were, and continue to be, renowned as both lamas and doctors (Tib. *am chi*). The favourable terms on which the first occupant and his family were allowed to occupy the property are set out in a contract. The archive contains a number of items of correspondence between members of this family and individuals from neighbouring communities.

Dzar

The Tibetan section of the Dzar archive contains just twelve documents. Given the political importance of the village in the Muktinath Valley and in Baragaon as a whole, it is clear that this collection must be just a fraction of a much larger corpus. The house in which the archive is contained is located directly next door to the former palace of Dzar, and belongs to the descendants of Trowo Kyabpa, the first representatives of the rulers of Lo to come to Baragaon in the sixteenth century (see chapter 2). In accordance with the Tibetan custom of giving names to houses of aristocrats and other dignitaries, this is one of several houses in Dzar to have a name: Zimkhang Nya (gZim khang gnya'), the "upper mansion". Whereas most archival collections contain a large number of documents that could not possibly have any current relevance, almost all those in the Dzar archive have some potential public or private significance. Owners of private archives do periodically weed out obsolete items (our colleague Nyima Drandul, a former resident of Chongkhor and co-author of several works with the present authors, admits to having thrown away his entire domestic archive in the 1980s), and it is very possible that the Dzar collection is the remnant of such a clearance.

Only three of the documents are private, and all relate to loans that were made by members of the family to outsiders. If they were not discarded during the conjectured rationalisation of the collection, that may be because those responsible for sorting them were unsure about whether the outstanding debts had ever been repaid. Mention has already been made of MA/Dzar/Tib/4, which contains a list of public accounts spanning an indeterminate number of years. Another records the sale of an area of land by a village corporation to the community as a whole, and a third confirms the inheritance of the house of a deceased palace official by his son. All the other documents deal with external affairs. It is clear from these documents that the Zimkhang Nya house was the heart of civic life in Dzar, and a centre of ceremonial activity in Baragaon as a whole. It may be that some of the documents are copies of resolutions that were also kept in the archives of some of the other "capitals." This could be the case of MA/Dzar/Tib/1, for example, which sets out the newly agreed procedures for the participation of nuns from Tiri convent and the monks from Kag and Dzong monasteries at funerary rituals. MA/Dzar/Tib/2 contains a list of donations to several monasteries, not only that of Dzar itself. The remaining documents concern the organisation and financing of two ceremonies, both now obsolete, that involved several other villages in the Muktinath Valley: one of these was the Demdem archery festival, which was held in Dzar but included the villages of Purang and Khyenga, and the other was the Dögyab (Tib. *mdos rgyab*), an annual purification and exorcism rite of the sort that has been described earlier for Lubrak. The following is an excerpt from MA/Dzar/Tib/6, concerning the activities that are to be carried out on eleventh day of the month, the second day of the Demdem festival.

> On the 11th day at the first gun (*'bam gor*) there should be a [serving of beer] for clearing the head; at the second, food [should be served]; at the third gun, there should be archery, dancing and singing. The *dgra zor* ritual should be performed, and everyone should come; if anyone doesn't come, he (or she?) will pay a fine of one rupee each.
>
> Purang should bring yellow clay; Dzar should bring whitewash; Khyinga should bring black clay. On the 10th day, the people who set up the targets should be given a full bowl of beer (*stam ka* <*ltam ka*); the three people who paint the (different) *mchod rten* should be given 3 ladles of beer each; When the *dgra zor* is being performed, the Lama and the Lord should receive a beer allowance of first-quality beer (*snying khu*). The people who play the little cymbals shall receive one *zo ba* of chang.
>
> On the 10th day, when you go to request the spear with the flag from the Lama, you should give him a container [of flour] (*chab rkyan*) and when you return it to him again, another *chab rkyan* container [of flour]. It shall be the same when you request the bow and arrow from the Lord. If there is any angry or quarrelsome behaviour,
>
> *page 2*
>
> those responsible shall be fined 8 rupees, with no excuses. On the 9th day, after offering the performance [of songs and dances, each participant] shall receive 6 ladles [of beer]. On the 10th day [each person shall receive] 6 ladles of beer after food that does not form part of the allocation (*sma the* <*ma'thad*) of beer to accompany the long life ritual (*tshe phyang* <*tshe chang*).
>
> The stewards of each of the settlements should also, as above, soak the dry grain; if they do not wet the dry grain, and if they take even a single handful of grain or a small flask of beer home to their own communities; and if any of them is partial: may the protector Gönpo Yeshe; the glorious Makzor Gyalmo; the protector Ekajati; the protector of the [Bon] doctrine Abse Dungmar, [and of the Buddhist doctrine] Genyen Dorje Shugden; the holy place of Muktinath: may these swiftly inflict on the upper part of their bodies hot illnesses that are like fire; may the lower parts of their bodies be boiled with cold illnesses like water; and may they inflict on the middle parts of their bodies blood diseases with ferocious pains. If the three stewards are honest and avoid engaging in concealment, partiality or theft as described above, may they be free of hot illnesses in the upper parts of their bodies, cold illnesses in the lower parts of their bodies, and ferociously painful blood diseases in the middle parts of their bodies. May men enjoy long lives and may women be glorious. May they be constantly pleasantly drunk. Blessings and good fortune. May the beer from the earthenware jars be excellent.
>
> *page 3*
>
> The three stewards must receive a blessing from the hand of the lama with [this?] document and a *zo ba* measure.
>
> If anyone has not arrived by the third gun, they may be too late for the one ladle of beer or for two ladles of beer (of the three servings).

Geling

The Geling archive resembles that of Dzar to the extent that it is kept in the house of a village dignitary – in this case not an aristocrat but the hereditary headman – and consists of both private and public documents. However, with 172 documents it is considerably larger and its contents more diverse. As noted in chapter 2, Geling was part of Upper Lo until 1754, when it broke away from the kingdom shortly after the secession of Baragaon. It did not join Baragaon, but remained autonomous, albeit with close and for the most part amicable relations with its northern and southern neighbours.

The private chaplains of the Kings of Lo belonged to a family named Drangsong (Drang srong), whose original seat is said to have been the small settlement named Jaragang (Bya ra sgang) a short distance to the west of Monthang, the capital city of Lo. One of the clans in Lubrak is named Jaragang, and claims to be a branch of the same clan, and in 1880 the King of Lo arranged for a young man of the family, named Shilog, to marry an heiress from Geling and to act as his private chaplain. The Jaragang/Drangsong family in Lo Monthang continued to provide chaplains until the 1950s or 1960s, so if in 1880 the king thought it necessary to turn to an outsider, we can only surmise that had been a temporary problem – such as the premature death of a serving chaplain. The edict issued by the king in 1880 contains the following passage:

> Since Drangsong Shilog, the holder of a Bonpo lineage from Lubrak, is to come here as the husband of Palzang [who dwells] at the main entrance of Geling, in our dominion, and will now be the royal chaplain of Lo, he shall be sent up here. No taxes whatsoever – such as transportation duty, beer-brewing, constabulary duty, water mill duty, gathering community firewood or acting as long-distance or short-distance messenger – shall be imposed on [his future wife] Palzang of Geling.

Geling at this time was ruled by a branch of the royal family of Lo whose scions had the title of Dewa (*sde pa*). An undated document from around the turn of the twentieth century (MA/Geling/Tib/153) records a decision by the council to the effect that the hereditary lord (*dpon po*) – a reference to the Dewa – should no longer hold power, but that authority should henceforth be with the headman, a relative of Shilog named Taglha. We do not know the circumstances in which this transfer of power occurred, but the situation was apparently acrimonious. A letter (also unfortunately undated) from the last Dewa, named Karma De, denies charges of murder that have been levelled at him, states that he will return to Geling just to remove the timbers of his palace, and warns that "even though the tiger may be dead, his claws have not yet dried out" (MA/Geling/Tib/75), a clear threat that he intended somehow to avenge himself on the community that had deposed him (Fig. 58). As far as it is possible to tell from the documents, nothing ever came of this threat.

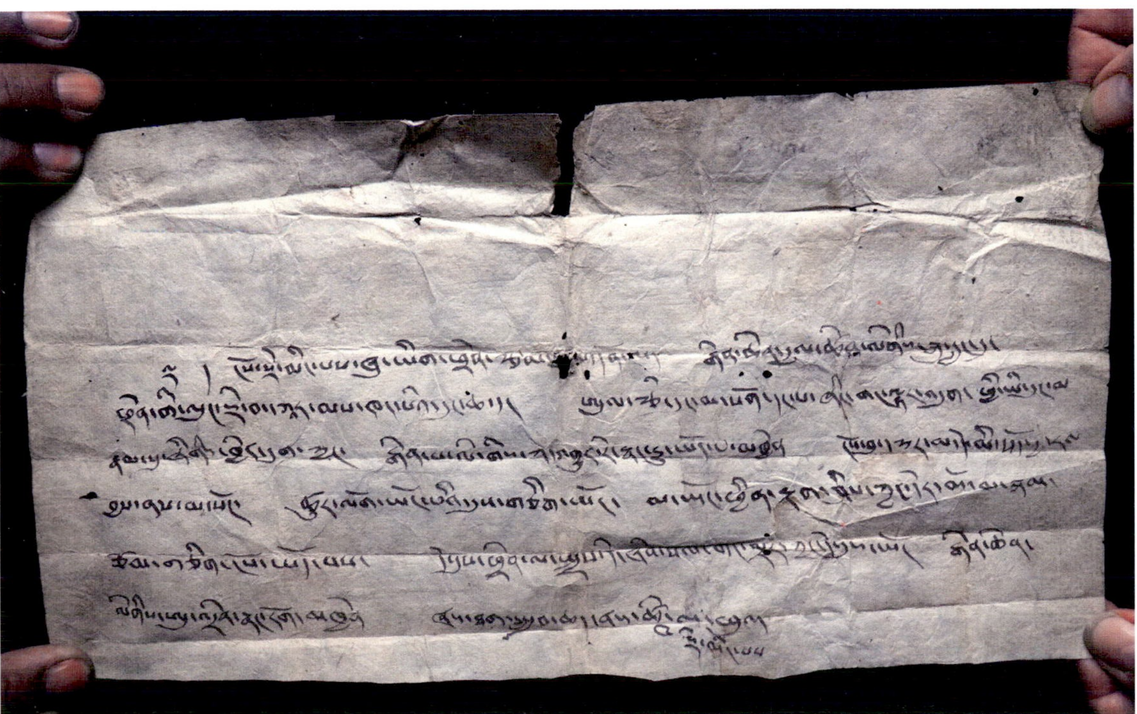

Fig. 58. The document archived as MA/Geling/Tib/75. Undated threat by Karma De, the last ruler of Geling, that he will return one day to reclaim his position. Photograph by Kemi Tsewang.

Private documents actually form a rather small proportion of the collection, and for the most part concern contracts for loans and for the purchase of land and property by members of the family. In the early part of the nineteenth century one of the sons of the household was a monk in Ngor Ewam Chöden monastery in Tibet, and half a dozen of the letters he sent to his parents and family are preserved in the collection. Some of these provide valuable information about the situation north of the border at the time of writing. In one case, for example, he advises his parents to cancel a projected visit because of a famine in the country, and in another he expresses his relief and gratitude at surviving a smallpox epidemic that has left two out of three people dead in the region.

More than twenty documents relate to disputes of one sort or another between members of the community, though to a certain extent also with outsiders. The subjects of these disputes are very varied, and include quarrels over ownership of land, houses and moveable goods, accusations by plaintiffs that they had been insulted, or paid in low-quality tea, or given inferior tsampa. A rather unusual – and surprising – feature of the collection is the extent to which private and domestic issues are made matters of public concern. MA/Geling/Tib/154, for example, records the resolution of a quarrel between a woman and her daughter-in-law: if the latter is insulting or abusive she agrees to pay a fine of 50 rupees, while the former promises to desist from beating the younger woman on pain of paying a similar fine. In another case from 1918 (MA/Geling/Tib/102), a woman named Tenzin Wangmo agrees to terminate her extramarital affair and to remain with her husband Dondrub; Dondrub in turn undertakes to eschew domestic violence (Fig. 59). This document may be cited in full as a good example of such a case.

> *Verso*
>
> Written agreement concerning three people: Gara Dondrub of Tshug, Tenzin Wangmo, and Trashi. Blessings.
>
> *Recto*
>
> Earth Horse year (1918), 8th month, 15th day. To the assembly of the War Company[4] that is led by headman of Geling, the supreme holder of the law of the two traditions. We, whose names are set out clearly below, freely and willingly submit the following covenant. Concerning Tenzin Wangmo, the wife of Tsera Trashi, since she has become the girlfriend of Gara Dondrub of Tshug, copies of the same document have been issued by both Gara Dondrub of Tshug and by Tenzin Wangmo to the effect that, with regard to Tsera Trashi, we shall put behind us what we have done in the past and, in the future, shall meet neither by day nor by night. Furthermore, if we should happen to forget, and talk about the possibility of meeting, on top of the fine that we shall pay in accordance the national law (Nep. *ain bamojim*), we shall also pay 3 *zho* (24 rupees) each in accordance with local custom. Should either of us, Gara Dondrub or Tenzin Wangmo, violate this undertaking, we shall pay a fine according to the law of the lamas and lords, and to this we, Gara Dondrub and Tenzin Wangmo, whose names are given above, willingly set our respective marks. The witnesses were Kunga Trashi and Trinle. The scribe was Gyaltsen.
>
> *Part 2*
>
> Earth Horse year, on the day in the 8th month. To the assembly of the War Company that is led by our headman, who is endowed with the law of the two traditions. The purpose of this convenant is as follows. Even if I, Trashi, may have beaten my wife Tenzin Wangmo, I shall henceforth put this past behaviour behind me, and shall not in future beat Tenzin Wangmo, nor shall I smash property or her jewellery at home. Furthermore, should I happen to forget and beat her and break property, or engage in domestic violence, I, Trashi, shall pay 2 *zho* (16 rupees) to the court of Geling, and shall pay a fine according to the law of the lamas and the lords, and to this I, Trashi, willingly set my mark. In accordance with this abovementioned undertaking, Tenzin Wangmo shall not leave, and if she does leave she shall pay a similar fine of 2 *zho*, and to this Tenzin Wangmo, who is named above, sets her mark. The scribe was Gyaltsen, as above.

[4] The term "War Company" denotes a category of village meeting that comprises all men between the ages of thirteen and sixty.

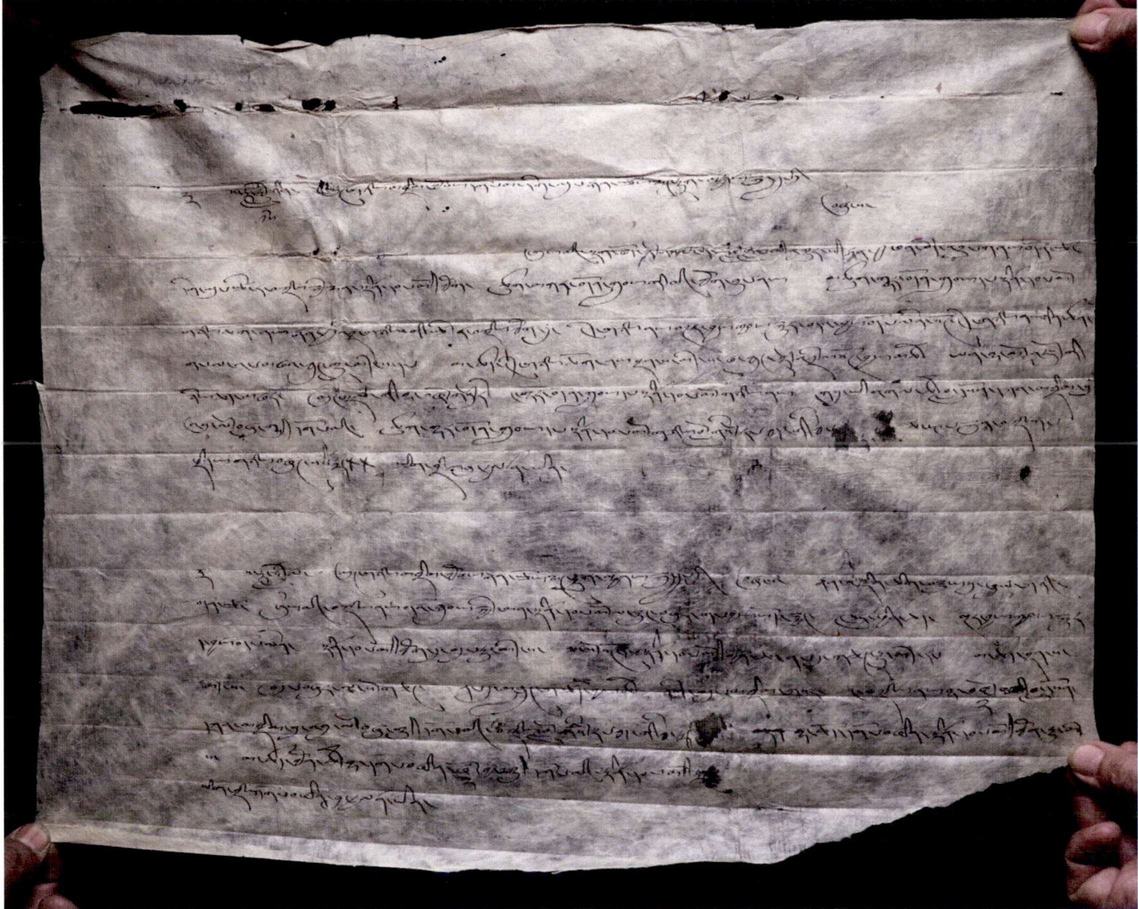

Fig. 59. The document archived as MA/Geling/Tib/102. An agreement between a husband and wife that she will cease to have extra-marital affairs if he promises to desist from domestic violence, 1918. Photograph by Kemi Tsewang.

There are also numerous accusations – and denials – of immoral conduct, notably illicit liaisons, a topic that is almost completely absent from all other archives. One such case (MA/Geling/Tib/106) concerned a single woman named Namgyal who was seven months pregnant. The village held an inquiry to determine the paternity of the child, and in doing so established that the woman had had relations with two other men:

> *Verso*
> Written agreement concerning the young woman Namgyal and Dawa of Kag.
> *Recto*
> Wood Hare year, 8th month, 28th day. To the general War Company of Geling that is led by the headman Taglha, the holder of the law who knows the two traditions. We whose names are set out clearly below freely and willingly submit this covenant, the purpose of which is as follows. When the young woman Namgyal of Geling found herself with child, an investigation concerning the paternity was carried out in the Geling court. It was determined to be Dawa the Younger of Kag. Regarding their cohabitation, they spent the day together on the 13th day of the 1st month. I, Dawa, willingly set my mark in confirmation that there is nothing further to be said on this matter. The witnesses to this, Gara and Darpo of Kag, both set their mark. In accordance with the above declaration, the young woman Namgyal states that since Dawa stayed with her, not a single person apart from Gyamtso and Tshang Namgyal has slept with her (lit. skinned her, i.e. removed her clothing), and that if it should later transpire that someone else has "skinned" her may the law of the lamas and the lords be brought to bear on her, and to this Namgyal willingly sets her mark.

> *Part 2*
> According to the law, because the woman Namgyal has lapsed into decadent immorality (lit. "gone to black skinning of the flesh"), she has been fined 25 rupees...

Occurrences of theft by both villagers and outsiders are also exceptionally common. In most instances the offender pays reparation (*rkun 'jal*) and promises not to reoffend, but in at least two cases the thief was an indigent who had neither money nor land with which to pay the fine. In one of these, the thief's father had to give his house – a house that he himself had built many years previously – to the community as a civic building; in another, the offender – a Tibetan – was sentenced have his hand cut off but was rescued from this fate by his common-law wife, who gave her fourteen-year-old daughter to the village as a slave in compensation for her partner's crime.

As we would expect, many of the documents deal with regulations for the use of natural resources such as pasture and water (unlike Lubrak, Geling has no forest to speak of), as well as rules for herding goats and cattle. One document (MA/Geling/Tib/151), dating from 1889 and relating to internal affairs, is especially interesting for two reasons. The first is that it sets out the protocol for attendance at village meetings. In brief, two town criers must go to opposite ends of the village – east and west – and summon household representatives to the assembly. The householders must prepare themselves by donning appropriate attire – the chuba (*gos*) – and, after a second call, make their way to the assembly place. At this point, an official pours water onto a standing stone (*rdo ring*). Anyone who has not turned up for the meeting by the time the stone has dried must pay a fine for lateness. An even more interesting feature of the document is that it records a government concession granting Geling legal autonomy for three years. During this period there was no requirement for any legal issues to be referred to an external authority. The archives of several villages contain an agreement to the effect that legal matters should be settled internally with fines payable by anyone who might take a case to a government court, but such decrees were internal to communities and clandestine, and this is the only example we know of in which such local autonomy was officially sanctioned.

Chapter 5
A Codicological Study of the Documents

The Tibetan diplomatic tradition recognises a large number of categories of documents. One of the main differences between the archives from Central Tibet under the Ganden Phodrang, the government of the Dalai Lamas, which ran from 1642 to 1959, on the one hand, and those from Mustang, on the other, is that the former include relatively few documents concerning dealings between villagers, the overwhelming majority consisting of different categories of communication from institutions or individuals in positions of authority to lower-ranking members of the population, such as the peasantry, whereas among the archives from Mustang the opposite is true. Most documents in the Mustang archives belong to the category *gan rgya*, a term that may be translated as "contract", "covenant" or "written obligation" according to the context. In view of the wide-ranging application of the *gan rgya* genre, the documents under consideration were classified into ad hoc categories based on their actual function and the identities of the parties involved or by date in order to check for particular codicological features that may not be obvious when using other criteria. Private archives typically consist of documents such as contracts for loans of grain or cash, sales of land, wills, disputes over ownership and inheritance of property. Community archives may be classified according to various criteria, but broadly fall into two categories: documents relating to internal affairs and those concerned with dealings with outsiders. The former includes records of community gatherings, rules for local natural resource management, such as forests, water and grazing, disputes between fellow-villagers that were mediated by the community, and annual grain taxes to the communal fund. It may also include pasture boundary agreements between neighbours, and directives or other correspondence from political authorities such as the King of Lo or the Government of Nepal.

Searching for connections among all documents with respect to codicological features such as format and size, scribal hands, owners' authentication marks and paper type greatly helped us to see these documents from a different perspective and then to reconstruct the history of paper in Mustang, as set out in chapter 7. As this study progressed, it became apparent that the interpretation of data regarding the reconstruction of the history of paper was more complex than we had expected. Our original idea worked better when documents were approached as a collection of "case studies" rather than by using a general statistical approach for a singular codicological feature. We therefore decided to group the documents according to particular features (preliminary typology), and then test what was specific to the particular documents, archives or locations. When studying documents within smaller groups, we noticed a connection between features such as format and size, scribe and type of paper, as well as the function of documents and their textual content, number of folds and the size of documents among other things. At the same time, however, we also looked at our tables and looked at all documents by particular feature.

Documents and their dating

A variety of features may be used when examining documents in order to help with dating, notably textual content (names of people whose life spans we know), palaeography, codicology, and materials, as radiocarbon dating may be used as a control method. Some documents contained no date in the text, and some displayed physical features that distinguished them from others. Thus, to better understand the possibilities of cross-disciplinary usage of various dating methods we selected five samples for radiocarbon dating, which was performed by the University of Arizona AMS Laboratory in Tucson (see Appendix 5). As shown in figure 60, the documents archived as MA/LTshognam/Tib/1, MA/LTshognam/Tib/15, MA/

Geling/Nep/116, MA/Lubrak/Tib/1 and MA/Lubrak/Tib/6, the results of ^{14}C dating all fall within a plateau spanning 225 to 354 years (Fig. 60).[1]

For this period radiocarbon dating was little help, but it was important to compare both methods, especially since the majority of the 330 documents in our sample contained the date of composition in the body of the text. It is rare to have the opportunity to compare these dates with those obtained by ^{14}C measurement. This is seen in figure 61, where dates included in text are marked with red arrows and circles on the radiocarbon graph (Fig. 61).

The "Copy of covenant among the five Shöyul" archived as MA/LTshognam/Tib/1 from the Lower Tshognam, dated to 1816 within the text, was thus dated by radiocarbon to a period of time between 1666 to the present.[2] The "Description of a monastery in Tibet" archived as MA/LTshognam/Tib/15 from Lower Tshognam, bearing the date of 1898, was dated by radiocarbon to between 1689 and 1926.[3] The "Land tax document" archived as MA/Lubrak/Tib/6 from Lubrak is dated in text to the Iron Hare year, i.e. 1951, but by radiocarbon to between 1666 and the present.[4] The document archived as MA/Geling/Nep/116 from Geling contains no information about when it was written, and was dated by radiocarbon to between 1694 and 1919.[5] The "Land tax document" from Lubrak, archived as MA/Lubrak/Tib/1, is similarly undated, and is placed by radiocarbon dating between 1663 and the present.[6]

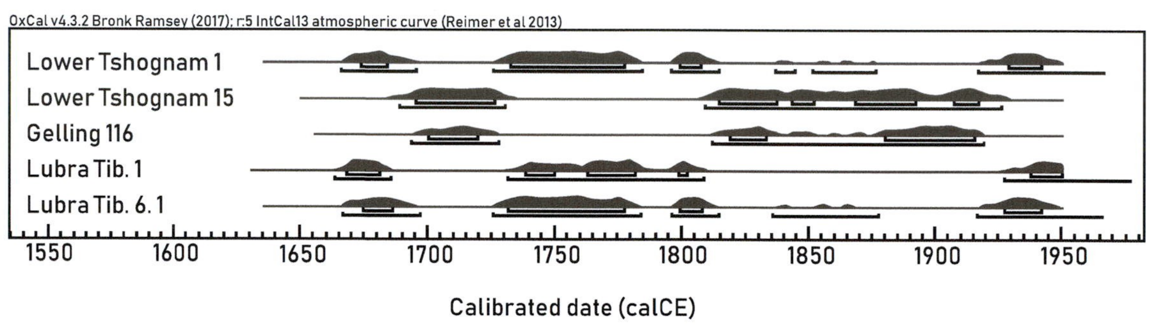

Fig. 60. Radiocarbon dating of the documents archived as MA/LTshognam/Tib/1, MA/LTshognam/Tib/15, MA/Geling/Nep/116, MA/Lubrak/Tib/1 and MA/Lubrak/Tib/6 selected from Lower Tshognam, Geling and Lubrak archives. Graph by Gregory Hodgins, University of Arizona, Report Helman-Wazny, A. (AA109961-AA109966), 12/22/2017.

[1] Conversion of radiocarbon ages into calendar years is not always straightforward. A high degree of accuracy in the conversion data does not necessarily result in the same accuracy in calendar ages. On account of short-term wiggles there are periods in which the accuracy of the latter is enhanced, other periods in which it is degraded, and yet others in which the ambiguity is substantial. A rapid decrease in concentration with decreasing calendar age may result in the radiocarbon age for a sample being greater than that for an older sample, i.e. the radiocarbon clock going backwards. Where the decrease in ^{14}C activity is prolonged but slower a "plateau" may result: a calendar period when there is little change in radiocarbon age. A notable example is provided by the activity decrease that occurs roughly between 800 BCE and 400 BCE, another being the decrease from 1660 CE to 1950 CE, with the result that radiocarbon dating is unsuitable for recent samples.

[2] This document was written in *'khyug ma tshugs (kmt)* script and consists of 15 text lines per page on a one single-layer sheet of paper measuring 43.5 × 41.5 cm folded 10 times. The paper is 0.09–0.16mm thick and composed of *Daphne* fibres that display an even distribution of fibres. The results of calibration give two periods, i.e Calendar Age Range (68%): between 1674 calCE and 1942 calCE and Calendar Age Range (95%): between 1666 calCE and the present.

[3] This document was written in *'khyug* script and consists of 23 text lines per page on one single-layer sheet of paper measuring 31 × 34 cm. The paper is 0.09–0.11 mm thick and composed of a mixture of *Stellera* and *Daphne* fibres that display an uneven distribution of fibres. The results of calibration give two periods, i.e. Calendar Age Range (68%): between 1695 calCE and 1917 calCE and Calendar Age Range (95%): between 1689 calCE and 1926 calCE.

[4] This is a single sheet of paper with text in *kmt* script, 7 lines per page with 7 crosses.
The results of calibration gave two periods, i.e. Calendar Age Range (68%): between 1675 calCE and 1942 calCE and Calendar Age Range (95%): between 1666 calCE and the present.

[5] This is a single sheet of paper 0.18–0.26 mm thick, measuring 51 × 21.5 cm and folded 11 times. The results of calibration give two periods, i.e. Calendar Age Range (68%): between 1700 calCE and 1915 calCE and Calendar Age Range (95%): between 1694 calCE and 1919 calCE.

[6] This is written in *tshugs* script in 26 text lines. The results of calibration give two periods, i.e. Calendar Age Range (68%): between 1668 calCE and 1950 calCE and Calendar Age Range (95%): between 1663 calCE and the present.

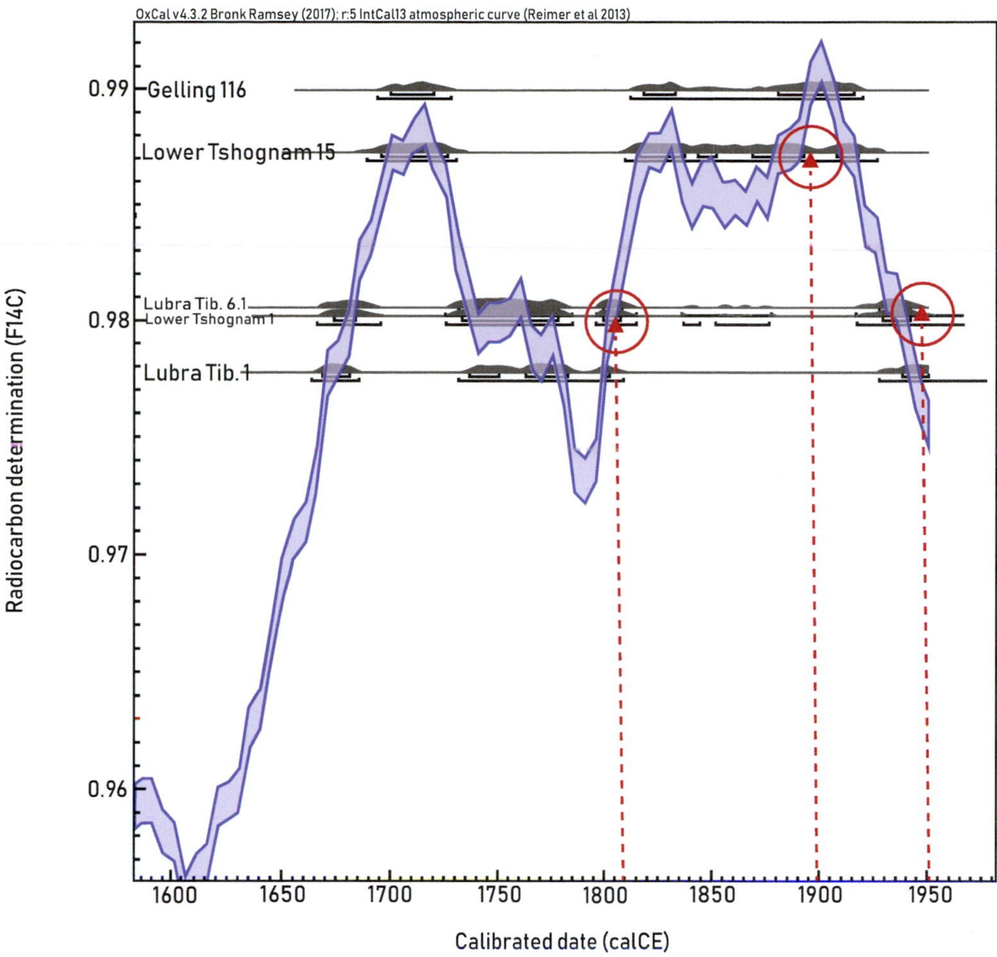

Fig. 61. Radiocarbon dating of the documents archived as MA/LTshognam/Tib/1, MA/LTshognam/Tib/15, MA/Geling/Nep/116, MA/Lubrak/Tib/1 and MA/Lubrak/Tib/6 crossed with dates derived from text marked with red arrows and circles. Original ^{14}C graph by Gregory Hodgins, University of Arizona, Report Helman-Wazny, A. (AA109961-AA109966), 12/22/2017.

From all the archives we were able to confirm that 44 documents from Upper Tshognam range in date between 1875 and 1914; 20 documents from Lower Tshognam between 1832 and 1927; 172 documents from Geling mostly between 1852 and 1969, with two examples possibly dated to the eighteenth century; 12 documents from Dzar between 1870 and 1906, and 82 documents from Lubrak between 1853 and 1994.

Format and layout

Various formats and sizes were registered in our sample, depending on the content and function of the documents. The majority of documents, however, were written on single sheets of paper which were then folded into small packages, as described in chapter 1. This format was found in 61 documents from Tshognam, 8 from Dzar, 172 from Geling and 80 from Lubrak (Fig. 62). They were of various sizes of recumbent or standing rectangles, as well as other specific polygonal shapes which varied substantially in size. We registered 201 single-sheet documents (comprising the majority of our sample) in a recumbent-rectangle shape and 87 in a standing rectangle shape. We also have a group of documents in approximately square format, exemplified by 15 documents from Tshognam, 3 from Dzar, 31 from Geling and 21 from Lubrak. A much smaller group of nine documents was in a sewn book format called *mgo tshem* or *mgo lteb ma*. There were 3 sewn books in Tshognam, 4 in Dzar, and 2 in Lubrak. The variety of layouts suggests that these features are not standardised.

Fig. 62. Documents written on a single sheet of paper, then folded into little packages, in the Geling archive. Photograph by Agnieszka Helman-Ważny.

Upper and Lower Tshognam

The majority of documents in the smaller single-sheet format contain texts of contracts between individuals or records of the acquisition of land in the village of Tshug. These documents usually measure between 10 cm and 15 cm by between 21 cm and 34 cm and most of them are folded four times (MA/UTshognam/Tib/6, MA/UTshognam/Tib/8, MA/UTshognam/Tib/16, MA/UTshognam/Tib/19, MA/UTshognam/Tib/34, MA/UTshognam/Tib/45). The majority of such documents contain 5, 6 or 7 lines of text aligned with the left margin, with the exception of two documents which consist of 11 lines of text.

By contrast, documents recording plenary gatherings were larger, written on vertical rectangular sheets measuring about 43.5 cm × 41.5 cm (MA/LTshognam/Tib/1) and 41 cm × 37 cm (MA/LTshognam/Tib/2). MA/LTshognam/Tib/1 contains 15 text lines organised into three paragraphs, written evenly and composed centrally with an upper margin with a width of a double fold, and a lower margin the width of a single fold. MA/LTshognam/Tib/2 is prepared in a rather sloppy way: its 23 lines, organised into two paragraphs, are not straight, and the text is not centred.

The largest document in our sample, with a nearly square format, folded 15 times, measures 63.5 cm × 58 cm (MA/UTshognam/Tib/24). It is a private contract between external parties, containing 6 lines of text on the recto and one line on the verso.

Other roughly square documents are MA/UTshognam/Tib/13 (29.8 cm × 31.8 cm), MA/UTshognam/Tib/31 (38 cm × 38 cm), MA/UTshognam/Tib/32 (38.6 cm × 41 cm) and MA/LTshognam/Tib/1 (43.5 cm × 41.5 cm). All, except MA/LTshognam/Tib/1, contain more than 20 lines on the page, and, although they lack side margins, they have an upper margin that is clearly marked.

The booklet format is seen in MA/UTshognam/Tib/46, MA/UTshognam/Tib/47 and MA/LTshognam/Tib/9 (Fig. 63). MA/UTshognam/Tib/46 is a ritual manual, a 20-page book of 9.5 cm × 44 cm, sewn along the left side (between 6 and 8 text lines per page). MA/UTshognam/Tib/47 (Songs of the Sixth Dalai Lama) is a book measuring 8.5 cm × 19 cm containing 14 bi-folios (16 cm × 19 cm) and sewn along the top.

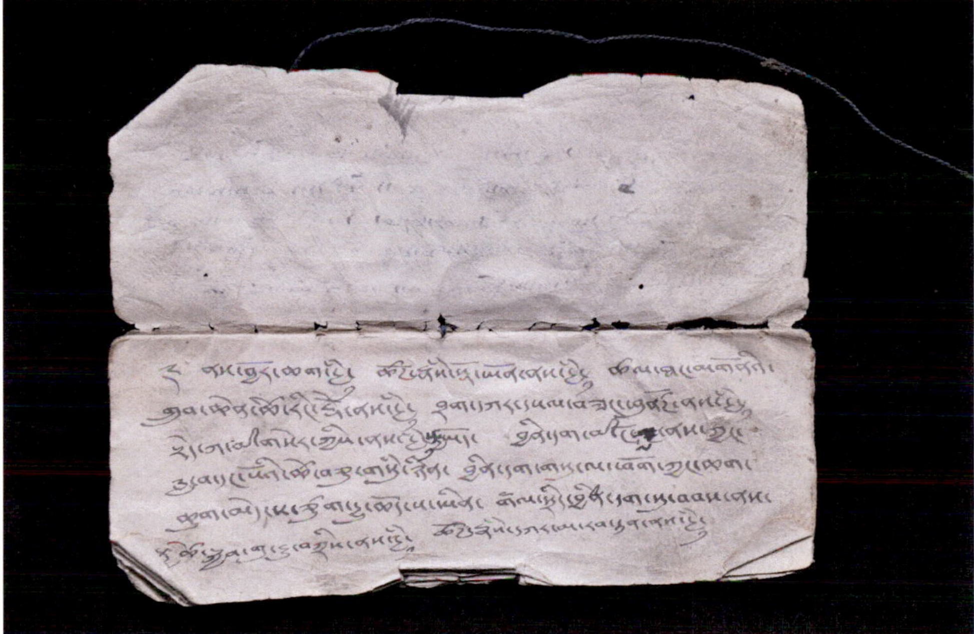

Figs 63 a–b. Document MA/LTshognam/Tib/9, representing the typical format of a stitched Tibetan book (*mgo tshem*). Photographs by Agnieszka Helman-Ważny.

Dzar

Eight single-sheet documents measure between 13 cm and 91 cm in height and between 19 cm and 63 cm in width, and are folded between six and twenty-seven times (MA/Dzar/Tib/1, MA/Dzar/Tib/2, MA/Dzar/Tib/3, MA/Dzar/Tib/7, MA/Dzar/Tib/8, MA/Dzar/Tib/9, MA/Dzar/Tib/11, MA/Dzar/Tib/12). The only roughly square document, MA/Dzar/Tib/12, with 11 lines of text, is between 21 cm and 22.2 × 19 cm and is folded eight times. The largest document in this collection, archived as MA/Dzar/Tib/11, contains "Rules for the annual *dö* (*mdos*) ceremony." It consists of a single sheet and measures 91 cm × 63 cm folded *c.* 27 times with a cloth backing on 4 outer folds (Fig. 64).

Unlike the other studied archives, there is a significant representation of stitched Tibetan books (*mgo tshem*) in the Dzar archive. Of twelve such documents four are in *mgo tshem* format (MA/Dzar/Tib/4, MA/Dzar/Tib/5, MA/Dzar/Tib/6, MA/Dzar/Tib/10). "Rules for ceremonies"

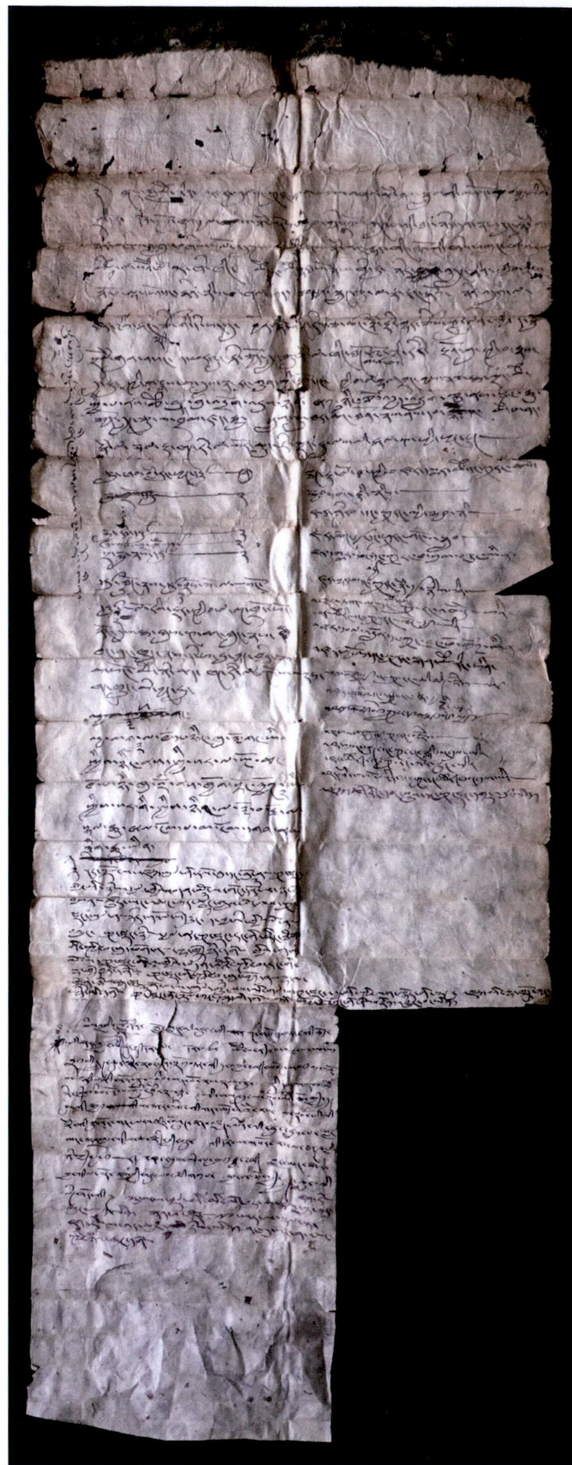

Fig. 64. "Rules for the annual *dö* (*mdos*) ceremony", archived as MA/Dzar/Tib/11. Photograph by Kemi Tsewang.

archived as MA/Dzar/Tib/4 measures between 10.3 cm and 11 cm × 28.6 cm contains 18 pages and is dated to 1878. It contains 9 bifolios measuring 22.4 cm × 28.6 cm. There are 6 or 7 lines of text per page in both *kmt* and Devanāgarī scripts. We registered 7 scribal hands and 1 thumbprint in the body of text. This book is on a woven type of paper between 0.11 mm and 0.18 mm thick, composed of *Daphne* fibres, with an even distribution of fibres within the sheet. Other examples of the same format are "Internal tax payments" archived as MA/Dzar/Tib/5, "Rules for ceremonies" archived as MA/Dzar/Tib/6, as well as a copy of the same text archived as MA/Dzar/Tib/10. MA/Dzar/Tib/5, a 6-page book dated to 1878, measures between 18.2 cm and 13.6 cm × 30.2 cm and is written in one hand in 6 or 7 lines of *kmt* script per page (Fig. 65). It contains three bifolios measuring 27 cm × 30.2 cm. The paper (between 0.10 mm and 0.46mm thick) is composed of *Daphne* fibres, with an even distribution of fibres within the sheet. MA/Dzar/Tib/6, dated to *c.* 1860, contains 10 pages which measure 21.5 cm × 13.3 cm (Fig. 66). It is written in at least 8 hands in *tshugs* script on a single-layer woven type of paper, between 0.14 and 0.18 mm thick, composed of *Daphne* fibres with an even distribution of fibres within the sheet. This form of book is reminiscent of spiral binding. The same text written in between 7 and 21 lines of *kmt* script (possibly by 5 or 6 scribal hands) is found in the book archived as MA/Dzar/Tib/10. This document has a similar type of binding to MA/Dzar/Tib/6, but each leaf is the same size, 30.2 cm × between 17.5 and 19 cm (Fig. 67). Like MA/Dzar/Tib/6 this book contains 6 pages of a single-layered woven type of paper, 0.09 mm and 0.27 mm thick, with felt print composed of *Daphne* fibres with an even distribution of fibres within the sheet.

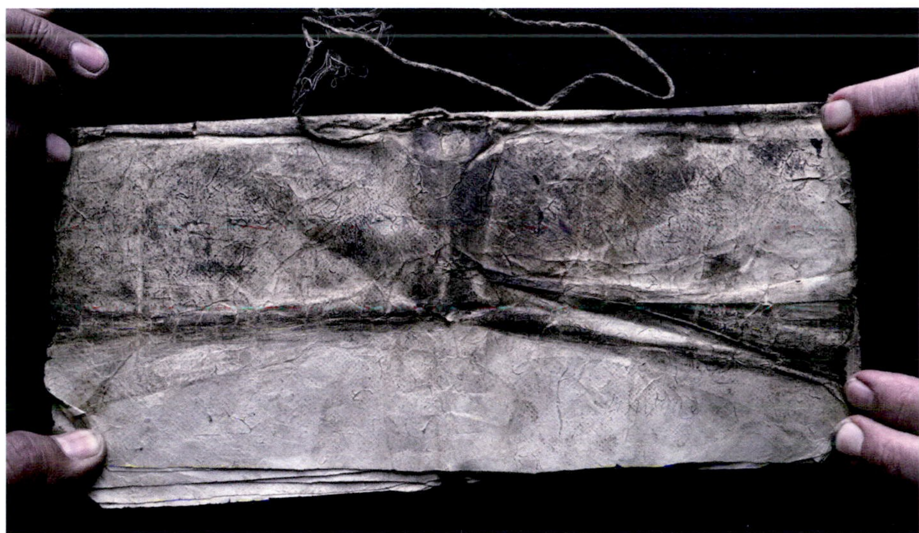

Figs 65 a–b. "Internal tax payments", archived as MA/Dzar/Tib/5. Photographs by Kemi Tsewang.

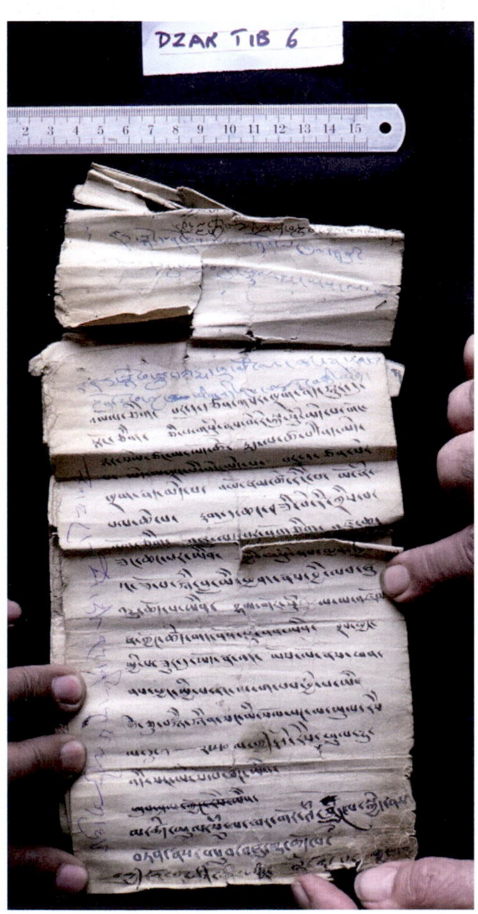

Figs 66 a–c. "Rules for ceremonies," archived as MA/Dzar/Tib/6. Photographs by Kemi Tsewang.

Figs 67 a–b. "Rules for ceremonies," archived as MA/Dzar/Tib/10 (copy of MA/Dzar/Tib/6). Photographs by Kemi Tsewang.

Geling

Most of the documents from the Geling archive are in traditional single-sheet format: the majority, 123 documents, in a recumbent-rectangle shape, 37 in a standing-rectangle shape, and 11 in roughly square format. These documents usually measure between 4 cm and 106.4 cm in height and between 18.8 cm and 70.8 cm in width. Other roughly square documents usually measure between 27.6 cm and 43 cm × between 29.5 cm and 42.2 cm. These are MA/Geling/Tib/3, MA/Geling/Tib/11, MA/Geling/Tib/20, MA/Geling/Tib/41, MA/Geling/Tib/42, MA/Geling/Tib/83, MA/Geling/Tib/84, MA/Geling/Tib/96, MA/Geling/Tib/119, MA/Geling/Tib/160, MA/Geling/Tib/170. There are a couple of especially large documents, such as "Letter home from a monk in Ewam Chöden, Tibet" archived as MA/Geling/Tib/124 measuring 106.4 cm × 51.7 cm (Fig. 68), "List of debts in cash, grain and other commodities" archived as MA/Geling/Tib/110 measuring 73.7 cm × 18.8 cm, or MA/Geling/Tib/164 measuring 66.2 cm × 43.4 cm. The last document deals with an offering by the village to the lama of a field that was to be worked by the nuns, who would also pay taxes on it. In the second part, a certain Gyatso is to marry one of the nuns, and was to pay a fine to the village and the religious community in the form of a pregnant cow worth 15 rupees.

As described above, there is a wide variety in sizes and shapes, including specific polygonal shapes such as MA/Geling/Tib/141, containing the record of "Sums of money received following the death of an unnamed individual" (Fig. 69). The layout usually follows the format of document, according to the amount and type of text contained. The text is usually centred, and margins differ significantly in size from one document to another. The layout of numerous Geling documents is characterised by large upper margins and a clearly visible left margin with text aligned. Such a layout may be seen in documents MA/Geling/Tib/32, MA/Geling/Tib/51, and MA/Geling/Tib/89 (Fig. 70). Documents with an especially large upper margin include MA/Geling/Tib/43, MA/Geling/Tib/47, MA/Geling/Tib/57, MA/Geling/Tib/70, MA/Geling/Tib/75, MA/Geling/Tib/100, MA/Geling/Tib/135, and MA/Geling/Tib/160. Sometimes the lower margins were significantly larger than others, as may be observed in MA/Geling/Tib/3, MA/Geling/Tib/64, MA/Geling/Tib/85, MA/Geling/Tib/86, MA/Geling/Tib/96, MA/Geling/Tib/157, and MA/Geling/Tib/165.

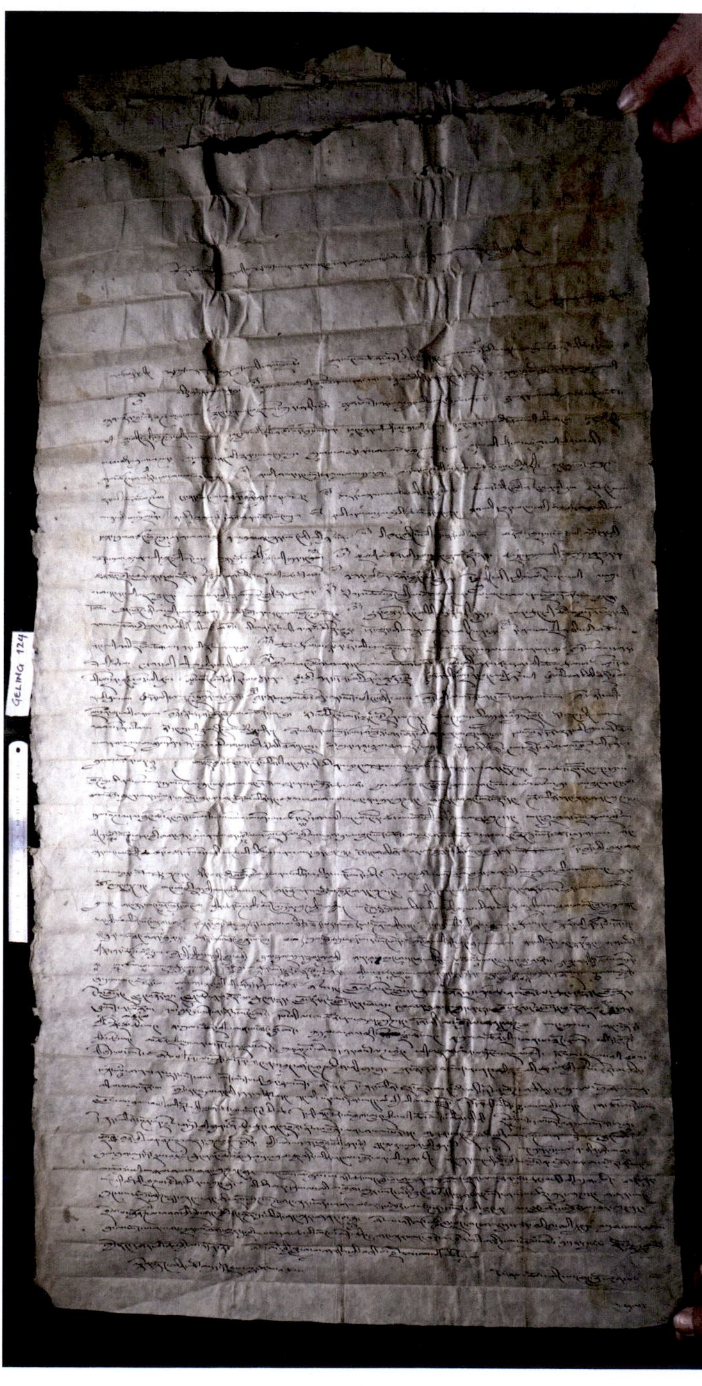

Fig. 68. "Letter home from a monk in Ewam Chöden, Tibet," from Geling, archived as MA/Geling/Tib/124. Photograph by Kemi Tsewang.

Fig. 69. The document containing the record of "Sums of money received following the death of an unnamed individual" archived as MA/Geling/Tib/141. Photograph by Kemi Tsewang.

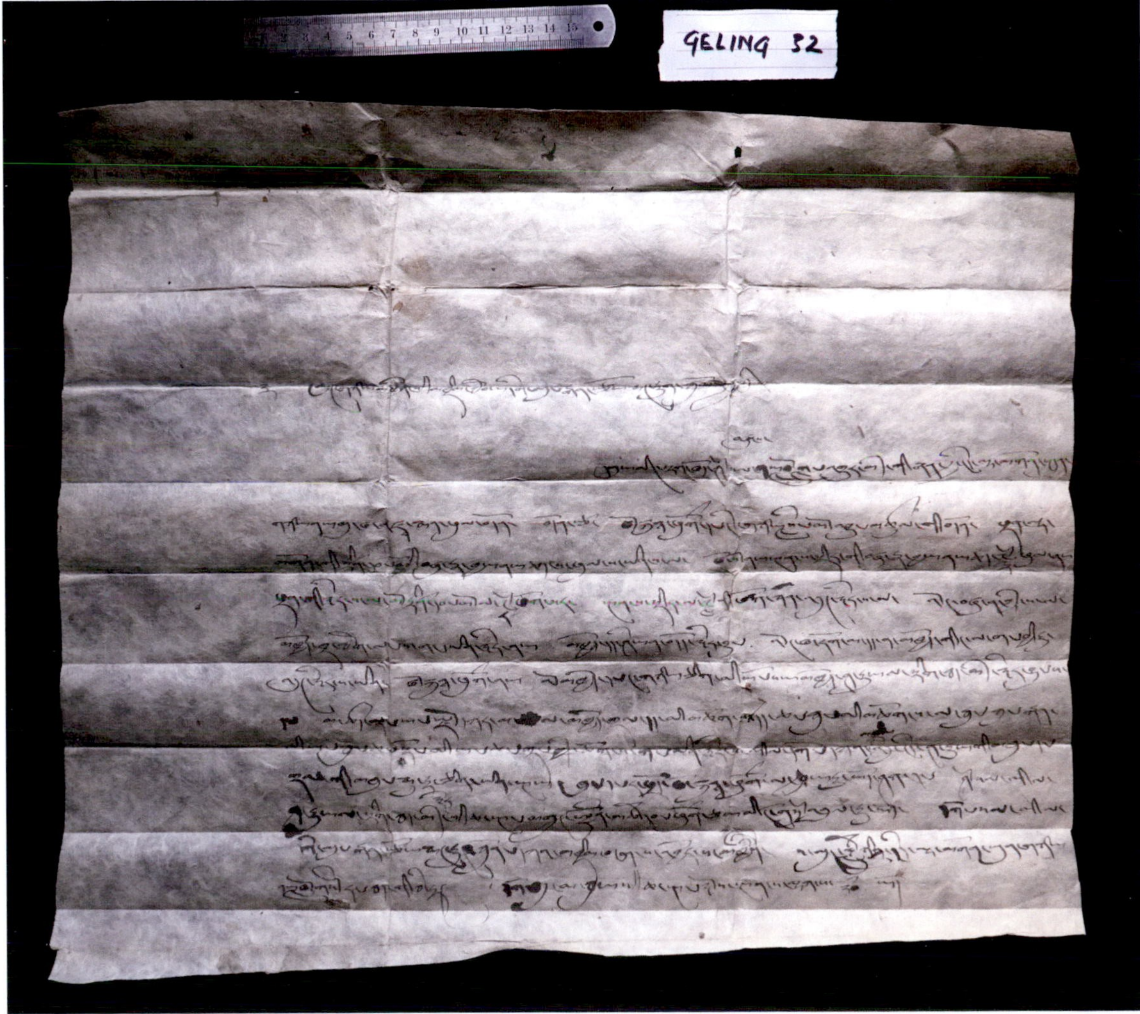

Fig. 70. "Statement by a party in a dispute," archived as MA/Geling/Tib/32. Photograph by Kemi Tsewang.

Lubrak

Like the other archives, the majority of documents from Lubrak represent single-sheet format. These documents usually measure between 6.4 cm and 136 cm in height and between 13.5 cm and 53.5 cm in width. The "land tax document" archived as MA/Lubrak/Tib/17 is in traditional single-sheet format measuring 33.5 cm × 32 cm and supported with textile attached to the upper part of the paper (Fig. 71).

Other roughly square documents are: MA/Lubrak/Tib/2A (38.3 cm × 39.2 cm), MA/Lubrak/Tib/4 (18.2 cm × 18 cm), MA/Lubrak/Tib/16 (20.8 cm × 23.2 cm), MA/Lubrak/Tib/17 (33.5 cm × 32 cm), MA/Lubrak/Tib/20 (26.5 cm × 28.6 cm), MA/Lubrak/Tib/50 (35.1 cm × 37 cm), MA/Lubrak/Tib/62 (20.9 cm × 19.1 cm), MA/Lubrak/Tib/65 (36.6 cm × 35.7 cm), MA/Lubrak/Tib/69 (14.2 cm × 15.6 cm), MA/Lubrak/Tib/71 (19.3 cm × 21.8 cm). The large format documents may be exampled by "Rules for conduct during temple ceremonies" archived as MA/Lubrak/Tib/15 measuring 130.2 cm × 36.4 cm and dated to between 1881/1941 or "Temple property list" archived as MA/Lubrak/Tib/58 measuring 136 cm × 49 cm. Only two documents have a *mgo tshem* form. Both measure 11 cm × 24 cm.

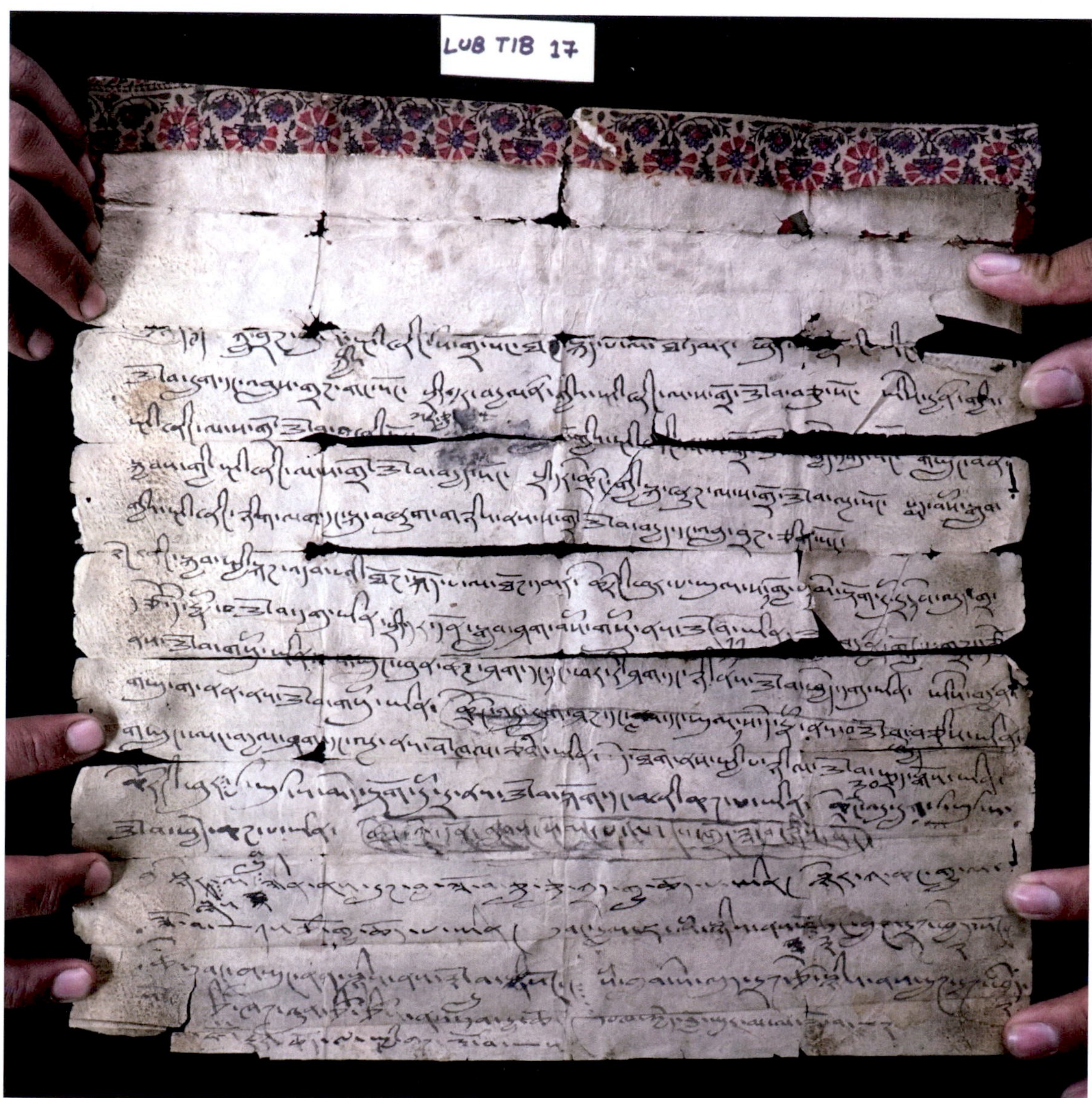

Fig. 71. "Land tax document" from Lubrak, archived as MA/Lubrak/Tib/17. Photograph by Kemi Tsewang.

Script and scribal hands

Perhaps the most succinct presentation of the varieties of the Tibetan script is to be found in a well-known nineteenth-century Tibetan encyclopaedia:

> In Tibetan calligraphy, all [writing systems] can be subsumed within the following six scripts: The headed block-letter script, the headless [block-letter] script, the headless thick and thin italic scripts, the formal handwriting script, and the cursive shorthand script. Although there are many different categories of Tibetan script that gradually gained currency in recent times, all of them may be subsumed within the following six: the basic headed block-letter script (*gzab chen*) and its headless form (*gzab chung*), the headless thick-stroked italic script (*'bru chen*) and its thin-stroked form (*'bru chung*), the [formal] handwriting script (*bshur ma*), and the cursive shorthand script (*'khyug yig*) [which is a derivative of common writing, *dkyus yig*].[7]

The author then goes on to give concise descriptions of the many categories of scripts that fall under each of these rubrics.[8] The headless category includes a wide variety of styles, ranging from clearly formed, unconnected letters to a fluid hand that can properly be described as cursive. Tibetan has names to describe numerous sub-categories of headless script, depending on features such as the length of the descenders, the form of the vowels and so forth. The great majority of official documents were written in the cursive script known as *'khyug* (Fig. 72). This script was a requirement of private documents in Central Tibet, though a slightly more formal version, known as *gshar ma* (Fig. 73), was sometimes used until the end of the nineteenth century.[9] An obstacle facing any attempt to classify scripts in the Mustang archives is that the formal Tibetan scriptural categories denote ideal types, whereas in reality, there are numerous intermediate forms that do not correspond precisely to any category. Whereas some documents are written in *'khyug*, and in others the script is closer to the more rounded, larger-lettered *tshugs*, most fall into the category called *'khyug ma tshugs* (abbreviated here as *kmt*), a script that exhibits features of both (Fig. 74). It may be noted that the tendency to depart from clear scribal categories is by no means unique to Mustang or other borderland areas, and even official documents issued by the Tibetan government sometimes used "hybrid" scripts (see Fig. 75).

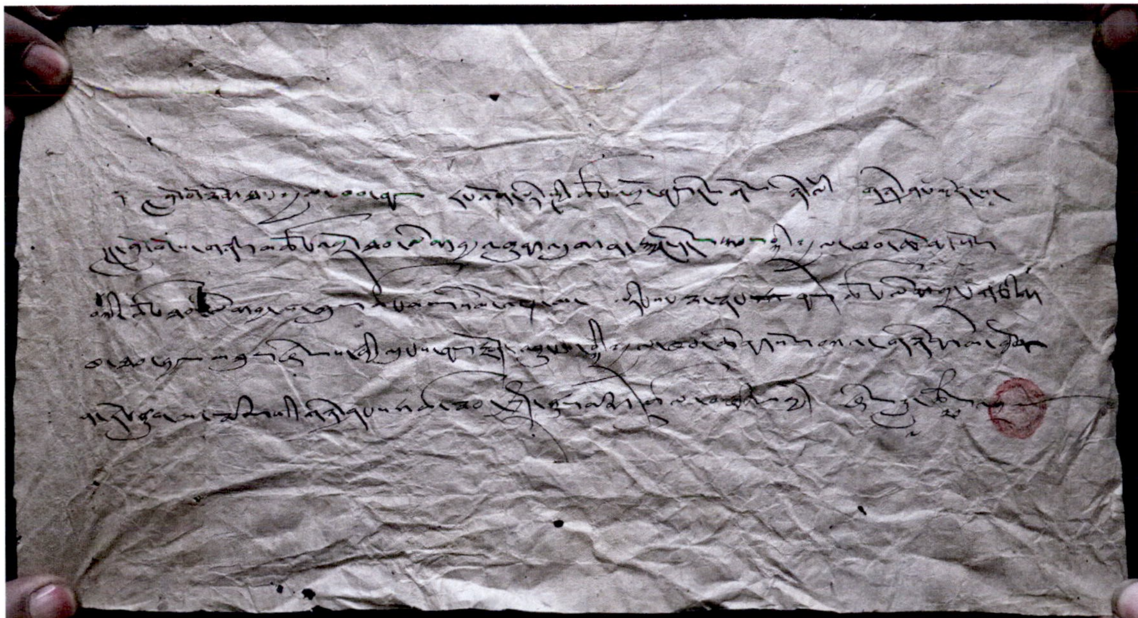

Fig. 72. MA/Geling/Tib/168, a document written in the cursive *'khyug* script, issued by the King of Lo and bearing his seal. Photograph by Kemi Tsewang.

[7] Jamgön 2012: 251.

[8] Jamgön 2012: 251–59.

[9] Schneider 2002: 417.

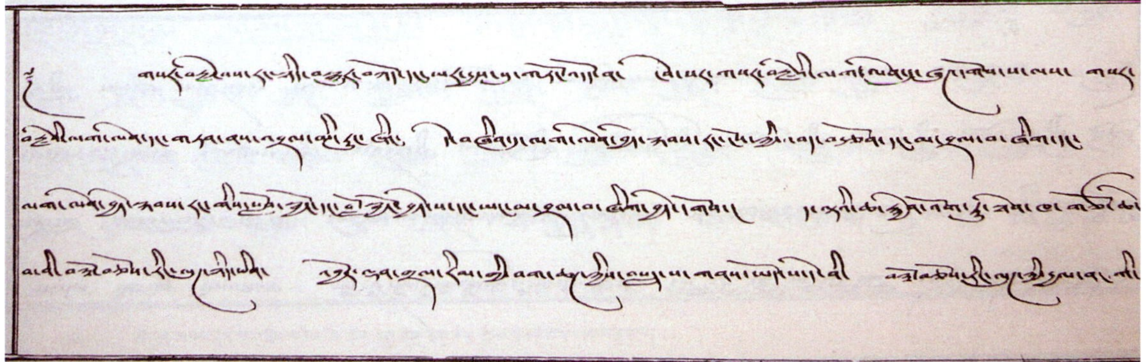

Fig. 73. Example of *gshar ma* script from a manual of calligraphy.

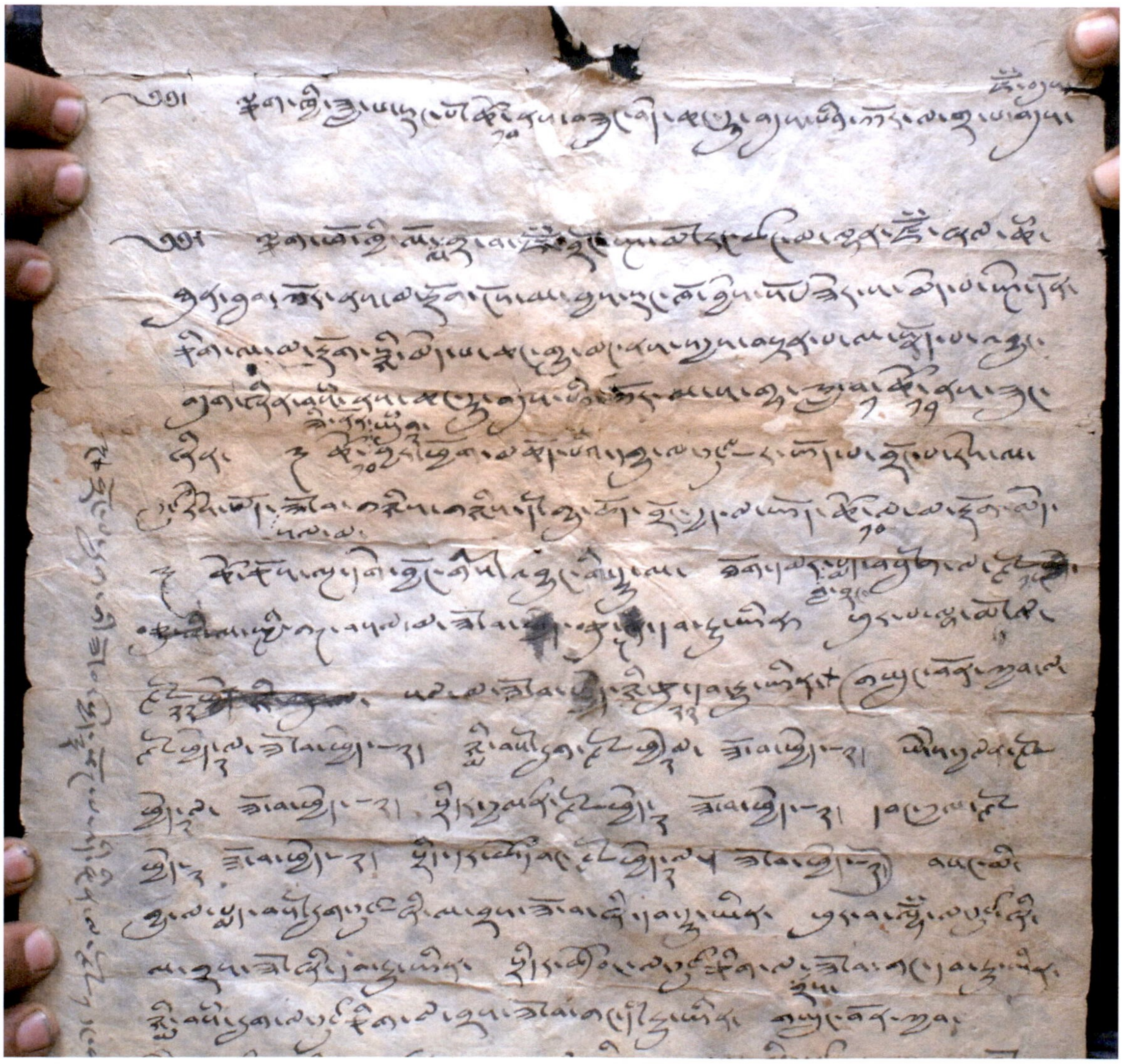

Fig. 74. MA/Lubrak/Tib/18, an example of *'khyug ma tshugs*, the "hybrid" script – between the relatively formal *tshugs* and the most cursive script, *'khyug* – in which the majority of documents in South Mustang are written. Photograph by Kemi Tsewang.

Fig. 75. Detail of an edict from western Tibet issued in 1931, bearing the seal of the 13th Dalai Lama and written in a script that has features of both *tshugs thung* and *gshar ma*. Photograph by Charles Ramble.

In a number of cases we also find documents that use a combination of different scripts. For example, a more "formal" script may be used for the title of a document, inscribed on the verso (Fig. 76), or for an opening invocation (Fig. 77).

Over recent years scholars have made some attempts at analysing handwriting styles in Tibetan manuscripts. From a range of auxiliary tools available they have turned to palaeography in order to define styles of Tibetan writing. Such attempts, together with analyses of other physical features, can help to link documents in meaningful ways or determine the age of the manuscripts or documents that are currently undated. Sam van Schaik has described several imperial-period writing styles found in Dunhuang manuscripts that are particular to certain genres based on palaeographic features.[10] Together with Jacob Dalton and Tom Davis, van Schaik has also applied the techniques of forensic handwriting analysis in order to identify individual scribal hands.[11] This has made it possible to see particular manuscripts in the context of their genre, origin and scribal habits.

The application of these techniques to Tibetan writing, however, is still in its early stages, and we must be cautious in maintaining the distinction between the standardised features of a particular script (imposed from the stylistic norms of different scripts) and the idiosyncracies of a particular scribe. Handwriting, understood as the extension of the scribe's personality defined by very detailed individual features, can help us to attribute manuscripts to specific scribes and consequently group them in ways that otherwise would not have been justifiable or even imaginable. At the same time these detailed studies have a direct impact on our understanding of local written traditions. The comparison and evaluation of these individual features or habits enable forensic analysts of

[10] van Schaik 2014.

[11] Dalton et al. 2007.

Fig. 76. Document MA/Lubrak/Tib/68 written in *'khyug* on recto, with the title on verso written in the more formal, angular *'bru tsha* script. Photograph by Kemi Tsewang.

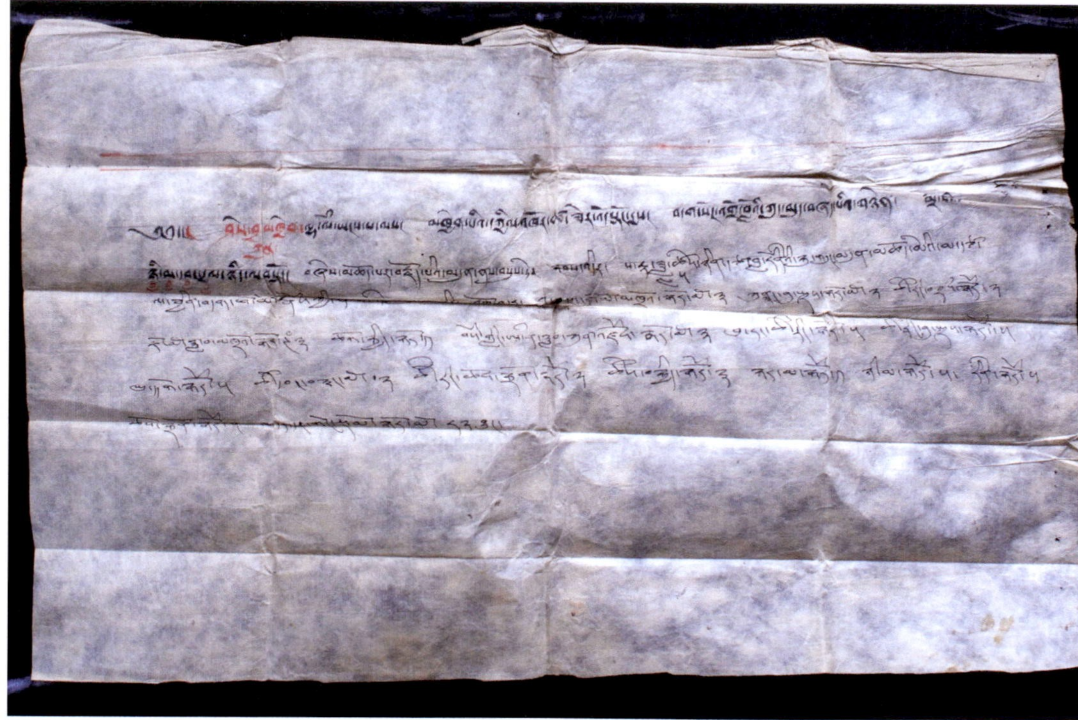

Fig. 77. Document MA/Lubrak/Tib/13, a document recording funds collected for a new ceremony. The opening invocation is written in a type of headless script known as *khyung yig*, while the details of the payments are given in a more informal *'khyug ma tshugs*. Photograph by Kemi Tsewang.

documents to identify the same scribal hands. The average person may recognise the handwriting of an individual and differentiate between individuals to some degree; however, only the gross features of the handwriting, such as letter formation, size, or slope of the handwriting is observed in such cases.[12] However, such an approach fails to consider the subtleties in the writing that may differentiate it from other very similar hands.

[12] On methods for analysing handwriting, see: Morris 2000 or Purdy 2006: 47–74.

Scribal identity cannot be established through the confirmation of single individual feature in the writing. Rather, it is established through a combination of the significant features shared by examples of writing, with no significant differences. Moreover, the writing of a single scribe will vary depending on a range of factors, such as the material support, writing tool, the script style (e.g., headed or headless, the size and slope of the writing), the perceived importance of the work, pen pressure, pen lifts, the spacing between words and letters, the position of the writing on the real or imaginary baseline, height relationships, beginning and ending strokes, and any number of other factors not to mention personal handwriting character change over time. Defining these features for Tibetan texts entails a letter-by-letter comparison of the same type of writing, and this must be carried out before we can even consider the possibility of identifying scribal hands.

The Mustang archives afford a rare opportunity to test the extent to which we can or cannot identify the same scribal hands. It should be noted that most of these documents were produced by a small community of local scribes using a very narrow selection of materials and tools and not subjected to restricted script standards. Thus in our sample we deal with personal handwriting rather than any standardised script. By examining documents written by the same scribe we tested how, if at all, writing materials influence the final result, as well as the degree to which an individual's handwriting might vary over time and according to the casualness or formality of the document. Our main aim is to develop a methodology by producing the reference material, and point to features which cannot be ignored, rather than to identify the same scribal hands from among anonymous documents.

The examined documents constitute a fertile arena for the study of Tibetan handwriting. This is thanks to a number of factors, the most important of which are, first, those in which the identity of the scribes of several of the documents is known and, second, that these same scribes display different hands. The following general observations could be profitably applied to other manuscript collections. Because the general appearance of an individual's handwriting is not a reliable indicator of the scribe's identity, close attention must be paid to the construction of individual letters. While it is the case that certain letters are diagnostic of a particular scribe insofar as they retain idiosyncratic features in different scripts and over the course of time, other letters are subject to variation. Identification of the same scribes in a number of documents also opened the possibility to learn about a scribe's preference for using a particular type of paper. In spite of the fact that the selection of raw materials and technology of papermaking thus far identified shows limited variety, being able to identify and follow a particular scribe has enabled us to understand to some extent the processes of making archival documents, the transfer of technological knowledge, the trade of materials, and the socio-historical background concerned (from the textual content of documents).

Understanding consistency and variation in handwriting is greatly assisted by documents in which the scribe identifies himself, invariably at the very end of the text. The handwriting in several documents was so different that there would have been few grounds on which to attribute the items to a single writer; however, the presence of the name left no doubt that the identity of the scribe was the same in each case, and the differences had to be attributed to circumstances such as the lengthy period between the earliest and latest examples, as well as the fact that some documents were intended as rough drafts of more careful scripts.

Documents issued by the Ganden Phodrang government of the Dalai Lamas are in some cases signed by the scribe and in others not. In Mustang, at least, whether a scribe chooses to identify himself or not seems to be a random affair, and may reflect the preferences of a particular writer or the prevailing practice in a given community. In Lubrak, for example, only two documents name the scribe, and in one case this was an outsider; in Dzar, only one document bears the scribe's name; in Tshognam there are eighteen documents. In Geling by contrast, there were twenty-three different scribes mentioned in thirty-two documents, with a number of these featuring on several documents, so that we have altogether fifty-three signed items.

Where scribal identities were not recorded, recognition of similar hands was facilitated by the expedient of organising the documents in chronological order and comparing those that were produced within a given tranche of time. In this way, it was possible to identify anonymous scribes by assigning letters (A, B, C, D, E, F) to the hands. A scribe did not belong to a particular class of people but could be anyone who was literate, though in practice this field would be limited to clerics, either monks or village lamas, or members of better-off families (such as aristocrats) who would have had private tutors. In Tshognam – a priestly settlement – most of the scribes were lamas, either from Tshognam itself or from other villages; the lamas were not only religious figures but acted as doctors, astrologers and scribes for their illiterate parishioners. The only document in Dzar in which the scribe identifies himself is a loan contract drawn up between the lord of Baragaon, Kuzhab Trogyal, and a nomad from the Tibetan border, and in this case the writer – the lord himself – states simply that "I myself was the scribe." In the case of Geling the range is very varied, including monks in Tibet who were the authors of private correspondence with their families, village headmen and others whose identity is not known. Many nuns would also have been literate, and while it is very likely that documents in the archives of Kunzang Chöling convent were written by women, we have not encountered any documents in which the name of a female scribe is given.

Independently of our analyses we tested a selection of samples of identifiable handwriting from the Tshognam and Geling archives with the Handwriting Analysis Tool v3.0 (HAT 3) mentioned in chapter 1 on methods. Hussein Adnan Mohammed from the Centre for the Study of Manuscript Cultures (CSMC) at the University of Hamburg, with whom we collaborated, measured the similarities between confirmed hands in several samples. Thus the following handwriting samples were analysed by HAT 3: "the man Gyaltsen" (*bu rgyal mtshan*, found in two documents MA/Geling/Tib/102 and MA/Geling/Tib/150), Lama of Tshognam (found in document MA/UTshognam/Tib/7), Lama Ösal Dorje (found in four documents MA/UTshognam/Tib/10- MA/UTshognam/Tib/11, MA/UTshognam/Tib/19, and MA/UTshognam/Tib/21), Lama Thutob (found in two documents MA/UTshognam/Tib/5 and MA/UTshognam/Tib/8), Gyaltsen (found in three documents MA/Geling/Tib/13, MA/Geling/Tib/24, MA/Geling/Tib/50), and Tenpa Gyaltsen, who was Ösal Dorje's son (found in document MA/UTshognam/Tib/28).

Regarding the measured similarities, they are generated by comparing the first sample from each style with all others. The results obtained by computer agree with our observations. The first sample of handwriting by Gyaltsen (MA/Geling/Tib/13) is very different from the other samples (MA/Geling/Tib/24, MA/Geling/Tib/50) (based on the similarity values), while the other two samples are similar to each other. It could be the case that the Gyaltsen of MA/Geling/Tib/13 is a different person – Gyaltsen is a common name – from the scribe of the other two.

Although we examined documents written by the same scribe, we were unfortunately unable to find large collections written by the same person (a maximum of four documents). Thus, due to a lack of sufficient data, it was difficult to say how writing materials may have influenced the final result, or the degree to which an individual's handwriting might vary over time and according to the casualness or formality of the document. However, this project contributed to the development of our methodology and produced valuable reference materials for any future study on identification of the same scribal hands from among anonymous documents.

Authentication marks: seals, crosses and digital prints

The documents bear a variety of marks that are intended to certify ownership or validate the document. These are seals, fingerprints and other signatures, such as written names or crosses, which when compared helped to know which documents were certified by the same person. We photographed these marks as close-up images, and preserved them in the CSMC data repository together with other data related to relevant documents.

For the same reason we recorded digital prints (finger- and thumbprints) and worked on adaptation of fingerprint recognition software to test if there was any chance of identifying the same fingerprints on different documents. As mentioned in chapter 1, at this point the quality of images of digital prints impressed on paper was not sufficient to obtain straightforward results.

Various devices are used for the authentication of documents, and here we have given particular attention to the use of seals (Fig. 78). Although there is a growing body of published

Fig. 78. Official seal of the village of Tshug. Photograph by Kemi Tsewang.

research on the subject of Tibetan seals, their use in borderland areas such as Mustang merits closer attention. The brief examination of a selection of seals appearing in the Tshognam archives identified certain areas that deserve further investigation, and within the project prolongation we undertook a more extensive survey based on a larger sample from several archives. This enquiry made it possible to shed light on features such as the shape of the seals, the choice of the language (Tibetan, Nepali) and script (which includes examples of Arabic and Roman), the incidence and relevance of certain motifs, and the extent to which the content of the seal was implicated in the identity of the owner. Further, it is clear that digital prints (finger- and thumbprints) were used to authenticate documents. This fact opened another potential avenue of investigation – the use of individual fingerprints to detect whether there were other similarities among this group of documents.

The increasing incidence of Nepali administrative and other vocabulary mentioned in Chapter 3 are a sign of the closer integration of Mustang into the orbit of national institutions. A further indicator is the range of marks that are used to validate documents. This section will examine the types of marks that appear in the documents contained in the collections under consideration here in an attempt to discern a pattern in changing usage.

Seals

The use of seals as a method of validating documents in Mustang has been largely discontinued for reasons that will be discussed below, but the collections considered in this work show that they were extensively used in both Tibetan and Nepali documents over an extended period by different categories of individuals and institutions. Before examining these seals more closely, a point of clarification may be made. The term "seal" is ambiguous inasmuch as it may denote both the object that creates the impression and the impression itself. In the present section, the word will usually signify the impression. However, when a distinction needs to be made, the terms "matrix" and "impression" will be used in order to overcome any ambiguity. For the sake of clarity of presentation, the seals to be discussed in this section will be grouped into eight categories, and this grouping is reflected in the table of seals contained in Appendix 4. In most cases there are no formal differences between the seals used by each category, and the definition of these user-groups is partly a matter of convenience for the reader. The groups proposed are as follows:

1. The rulers of Nepal (specifically, the Prime Minister and other high-ranking officials during the Rana era);
2. Nepalese government offices of different levels;
3. The rulers of polities that were, or would become, part of the Nepalese state;
4. Monks or officials from Tibet;
5. Local aristocrats and other prominent individuals;
6. Village communities in Mustang;
7. Lamas and their private temples or households;
8. Laypeople and their households.

Since all communications from Kathmandu, and most of those from local and intermediate government offices, used the medium of Nepali, it is not surprising that most of these official seals are to be found on Nepali-language documents. It is clear that certain items in Tibetan are intended for translation into Nepali before submission to government offices (such as court depositions in legal disputes), while others are translations from Nepali into Tibetan, and these do not bear seals.

MA/Geling/Tib/166 is an official printed government communiqué dealing with the abolition of pasture taxes, dating from February or March 1920, that bears eight or nine seals, of which the most imposing is that of the Prime Minister himself. The seal is elliptical in shape, black, and measures 12 cm at its longest diameter (Fig. 79). The main central space has three horizontally-arranged blocks of lettering, respectively in Devanāgarī, Roman capitals, and Arabic script. The impression is very faint to the left, but it is possible to read the second block as MAHARAJA HONORARY LIEUTENANT GENERAL SIR / CHANDRA SHUMSHERE JUNG BAHADUR RANA C.C. / ...PRIME MINISTER... MARSHAL / NEPAL 1916.

The outer border contains Tibetan script, and though any other scripts this band may contain are too faint to be read it is possible to see clearly, in the right-hand part, the syllables "SHAM SHER JANG+GA BHA DUR RĀ ṆA." Chandra Shumshere was Prime Minister from 1901 to 1929, when he was succeeded by his younger brother Bhim Shumshere, whose seal also appears on the document (Fig. 80). In fact it was Bhim who issued this order, and the Prime Minister's seal is an endorsement. Measuring 9 cm at its longest diameter, this elliptical seal is smaller than that of the Prime Minister but imposing nevertheless. The central area of the seal contains two horizontally arranged blocks of text, in Devanāgarī and in Arabic script. The border contains capital Roman lettering, which reads: "GENERAL BHIM SHUM SHERE JUNG RANA BAHADUR COMMANDER-IN-CHIEF NEPAL 1901."

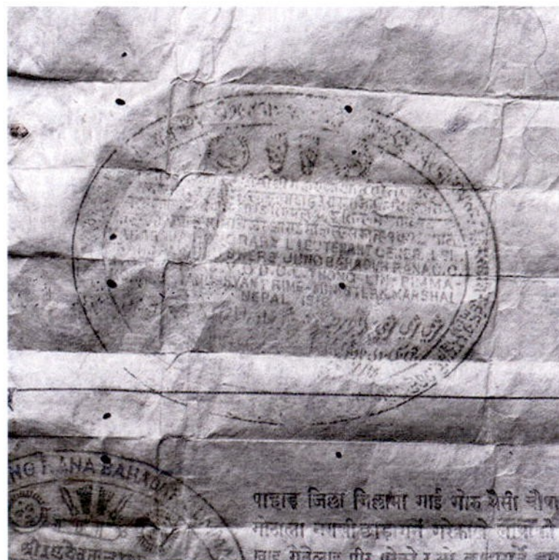

Fig. 79. Seal of the Rana Prime Minister, Chandra Shumshere Rana on the document from Geling archived as MA/Geling/Tib/166. Photograph by Agnieszka Helman-Ważny.

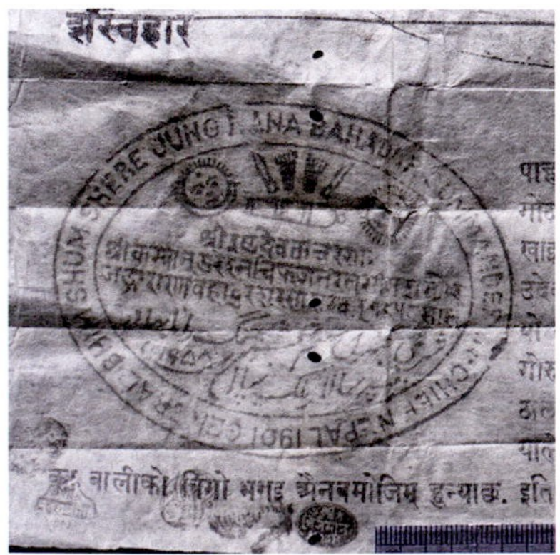

Fig. 80. The seal of Bhim Shumshere Rana, Commander-in-Chief of the Army on the document from Geling archived as MA/Geling/Tib/166. Photograph by Agnieszka Helman-Ważny.

The significance of the date 1901 in the seal is not clear. From 1901 to 1907 Bhim was the senior commanding general of the western command and chief of army staff, but at the time of this document he was commander-in-chief of the army, a position he held from 1907 until his accession to the prime ministership in 1929.[13] The horizontal cannon barrel and the two khukuris in the upper part of the central space, on either side of an impression representing the footprints of the goddess Lakshmi and between the symbols of the sun and moon, signify his association with the military. The six or seven smaller seals along the lower edge of the document presumably belong to government departments or officials.

A feature of these two large seals that may be noted here is that the lettering and motifs in the impressions are formed by ink (or some other medium) against the plain paper background, indicating that the mirror-image forms of the matrix are in relief, standing proud of their background. This is a rather unusual feature that appears in relatively few examples, most of them representing institutions of some importance – such as the Kingdom of Jumla before the Gorkha conquests and the principality of Manang. The letters and motifs in the great majority of cases are "negative," in the sense that they are formed by the plain paper against an inked background, indicating that the design on the matrix is in intaglio – cut below its flat surface.

A number of government offices may be identified in seals from other documents in collections here. One that appears with relative frequency, on both Tibetan and Nepali documents, is that of the customs office (*bhansār aḍḍā*) in Kag (Fig. 81). The seal is elliptical in shape and bears three lines of Devanāgarī: SRĪ/ KĀGBENI BHAN/ SĀR AḌḌĀ.

All the documents in question are tax receipts. Some of the Nepali documents appear to be receipts for the same payments that were made at Kagbeni from an office at the higher level of the administrative pyramid. The main seal here (seen in MA/Lubrak/Nep/8) is a horizontally-oriented rectangle with three vertically stacked sections of which the first and third are indistinct due to smudging (Fig. 82). The middle section contains Devanāgarī lettering, SRĪ MĀL, and may therefore represent a government land revenue (*mālpot*) office, perhaps at the district or zonal, rather than local, level. Unusually, as in the case of the two Rana seals, the impression is a positive one formed by ink against a plain background.

Fig. 81. Seal of the customs office in Kag on the document from Lubrak archived as MA/Lubrak/Tib/8. Photograph by Agnieszka Helman-Ważny.

Fig. 82. Seal of a Nepalese government body, possibly a zonal-level tax office on the document from Lubrak archived as MA/Lubrak/Nep/8. Photograph by Agnieszka Helman-Ważny.

[13] Buyers, Christopher, "Lambjang and Kaski", www.royalark.net/Nepal/lamb7.htm, last consulted 3 May 2020.

South Mustang was under the authority of powers other than the central government in Kathmandu at different periods in its history. MA/Geling/Nep/116 is a bilingual document, in Nepali followed by a Tibetan translation, issued to the people of Geling by someone who is identified simply as "the great king who leads us" (*ma hā ra dza mgo' mdren* [<*mgo 'dren*]). The document mentions a number of tax concessions, but specifies that the community must nevertheless provision the "*'o khom pa* and messengers with fodder for their horses, firewood and food." The term *'o khom pa* – derived from the Nepali term *hukum*, "order, government," – appears in other documents or texts as the local representative of the King of Jumla. The same seal appears on a document from 1733 that is published in Ramesh Dhungel's *The Kingdom of Lo (Mustang)*, where it is identified as the seal of King Surath Shah of Jumla.[14] Like those of the Ranas described above, this seal consists of black lettering on a plain background (Fig. 83). It is rectangular, oriented horizontally, with Devanāgarī text around the inside border. The central space is occuped by the image of a conch.

Another principality that appears to have had some authority over at least the southern part of Mustang was Manang, situated in the Marsyangdi Valley on the eastern side of the Annapurna watershed. The Lubrak archive contains a document from Manang that grants permission to the inhabitants of the village to reside on their land – which, by implication, belongs to Manang – on condition of their payment of a symbolic tax consisting of forest products. The document bears two seals, both consisting of inked designs on a plain background. One of these, unfortunately incomplete owing to damage to the paper, has a complex spiral motif and other features (Fig. 84). The other is square and contains geometric motifs in two central columns (Fig. 85). The motifs

Fig. 83. Seal of a ruler of Jumla, possibly King Surath Shah on the document from Geling archived as MA/Geling/Nep/116. Photograph by Agnieszka Helman-Ważny.

Fig. 84. Seal belonging to the principality of Manang found on the document from Lubrak archived as MA/Lubrak/Tib/61. Photograph by Agnieszka Helman-Ważny.

Fig. 85. Seal belonging to the principality of Manang on the document from Lubrak archived as MA/Lubrak/Tib/61. Photograph by Agnieszka Helman-Ważny.

[14] Dhungel 2002, Photo plates and facsimiles, Doc. No. 10 Nepali.

resemble letters, but in fact are probaby abstract designs that may have been intended to resemble the Phagpa (*'phags pa*) script that features on many Tibetan seals.

The third provincial power that had authority over the communities where our archives are kept was of course the King of Lo. The seal appears on five documents, four from Geling and one from Tshognam.[15] It is relatively small, round, and features a crossed vajra at the centre (Figs 86 a–b). Although the spread of time covered by these documents indicates that different kings must have used this seal, documents issued by the King of Lo in other collections show that other seals were sometimes used.[16]

The seal is one of only five in the collection that are red. One appears on a number of Nepali documents, invariably placed in the middle of the upper edge. The seal is stadium-shaped – that is to say, rectangular with rounded ends – with a blank rectangle in the centre bearing Devanāgarī lettering (Fig. 87). In the only example where the impression is relatively distinct, the text is damaged but may read NAMBAR, representing the English word "number", and therefore one in a series of government-issued documents.

Two of the remaining seals are from Tibet. One belongs to Ngor Ewam Khangsar (Ngor e wam khang gsar), a college of Ngor Ewam Chöden (Ngor e wam chos ldan) monastery in Tibet. It is round and contains the motif of crossed vajras inside two concentric rings (Fig. 88). In the centre is the Tibetan syllable *E*, presumably for Ewam. The seal appears on several documents in the collections of Tshognam and Geling. In all cases the documents are receipts for donations to the college for the performance of merit-making rituals for deceased persons, and contain the assurance that the karmic defilements accruing to the beneficiary have been removed.

Figs 86 a–b. The seal used by the King of Lo authority found in a) document from Geling archived as MA/Geling/Tib/128 and b) document from Lower Tshognam archived as MA/LTshognam/Tib/10. Photographs by Agnieszka Helman-Ważny.

Fig. 87. Seal or stamp of a Nepalese government office, perhaps representing a serial number on the document from Lubrak archived as MA/Lubrak/Nep/7. Photograph by Agnieszka Helman-Ważny.

Fig. 88. Seal of Ngor Ewam Khangsar college of Ewam Chöden monastery in Tibet on the document from Geling archived as MA/Geling/Tib/27. Photograph by Agnieszka Helman-Ważny.

[15] These were: MA/Geling/Tib/16, MA/Geling/Tib/127, MA/Geling/Tib/128, MA/Geling/Tib/168, MA/LTshognam/Tib/10.

[16] See Dhungel 2002, unnumbered reproductions of texts given in the plates section of the book.

The other red seal from Tibet belongs to the *garpön* (*gar dpon*) – a local governor – of Trarik (Khra rigs). The document is a receipt from the *garpön* to the headman of Geling, acknowledging the return of a Japanese gun he had borrowed. The seal depicts a vertically-oriented conch motif with lateral flourishes inside two concentric rings, and topped by a sun-and-moon motif in the outer rim (Fig. 89). Trarik is located in Yushu, in Qinghai province, and it highly unlikely that there would have been such cordial personal relations between its local chief and the headman of Geling over such a distance. The document is undated, but the headman in question was probably born some time in the1930s, and the letter may have been written within Nepal when the *garpön* was in exile. In 1960, a contingent of prominent people from Trarik, including clerics and officials, did arrive in Kathmandu, where they established a Sakyapa monastery in Bouddhanath in 1969.

The last red seal appears on a Nepali document from Dzar. It is round, and features the Tibetan letter *A* at the centre of an eight-petalled lotus (Fig. 90). The identity of the seal's owner is uncertain.

Like the kings of Lo, even after the Gorkha conquests, the aristocracy of Baragaon retained a certain amount of their former power under the aegis of the government in Kathmandu, either in their own right or as the local agents of outsiders who held contracts to collect revenues in the region. One of these nobles was a certain Zangpo Dorje (bZang po rdo rje), a member of the main noble family from Dzar, whose seal appears on a document from 1893, in which he appears as the witness to an agreement by the village of Te to grant residential and other rights to a new lama. The seal is round and rather modest, but unfortunately the impression is too unclear for any motif or lettering to be distinguishable (Fig. 91).

Fig. 89. Seal of the *garpön* of Trarik (Khra rigs), in Amdo on the document from Geling archived as MA/Geling/Tib/169. Photograph by Agnieszka Helman-Ważny.

Fig. 90. Seal of an unidentified individual or institution from Dzar found on the document from Dzar archived as MA/Dzar/Nep/22. Photograph by Agnieszka Helman-Ważny.

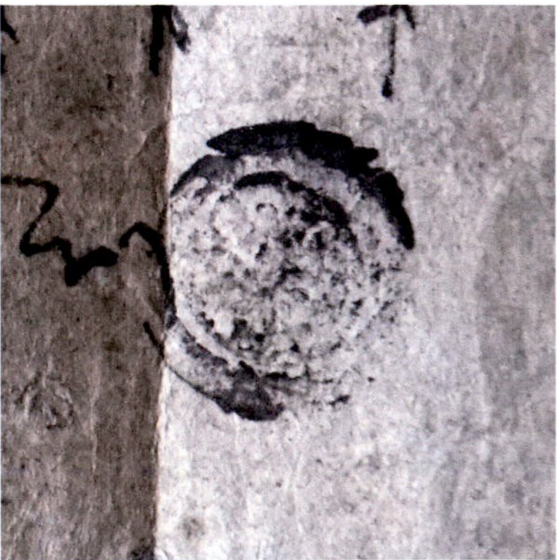

Fig. 91. Seal of Zangpo Dorje, a nobleman of Dzar found on the document from Upper Tshognam archived as MA/UTshognam/Tib/37. Photograph by Agnieszka Helman-Ważny.

Fig. 92. Seal of Candra Bir, a nobleman from Dzar found on the document from Upper Tshognam archived as MA/UTshognam/Tib/45. Photograph by Agnieszka Helman-Ważny.

Fig. 93. Seal of Kuzhab Trogyal, a nobleman of Dzar found on the document from Lower Tshognam archived as MA/LTshognam/Tib/20. Photograph by Agnieszka Helman-Ważny.

Fig. 94. Seal possibly belonging to a *subbā* named Candra Singh found on the document from Geling catalogued as MA/Geling/Tib/100. Photograph by Agnieszka Helman-Ważny.

Another lord of Baragaon whose name appears in several documents has the Nepali name Candra Bir. His seal features on a property settlement document from 1871. It is elliptical, and in spite of smudging it is possible to make out Devanāgarī lettering that reads SRĪ PṚTHVĪ (Fig. 92).

The last example of a seal belonging to a nobleman appears on an agreement relating to the repayment of a debt for which Kuzhab Trogyal (sKu zhabs Khro rgyal) acts as one of the witnesses. The seal is square and contains three lines of Devanāgarī lettering (Fig. 93).

The different *subbās* who held the monopoly on the salt trade that passed through Mustang also had their own seals. An undated letter from a certain Subbā Candra Singh (*su bha tsan tar shing*) bears a seal that is likely to be his own. It is unusual inasmuch as part of the design is "positive" and part "negative." The shape is elliptical, with an elliptical space at the top containing what may be an impression of the syllable SRĪ (Fig. 94). Below this is a name or word in Devanāgarī against an inked background. Although no *subbā* by this name is recorded in the available secondary sources, it is just possible that *tsan tar* in the document is a deformation of Champa rather than Candra; there was a *subbā* named Champa Singh Khadga Chetri who held the salt monopoly in the 1860s.[17] However, this identification remains highly uncertain.

In addition to individuals, certain groups also had seals, notably monasteries and settlements. Document MA/LTshognam/Tib/2 offers a good illustration of the use of seals by communities. Dated 1832, it is one of the oldest documents in the archives of Tshognam, and consists of two parts. The first part is an agreement among the five communities comprising the Shöyul concerning procedures for coordination in the event of a crisis. Each of the communities has endorsed the document with what appears to be its own seal, but in the case of Gyaga, Te and Tshug the same seal is placed twice in each case: from a later document we know that Te and Tshug, as the largest of the five, each had two officials called *centsug* (*spyan btsug*, etc.), whereas the others had only one each (MA/LTshognam/Tib/26). However, the latter document names only one *centsug* for Gyaga. In the second part of MA/LTshognam/Tib/2, the scribe has simply placed five crosses representing the five communities that have given their approval to an agreement concerning trade regulations. In the first part of the document, Figs 95–99 show respectively the seals of the communities of: 95. Taye, 96. Tshug 97. Gyaga 98. Tsele and 99. Te. The motifs in Figs 95 and 96 are illegible. Fig. 96 contains Devanāgarī letters, possibly featuring the words ŚRĪ SIVA; Fig. 98 seems to contain the words ŚRĪ BHŪPALA, and the word GAṆEṢ may also appear in Fig. 99.

[17] Vinding 1998: 74–75.

Fig. 95. The seal of Taye or one of its representatives found on the document from Lower Tshognam catalogued as MA/LTshognam/Tib/2. Photograph by Agnieszka Helman-Ważny.

Fig. 96. Seals representing the community of Tshug, possibly belonging to two of its officials found on the document from Lower Tshognam catalogued as MA/LTshognam/Tib/2. Photograph by Agnieszka Helman-Ważny.

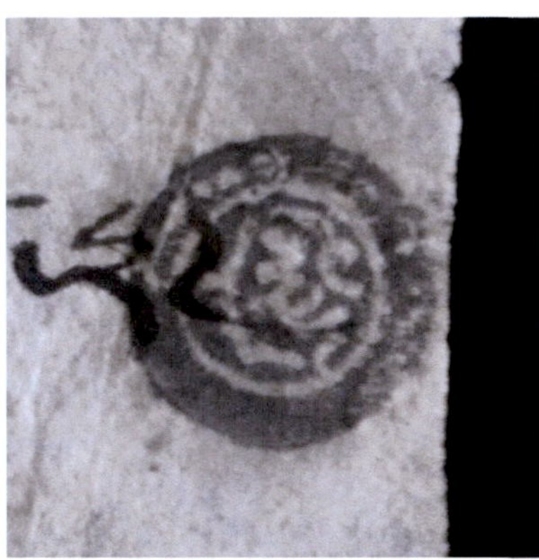

Figs 97 a–b. Seals representing the community of Gyaga, possibly belonging to two of its officials both found on the document from Lower Tshognam catalogued as MA/LTshognam/Tib/2. Photographs by Agnieszka Helman-Ważny.

Fig. 98. Seal of Tsele or one of its representatives found on the document from Lower Tshognam catalogued as MA/LTshognam/Tib/2. Photograph by Agnieszka Helman-Ważny.

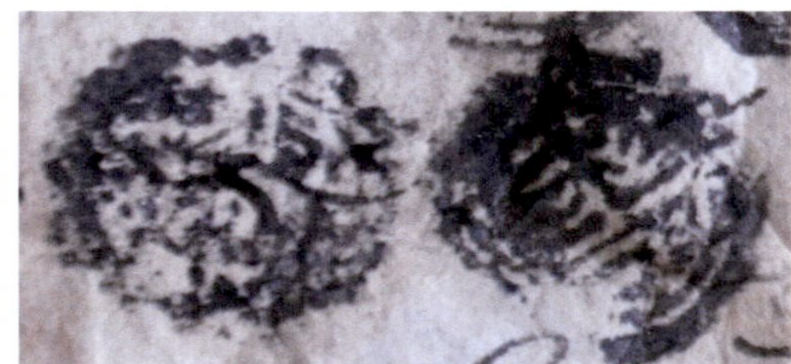

Fig. 99. Seals representing the community of Te, possibly belonging to two of its officials, found on the document from Lower Tshognam catalogued as MA/LTshognam/Tib/2. Photograph by Agnieszka Helman-Ważny.

We cannot be sure that the seals representing the five settlements were indeed community seals, or seals belonging to individuals that were used provisionally for the occasion. Whatever the case, in 1910 we find Tshug using a seal that is unequivocally its own. The document, MA/LTshognam/Tib/17, is an

Figs 100 a–b. Teardrop-shaped seal of the community of Tshug found on the document from Lower Tshognam catalogued as MA/LTshognam/Tib/17. Photographs by Agnieszka Helman-Ważny.

Fig. 101. Seal of the community of Te, bearing the name of the village, found on the document from Upper Tshognam catalogued as MA/UTshognam/Tib/36. Photograph by Agnieszka Helman-Ważny.

Fig. 102. Seal of Te from 1893 found on the document from Upper Tshognam catalogued as MA/UTshognam/Tib/37. Photograph by Agnieszka Helman-Ważny.

agreement by the whole community to grant a newly-arrived lama tenancy of an abandoned estate. The seal, which is placed twice, has an unusual teardrop shape. It bears a bilingual inscription in three lines. The first and third lines are in Devanāgarī. The first reads simply SRĪ and the third is illegible. The second line, in Tibetan, reads TSHUG YUL SPYI = (the last letter being illegible), meaning "the community of Tshug in general" (Fig. 100). One of the headmen of Tshug informed us that at some point this seal was lost, and was replaced by the one that he is seen holding in Fig. 78.

Like Tshug, Te had its own seal with lettering that identified it as belonging to the village. It appears on a document from 1916 (MA/UTshognam/Tib/36). The seal is square and contains two lines of Tibetan framed by a square surround (Fig. 101). The lettering reads GTER/ LUNG, "Te community."

An earlier document, from 1893 (MA/UTshognam/Tib/37), is validated by Te using a different seal. The seal is square with the motif of a diagonally-oriented conch (Fig. 102).[18] This may suggest that the seal bearing the community's name was an innovation that was created between the dates of these two documents.

The community seal that appears with the greatest frequency is that of Geling, which features on at least twelve documents from the village archive (Fig. 103). The seal, which is square and "positive", does not obviously bear the name of the village but consists of three or four (depending on which way it is meant to be "read") of double columns or rows of letters, or motifs that are designed to look like letters (as

[18] Wolfgang Bertsch notes that the conch, together with swastikas, is one of the commonest motifs in anepigrapic Tibetan seals (Bertsch 2005).

Fig. 103. The seal of the community of Geling, with motifs resembling the decorative Zhangzhung Marchen script, found on the document from Geling catalogued as MA/Geling/Tib/24. Photograph by Agnieszka Helman-Ważny.

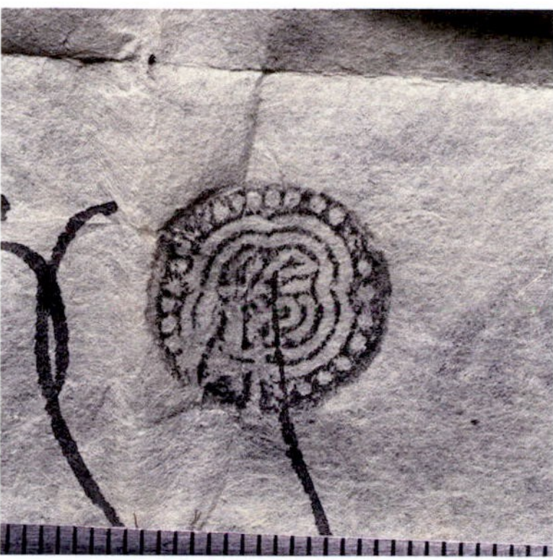

Fig. 104. The seal of a monk from Marpha found on the document from Geling catalogued as MA/Geling/Tib/125. Photograph by Agnieszka Helman-Ważny.

Fig. 105. Seal on a letter sent by two monks in Tibet on the document from Geling catalogued as MA/Geling/Tib/104. Photograph by Agnieszka Helman-Ważny.

Fig. 106. Seal "borrowed from Gatrug", bearing the syllable CHOS, found on the document from Geling archived as MA/Geling/Tib/1. Photograph by Agnieszka Helman-Ważny.

in the case of the seal of Manang, described above). In the present case, however, the design is reminiscent not so much of Phagpa as of the Zhangzhung script known as Marchen (*smar chen*), a decorative script that is used in some Bonpo texts. The hereditary headmen of Geling come from two families, both of which are Bonpo, and we should not discount the possibility that one of them asked a Bonpo lama to design a seal for the community.[19]

Religious specialists in Mustang are represented by celibate monks and nuns, and also married householder-lamas. For reasons that we need not go into here, the village of Geling had close connections with the monastic community of Marpha, in the south of Mustang, and one of the documents in the Geling archive bears the seal of a Marpha monk. The document, MA/Geling/Tib/125, is a contract in which the monk, named Cangdrug, agrees to lease a field in Geling in 1913. The seal is round and features the Tibetan syllable CHOS in the centre, surrounded by two four-lobed concentric rings (Fig. 104). *Chos* is the Tibetan term for "dharma," and may perhaps signify *chos pa*, "religious person," and hence monk, the title by which Cangdrug is identified in the document.

MA/Geling/Tib/104 is a letter sent by two monks in Tibet to their family or families in Geling. The verso of the document bears a seal of very similar design to the last, also with the term CHOS in the centre (Fig. 105).

A third seal with the same design and motif appears in another document from Geling (MA/Geling/Tib/1), an inheritance agreement from 1907. Three of the parties validate the document using

[19] For examples of this script, see Blezer et al. 2013.

Figs 107 a–b. Seals of two ordained monks, Palden Chöphel and Ngawang Rabsal, found on the document from Geling archived as MA/Geling/Tib/130. Photographs by Agnieszka Helman-Ważny.

Fig. 108. Seal of the community of nuns of Geling found on the document from Geling archived as MA/Geling/Tib/164. Photograph by Agnieszka Helman-Ważny.

the same seal, which also features the syllable CHOS, although the design is slightly different from those in two preceding documents (Fig. 106). A note in the margin informs us that "the seal [matrix] was borrowed from Gatrug." Unfortunately we are not informed whether Gatrug was a monk or a layman.

In all three cases the seals are very similar in design and content but are clearly not identical. If the owner of the last one, Gatrug, was indeed a monk, it would seem likely that there was a tradition of certain monks using a seal that identified their clerical status without giving any indication of their individual identity. Whatever the case, the practice would have been confined to only certain monastic communities. A document from 1921 bears the seals of two fully-ordained monks from Geling, and each is distinctive (MA/Geling/Tib/130). One is round, with a sun-and-moon motif atop a vertical axis (Fig. 107 a). The central design is indistinct, but is clearly surrounded by two four-lobed concentric rings. The other is square, with indistinct motifs in the centre surrounded by a square border (Fig. 107 b). The monks are named Palden Chöphel and Ngawang Rabsal. It is not clear which seal represents which monk.

Only one document (MA/Geling/Tib/164) bears a seal that, from the context, represents the community of nuns from Geling (Fig. 108). The seal closely resembles those described above that feature the syllable CHOS. In this case, however, the lettering appears to be either LOS or MOS, neither of which has any obvious meaning in the context.

In the traditional social hierarchy of Mustang, hereditary lamas are ranked below the aristocrats and above the commoners. Whereas many commoners did have seals, it appears that all, or almost all, members of the priestly class did. In some cases the seals belonged to individuals, and in others to the households that they shared. This is illustrated by one of the earliest documents from Tshognam, MA/UTshognam/Tib/43, which dates from 1837. The document is partly a will and partly a property a settlement between two brothers and their sister, who is to inhabit a dependency on the family estate. The two brothers, Lama Rigden and Lama Rangdrol, validate the

Figs 109 a–b. A seal applied successively to represent two brothers, Lama Rigden and Lama Rangdrol, found on the document from Upper Tshognam archived as MA/UTshognam/Tib/43. Photographs by Agnieszka Helman-Ważny.

Fig. 110. A seal used by Phurba Angmo, from the priestly family of Tshognam, found on the document from Upper Tshognam archived as MA/UTshognam/Tib/43. Photograph by Agnieszka Helman-Ważny.

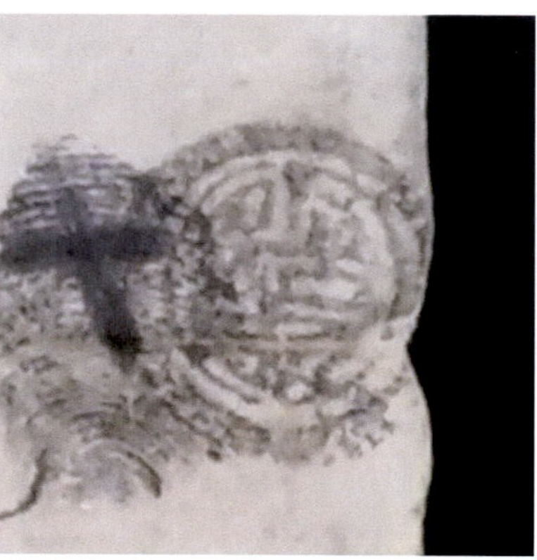

Fig. 111. The seal of Lama Tshewang Bumpa found on the document from Upper Tshognam archived as MA/UTshognam/Tib/5. Photograph by Agnieszka Helman-Ważny.

document using one seal that the younger brother, Rangdrol, applied immediately after Rigden, apparently without inking the surface of the matrix again. The seal is square, with an indistinct motif that may be a swastika (Figs 109 a–b). Their sister, Phurba Angmo, uses a round seal, but here, too, the motif is unclear because of smudging and due to the age of the document (Fig. 110).

The house that the two brothers inhabited was inherited by Rangdrol's son, Lama Tshewang Bumpa. The seal that the latter used on a document from 1876, round and containing a geometric motif, is different from that of his father and uncle (Fig. 111).

The same document also features a seal used by Lama Ösal Dorje, the natural son of Phurba Angmo. The seal is round and contains a five-lobed ring with an obscure central motif (Fig. 112). Unfortunately, the impression of his mother's seal on the 1837 document is not clear enough to allow us to determine whether the two are the same.

Ösal Dorje's son, Lama Tenpai Gyaltsen, also seems to have had his own seal, and did not use his father's. MA/UTshognam/Tib/42 is an undated excerpt from a religious work possibly (to judge from the handwriting) written by Tenpai Gyaltsen himself. The upper line of the seal contains the consonants P and Z, and the lower line the letter NG (Fig. 113). Also present are two other marks: a superscript curve that may stand for the letter E, and a concluding half-circle. If these are not alphabetical signs, the letters may stand for the name *[d]pa[l b]zang*.

Like noblemen, lamas were often called upon as respectable members of the community to act as witnesses to contracts and agreements. Document MA/LTshognam/Tib/2, presented above, is an agreement reached by a group of communities and witnessed by a lama by the name of Jamyang

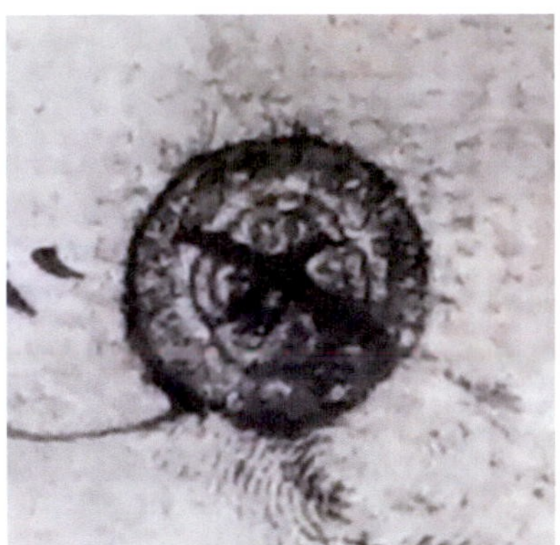

Fig. 112. The seal of Lama Ösal Dorje found on the document from Upper Tshognam archived as MA/UTshognam/Tib/5. Photograph by Agnieszka Helman-Ważny.

Fig. 113. A seal, probably belonging to Lama Tenpai Gyaltsen, found on the document from Upper Tshognam archived as MA/UTshognam/Tib/5. Photograph by Agnieszka Helman-Ważny.

Fig. 114. The seal of Lama Jamyang Wangdü, acting as witness to an agreement on the document from Lower Tshognam archived as MA/LTshognam/Tib/2. Photograph by Agnieszka Helman-Ważny.

Fig. 115. The seal of a commoner from Te named Tshering Trashi, found on the document from Lower Tshognam archived as MA/LTshognam/Tib/18. Photograph by Agnieszka Helman-Ważny.

Fig. 116. The seal of a commoner from Tshug, Phurba Dorje, a commoner, apparently with conch motif, found on the document from Upper Tshognam archived as MA/UTshognam/Tib/2. Photograph by Agnieszka Helman-Ważny.

Wangdü. His seal is square with a complex "positive" central motif that may be lettering, surrounded by two concentric squares (Fig. 114).

There are a few instances in which private individuals with the social rank of commoners, not priests or aristocrats, have used seals. An example of this is to be seen in MA/LTshognam/Tib/18, a document from 1910 in which a man from Te and another from Tshug agree to exchange fields for a period of ten years. The seal of the former, Tshering Trashi, contains three lines of script: PAD/ MA/ KHA' GRO, and therefore probably representing the words *padma mkha''gro*, a personal name (Fig. 115).

MA/UTshognam/Tib/2, a document from 1869, offers another example of a commoner with a seal. A mother and her two sons are selling a field, and all the parties concerned sign with a cross except one of the sons, Phurba Dorje, who applies a seal. Apart from an abstract spiral motif that may represent a conch, it is not clear if the seal also contains lettering. (Fig. 116)

The use of seals coexisted with, and later came to be superseded by, others forms of validation. Before embarking on a discussion of these other methods, we may illustrate this shift by comparing two documents from the same community, the priestly village of Lubrak.

Document SH/Lubrak/Tib/3946 (Fig. 117) is an internal agreement among the seventeen households of Lubrak, a community of hereditary Bonpo priests.

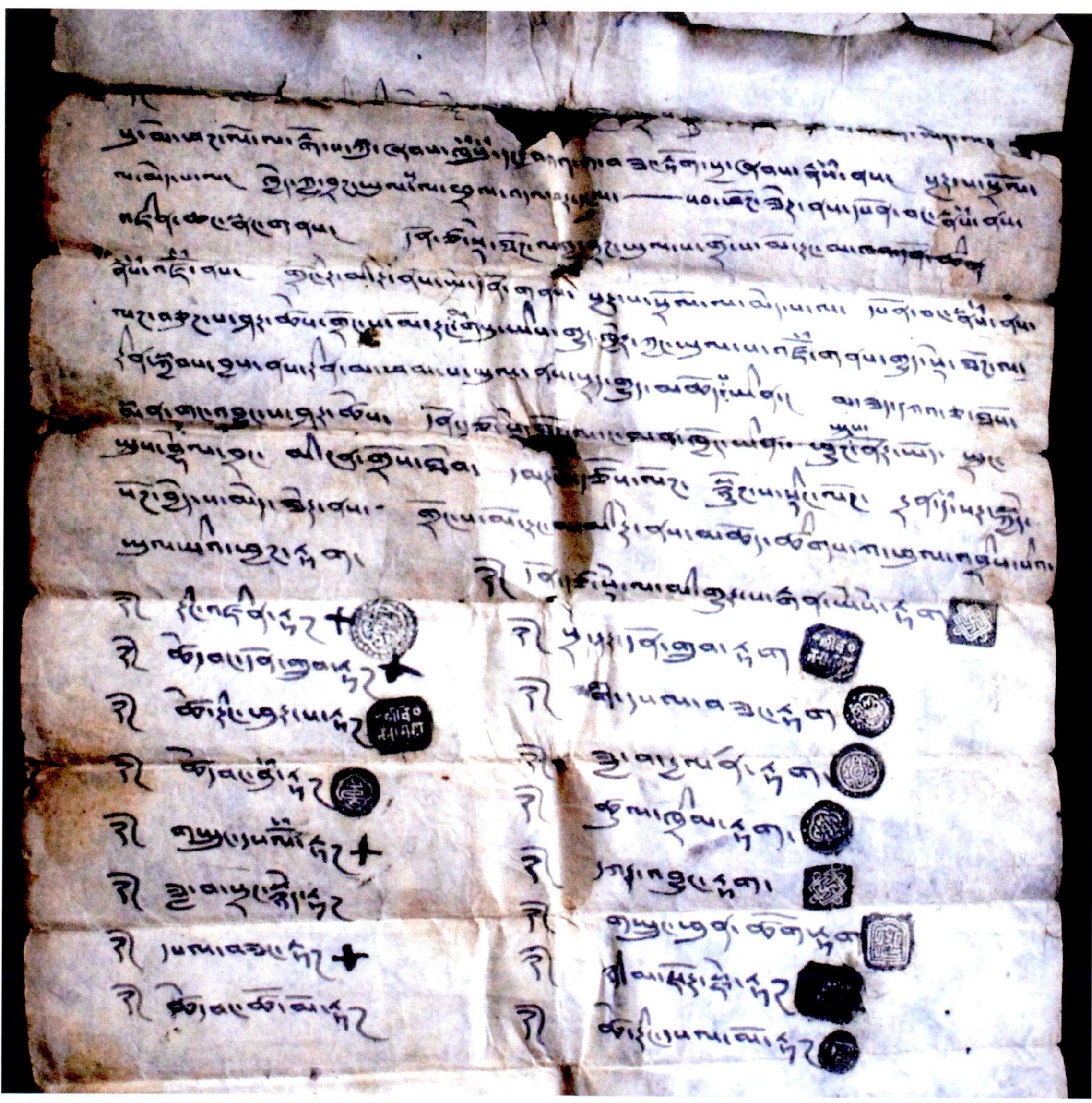

Fig. 117. SH/Lubrak/Tib/3946. Agreement among the 17 households, authenticated with seals and crosses. Photograph by Kemi Tsewang.

Until 1887, the community had been exempt from taxation, but in this year the *sku zhabs* (or the contractor whom he represented) withdrew the privilege and imposed on the priests an annual tax of 31 rupees. The village opposed the tax. This document registers the decision to refuse to pay the sum, and also to compensate, from the public coffers, any household that might be raided by the *sku zhabs*' bailiffs with a view to seizing property to the value of the tax owed. Each of the names is followed by a seal, signifying endorsement of the resolution by the representative of the corresponding household. A few features of this document – to which we shall return below – deserve further comment at this stage.

1. The sixth and eighth names in the left row are not endorsed. The numerous possible explanations for the omission include absence from the meeting and simple oversight when the document was being circulated for signature.
2. Four of the signatories have signed with crosses. The name in line 5 of the left column is that of a woman, but we cannot conclude from this that seals were reserved for men and crosses for women. The first two names in the left column belong to men, while the seventh (*dpal bzang*) could be either a man or a woman. The last signatory in the right column, a woman named Tshe ring dpal mo, has used a seal.
3. Why the first signatory should have both a cross and seal after his name must remain a matter of conjecture.
4. In a number of cases the same seal is used by more than one signatory. The significance of this will be addressed below.

It is instructive to compare Fig. 117, SH/Lubrak/Tib/3946, with the following document (Fig. 118, MA/Lubrak/Tib/29), from the same community, but drawn up almost seventy years later in 1956. All the same households are represented, but now they no longer mark their assent with crosses or seals. Almost all use thumbprints.

A history of digital prints

Digital prints – that is to say, thumb- and fingerprints – as well as handprints have long been used in many parts of the world to validate documents, on paper, clay or silk. As early as the thirteenth century, the Persian doctor Rashideddin observed that "no two individuals have fingers exactly alike."[20] Rashiddin was speaking about validation methods in China, but similar procedures were also used in Persia. What, if any, influence these traditions may have had on Tibetan usage is not yet known.

Digital and hand-prints were quite commonly used in Tibet. Although "finger seals" on contracts are known from as long ago as the Imperial Period (sixth to ninth centuries),[21] the best-known examples are related not to the validation of documents but to the blessing of religious texts and paintings.[22]

The expansion of the use of the thumbprints as signatures on legal documents in Mustang is likely to be related to the development of the practice in Nepalese legal usage. It is not known when the use of fingerprinting as a way of signing legal documents became generalised in Nepal, but there is a narrative concerning the origin of the practice that contains some intriguing clues. The background to the story is provided by Saul Mullard, who recounts the events that followed the assassination of the Sikkimese chancellor Bho lod rNam rgyal phun tshogs. After the chancellor had been killed around 1826 at the orders of the seventh Chos rgyal, a faction of Lepchas under a certain Yug Drathub rebelled against the government. In 1835, after the uprising had been put

[20] Cole 2001: 60–61.

[21] See Takeuchi 1995.

[22] Numerous examples of such manual benedictions may be found on the HAR (Himalayan Art Resources) website (http://www.himalayanart.org/ [accessed 10 July 2017]).

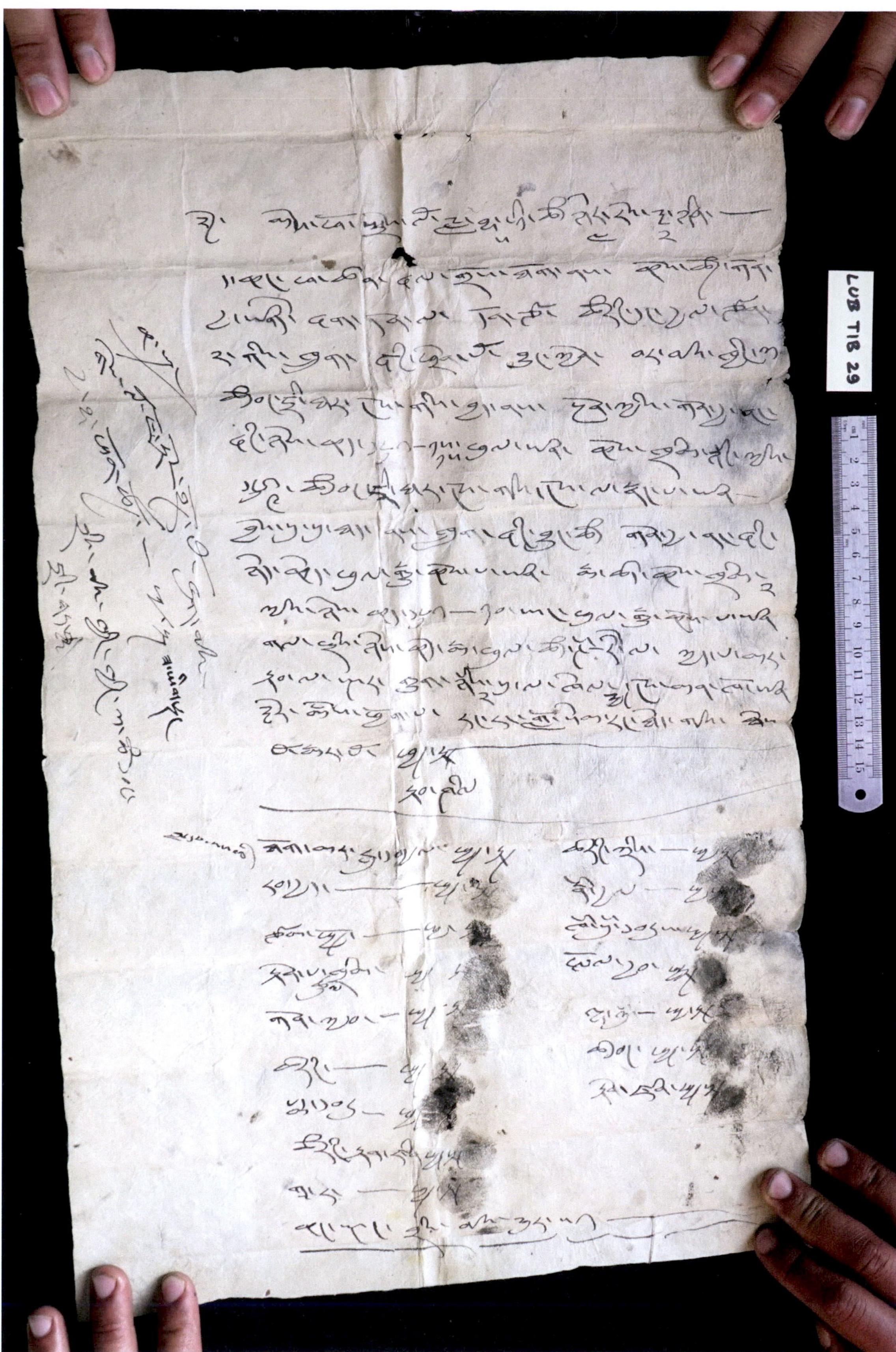

Fig. 118. MA/Lubrak/Tib/29. Agreement among the households from 1956, authenticated with digital prints. Photograph by Kemi Tsewang.

down, several hundred households of Lepchas sought refuge in Nepal.[23] They were given land on which to settle in eastern Nepal, and signed an agreement setting out the terms of their acceptance. According to a story that is recounted in Nepal about this episode,[24] they did so by marking crosses against their names, but were told by the Nepalese authorities that this form of signature – which was considered to be a Tibetan, and therefore alien, practice – was unacceptable, and that they should apply thumbprints instead. There are two Nepali expressions for thumbprint: one is *buḍhī-aũloko chāp*, literally "thumb stamp"; the other is *lepcā* or *lāpce chāp*, which is said to mean "Lepcha stamp". It is not at all clear why the fugitive Lepchas should have given their name to a procedure that was not only unfamiliar to them but supposedly an established procedure in Nepal. If the use of fingerprinting was, as the story implies, a tradition that was imported or reinforced by foreign influences – specifically from Sikkim – then the Lepcha story may have been associated with it in order to explain the unfamiliar term *lāpce*. We may consider the possibility that *lāpce* may be derived from a Tibetan term, such as *lag rjes* (pronounced *lakche*), meaning "hand print".

Colonial influences

Although the practice of validation of documents by digital prints seems to have received a significant boost from British India in the late nineteenth century, it should be noted that the technique was used before that time in parts of the Indian subcontinent. Saul Mullard has informed us of the existence of fingerprinted documents from Sikkim prior to this period. These include a tax agreement of 1789 from Morang (East Nepal), in a north Indian script, and several in both Nepali and Tibetan from the 1840s. However, it seems that the use of thumbprinting in Nepalese diplomatic practice during the Rana period (1846 to 1951) may have been inspired by contemporary developments in British India. The suggestion may find some support in the fact that documents of the Rana period made extensive use of British titles and even English-language seals.

The use of digital and hand-prints to identify suspects in legal and criminal cases was substantially pioneered in India. In the mid-nineteenth century, the police and judiciary faced persistent problems arising from the difficulty of identifying criminals. These problems took the form of wealthy individuals paying substitutes to serve their prison sentences, families continuing to claim the pensions of deceased relatives, and parties to agreements repudiating their signatures. A watershed moment occurred in 1858, when William (later Sir William) Herschel, an officer of the Indian Civil Service in Bengal, drew up a contract for 2000 maunds of road metalling with a certain Rajyadhar Konai, and asked the contractor to validate the document with his hand-print.

The practice of using fingerprints on documents was subsequently initiated in Calcutta in 1877, and was "in full use" by 1878.[25] None of the documents bearing thumbprints in the collections considered in this study predates 1878. In fact there is just one document prior to this time from all the collections examined in Baragaon and Geling that bears marks that might be fingerprints; but they are certainly not thumbprints, and it is equally possible that some makeshift seal may have been used. It may be the case that we are dealing with two different traditions: an older, "indigenous" form that entailed the application of a mark using a fingertip, and a later, British colonial practice of using the pad of the thumb. For the present, however, this suggestion must remain speculative.

Among the Nepali documents from Mustang published by the late Madhav Karmacharya, the earliest that can be reliably dated to feature a thumbprint is from 1911.[26] But it is in a later document, from 1924, that we find unequivocal evidence that the thumbprint is regarded not just as a substitute for a seal, but as an inalienable token of an individual's identity. The document is described as a public notice about the abolition of slavery, after the Prime Minister, Chandra Shamsher Jang Bahadur Rana, had officially declared an end to the practice on 13 April of that year. The process of emancipation entailed the validation of a designated form by various parties, notably the slave owner and the slave, and the procedure is prescribed as follows:

[23] Mullard 2015.

[24] Ramesh Dhungel, personal communication.

[25] Herschel 1916: 20, 22.

[26] Karmacharya 1996, 2001a, 2001b.

> If … the names and addresses of the owners and the names and age of the slaves who have or have been presented are found to be correct, the printed forms designed after the regulations shall be filled in, and the owners, land-agents and people in the neighbourhood shall be made to put their signatures on it [under their handwriting] and the slaves to do so with thumb-impressions of both hands put in a way to make conch and circle marks (*saṇkha-cakra*) come out distinct, and (on completion of which) the statutory price of the slaves shall be paid to the owners, and the slaves shall be declared liberated.[27]

The "conch and circle" motifs refer to the loops and whorls of the slave's thumbprints, and the stipulation that they should be clearly visible indicates that the prints were not merely symbolic, but a means of identifying the individual in question. As we shall see presently, the practice of validation by signature alone, which is enjoined on the slave owners, became a part of diplomatic practice in Tibetan documents of Mustang only much later.

While the principle of using thumbprints is that they are specific to the person who applied them, seals may be associated either with an individual or an institution, such as an office or an enterprise – or in the Mustang archives, a village community. Some of the seals to be found in the archives considered here are clearly personal. By contrast, we know that certain seals that were presented to particular Dalai Lamas, for example, were also used by some of their successors.[28]

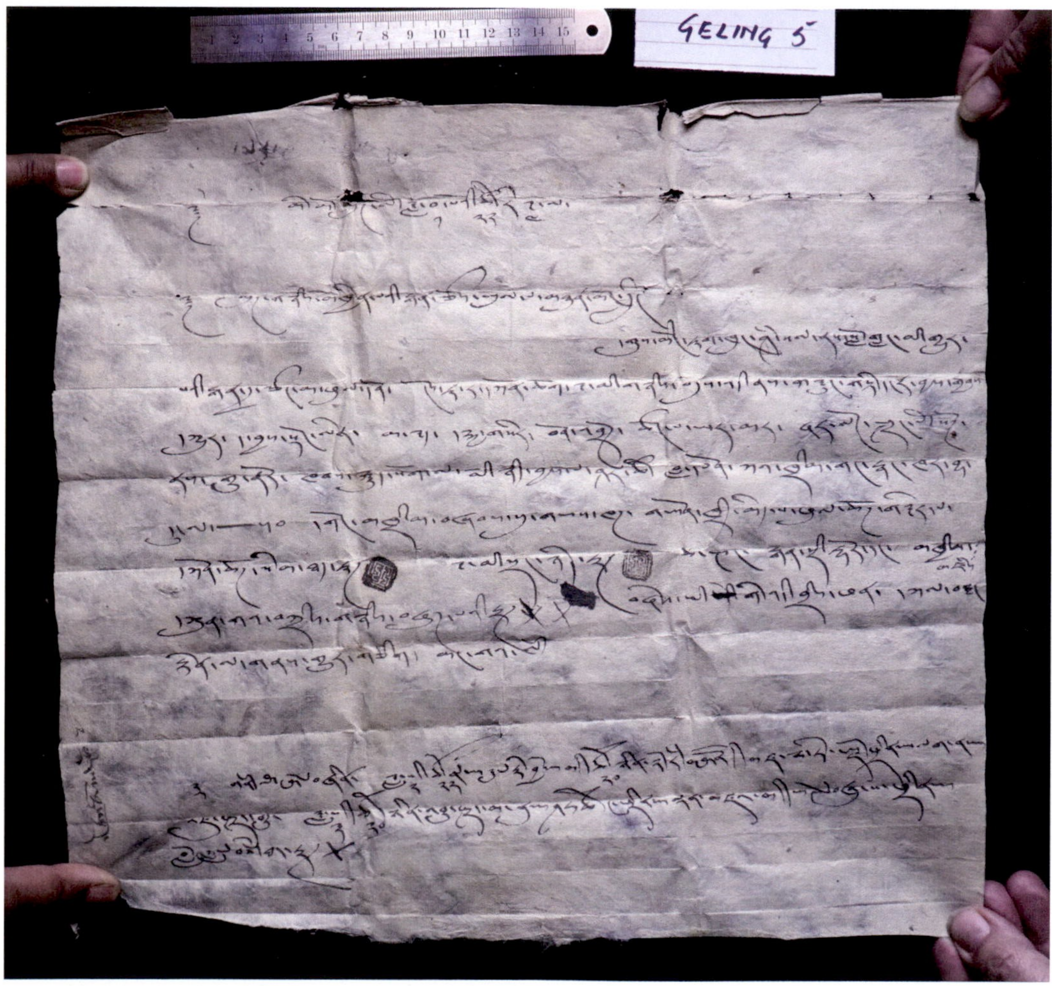

Fig. 119. MA/Geling/Tib/5. An undertaking by two thieves that they will never steal again. Photograph by Kemi Tsewang.

[27] Karmacharya 2001a: 59, lines 59–62. We are indebted to Axel Michaels for drawing our attention to this document.

[28] Schuh 1981.

In one of the documents from the Tshognam archive, dated 1898, we see the same seal appearing after the names of two different people. These two are a married couple, and the document is a contract for the sale of a field. It is clear, then, that the seal represents not the individuals but their household. In another case, MA/Geling/Tib/5 (Fig. 119), a couple who have been found guilty of stealing each promise that they will never steal again, and validate their undertaking with the same seal.

These examples explain why the same seal was used by different signatories in the document shown in SH/Lubrak/Tib/3946 (Fig. 117). Since the signatories are from different houses, the pairs cannot represent married couples. In fact, villages in Mustang share with other culturally Tibetan communities the feature that there are different categories of households. Each of the signatories in SH/Lubrak/Tib/3946 (Fig. 117) represents the domestic unit known as a "house" (*khang pa*). A higher-order category of household is the "estate" (*grong pa*). Some of the houses in the list are full *grong pa*, while others are the components of such estates that have split. The fact that seals are shared by the component houses of certain estates suggests, among other things, that the association of these seals with particular estates existed before these estates split into subsidiary houses.

Fingerprints are, in theory at least, inseparable from the individual, while seals may be either personal or institutional. Sometimes validation is indicated without any mark but by a statement to the effect that the document has been passed from hand to hand around the assembly; the declaration that it has been circulated among those present is taken as confirmation of endorsement. This is the case with MA/Geling/Tib/96 (Fig. 120), which contains the formula *lag skor gi rtags*, "a sign that this has been circulated [from] hand [to hand]", although there is in fact no sign.

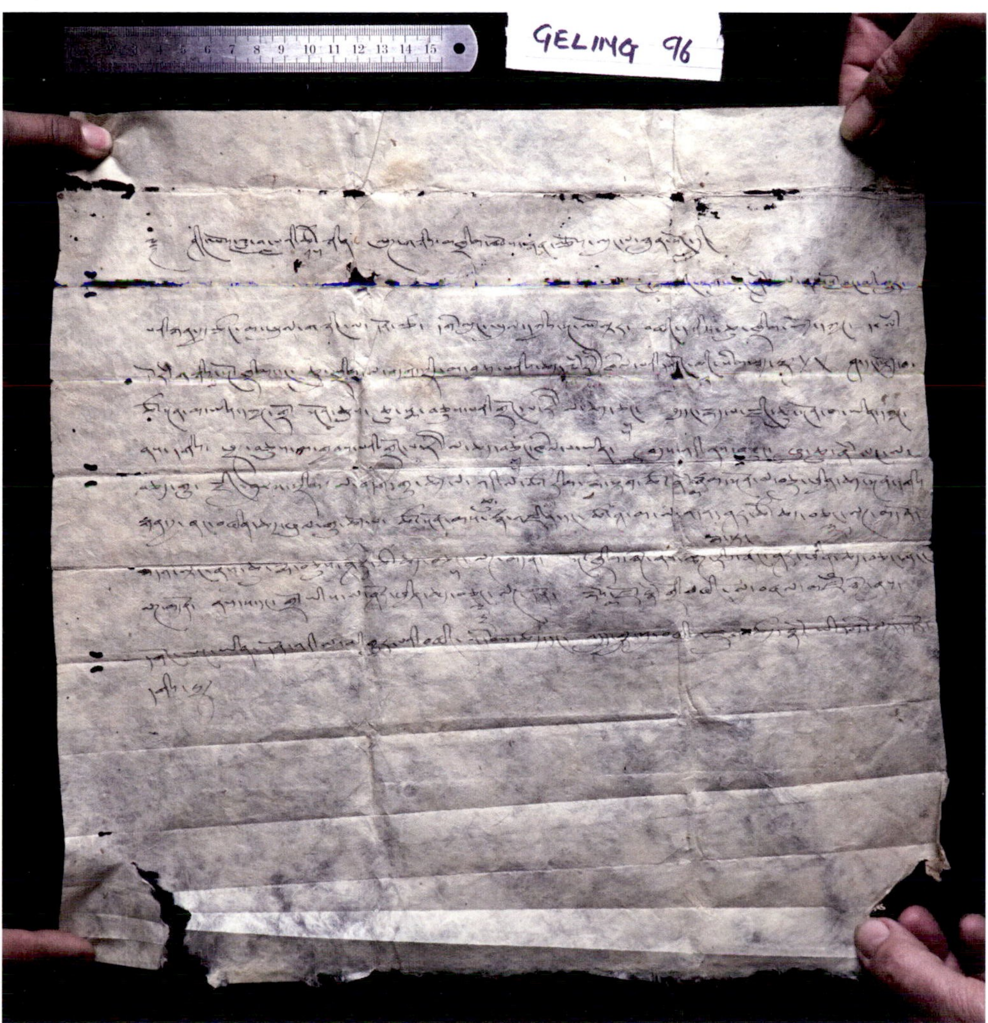

Fig. 120. MA/Geling/Tib/96. A document that has been validated by "being circulated from hand to hand" (*lag skor*). Photograph by Kemi Tsewang.

In other cases, a mark is made on the document after a formula to the effect that the item used to make the mark has been touched by all the members of the assembly before being applied. Thus MA/Geling/Tib/153 (Fig. 121) has three seal impressions, one of which is imposed after the statement *the se lag kor kis the rtags*, "the seal has been applied after being circulated from hand to hand."

Many documents reveal an interesting form of endorsement that combines two different modes of validation. MA/UTshognam/Tib/19 (Fig. 122) is a contract for the sale of a field in 1890. After the name of the vendor, "Uncle Namkha" (*a kyis nam mkha'*), is a smudged cross. The curved striations to the lower right are the epidermal ridges of a thumb. The sign has been produced by marking a cross on the thumb and then, while the ink is still wet, pressing it to the paper.

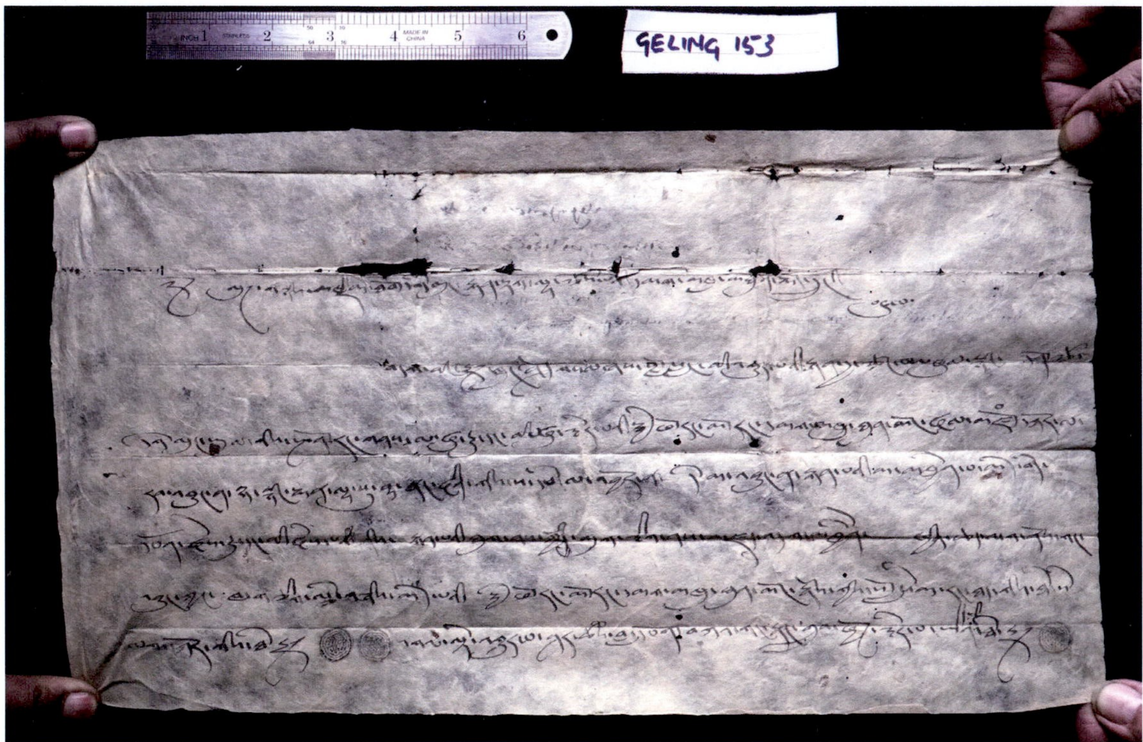

Fig. 121. MA/Geling/Tib/153. A document validated by means of a seal that has first been touched by all the participants. Photograph by Kemi Tsewang.

Fig. 122. MA/UTshognam/Tib/19. The validation has been made by drawing a cross on the signatory's thumb and applying it to the paper. Photograph by Kemi Tsewang.

In other cases we find that seal impression has been superimposed on a cross (or vice versa), as in the case of MA/Geling/Tib/57 (Fig. 123) and MA/Geling/Tib/80 (Fig. 124).

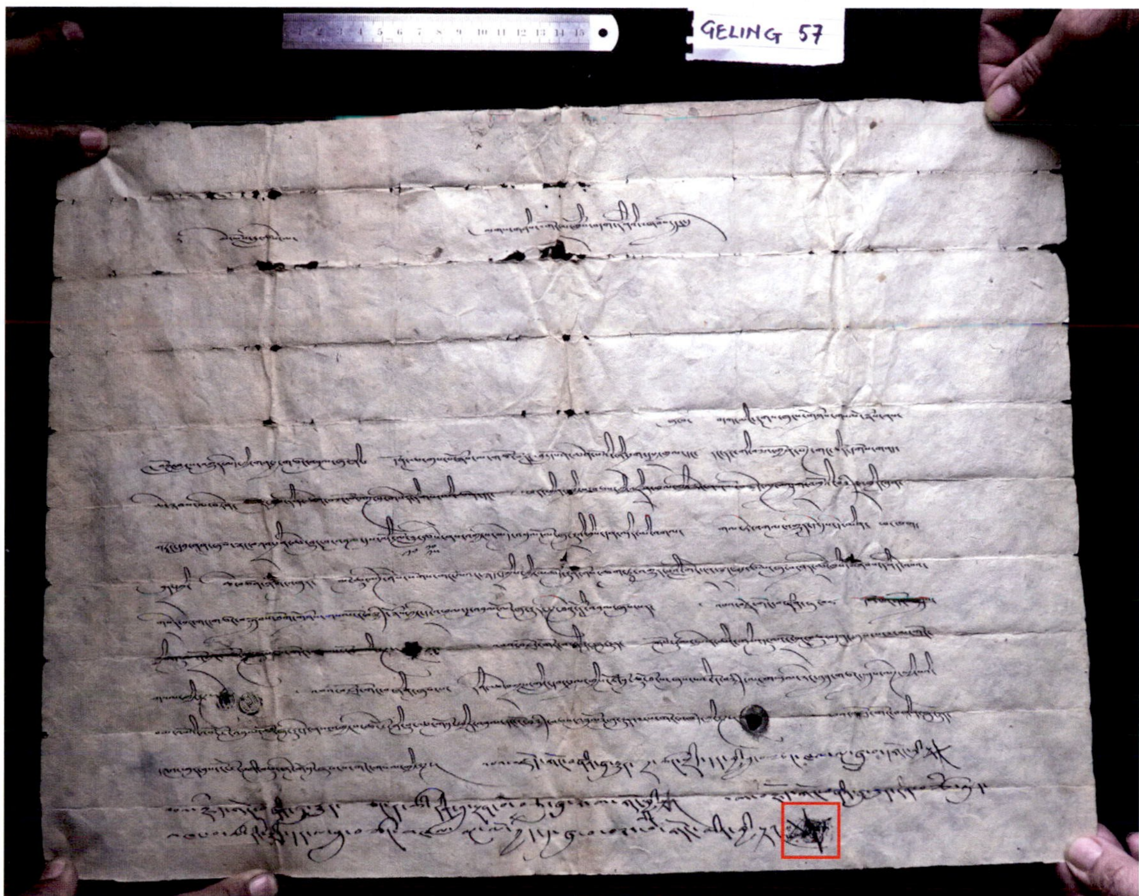

Fig. 123. MA/Geling/Tib/57, showing validation with superimposed seal and cross. Photograph by Agnieszka Helman-Ważny.

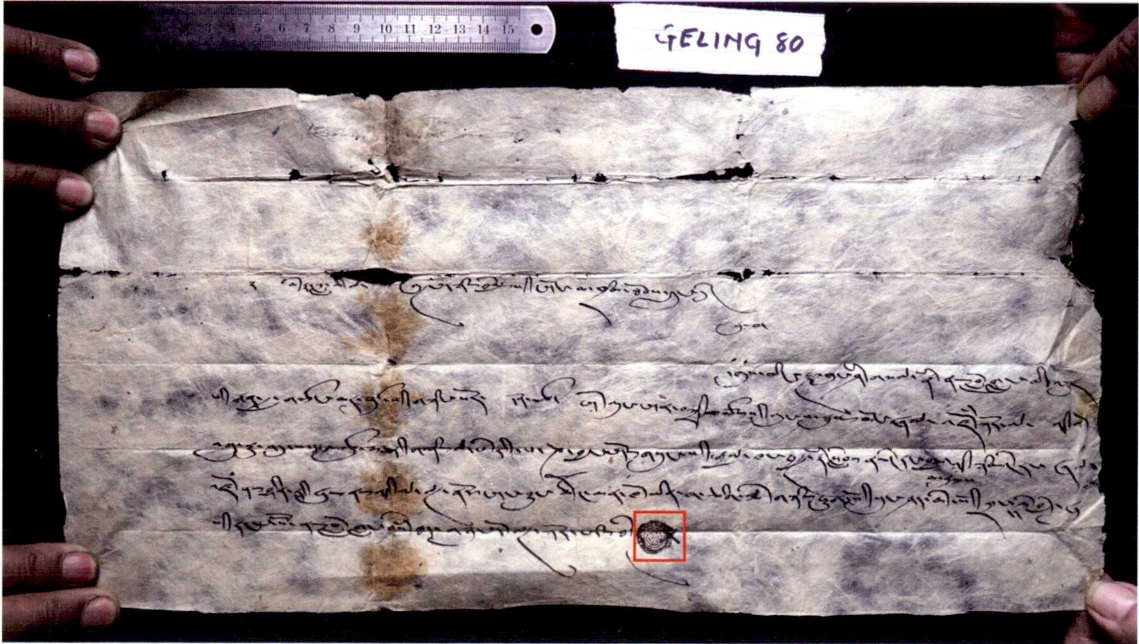

Fig. 124. MA/Geling/Tib/80, showing superimposed seal and cross. Photograph by Agnieszka Helman-Ważny.

If, as suggested above, the use of thumbprints in validating documents reflects the growing influence of Nepalese diplomatic conventions, this influence is even more apparent in the increasing incidence of Nepali terms over the course of time. Before developing this point further, a note of caution should be sounded. The degree to which Tibetan documents exhibit Nepalese features depends on a number of factors, notably the purpose of the document and the identity of the writer and intended readership. As we might expect, documents dealing with local religious affairs, such as the organisation of community rituals, are likely to retain their consistency with traditional Tibetan practice, while those that relate to national institutions have a more Nepalese character in terms of both vocabulary and formulation.

In one of the documents from Lubrak considered above (MA/Lubrak/Tib/29, Fig. 118), it was seen that the first of the signatories and one of the witnesses had marked their endorsements not with a seal, thumbprint or cross, but with the syllables *sas yig*. A clue to the meaning of this expression is given in the choice of script that the signatory has used – not the cursive *'khyug* of the rest of the text, but a more formal headless script. It is sometimes the case that a change of script signifies a formal statement in a language other than Tibetan. In MA/LTshognam/Tib/20 (Fig. 125, the final word), we see that the same word has been written in Devanāgari script: *sahi*. *Sahi* is in fact a Nepali term meaning "signature" (derived from the Arabic *ṣaḥīḥ*).

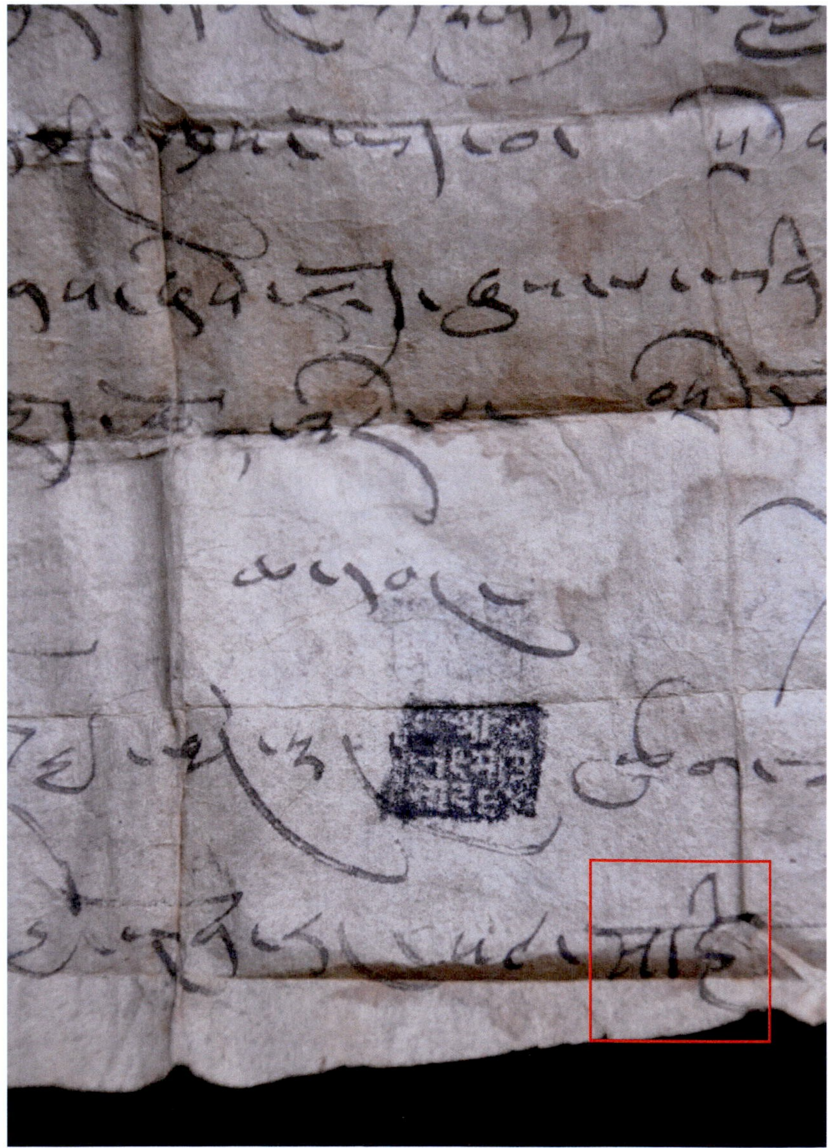

Fig. 125. MA/LTshognam/Tib/20 (detail). Document validated by means of the word *sahi* written in Devanāgarī script. Photograph by Agnieszka Helman-Ważny.

The word does appear in documents from the pre-Rana era, as in the following excerpt from MA/LTshognam/Tib/2 (Fig. 126), the second-earliest item (from 1832) in the Tshognam archives:[29]

'don cha'di la mi gyur zer nas | *bsas tshogs rnaṃ blaṃ (bla ma) la phul pa yin* | (lines 22–23)

Having stated that [this agreement] is not to be altered, it is confirmed (*bsas*, i.e. *sahi*), and offered to the lama of Tshognam.

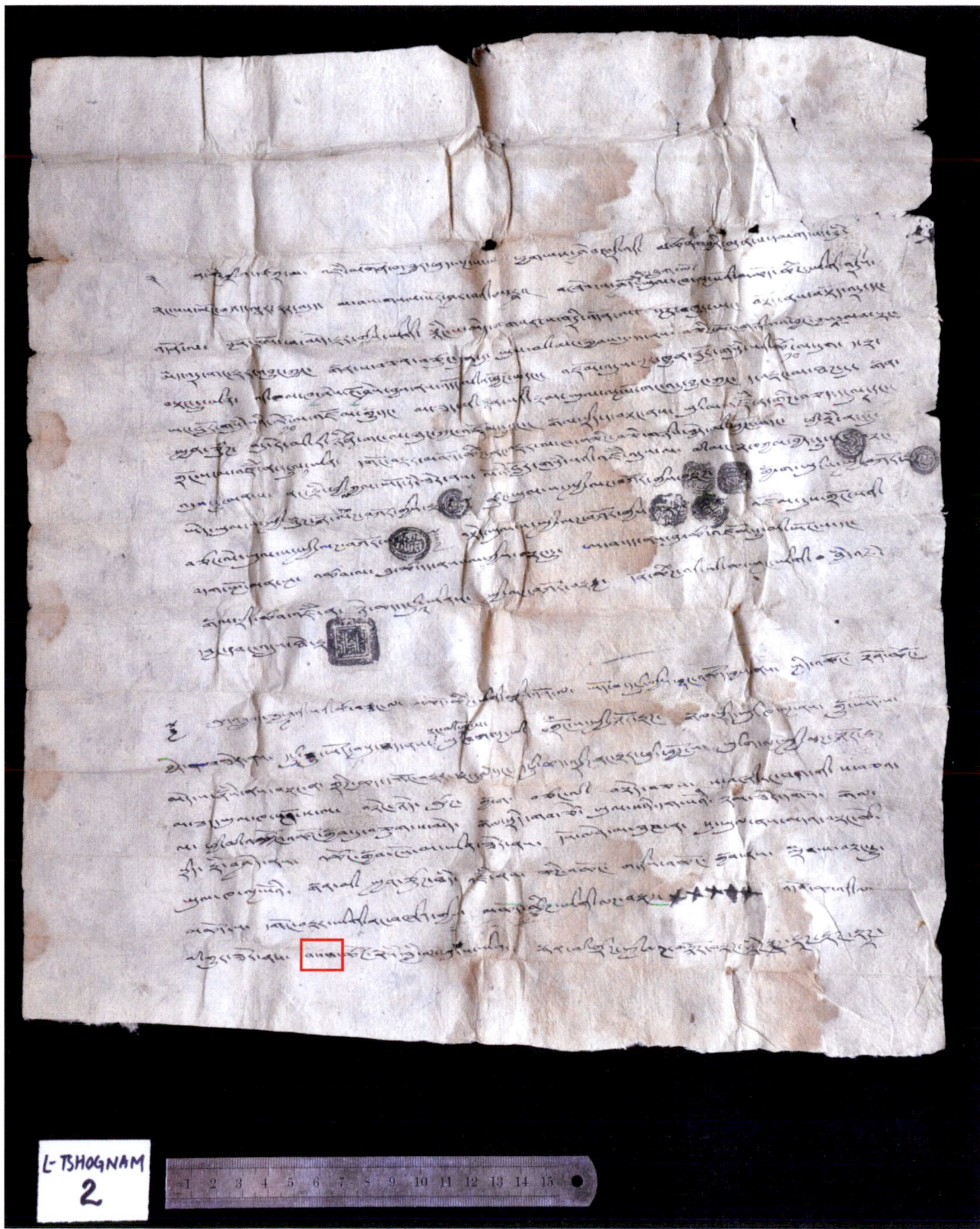

Fig. 126. MA/LTshognam/Tib/2 (detail). Document validated by means of the syllable *bsas*, representing the Nepali *sahi*, on the last line. Photograph by Agnieszka Helman-Ważny.

[29] The document is a copy, and we should not overlook the possibility that this last sentence was not present in the original.

However, it is only later that it comes to be used more systematically as a personal mark of validation to the extent of replacing a seal, a thumbprint or a cross. MA/Geling/Tib/67 (Fig. 127) is a particularly interesting example of three modes of validation: it bears one seal, several thumbprints, and at the end of the penultimate line, following the name of one of the signatories, *brtsis bdrung* (*recte*: *rtsis drung*, "the secretary") Ka mi, the expression *sa hī (sic)* in Devanāgarī.

Fig. 127. MA/Geling/Tib/67 (detail). Document exhibiting different modes of validation: a thumbprint in the second line and the word *sahī* in Devanāgarī in the third. Photograph by Agnieszka Helman-Ważny.

By 1993, we see a more advanced integration of Mustang into the national and global arena. In this document, MA/Lubrak/Tib/21 (Fig. 128), an agreement regarding the use of the community forest, there are only three thumbprints, all placed by elderly illiterate men (one of whom is the village blacksmith). The others are signatures in Devanāgarī and Tibetan, and now, to the lower right, Roman letters representing the name "Yungdrung".

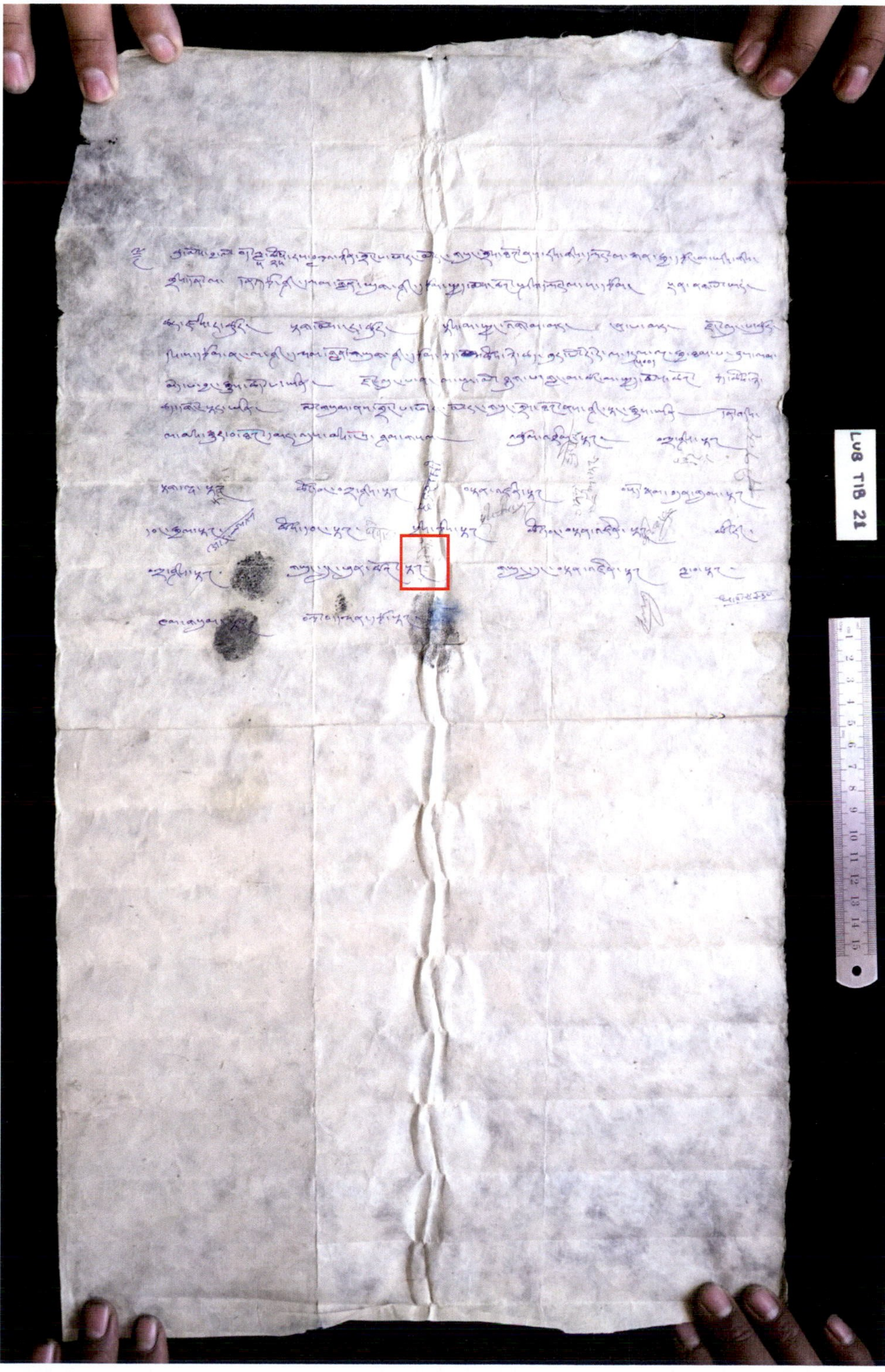

Fig. 128. MA/Lubrak/Tib/21. Document validated by means of a Tibetan rendering of the word *sahi* as *sa yig* (in red frame), as well as signatures in Tibetan, Devanāgarī and Roman scripts. Photograph by Kemi Tsewang.

A further illustration of the impending displacement of Tibetan by Nepali is provided by a comparison of the first (4b) and last (4p) pages of a booklet from Dzar, MA/Dzar/Tib/4 (Figs 129 a–b). The document is a record of financial transactions by the community over a number of years. There is no date for the earliest entries, but from the names of recognisable individuals in the last pages it is likely that this part was written in the mid- to late 1990s. While the basic text is in Tibetan, many of the additions and annotations are in Devanāgarī script, and both are written in blue and black ballpoint pen.

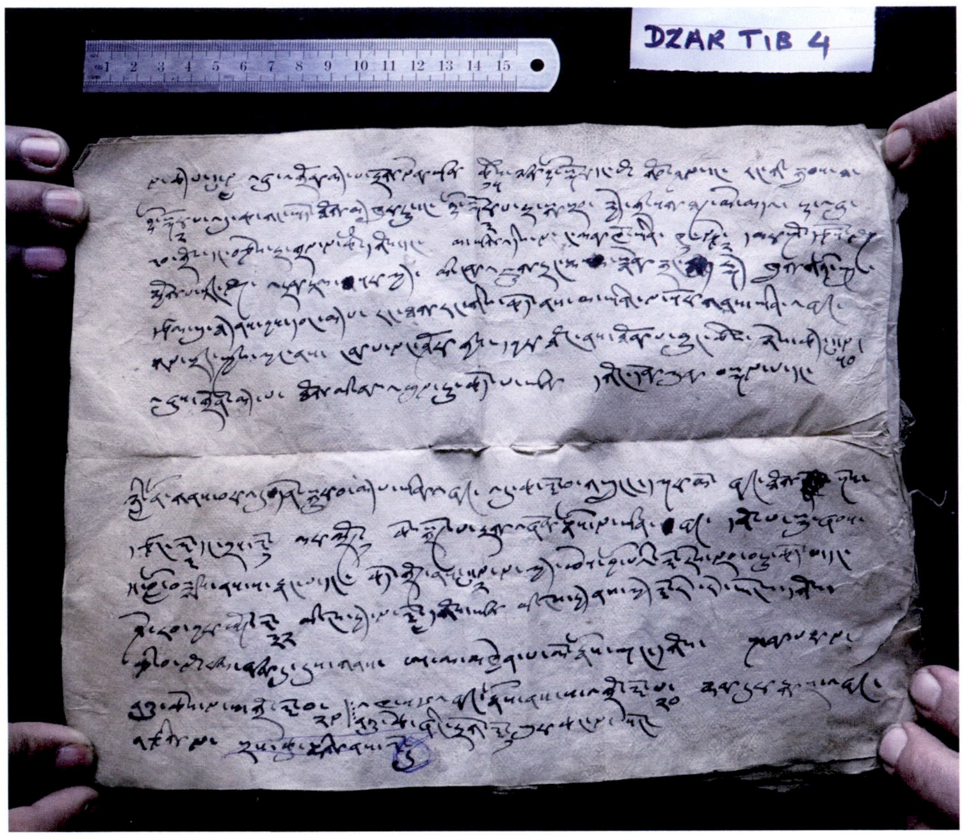

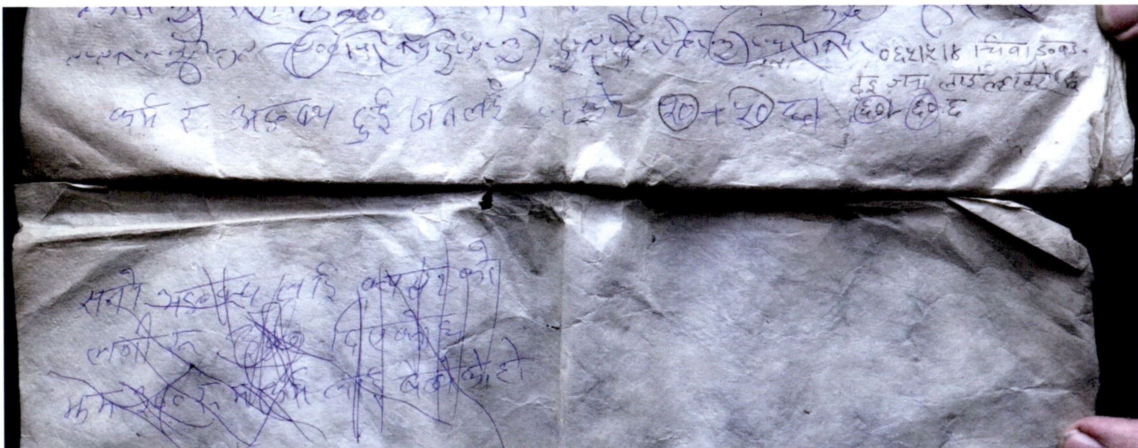

Figs 129 a–b. MA/Dzar/Tib/4b and 4q, illustrating the increasing use of Nepali at the expense of Tibetan over time. Photograph by Kemi Tsewang.

Numerals in "hybrid" Nepali/Tibetan documents

Tibetan has its own system of numbers, but even in documents in which the text itself is Tibetan, Nepali digits are sometimes used. This is the case with two documents that we may take as examples: MA/Lubrak/Tib/62 and MA/Lubrak/Tib/4 (Fig. 130).

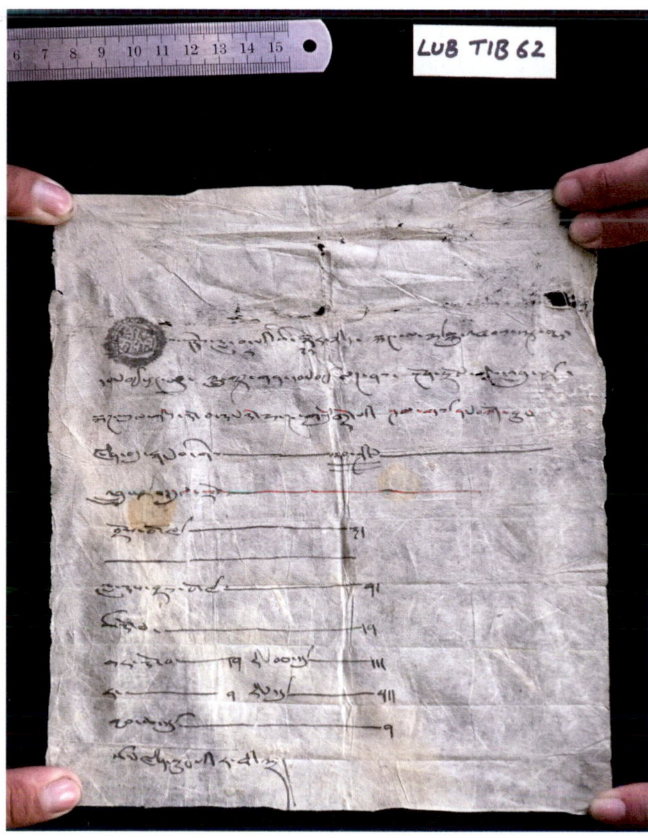

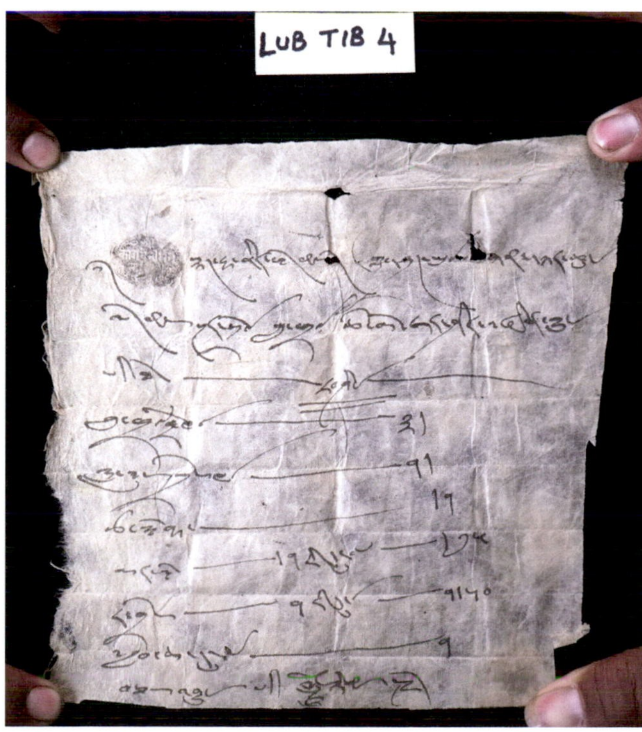

Figs 130 a–b. MA/Lubrak/Tib/62 and MA/Lubrak/Tib/4, showing different conventions for expressing quantities. Photographs by Kemi Tsewang.

From the mid-1880s onwards two previously unseen categories of taxes make their appearance in the archives of Lubrak. One of these was the "Great Government Tax" (*gzhung khral chen mo*), which has been mentioned above. The other is the "Great Grain Tax" (*'bru khral chen mo*). Document MA/Lubrak/Tib/62 (Fig. 130 a) is a receipt from 1906 for the payment of this tax to the authorities in Kag in the form of grain, salt and cash (1 *zo ba* is equal to roughly 1.53 litres, and 20 *zo ba* equal 1 *'bo khal*). Following each item in the list, *stab shil* (Nep. *tapsil*), is a number in Nepali numerals. In addition to the number 1 there is the frequent appearance of a simple vertical line that does not correspond to any numeral, and its location in relation to the numbers themselves varies. In the following translation of lines 6 to 13 of the document, the line is represented by a vertical stroke:

6. *dngul rdoṃ* –
7. *'bro bho khal* – 3
8. *zla zas dngul rdoṃ* – 3 |
9. *bras bho khal* – 1
10. *tsha zo pa* – | 1
11. *gyab cha dngul* – 1
12. *ra* – 1 – *rin dngul* 1 | |
13. *mar zo pa* – 1 – *rin dngul* – | | |

6. Cash total –
7. *'Bo khal* of wheat – 3
8. Total rupees for Dasain [ceremony] – 3 |
9. *'Bo khal* of rice – 1
10. *Zo ba* of salt – | 1
11. Rupees for *gyab cha* – 1
12. Rupees as cost of one goat – 1 | |
13. Rupees as cost of 1 *zo ba* of butter – | | |

The line is clearly not a number, nor can it be understood simply as a *ḍaṇḍa* punctuation mark, since there are two of them after the digit in line 12, and three without any digit at all in line 13. The tax receipt for 1904 has a similarly enigmatic presentation, but for 1905 we are fortunate to have a scribe who adopted a different convention for representing the same quantitites. In this document, MA/Lubrak/Tib/4 (Fig. 130 b) we see:

4. *gru khral bre khal* – 3 |
5. *zla zes bres khal* – 1 |
6. *tsha zo bha* – | 1
7. *mar zo* – | 1 *ring dngul* – | 75
8. *ra bre* – 1 *ring dngul* – 1 | 50
9. *'rgyab cha dngul* – 1

4. [*Bo*] *khal* of wheat as the grain tax – 3 |
5. [*Bo*] *khal* of rice for the Dasain festival – 1 |
6. *Zo ba* of salt – | 1

7. Rupees cost of | 1 *zo ba* of butter – | 75
8. Rupee cost of 1 yearling goat – 1 | 50
9. Rupees for *rgyab cha* – 1

From this document it is clear that the stroke has a dual function. On the one hand it operates as the separator between different units of the same currency, as we see in line 8, where it marks the divide between the rupee to the left and the paise to the right. For volumetric measures, it likewise separates the larger unit – the *'bo khal* – from the *zo ba*. When there are no *zo ba* (as in lines 4 and 5) there is nothing after the stroke, and when there are no *'bo khal*, but only *zo ba*, the figure is written after the stroke with nothing preceding it. Lines 7 and 8 of MA/Lubrak/Tib/4 (Fig. 130 b) give us the answer to the other function of the stroke that we find in the corresponding locations in MA/Lubrak/Tib/62, that is, lines 12 and 13. In MA/Lubrak/Tib/62 the cash equivalent of the butter is represented as "| | |" and that of the goat as "1 | |"; in MA/Lubrak/Tib/4 these quantities are given respectively as "| 75" and "1 | 50". From this we can conclude that, in MA/Lubrak/Tib/62 the stroke denotes a quarter of a rupee.

The decline of the "South Mustang" diplomatic form

The replacement of Tibetan by Nepali as the written medium of secular communication and administration has been rapid and complete. This apparent suddenness conceals the fact that the shift was actually the culmination of a process of transition that had been taking place over the course of more than a century. Educated Tibetans who are familiar with the diplomatic conventions of the Ganden Phodrang government of the Dalai Lamas react with bafflement when confronted with documents from South Mustang. The confusing features include the arbitrariness of the spelling and the presence of terms in the local Tibetan dialect and the Tibeto-Burman Seke language, neither of which have standard written forms. These traits have been perennial features of local documents since the earliest times, and make up what we might think of as the diplomatic sociolect of Baragaon. While our educated Tibetan reader might be bewildered by these varieties, he or she would be completely confused by the unrecognisable words that occupied positions of prominence in the later documents: terms for the issuing office or the intended recipient, for the category of document, the legal status of the protagonists, and even the word for "law". It would also seem very strange to the reader that the documents were validated with thumbprints. Unlike some of the perpetuity clauses and dialect words, these features were not local, but rather symptomatic of the infusion of the conventions of the national Nepalese administration and judiciary into the local legal lexicon. The result was a truly hybrid Tibetan-Nepalese diplomatic practice whose main exponents were local lamas, aristocrats and their scribes. With the coming of age of a generation educated in Nepali in local government schools, the tradition was rapidly displaced. Not only is there no one in Baragaon who can write these documents, there is possibly no one now who can even read them.

Paper

Technically, paper is a material formed of a webbed and random network of fibres made out of the water suspension on a bamboo, textile or wire screen into a felted sheet, usually of cellulose fibres. The physical features of a final product are determined in the production process. The fibres of the paper typically have a very wide range of morphological properties, which can be detected during scientific examination depending upon the type of raw materials used and where those materials came from.

In the case of paper type, besides creating a general typology according to raw materials, it was impossible to observe any clear patterns until we arranged the documents within smaller groups organized by codicological features. After this grouping, it became obvious that this method was the only way to permit an understanding of the results of paper identification and typology. Without grouping these artefacts by textual and historical context, and finding all possible connections in between these documents, general typology informs us to a certain extent about the nature of paper produced and used in Mustang, but does not allow us to see the complexity of this research.

The paper typology was based on the combination of both the sieve print type and the raw materials used. From a technological point of view, the woven sieve print is recorded in almost all documents, suggesting that during the nineteenth and twentieth centuries the same technique was used locally in the Mustang area and also in other places from which this paper could have been brought. This technology involves a floating papermaking mould with a textile sieve attached to a wooden frame – the method that is still used in Western Nepal and Tibet. However, it is usually impossible to observe any pattern since fine cotton thread was traditionally used for such sieve, a material that does not usually leave any significant pattern in the paper structure, as do for example laid and chain lines left by a bamboo movable sieve. However, in our sample from Mustang a significant number of papers have the clear pattern of a textile woven from coarse threads as seen in figure 131.

When there are many woody fibre-bundles and outer bark particles in the pulp, as witnessed in document MA/Geling/Tib/29 (Fig. 132) from the Geling archive, these appear in the paper structure as thickenings or impurities, rendering the spread of the fibres uneven. In the paper structure these impurities give the impression of lower quality paper and may make it more difficult to write on such paper. This tends to be a result of the raw material having been insufficiently cooked and pulped. On the other hand, this is often the case with Himalayan paper due to the simple, natural methods used even today. Traditionally only ash was used for cooking and it was not as effective as caustic soda, which tends to be used today. This was confirmed by all our interviewees.

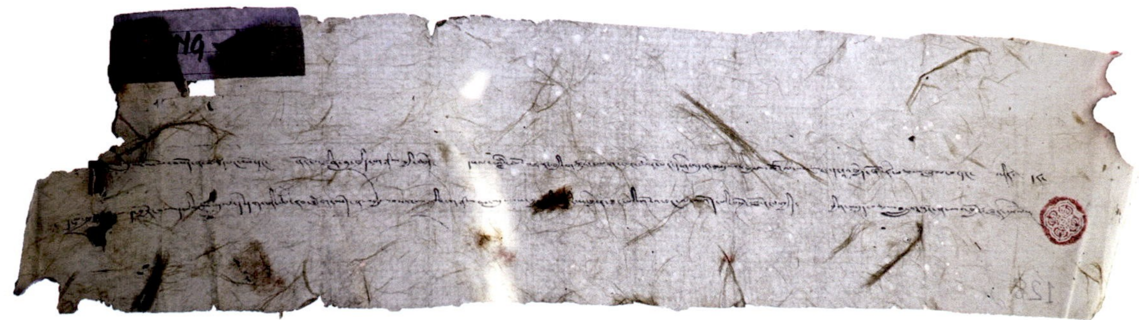

Fig. 131. Document MA/Geling/Tib/128 from the Geling archive, with the pattern of a textile woven from coarse threads. Photograph by Kemi Tsewang.

Fig. 132. Document MA/Geling/Tib/29 from the Geling archive, showing woody fibre-bundles which were not thoroughly pulped. Photograph by Kemi Tsewang.

Fig. 133. Document MA/Geling/Tib/13 from the Geling archive showing flaws appearing as light dots in the paper structure due to water being accidentally sprinkled on the surface of the paper while it was still on the sieve; the water had not yet drained away and the fibres were yet not fixed. Photograph by Kemi Tsewang.

These woody fibre-bundles, however, are so often observable that they have become the most distinguishable feature of Nepalese and Tibetan paper. Since the majority of paper in our sample displays this feature, we may conclude that even in nineteenth and twentieth centuries paper was produced according to traditional technology.

There are also purely accidental marks that are not produced by tools or any specific technologies. As seen on document MA/Geling/Tib/13 (Fig. 133) from the Geling archive, specific flaws (light dots in the paper structure) came from water being accidentally sprinkled on the surface of the paper while it was still wet on the sieve, and while the fibres were not tightly fixed together. Such marks allow for no other interpretation than that they bear witness to errors on the part of the papermaker.

With the exception of one document from Geling, all documents were written on a single layer of paper. The distribution of fibres shows some variety, mostly related to the preparation of the papermaking pulp, which produces a range of qualities. It is different from Tibetan manuscripts which were usually made of layers of paper glued together. It is clear that the form of the documents and their purpose required lighter writing support which was easy to fold and carry, as documents often were.

The raw material in our sample is mostly homogenous. The majority of documents are composed of *Daphne* and *Stellera* fibres alone or mixed with each other or with a small addition of other fibres. However, there are few exceptions of samples in the Lubrak archive composed of wood pulp and grasses, which clearly shows that those documents are more recent. There were the main types of documents written on paper made from: 1) pure *Daphne* sp. fibres; 2) pure *Stellera* sp. fibres; 3) *Daphne* sp. mixed with *Stellera* sp. fibres; 4) paper based on previous compositions with an addition of cotton or hemp recycled fibres; 5) wood pulp; and 6) documents on paper made with a variety of grasses.

Below is a list of all identified components plus microscopic description of those components illustrated with microscopic images:

Daphne

Although *Daphne* fibre is not described in either Marja-Sisko Ilvessalo-Pfäffli's book[30] or Juhua Wang's[31] – the main fibre atlases used for fibre analysies references – the descriptions of *Wikstroemia* and *Edgeworthia* fibres can offer help, since the morphologies of these two species are quite similar to that of *Daphne*. The descriptions of *Daphne* fibres illustrated with microscopic photographs can be found for example in Jasper Trier's *Ancient Paper of Nepal*[32] and Helman-Ważny's *The Archaeology of Tibetan Books*.[33]

An online database of Asian paper and fibres known as Khartasia (http://khartasia-crcc.mnhn.fr/en) can also offer some help, but there are few descriptions about *Daphne* fibre. Thus, we should note that the majority of fibre images consulted for reference during the fibre identification were samples from the collection of Agnieszka Helman-Ważny (pulp from identified plants, processed according to traditional papermaking procedure).[34]

Features of *Daphne* fibres

Anatomical peculiarities

The lumen of *Daphne* fibres varied in width and the fibre walls, however irregular, were usually thick, which was suggested by the rigid bending (Fig. 134). The most characteristic feature of the fibre was its broad central portion and this was shared by all papermaking plants from the

Fig. 134. Bending *Daphne* fibre from MA/Geling/Tib/15 in 200× magnification observed in polarised light. Photograph by Mengling Cai.

[30] Ilvessalo-Pfäffli, 1995: 350–51.

[31] Wang, 1999: 181–83.

[32] Trier 1972.

[33] Helman-Ważny 2014: 23–26.

[34] Microscopic fibre analyses were conducted in the CSMC Laboratories of the University of Hamburg by Agnieszka Helman-Ważny and her student Mengling Cai.

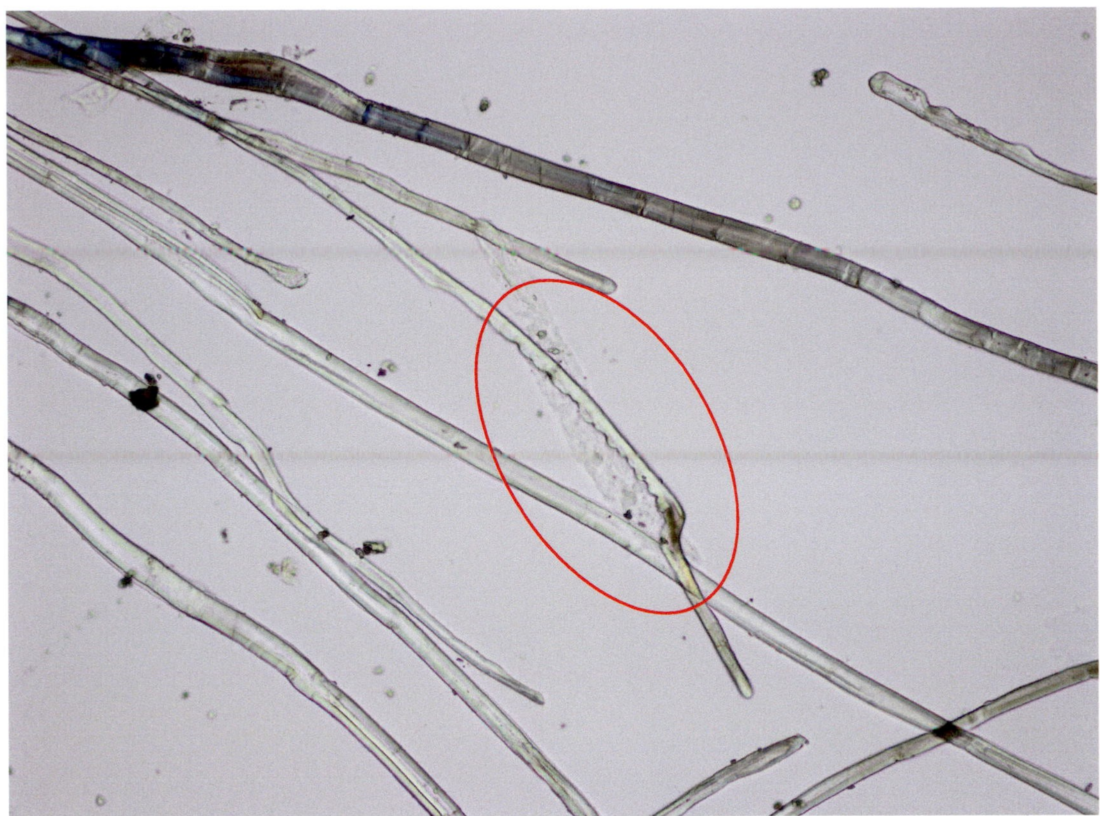

Fig. 135. *Daphne* fibre with scalloped wall and fibre ends from MA/Lubrak/Tib/Tib 62 in 200× magnification observed in polarised light. Photograph by Mengling Cai.

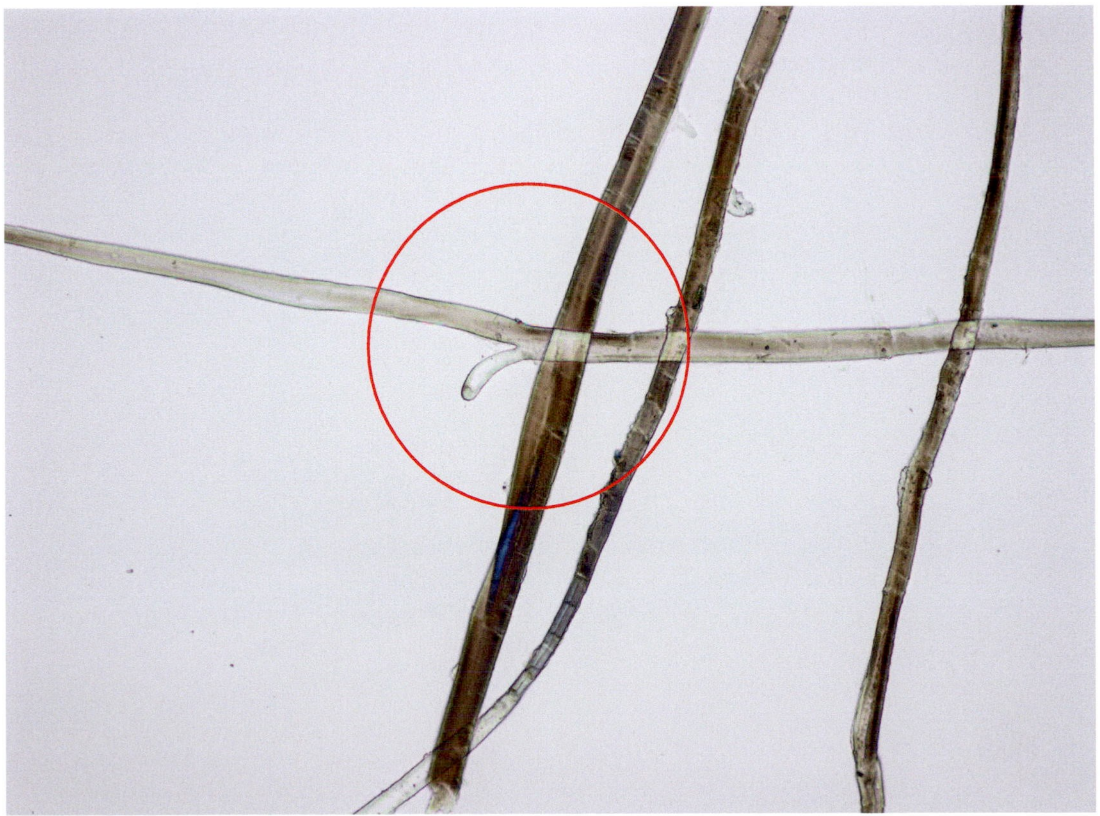

Fig. 136. Forked *Daphne* fibre wall from MA/Geling/Tib/46 in 200× magnification observed in polarised light. Photograph by Mengling Cai.

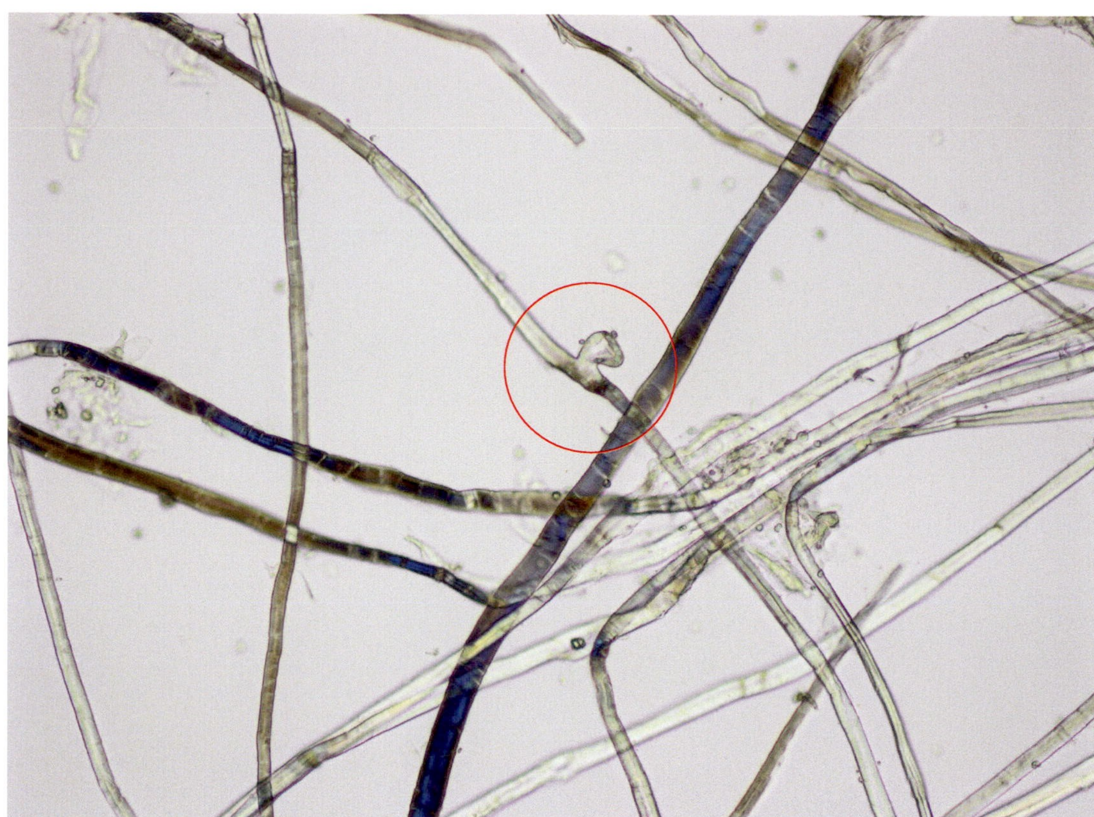

Fig. 137. Irregularity in the middle of *Daphne* fibre from MA/Geling/Tib/34 in 200× magnification observed in polarised light. Photograph by Mengling Cai.

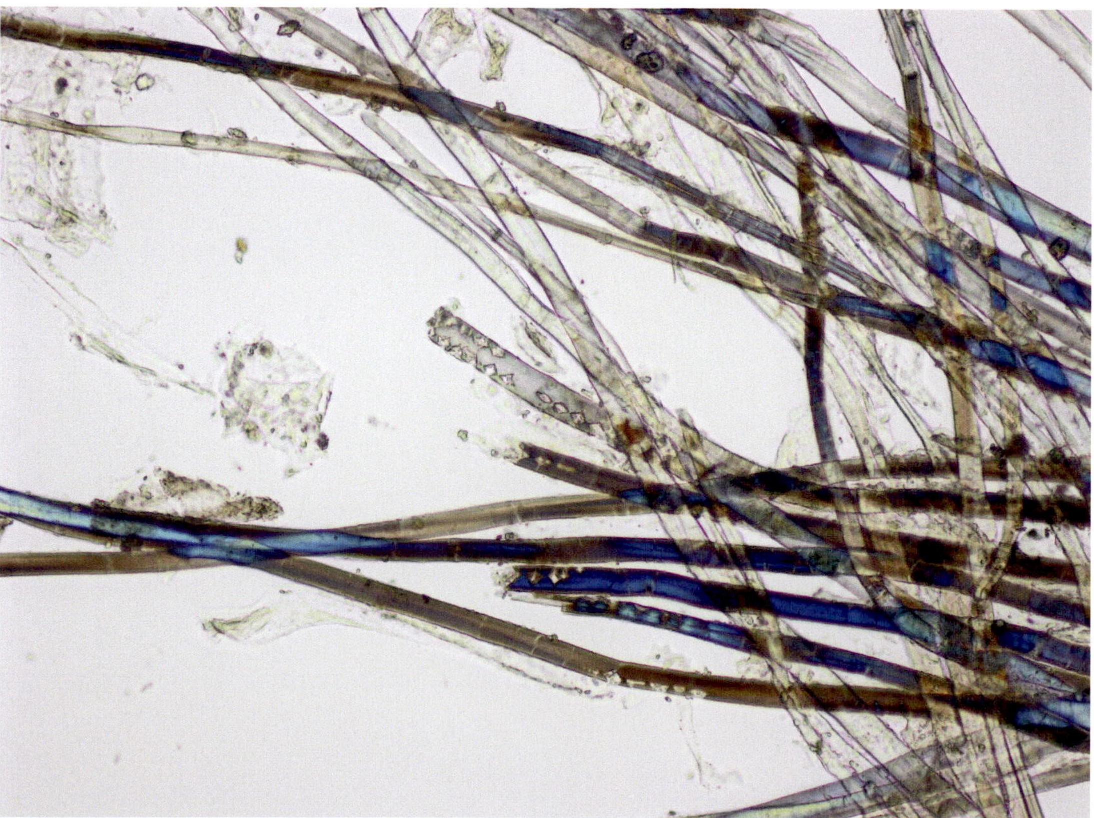

Fig. 138. Some small, irregular-shaped holes in *Daphne* fibres from MA/Lubrak/Tib/82 in 200× magnification observed in polarised light. Photograph by Mengling Cai.

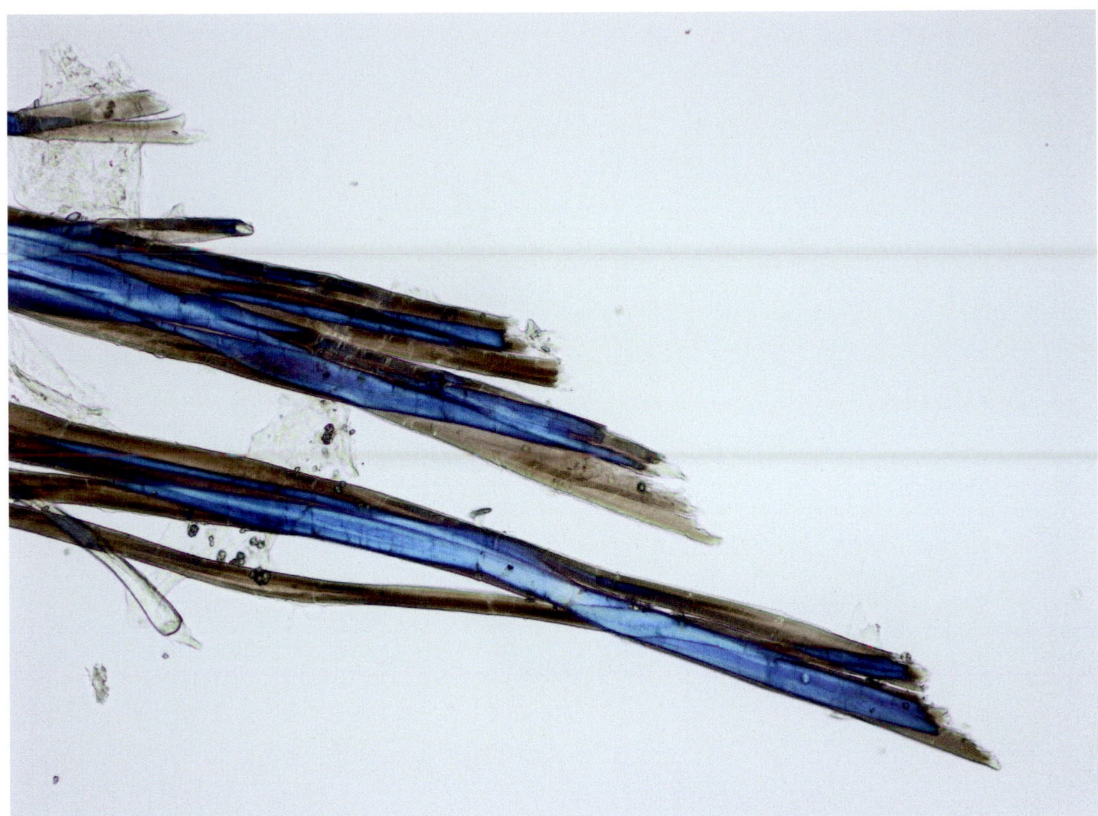

Fig. 139. Cut or broken fibres from MA/Geling/Tib/41 in 200× magnification observed in polarised light. Photograph by Mengling Cai.

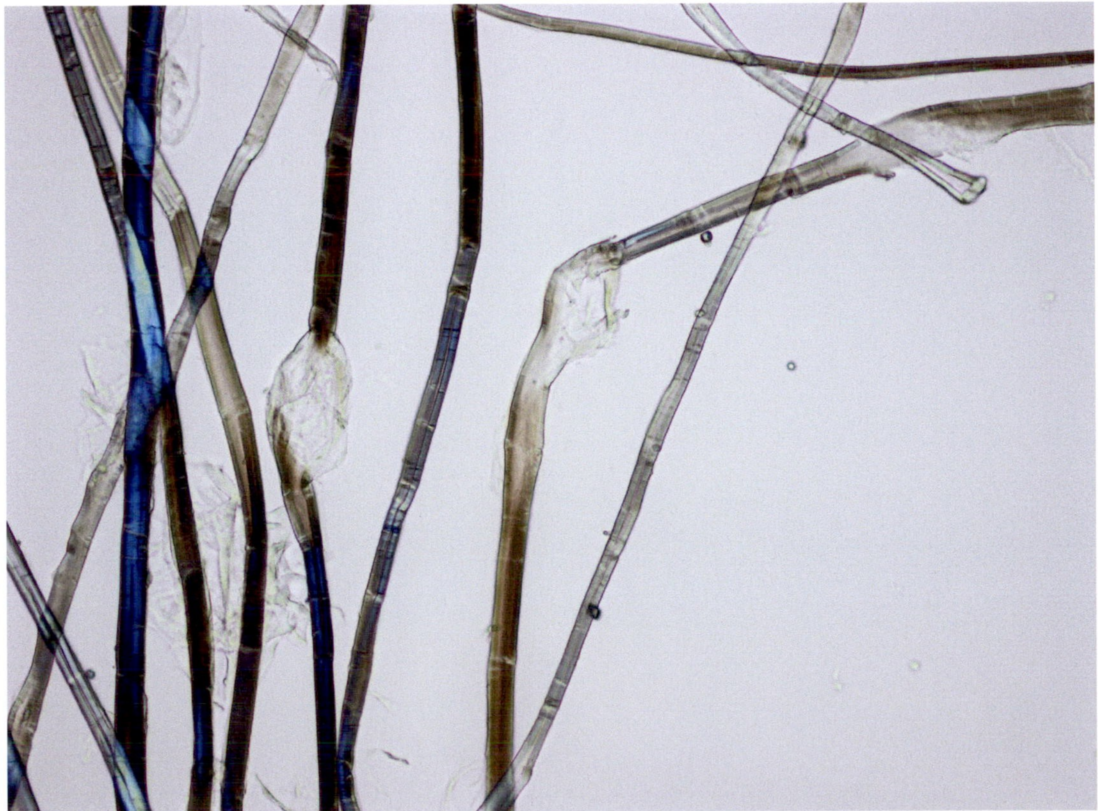

Fig. 140. Swelling and broken fibres from MA/Geling/Tib/29 in 200× magnification observed in polarised light. Photograph by Agnieszka Helman-Ważny.

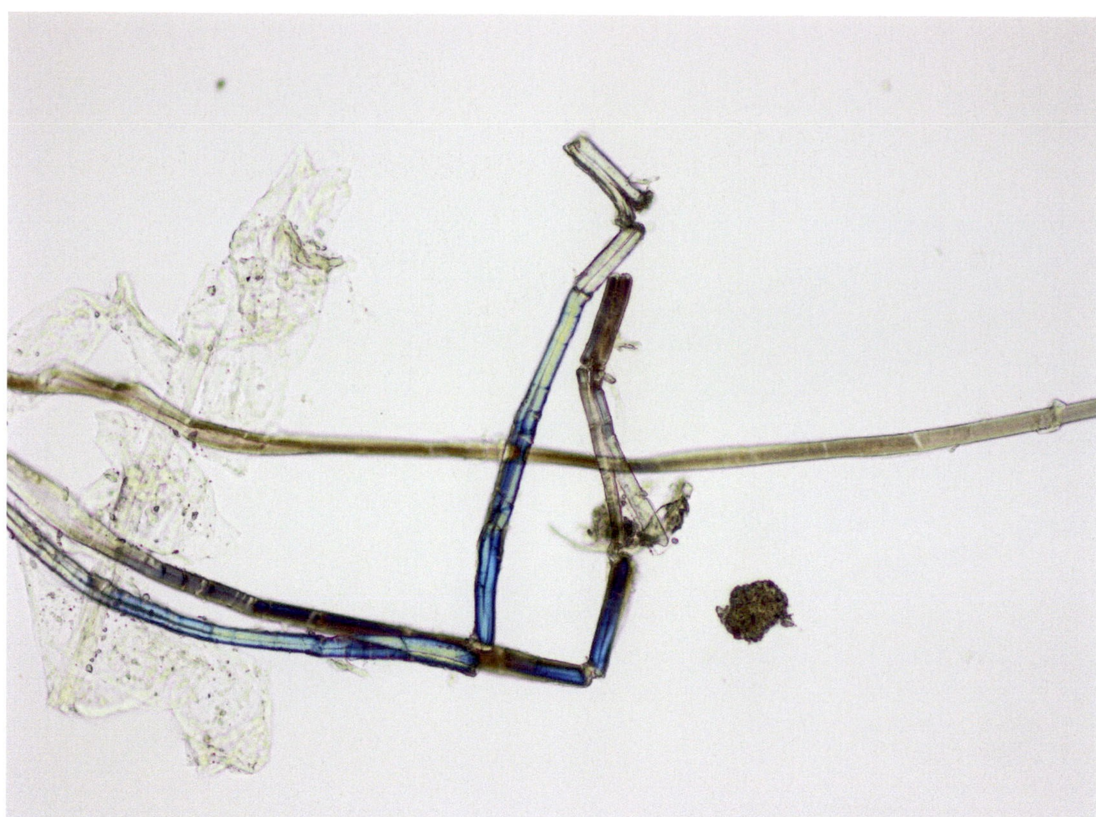

Fig. 141. Fibres fractured in the middle from MA/Geling/Tib/37 in 200× magnification observed in polarised light. Photograph by Mengling Cai.

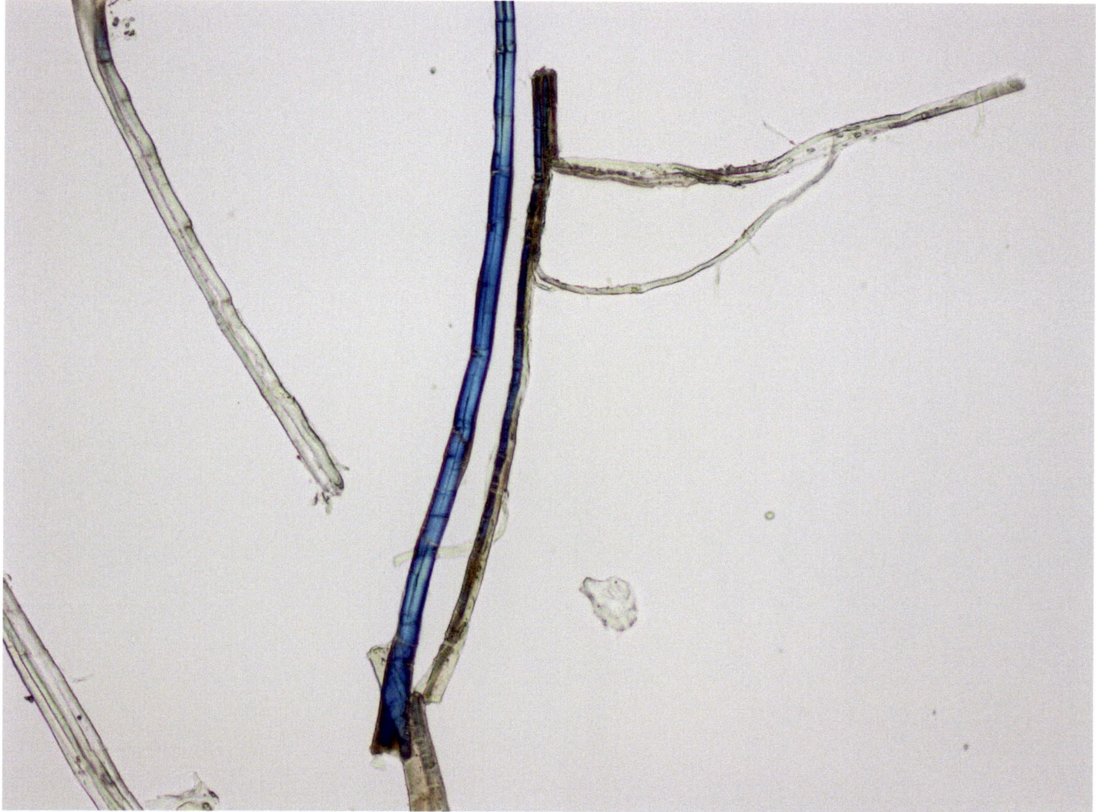

Fig. 142. Fibre split in the middle from MA/Geling/Tib/27 in 200× magnification observed in polarised light. Photograph by Mengling Cai.

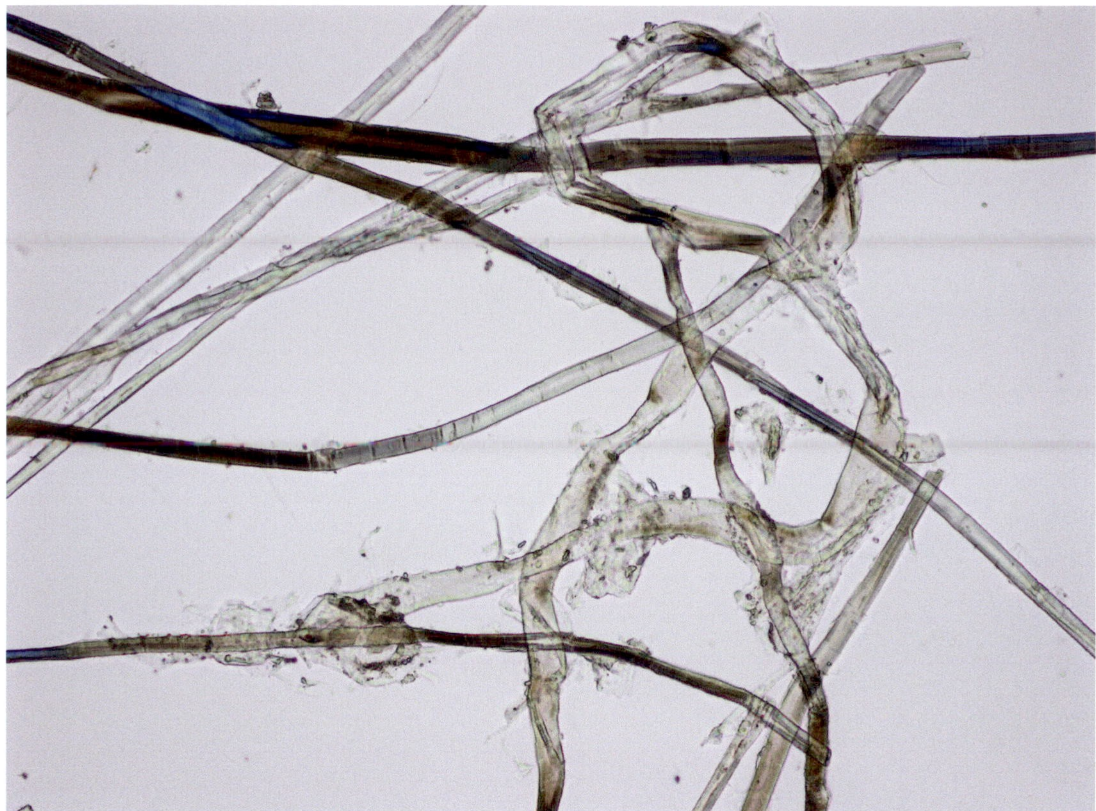

Fig. 143. Flatter *Daphne* fibres from MA/Lubrak/Tib/65 in 200× magnification observed in polarised light. Photograph by Mengling Cai.

Thymelaeaceae family. Dislocations and cross-markings were clearly visible. Besides, *Daphne* fibres sometimes showed scalloped walls (Fig. 135). Forked shapes (Fig. 136) and other irregularities (Fig. 137) could also be observed in the middle of the fibre. This can be illustrated by some small, irregular shaped holes in *Daphne* fibres from MA/Lubrak/Tib/82 (Fig. 138).

In our samples, several fibres were cut or broken (Fig. 139), with the result that sometimes very short *Daphne* fibres or fibres without complete fibre ends could be seen. Swelling or broken fibres were observed (Fig. 140), and fibres swelled easily in the broad central portion. Some fibres were fractured (Fig. 141) or split (Fig. 142) in the middle or at the end due to the papermaking process or fibre aging. Some *Daphne* fibres became flatter especially in the broad portions (Fig. 143) because of the beating and pounding processes during papermaking.

Fibres endings

The ends of *Daphne* fibres have pointed, blunt, rounded, forked, spatulate or scalloped shapes. The entire range of above-mentioned irregularities in fibre ends were frequently observed in our samples. Examples typical for *Daphne* fibres are shown in Fig. 144. Occasionally the fibre ends were changed by beating or pounding. However, it is not always easy to differentiate natural anomalies from modifications resulting from mechanical processes (Fig. 145).

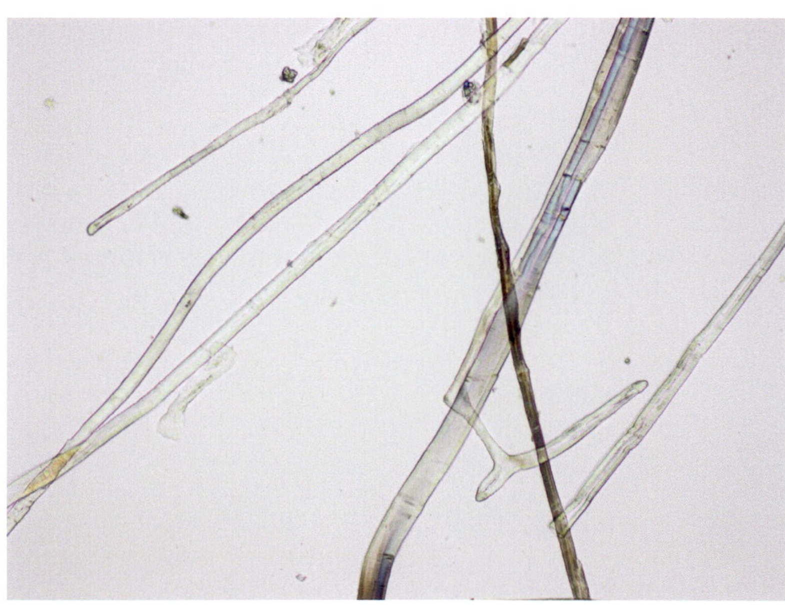

Figs 144 a–c. Examples of irregular fibre endings typical for *Daphne* sp. in paper a) from MA/Geling/Tib/36 in 200× magnification observed in polarised light, b) from MA/Geling/Tib/14 in 200× magnification observed in polarised light, c) from MA/Lubrak/Tib/19 in 200× magnification observed in polarised light. Photographs by Mengling Cai.

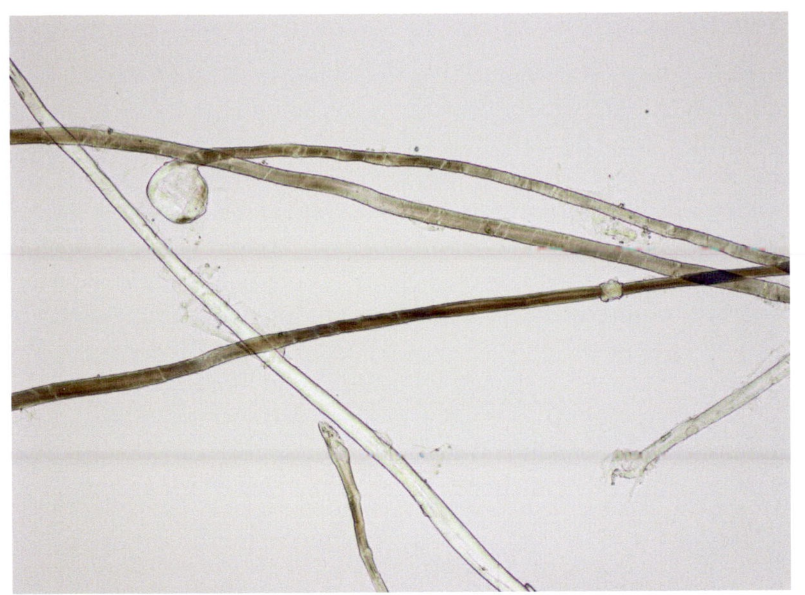

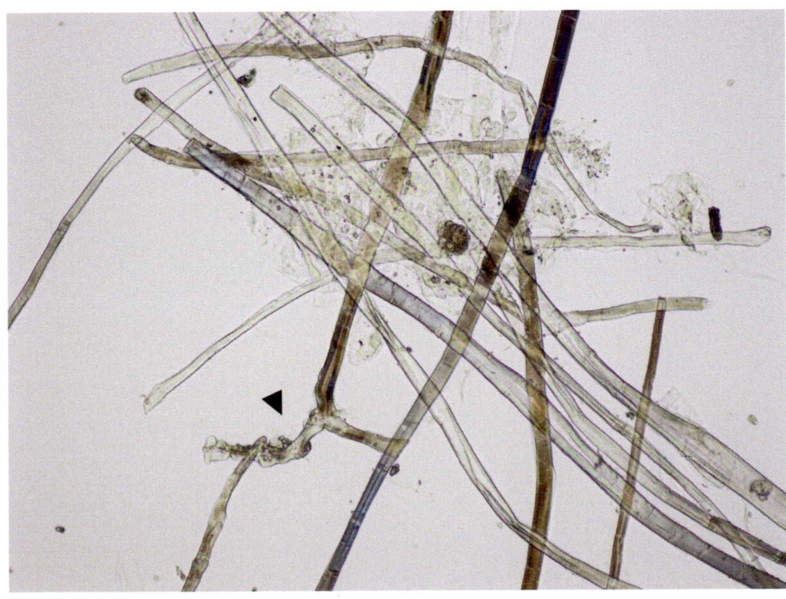

Figs 145 a-c. Fibre endings possibly also shaped by mechanical process a) from MA/Geling/Tib/40 in 200× magnification, b) from MA/Geling/Tib/68 in 200× magnification, c) from MA/Geling/Tib/15 in 200× magnification, all observed in polarised light. Photograph by Mengling Cai.

Associated cells and other substances

Parenchyma cells or remains of them and crystals were common associated elements in *Daphne* pulp. They were not only loosely dispersed between fibres in the pulp, but also appeared within the fibre cells (suggesting that they came from the plant and not from extraneous substances added during the production process). As was shown in Fig. 146, crystals inside *Daphne* fibres changed the shape of this fibre making it swell in the portions where crystal was located (Fig. 146 a) or dislocation on hemp fibres (Fig. 146 b). In addition, different shapes of sclereid were also found. In most cases, they had very thick walls and narrow lumens with two ends tapering and pointed (Fig. 147 a), and they usually were short, but there were comparatively long ones (Fig. 147 b) as well. Sclereids with thin walls and wide lumens (Fig. 147 c) were also observed but were quite rare. A sclereid that was tested became yellow when stained with Herzberg. Since we found such cells in sample MA/Geling/Tib/13, which was made of pure *Daphne*, and in other *Daphne* and *Stellera* mixed samples, though not in pure *Stellera* pulp, it could be assumed that sclereid might be associated with *Daphne*, but not *Stellera*.

Fig. 146 a. Crystals in the pulp of document MA/Geling/Tib/53 in 50× magnification observed in polarised light. Photograph by Agnieszka Helman-Ważny.

Fig. 146 b. Crystals in the *Daphne* fibres from MA/Lubrak/Tib/57 in 200× magnification observed in polarised light. Photograph by Agnieszka Helman-Ważny.

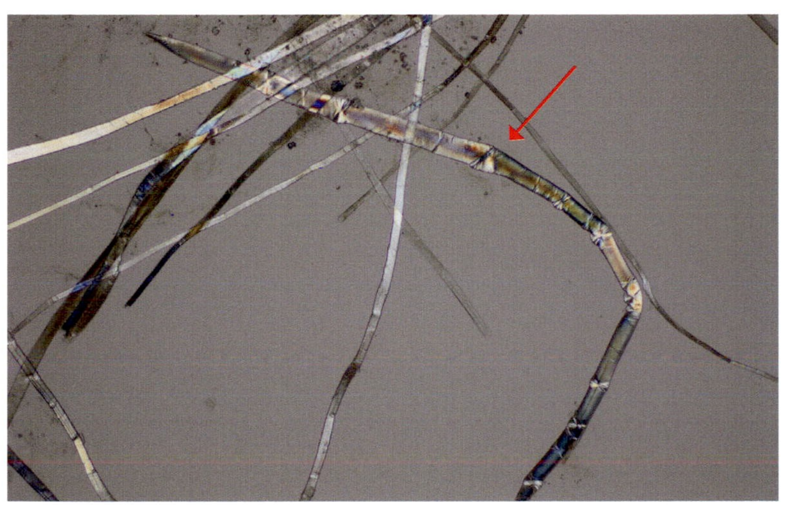

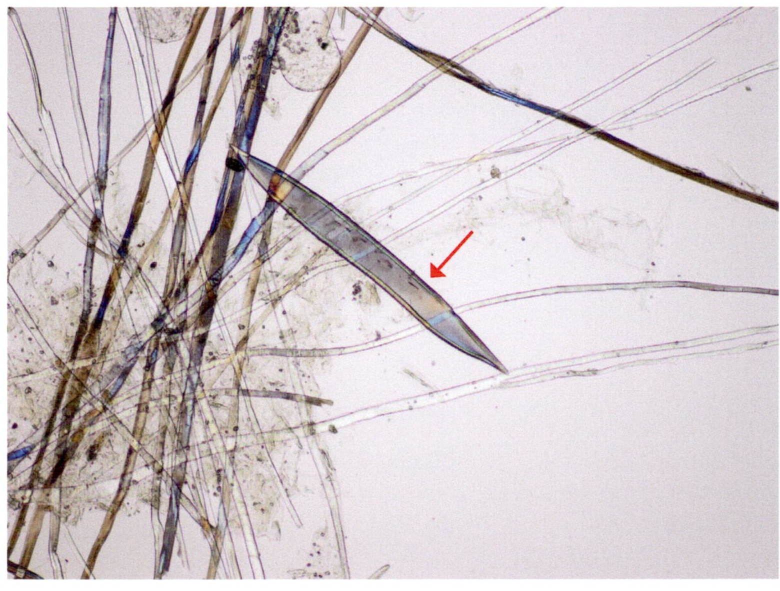

Figs 147 a–c. a) Short sclereid from MA/Lubrak/Tib/4 in 100× magnification, b) comparatively long sclereid (arrow) from MA/Geling/Tib/21 in 100× magnification, c) sclereid with thin wall and wide lumen (arrow) from MA/Geling/Tib/38 in 100× magnification, all observed in polarised light. Photographs by Agnieszka Helman-Ważny.

Furthermore, spiral vessel element was found in two samples from MA/Geling/Tib/48 and MA/Lubrak/Tib/74 respectively (Fig. 148). The raw materials of them were both identified as *Daphne* mixed with a small quantity of *Stellera* fibres. Neither of the references we used, however, mentioned this feature in the descriptions of *Daphne*, *Stellera* or other Thymelaeaceae family papermaking plants. It is usually described as unwound spiral vessels sometimes associated with hemp fibres, which were not found in our sample. It is why we cannot be sure of the source of this spiral element, and if it could be associated with *Daphne* or *Stellera*.

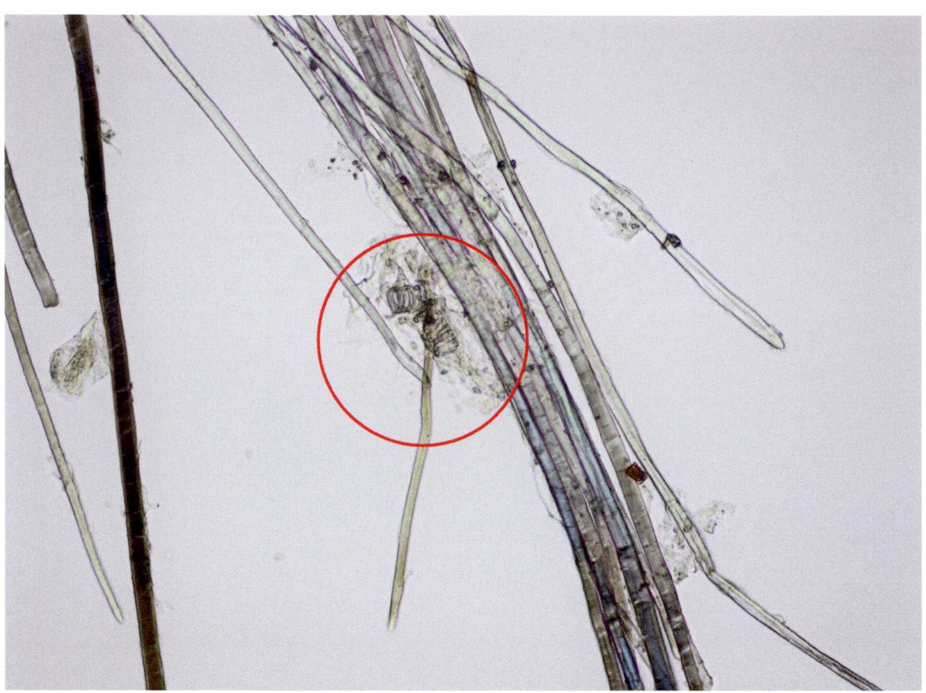

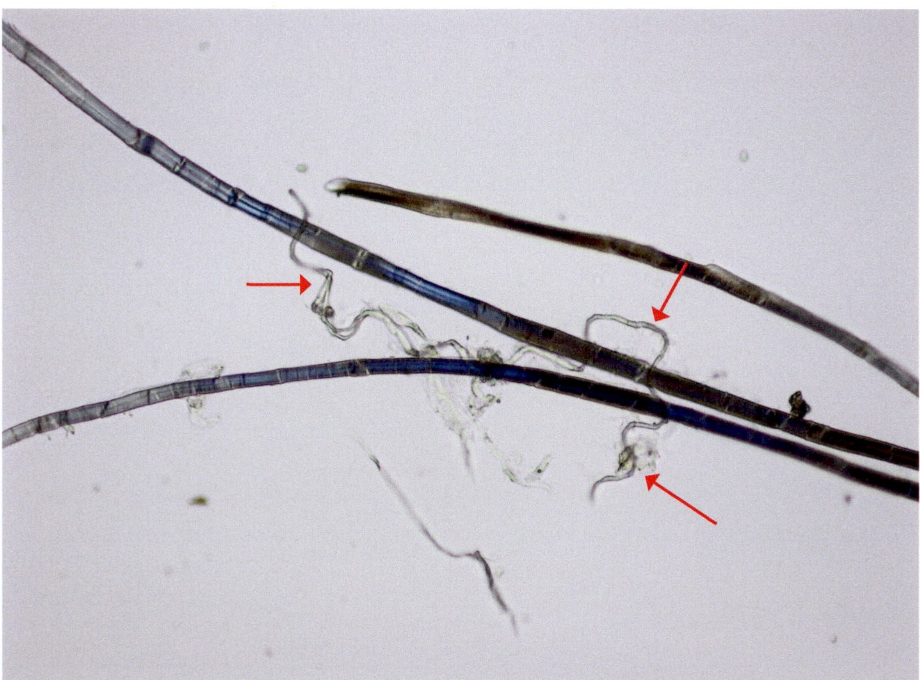

Figs 148 a–b. a) Spiral vessel element from MA/Geling/Tib/48 in 200× magnification observed in polarised light. b) Unwound spiral vessel element from MA/Lubrak/Tib/74 in 200× magnification observed in polarised light. Photographs by Mengling

Stellera

The microscopic description of *Stellera* can be found in Helman-Wazny's *The Archaeology of Tibetan Books*,[35] and in Khartasia database. As in the case of *Daphne* the slides prepared from *Stellera* paper acquired in the Nyemo papermaking workshop from the Helman-Ważny collection helped to distinguish it from other species in Thymelaeaceae family.

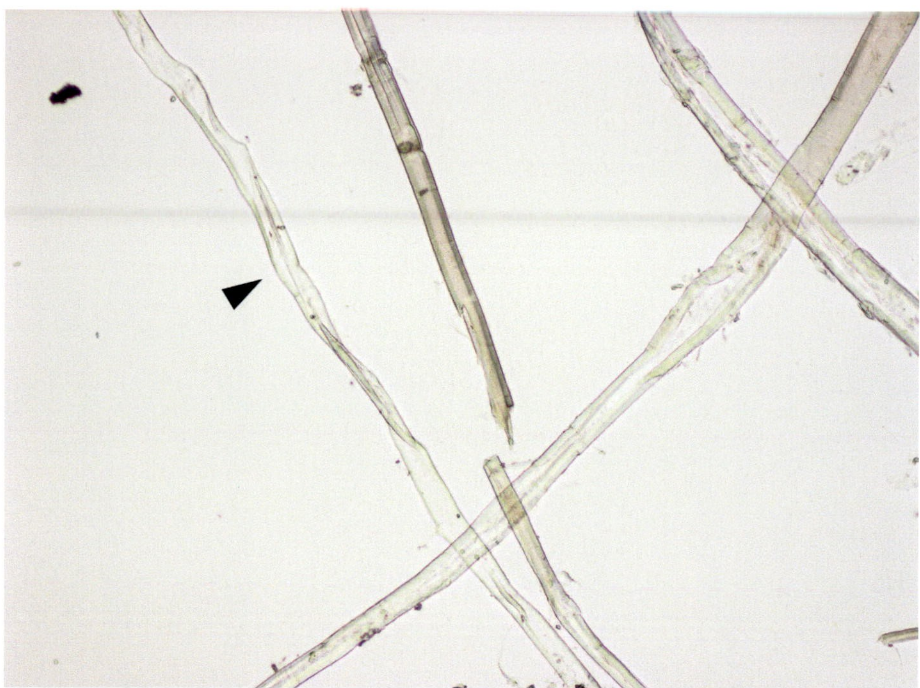

Fig. 149. *Stellera* fibre with ribbon-like shape (arrow) from MA/Geling/Tib/35 in 200× magnification observed in polarised light. Photograph by Mengling Cai.

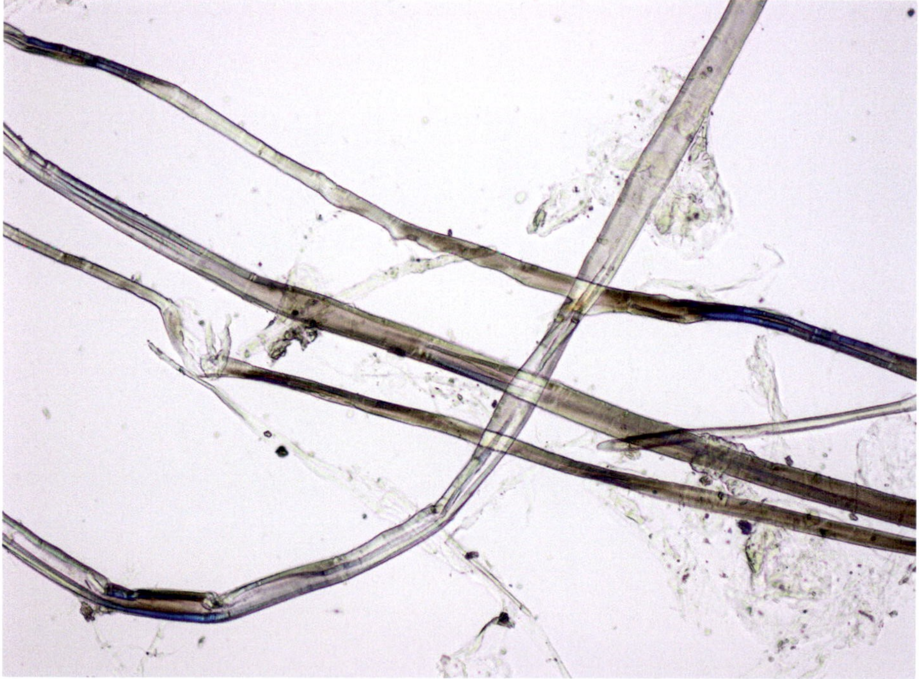

Fig. 150. Irregular fibre wall from MA/Lubrak/Tib/7 in 200× magnification observed in polarised light. Photograph by Agnieszka Helman-Ważny.

[35] Helman-Ważny 2014: 23–26.

Features of *Stellera* fibres

Anatomical peculiarities

Stellera, belonging to Thymelaeaceae family, shared the common characteristic of having a broad central portion. But compared to *Daphne*, it could be differentiated by its ribbon-like shape (Fig. 149), which was similar to flabby cotton fibres. Due to the thin fibre walls and wide lumens, the fibres were often observed twisted or in other irregular shapes. Besides, forked or other irregular fibre walls were also observed in *Stellera* fibres (Figs 150 and 151). Figure 152 shows the swelling on the *Stellera* fibres which can easily occur due to the thin fibre walls (Fig. 152).

Fig. 151. Irregular fibre wall from MA/Lubrak/Tib/28 in 200× magnification observed in polarised light. Photograph by Mengling Cai.

Fig. 152. Swelling *Stellera* fibre from MA/Lubrak/Tib/41 in 200× magnification observed in polarised light. Photograph by Mengling Cai.

Fibre endings

In our samples, the majority of *Stellera* fibres were cut and they had no natural endings. From the remaining ends we observed, the pointed, rounded and blunt shapes were the most common for *Stellera* fibres. Scimitarlike shapes (Fig. 153) were often observed as well. There were also some irregular-shaped endings which were shown in Figs 154 a–b.

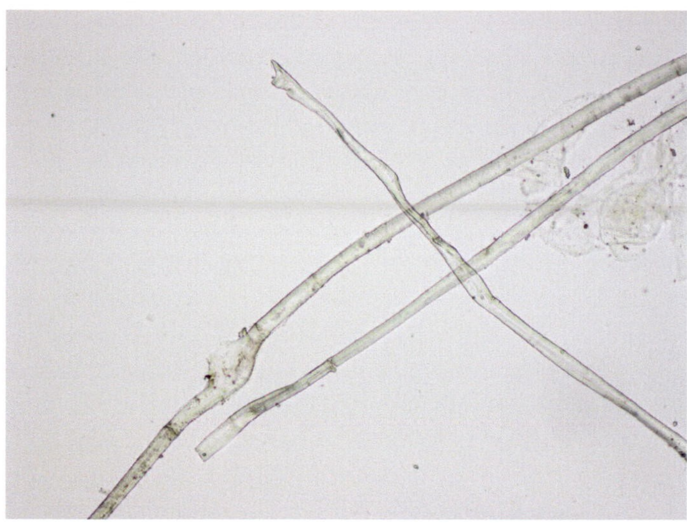

Fig. 153. Scimitarlike *Stellera* fibre end from MA/Lubrak/Tib/78 in 200× magnification observed in polarised light. Photograph by Agnieszka Helman-Ważny.

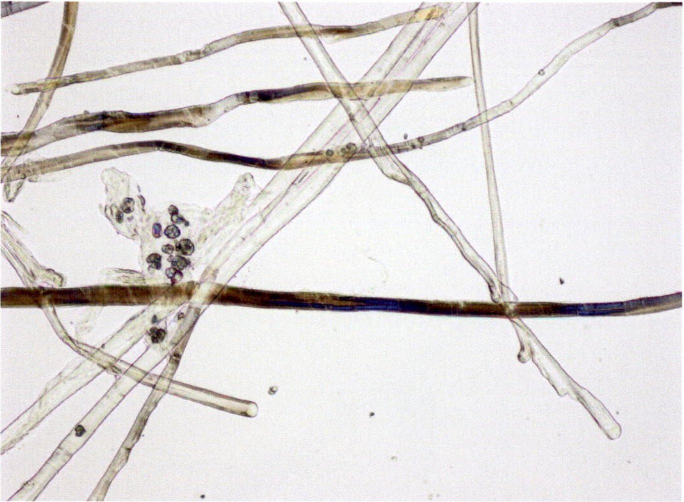

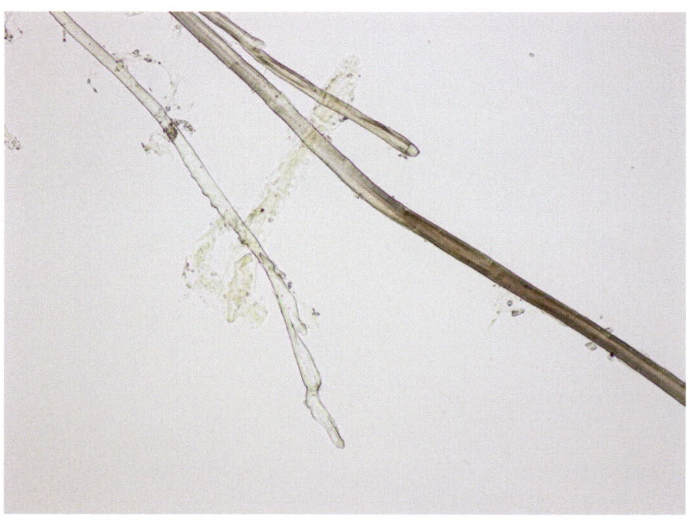

Figs 154 a–b. a) Irregular *Stellera* fibre end from MA/Geling/Tib/42 in 200× magnification observed in polarised light. b) Irregular *Stellera* fibre end from MA/Lubrak/Tib/19 in 200× magnification observed in polarised light. Photographs by Agnieszka Helman-Ważny.

Other species

According to results of fibre analyses, *Daphne* and *Stellera* were the main raw materials found in the studied documents. However, as illustrated by the paper of the documents archived as MA/Lubrak/Tib/20, MA/Lubrak/Tib/49 and MA/Lubrak/Tib/55 other components, such as grass, wood, sunn hemp and other unidentified species were detected as well. Grass mixed with *Daphne* and *Stellera* was found in document MA/Lubrak/Tib/10, while hardwood cells among other components were observed in the document archived as MA/Geling/Tib/61. Grass fibres were usually short, thin and regular with the thick, narrow fibre wall and pointed endings. The scalloped epidermal cells typical for grass were often detected. They had numerous small parenchyma cells and relatively long, pitted vessel elements. Regarding the identification of hardwood fibres, all the three reference resources focused on the morphology of its vessel elements, which showed structural variation between different genera, and there were few or even no descriptions for the fibre itself which was thought to be rarely a diagnostic feature. However, we didn't find the featured vessel with a small tail of hardwood except in MA/Lubrak/Tib/20. Since the vessel shown in figure 155 has been quite damaged, we initially assumed it came from one of *Betula* species according to the morphology of the pits (Fig. 155). We identified the fibre with the thick wall, pointed endings and faint cross-markings in figure 156 as libriform fibre of hardwood compared with the figures in references (Fig. 156). Softwood fibres often had thin walls and wide lumens with various types of pits, which indicated different genera. Based on the morphology of softwoods in figure 157, the fibres were respectively identified as *Pinus* sp. from MA/Lubrak/Tib/20 and *Larix* from MA/Lubrak/Tib/49 (Figs 157 a–b). Sunn (*Crotalaria juncea L.*) fibre was seldom used as the raw material for papermaking in other areas and the main reference of its fibre morphology was Ilvessalo-Pfäffli's book. The fibre mostly had varying wide lumens but some had thick walls and very narrow lumens with dislocations, cross-markings and longitudinal striations. Fibre ends tapered to a blunt point or were rounded. Many fibres showed slit-like axial pits which were obvious in thin-walled fibres (Fig. 158 a, b). But the characteristic long hairs were observed in neither MA/Lubrak/Tib/20 nor in MA/Lubrak/Tib/55.

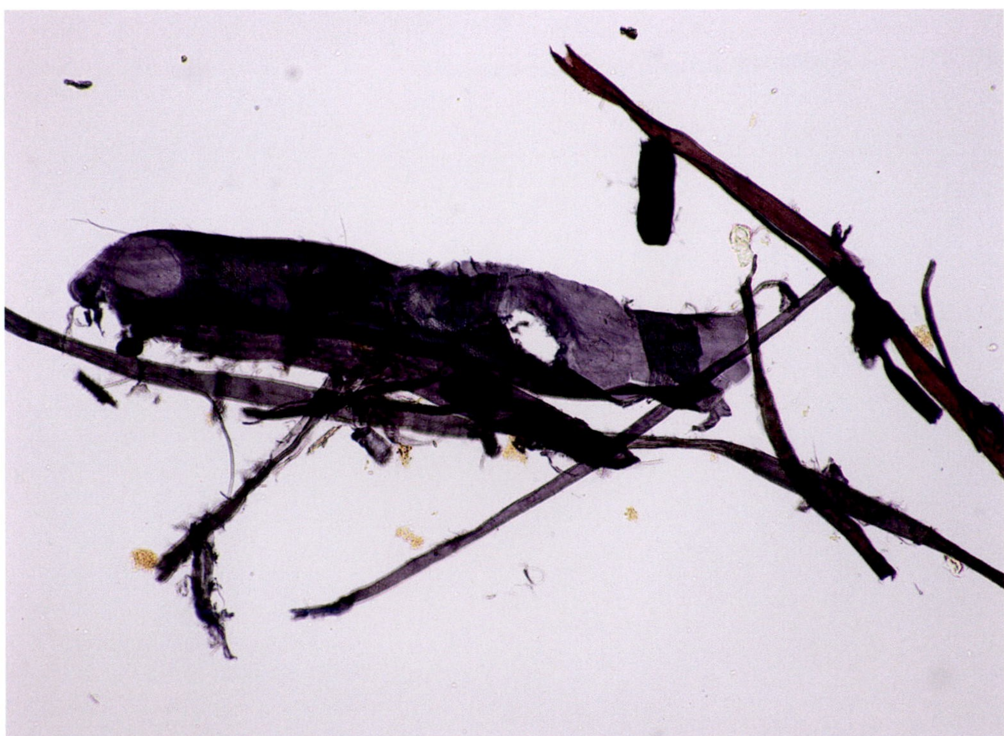

Fig. 155. Vessel element of hardwood from MA/Lubrak/Tib/20 in 100× magnification stained with Herzberg. Photograph by Agnieszka Helman-Ważny.

Fig. 156. Libriform fibre of hardwood from MA/Lubrak/Tib/49 in 100× magnification stained with Herzberg. Photograph by Mengling Cai.

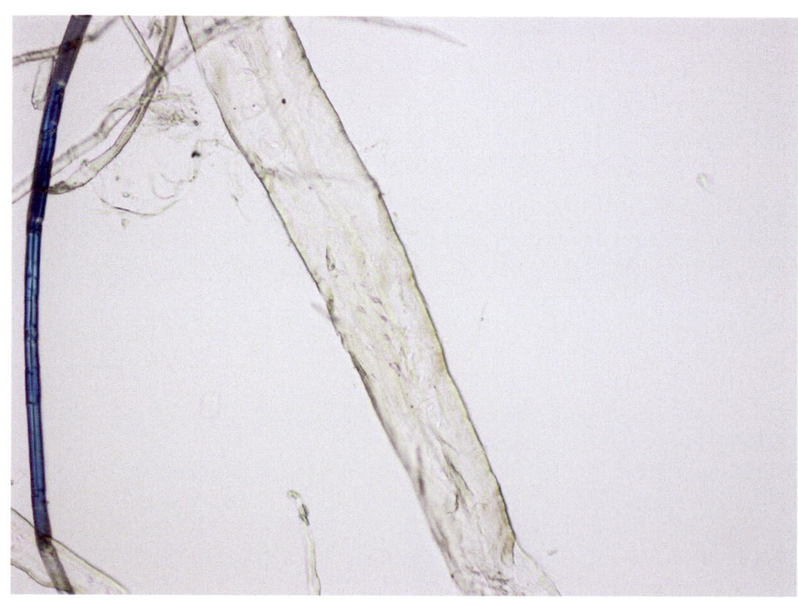

Figs 157 a–b. a) Mixed pulp from MA/Lubrak/Tib/20 in 200× magnification stained with Herzberg. b) Softwood fibre from MA/Lubrak/Tib/49 in 200× magnification observed in polarised light. Photographs by Agnieszka Helman-Ważny.

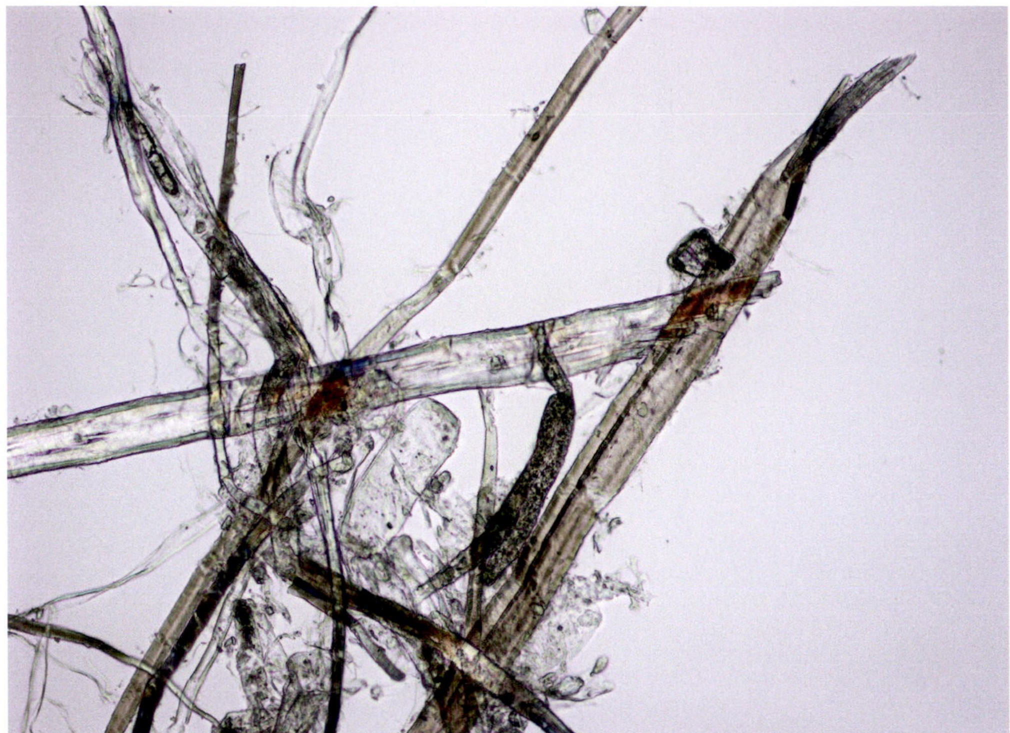

Fig. 158. Fibre with slit-like axial pits from MA/Lubrak/Tib/20 in 200× magnification observed in polarised light. Reference figure of sunn fibre from *Fibre atlas: identification of papermaking fibres* (page 341). Photograph by Mengling Cai.

Besides, there were small quantities of fibres we frequently observed (one or two fibres) in some samples, indicating they were probably added when the main raw materials were not sufficient and this also caused difficulty for us in identifying them. The morphologies of these fibres are shown in figure 159. Fibre A[36] (Fig. 159 a) shows a thick wall with wide lumen. In most cases, the fibre ends were damaged. The flabby morphology made it easy to twist or be pressed into different shapes. Cross-markings could sometimes be seen on the wall. It became reddish when stained with Herzberg. It is worth mentioning that we found some coloured fibre A in polarised light or in Herzberg: red and blue in MA/Geling/Tib/79, light purple in MA/Geling/Tib/99, which meant it might come from recycled paper. Fibre B[37] (Fig. 159 b) also had a thick wall and wide lumen, but there were light striations on the lumen. The fibre was cut into a short one with frequently split endings. The fibre turned olive when stained in Herzberg. Fibre C[38] (Fig. 159 c) was extremely thick walled and the lumen could hardly be seen. Pointed ends were observed. It was olive-grey if stained in Herzberg. Since very few fibre samples of C were found and they were damaged to some extent, the morphology was hard to recognize. Fibre D[39] (Fig. 159 d) had varying width, very thick but smooth fibre wall, and the narrow lumen sometimes disappeared. Striations were quite clear on the fibre walls and the fibre twisted frequently. The majority of fibre D in our samples had no natural ends and one with pointed ends. It is interesting that some coloured fibres D were also observed without Herzberg and polarised light: blue in MA/Geling/Tib/78 and MA/Lubrak/Tib/43, red in MA/Geling/Tib/88, dark grey in MA/Lubrak/Tib/21.

[36] Fibre A was found in MA/Geling/Tib/19, MA/Geling/Tib/35, MA/Geling/Tib/52, MA/Geling/Tib/64, MA/Geling/Tib/79, MA/Geling/Tib/99, MA/Lubrak/Tib/9, MA/Lubrak/Tib/30, MA/Lubrak/Tib/33, MA/Lubrak/Tib/45, MA/Lubrak/Tib/55 and MA/Lubrak/Tib/77.

[37] Fibre B was found in MA/Geling/Tib//52 and MA/Geling/Tib/89.

[38] Fibre C was found in MA/Geling/Tib/61 and MA/Lubrak/Tib/49.

[39] Fibre D was found in MA/Geling/Tib/62, MA/Geling/Tib/78, MA/Geling/Tib/83, MA/Geling/Tib/88, MA/Lubrak/Tib/16, MA/Lubrak/Tib/21, MA/Lubrak/Tib/29, MA/Lubrak/Tib/43, MA/Lubrak/Tib/50 and MA/Lubrak/Tib/77.

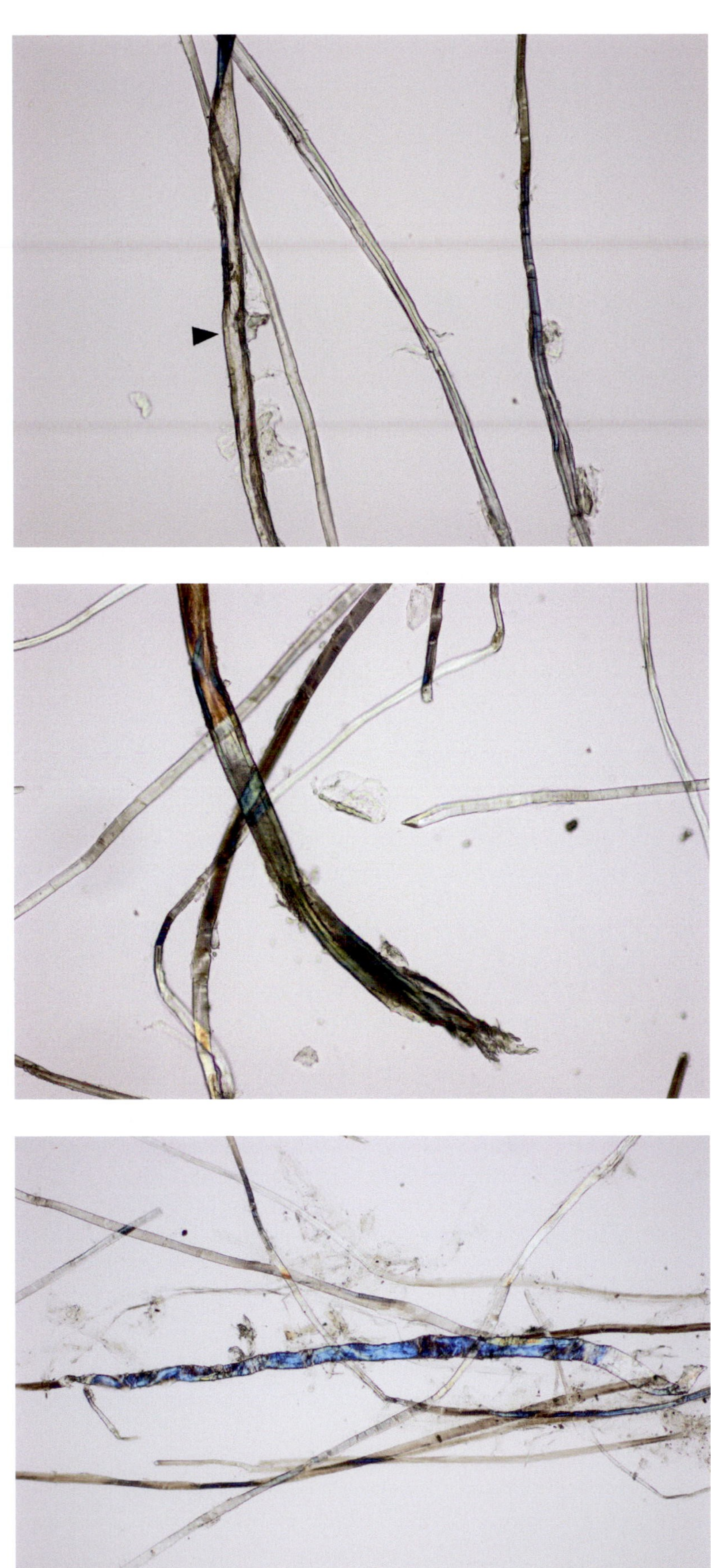

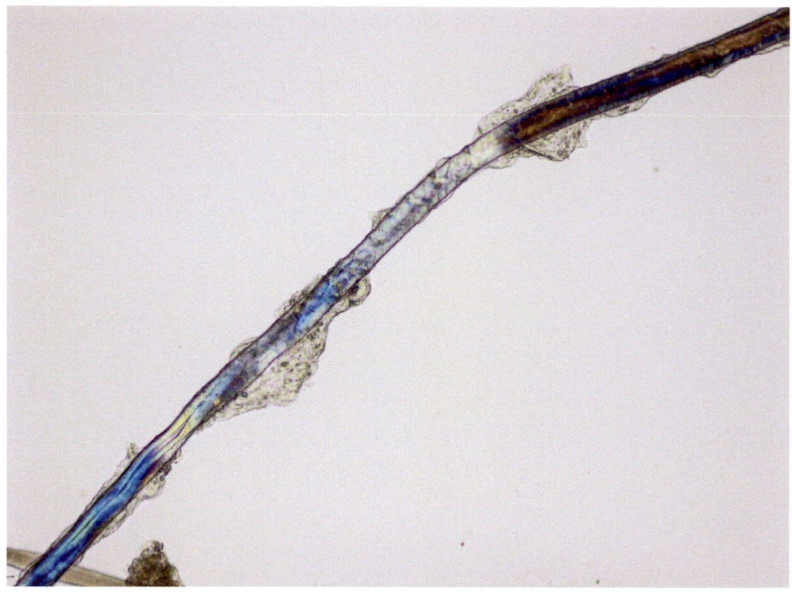

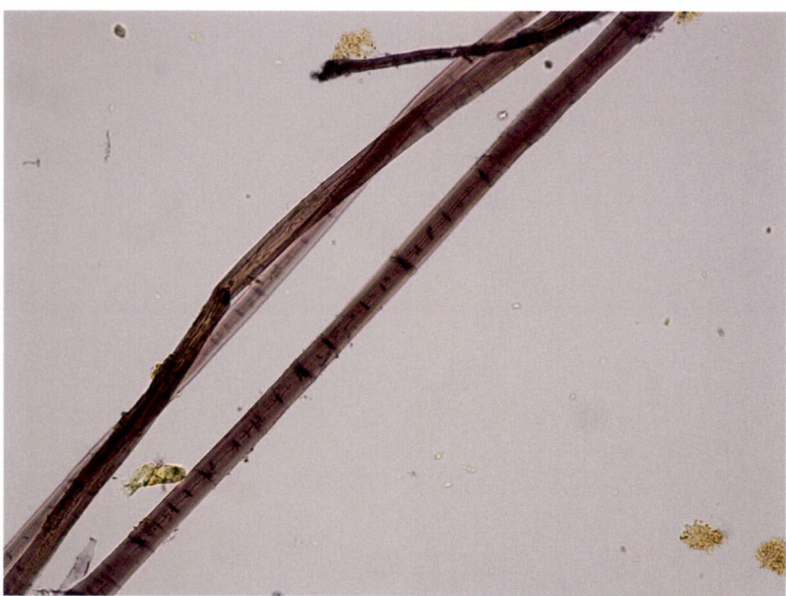

Figs 159 a–e. a) Fibre A from MA/Geling/Tib/64 in 200× magnification observed in polarised light. b) Fibre B from MA/Geling/Tib/89 in 200× magnification observed in polarised light. c) Fibre C from MA/Geling/Tib/61 in 100× magnification observed in polarised light. d) Fibre D from MA/Geling/Tib/83 in 200× magnification observed in polarised light. e) Fibre E from MA/Lubrak/Tib/20 in 200× magnification stained in Herzberg. Photographs by Mengling Cai.

Fibre E[40] (Fig. 159 e) was quite slim, rigid and regular with a thick wall and very narrow lumen. Cross-markings were clear and frequent. Endings tapered to a pointed or blunt shape. It turned red with Herzberg.

Additionally, the fibres in some samples exhibited a relatively high degree of fibrillation, suggesting that these documents may have been made from recycled components. The word "fibrillation" denotes both a process and the result of that process. Refining can be defined as the passage of a slurry of papermaking

[40] Fibre E was found in MA/Lubrak/Tib/20 and MA/Lubrak/Tib/55.

fibres between plates in relative motion to each other that have raised bars on their surfaces. The fibres are subjected to shearing and compression forces. One of the things that happens during refining of fibres is fibrillation, the partial delamination of the cell wall, resulting in a microscopically hairy appearance of the wetted fibre surfaces. The "hairs" are also referred to as fibrillation. Fibrillation tends to increase the relative bonded area between fibres after the paper has been dried.[41]

Despite observing some similarities in paper type within the examined groups of documents, it was not easy to see a clear pattern in the relationship between textual content, format or the function of the particular documents and the type of paper used. First we needed to gain an understanding of the connections between documents in order to group them into categories according to their specific features. With initial examination of papers during fieldwork followed by laboratory fibre analysis, it was possible to build a basic typology of identified papers, which, however, still did not allow for an understanding of further subtleties and reasons for particular paper usage or appearance in particular areas or villages. Only with the support of additional information, such as the identity of the scribes or parties involved or the function of a particular document, was it possible to make a step forward and understand more about conditions and circumstances surrounding the creation of these documents.

[41] Mini-Encyclopedia of Papermaking: https://projects.ncsu.edu/project/hubbepaperchem/Defnitns/Fibrilzn.htm (last accessed 27 December 2019).

Chapter 6
Papermaking Traditions in Nepal: The Spread of Technological Knowledge in Central Asia

We do not have exact dates for the adoption of Tibetan papermaking technology in Nepal, or consistent details on how methods and materials developed and spread over time. Our fragmentary information is based on written sources and more recent data from material studies of existing manuscripts found along the Silk Roads and in the Himalayas. Here we make an attempt to put together the information we have on the origin and spread of papermaking technologies, knowledge about plants used for making paper in Nepal, as well as the innovation and transmission of paper and its economic history to integrate an understanding of technologies with the historical development and transmission of social and cultural practices. The uniqueness of papermaking in Nepal was shaped by climatic extremes, the properties of the native plants, living conditions on the world's highest plateau and aspects of its culture that together create a distinctive craft. The trade connections between Tibet and other regions through corridors such as the Mustang-Kali Gandaki Valley and the Kyirong-Rasuwa Valley have contributed to distinctive paper- and bookmaking craftsmanship in the region. This chapter explores history, trade, modes of production, and the transfer of papermaking technologies across the Himalayas, the interaction of tradition with natural resources and climatic conditions, and the connection between the spread of paper and regional trade.

Origins and spread via the Silk Road

The history of paper has recently been popularised in books, where paper is regarded with sentiment as symbolic of a passing era, having now been replaced by a variety of electronic media. The year 105 CE is often cited as the date when paper technology began. It is a fascinating story of the way a simple two-thousand-year-old Chinese invention spread to the four corners of the world. According to historical records, the technique of making paper was reported to the Eastern Han Emperor Ho-di by Marquis Cai, an official of the Imperial Court. Archaeological records suggest, however, that paper had already been known in China since the second century BCE.[1] Regardless of its date of origin, it was clearly widely used in China soon after its invention and spread to the rest of world via the Silk Road. It is usually accepted that paper was unknown in India at that time. There are scholars, however, who claim paper originated in India.[2] Since 1984, paper technologist Prabhakar Gosavi has claimed that paper made of cotton was actually an Indian invention that was subsequently transferred to China via Turkestan.[3] He speculated that the Chinese did not know the art of beating cotton to make paper, while the Indians had been doing it since 327 BCE. He tells of Nearcticus (Nearchus), the ambassador of Alexander the Great in Punjab, who supposedly stated that Indians used to make paper by beating cotton derived from cloth.[4] However, when mentioning Nearchus, Strabo points out the contradiction between him and Megasthenes, who claimed that Indians at that time had no system of writing.[5] These sources alone are somewhat unconvincing, since writing materials could have been described in a symbolic way at that time. The Chinese monk Yijing, however, travelling to India from 671 to 695 CE witnessed the use of paper in India during his visit. In the message he sent home (translated by Takakusu in 1896) he wrote: "The priests and layman in India make *caitya*, or images with earth, or impress the Buddha´s image on silk or paper, and worship it with offerings wherever they go."[6]

[1] Pan 1981: 38–39.

[2] Gosavi 1984: 2000, Ramaseshan 1989: 104.

[3] Gosavi 1984: 42, Gosavi 2000: 54–56.

[4] Gosavi 1984.

[5] For all discussion on the knowledge and usage of letters by Indians based on Greek and Roman written sources, see Müller 1968, 472–73.

[6] Tsien 1985: 356 following Takakusu 1896: 150; Ramaseshan 1989: 104.

Yijing also included the word *kākali* for paper in his lexicon.[7] Konishi in 2013 refers to the same trip of Yijing and his record, but he gives slightly different dates (672–85).[8] He also explains that the original text in Chinese by no means confirms that the material mentioned was paper as we know it. Yijing's other note also mentioned the need to order paper and ink from China which rather suggests that paper was not at that time manufactured in the area.[9] Since another known Chinese traveller Xuanzang returned from India by 645 CE and made no mention of witnessing paper anywhere there, Tsien suggests that paper must have arrived in the Indian continent between 645 and 671 CE.[10] Most scholars, however, prefer to date the origins of paper in India to the time of the Muslim conquest, since that was a time from which paper has been extensively used for writing manuscripts in India.[11] This is probably the reason there is no indigenous term for paper in India. The Hindi word *kāgaj* or *kāgad* is a corruption of the Persian *kāghaz*, itself a derivation from the Chinese word *kog-dz*, the term for "paper made from the bark of the paper mulberry tree."[12] The term used for paper in Nepal is *kāgaj*.

As mentioned above, sources for the dates when paper could have been introduced to and then produced in India are sparse in the extreme. This, however, clearly offers no certainty regarding the origins of paper in India. The history of Indian literature may help us to understand the reason why it is so difficult to trace the origins of paper. The ancient Vedic texts, created when the Aryan tribes moved into India, are generally ascribed to the second half of the second millennium BCE.[13] This literature went on to grow over many centuries, but for many generations was handed down orally. First among India's preserved written documents are thousands of inscriptions on stone, copper, iron, silver, gold, brass, bronze, clay, bricks, crystals, ivory and other hard plates which are extremely difficult to date with any precision. Only much later do we have manuscripts written on organic materials such as birch bark, palm leaves, cotton and paper. Birch bark was available across the Himalayas and was favoured in and around Kashmir. It was used as a writing support as early as the last centuries BCE and is still used in parts of India for horoscopes, amulets and mantras.[14] The early employment of birch bark is attested by extant scroll fragments from ancient Gandhāra written in Kharoṣṭhī script and discovered in present-day Pakistan and Afghanistan. Earliest examples, dated by Richard Salomon to the first century CE, are preserved today in several collections including those of the British Library and the US Library of Congress.[15] Other birch-bark manuscripts in the Kharoṣṭhī script of roughly the first or second century CE and later have been also excavated in Khotan and elsewhere in Central Asia.[16] The manuscript referred to here is the Kharoṣṭhī manuscript (the *Dutreuil de Rhins Manuscript*) found in Khotan and preserved partly in Paris and partly in St Petersburg.[17] Also, palm-leaf or birch-bark manuscripts from the Bamiyan Valley (in present-day Afghanistan) were dated approxmiately from the second to the eighth centuries).[18]

Possibly the other extant examples of those early manuscripts are the *Bower manuscripts* and the *Bakhshālī manuscript*, both preserved in the Bodleian Library, Oxford. The *Bower manuscript* edited by Hoernle between 1893 and 1912 is dated to the Gupta era (between the fourth and the sixth centuries CE).[19] The date of the *Bakhshālī manuscript* is now the subject of heated dispute and

[7] Tsien 1985: 356.

[8] Konishi 2013: 22.

[9] Tsien 1985: 356.

[10] Tsien 1985: 357.

[11] Macdonell 1900: 18–19; Diringer 1982: 364.

[12] Diringer 1982: 364.

[13] Diringer 1982: 357.

[14] Konishi 2013: 6.

[15] Salomon 1999: 141–55; Salomon and Glass 2000: 23.

[16] Konishi 2013: 6.

[17] For more information see Diringer 1982: 354.

[18] Braarvig and Liland 2010.

[19] The original manuscript is written in the Gupta script on birch-bark in the fashion of traditional Indian *pothi* (loose leaves) and comprises fifty-one surviving leaves. It is enclosed between two wooden boards with a string holding the leaves together. The manuscript is known by the name of Col. H. Bower, who bought it in 1890 in Kucha. This manuscript was also previously dated to the second century BCE. See: Hoernle 1897; Pandey and Pandey 1988: 1–46.

is in fact dated anywhere from the third to the eleventh centuries by a variety of scholars.[20] David Diringer dates the earliest extant manuscripts on palm leaves to the fourth and sixth centuries CE. These are the fragments from Kashgar in the Godfrey Collection and the Horiuzji manuscripts, written in cursive letters of the Siddhamatṛka script.[21]

The manuscripts found in Jaina libraries in Gujarat and Rajasthan may be the earliest manuscripts written on paper. According to Macdonell (1900) the oldest known example of a Sanskrit manuscript written in India on paper is from Gujarat and belongs to the early part of the thirteenth century. According to Diringer (1982) the earliest of all preserved Indian manuscripts on paper is a manuscript dated to 1231 CE now in the Calcutta Sanskrit College (Library catalogue No. 582).[22] Unfortunately, there is little new research that allows for greater precision in dating these manuscripts.

The westward spread of papermaking through Tarim Basin along the Silk Road has been widely investigated, but its migration to the south towards the Himalayas, including Tibet and Nepal, to India remains to be studied in detail. When we consider the dissemination of papermaking technology to the south, most scholars assume two possibilities for the route via which papermaking reached India. One is from China through Central Asia, Tibet and Nepal; the second through Islamic traders in the Indian Ocean and, later, via the Muslim invaders who entered India from the thirteenth century onwards.[23] Possibly crucial for an understanding of the dissemination of papermaking from China to Tibet, Nepal, Bhutan, Burma and Thailand was the migration of Chinese communities that manufactured paper for their own needs. The development of papermaking in these countries was spurred on by Buddhist monks who copied vast tracts of religious literature. Many devout monks from all over Asia travelled to bring back the true words of the Buddha. Xuanzang, a Chinese monk and a scholar, traveller, and translator in the seventh century, who described the interaction between Chinese Buddhism and Indian Buddhism during the early Tang dynasty, was probably one of the best known, but many like him travelled to India at that time and spread technological knowledge, such as papermaking techniques, to the south and brought back religious thought and books.[24] Corridors connecting Tibet and other mountain regions across the Himalayas clearly facilitated the development of the distinctive crafts of paper- and bookmaking in the region. Jahar Sen, in accordance with Bal Chandra Sharma, puts the beginning of India's commercial relationship with Nepal and Tibet as early as the fifth century BCE.[25] He points to Zhang Qian, the Chinese general and explorer of Central Asia from 138 to 126 BCE, who is also depicted on a mural in the Mogao Caves (618–712 CE). He maintains that there was trade between north-eastern India and south-western China in Chinese silk cloth and Chinese bamboo flutes, among other things. These were brought into Eastern India and were carried the entire length of northern India to as far west as Afghanistan and Central Asia. A continuous flow of commerce along the overland trade route from Bihar to Tibet and China through Nepal has been conjectured and the Nepal route played a surprisingly prominent role in the ebb and flow of the trade of Central Asia.[26] However, actual figures are lacking.[27] Corneille Jest describes thirteen access roads that traversed the highest Himalayan passes (Fig. 160).[28]

[20] The Bakhshali manuscript was found in 1881, buried in a field in a village called Bakhshali, near Peshawar, in what is now a region of Pakistan. It was found by a local farmer and was acquired by the Indologist A. F. R. Hoernle, who presented it to the Bodleian Library in 1902, where it has been kept ever since. Scholars from the Bodleian Library recently dated the manuscript by radiocarbon to the 3rd or 4th century, making it approximately five centuries older than scholars previously believed. See: Bodleian Library (2017). Carbon Dating Finds Bakhshali Manuscript Contains Oldest Recorded Origins of the Symbol "zero". Ancient Indian mathematical text at Oxford's Bodleian Libraries revealed to be centuries older than previously thought. url: https://wayback.archive-it.org/6780/20210201212912/https://www.bodleian.ox.ac.uk/news/2017/sep-14. This gave rise to an important methodological discussion in scholarly circles, which clearly shows the importance of looking at things from all possible angles using cross-disciplinary tools and methods when dating a manuscript. For discussion see Plofker et al. 2017: 134–50. This manuscript is also referred to in Diringer 1982: 361.

[21] Diringer 1982: 358.

[22] Diringer 1982: 362.

[23] Bloom 2001.

[24] Schafer 1963: 273–75; van Schaik and Galambos 2012.

[25] Sen 1971: 21.

[26] Spengen 2013: 491–524, Graafen 2001: 247–52, Graafen and Seeber 1993: 34–48.

[27] Sen 1971: 35.

[28] Jest 1975: 35.

Fig. 160. Access passages between Tibet and Nepal. Drawing based on the map published by Corneille Jest in 1975.

As in the case of India, there are many and various claims that push back to early times the date of when the knowledge of papermaking in Nepal was acquired. Most of these claims, however, are unsupported by substantial evidence. Most commonly agreed is that Nepalese paper, used primarily for recording government documents and religious texts, has been recorded since the twelfth century CE. Manuscripts dated earlier would usually have been written on palm leaves, the oldest known of which are dated to the ninth century and are preserved at the National Archives in Kathmandu, Nepal,[29] the University of Cambridge, Cambridge, UK,[30] the British Museum in London, UK, and the Kaiser Library[31] in Kathmandu.

Manuscripts written on paper and said to be dated to the tenth century are preserved in the National Archives in Kathmandu.[32] There is, however, no certainty that those manuscripts written on good quality paper made of Thymelaeaceae fibres were not brought from somewhere else.[33] Konishi mentioned another manuscript in the Kaiser Library which is dated to *c.* 1000 CE, but there is again no certainty about that date.[34] Jesper Trier suggested that techniques of papermaking were transferred to Nepal around 1000 CE.[35] Probably the earliest datable example of twelfth century manuscripts is the illuminated *Pancarakṣā* manuscript at the Asutosh Museum in Calcutta, measuring 38 × 8.5 cm, which according to Konishi is written on paper made of four thin layers, glued together, consisting of Thymelaeaceae fibres akin to Daphne, as identified microscopically by Trier.[36] Losty (1982) and Ramaseshan (1989) probably referred to the same manuscript in the Asutosh Museum in Calcutta written on paper and dated to 1105 CE, stating that it is written in gold letters.[37] It is not known how this manuscript found its way to the Asutosh Museum.

[29] One of the oldest dated manuscript kept in the National Archives is the manuscript of the *Skandapurāṇa* (NAK 2/229 / NGMPP B 11/4) (Mānadeva Saṃvat 234, corresponding to 810/11 CE) (see Adriaensen et al. 1998: 33 as 810 CE; Harimoto 2011 as 811; Bhattarai 2020 as 811 CE following the date verified by Harimoto).

[30] Cambridge *Bodhisattvabhūmi* manuscript https://cudl.lib.cam.ac.uk/view/MS-ADD-01702/6 (last accessed 27 December 2019). Actually just one part of the manuscript of the *Bodhisattvabhūmi* is dated to Nepāla Saṃvat 914 (1794 CE) and the other part maybe datable to the 9th century on paleographic grounds (Harimoto 2017: 355–76).

[31] One of the oldest dated manuscripts kept in the Kaiser Library is the manuscript of the *Suśrutasaṃhitā* containing an āyurvedic text (KL 699 / NGMPP C 80/7) (Mānadeva Saṃvat 301, corresponding to 878 CE (see Petech 1984: 29; Harimoto 2011: 88; Harimoto 2014: 1087; Harimoto 2017: 363–64; Bhattarai 2020: 18). Other early palm-leaf manuscripts in the Kaiser Library are MS no. 118, dated to 1122 CE, and no. 161, dated to 1182 CE.

[32] Trier 1972: 13.

[33] Konishi 2013: 37.

[34] Konishi 2013: 38.

[35] Trier 1972.

[36] Konishi 2013: 38; Trier 1972: 132–33, 199.

[37] Losty 1982, Ramaseshan 1989: 104.

Interestingly, popular websites point to the earliest surviving *lokta* (*Daphne*) paper document roughly dated to somewhere between the first and the ninth centuries CE. It said to be the text of the Buddhist *Karaṇḍavyūhasūtra*, written in the *śāradā* script and preserved in Nepal's National Archives in Kathmandu. The provenance of this document, however, is unknown and this dating can be neither narrowed nor confirmed. The Nepal Handmade Paper Association (HANDPASS) stated in 2008 that the practice of making paper has been cultivated in Nepal since the thirteenth century.[38]

Despite uncertainty regarding the date of origin, we know that paper in Nepal began to supplant palm leaves as the most abundant writing material from about the twelfth century. A general increase in the production of manuscripts in Nepal took place from the fourteenth century. The progressive proliferation of paper as a writing material culminates in the seventeenth century, when paper replaced palm leaves almost completely.[39] In the second half of the fourteenth century, an unstable political situation in the neighbouring Tibetan kingdom of Mang yul Gung thang was accompanied by intense cultural activity. Both King bKra shis lde, who ruled between 1352 and 1363 CE, and King Khri rgyal bsod nams lde, who ruled between *c.* 1371 and 1404 CE, commissioned the production of a set of *bka' 'gyur* and *bstan 'gyur*, and the latter contributed also to the re-establishment of royal lineage and of Sakyapa patronage over Gung thang, also taking political control of the Glo bo (Mustang) and Dol po areas. He also founded the Gung thang chos sde (*c.* 1390) and the Shel dkar chos sde, where a printing house (*par khang*) was established. In order to complete such large editorial projects many people were involved, including craftsmen producing the writing materials such as paper and ink. This certainly intensified the development of the manufacture of traditional handmade paper in the region. This has been produced at several locations in the rural hills of Nepal.

As early as 1832 Brian Hodgson stated that paper had not been produced by Nepalese or the Newari craftsmen in the Kathmandu Valley, but by Lepcha or Murmi (Tamang) from the middle hills.[40] Trier also stated that among many ethnic groups in Nepal the Tamangs (Murmi) are the chief papermakers.[41] This may suggest where the technology of papermaking was learned from in Nepal. Maybe the fact that Nepalese papermaking workshops were in the hands of people of Tibetan origin even after 1800 draws a parallel with the situation in India, where the early paper mills were in the hands of the Muslims who introduced papermaking into the country. Nepalese paper itself is also substantially the same as Tibetan paper. What should be emphasised here is its locality, limited by specific raw material, technology and customs.

The historical origins of Tibetan papermaking are difficult to determine. Traditional Tibetan and Chinese historiography link paper to the arrival of the Chinese wife of Emperor Songtsen Gampo (Srong btsan sgam po).[42] The *Tang Annals* mention the date 648 CE in a report of the Tibetan emperor Songtsen Gampo's request for paper, ink and other writing equipment from the Chinese emperor.[43] Until the middle of the eighth century, however, most official Tibetan documents were written on wood. The entry for the years 744 and 745 in the *Old Tibetan Annals* records the transfer of official documents from wooden "tallies" (*khram*) to paper.[44] That entry also provides the first dated attestation of the word *shog* (paper) in Tibetan literature. It thus appears that by the time writing arrived in Tibet the technology of papermaking was already known not only in the Far East, but also in Central Asia. While there is a suggestion that paper was already available in the pre-existing Zhangzhung kingdom (i.e. prior to the formation of the Tibetan empire), and that the invitation letters to the Chinese imperial princess were already written on paper, this claim has so far been supported only by relatively late sources.[45]

[38] Sherpa et al. 2008.

[39] Konishi 2013: 187.

[40] Hodgson 1832: 8–11.

[41] Trier 1972: 21.

[42] Konishi 2013: 187.

[43] Pelliot 1961: 6.

[44] Uebach 2008: 61.

[45] Tsundru 2010.

During antiquity a vague knowledge of the Tibetan Plateau circulated in the West, while people probably already had far better contact with neighbouring countries than is generally supposed. Accounts of relations between Tibet and the non-Tibetan world, however, date only from the early seventh century. The earliest documented contact between Tibet and the world beyond the plateau comes during the Sui dynasty (581–618). Major relations with China date from the Tang dynasty (618–907), which framed the Tibetan imperial period. The Silk Road, which encouraged intellectual and religious exchange, was a trade route that existed for more purposes than trading in silk; many other commodities were also traded, among them paper. Of all the precious goods crossing this area, silk was perhaps the most remarkable for the people of the West. Paper was not yet known, and it took a thousand years before it was appreciated and properly valued by the West. During the imperial period Tibet intermittently gained control over crucial parts of the Silk Road, and was able at times to dominate trade between China and the West. At that time the production and circulation of manuscripts intensified. Luckily, thousands of manuscripts dated before the tenth century and written in the Tibetan language have been discovered at Dunhuang, in Gansu province. Earlier estimates date these manuscripts to the time of the Tibetan occupation of Dunhuang that occurred in between 781 and 848 CE, but recent research by Uray, Takeuchi and Dalton, Davis, and van Schaik has dated the majority of these manuscripts to the tenth century.[46] The earliest surviving examples of Tibetan paper, made of *Daphne* fibres and discovered in the Mogao caves near Dunhuang, are dated to the ninth century and were presumably produced in Central Tibet.[47]

A glance at the economic history of paper in Nepal

Papermaking is one of Nepal's traditional industries. High mountains and a harsh climate make this area suitable only for seasonal farming. In the Himalayas during the time when farming is impossible paper production has thus boosted farmers' livelihoods. The creation of workshops was most likely driven by demand. They would have been scattered, as the demand was not centralised. Although data is scarce, we may surmise that many small paper workshops existed in the Himalayas, sometimes family-run workshops, sometimes workshops run by a village, and in exceptional cases sometimes operated by a region. Nepal thus became famous for paper production.

Historically, the handcrafting of *lokta* paper took place in the rural areas of Nepal, most notably in Western Nepal. The existence of the right vegetation mostly limited this industry to mountain regions at an elevation from 2500 to 3000 meters above sea level. The administrative aspect of paper production in Nepal deserves closer study, since local papermaking traditions are steadily disappearing. Jesper Trier's book lists papermaking workshops involved in the production of traditional *lokta* paper which he personally visited in 1970.[48] Trier's book describes the local fibres and technology used, and provides a unique account of the living papermaking craft in Nepal at that time. A number of reports on papermaking methods in Nepal and the surrounding regions is also available.[49] Such reports are informative of the methods and technology of papermaking, as they have not changed over time as they have, for example, in Europe or in China. In fact, methods of papermaking in Nepal, Tibet, Bhutan, and even India are remarkably similar.[50]

Unfortunately, there exist very few historical documents that might shed light on the economic model of papermaking in Nepal and those that do exist, moreover, remain unexplored with respect to papermaking. As Holmberg and March argue, in the eighteenth century the villagers of Bomthang, Nepal, had an obligation to supply paper to the government administration offices of the Ranas in Kathmandu.[51] The village archive contains information about the regions where the raw materials were harvested, granted officially every few years depending on harvesting

[46] Uray 1988: 515–28; Takeuchi 2012.

[47] Helman-Ważny and van Schaik 2013: 735

[48] Trier 1972.

[49] Tschudin 1958: 679–89; Sandermann 1968; Hunter 1978; Rischel 1985; Koretsky 1986; Helman-Ważny 2001; Upreti 2004.

[50] Hunter 1978; Imaeda 1989; Premchand 1995; Soteriou 1999; Tsundru 2010.

[51] Holmberg and March 1999.

requirements. This shows that traditionally paper could be traded over long distances, while raw materials were harvested locally.

We have later confirmation, however, that semi-prepared pulp could also be traded over greater distances. On 25 March 1842 Brian Hodgson, the British Resident in Kathmandu, wrote a letter stating that

> by direction of Mr Secretary Halliday I have this day transmitted hence en route to Calcutta twenty-four packages of Nepalese paper pulp which will be delivered to you by my people and which I requested you will be pleased to forward to their destination in the most convenient manner, sending me your bill of charges for the same.

Elsewhere he writes:

> The raw produce or pulp [of paper], beaten into bricks, has been sent to England, and declared by the ablest persons to be of unrivalled excellence, as a material for the manufacture of that sort of paper upon which proof-engravings are taken off. The manufactured produce of Nepal is for office-records incomparable, better than any Indian paper, being as strong and durable as leather almost, and quite smooth enough to write on. It has been adopted in one or two offices in the plains, and ought to be generally substituted for the flimsy friable material to which we commit all our records.[52]

Most evidence concerning paper usage was gleaned from the *Regmi Research Series*, and related to times after 1742 (from the time of conquest by the Gorkhas).[53] Interestingly, Mahesh Chandra Regmi points to the use of paper in the firing mechanism of muzzle-loading guns in the eighteenth century.[54] Because flints were not available, Prithvi Narayan Shah introduced the practice of igniting muzzle-loading guns with paper wicks. Thereafter, he formed two companies of rifle-men. To begin with, each company had one hundred soldiers and seven officers. There were no more than five permanent companies during the reign of Prithvi Narayan Shah. Each company had no more than 150 troops. The companies must have had about 750 guns. With the help of these guns, the eastern territories of Nepal were annexed. Guns need frequent repair. Prithvi Narayan Shah employed three Muslim fugitives from India to repair guns, and gave them land grants. At that time Muslims were well known for their papermaking skills in India.

A contract issued in 1799 by King Rana Bahadur Shah (grandson of Prithvi Narayan Shah) to one Chhote Singh Newar, authorises the beneficiary "to collect the *nirkhi* levy on the sale and purchase of goods brought by traders throughout our territories, after appointing your agents at [a number of check points that are listed: it is worth noting that the checkpoints are not located on the border with either India or China, but are internal to Nepal]." The commodities listed include copper, iron, lead, wax, various medicinal herbs and spices, cotton, and paper.

In the eighteenth and nineteenth centuries diplomatic correspondence of the category known as *kharita* (i.e. letters sent in the name of His Majesty to foreign governments) would also use a particular variety of thick polished paper, black ink and an envelope bearing the Lal Mohar seal, as well as a wax impression of the Royal Seal called *lakhaut*. The letter was then put inside a covering made of perforated cloth and enclosed in a brocade bag.

There exists an excerpt from a list, drawn up around 1806, of items that were exported from Nepal to India, along with the quantities and prices.[55] The list includes ponies, ginger, cardamom and various other spices, prickly ash, ghee, musk, rice, yak tails, timber and paper. In that year 19 *maunds* (*c.* 709 kg) of bamboo paper were exported. The total price of this was 30 rupees (although it is unclear whether Indian or Nepalese). This is interesting since bamboo paper is usually associated with south-eastern China.

[52] Hodgson 1832: 11.

[53] Mulmi 2017: https://www.recordnepal.com/wire/features/the-making-of-the-gorkha-empire-part-i-land-nepal-unification/ (last accessed 27 December 2019).

[54] Regmi.

[55] *Regmi Research Series* 1989, Year 21, no. 1, p. 72.

In May 1862 a public notice was issued to village headmen and producers of wax and paper in parts of Gorkha District.[56] The notice stated, among other things, that, according to the terms of the paper monopoly, the holder of the monopoly was obliged to provide writing paper to the palace at a rate of one *anna* per 20 sheets. The document warns of reports received to the effect that landholders (*jagirdars* and *birta* owners) would not allow the monopoly holders to secure wax or paper produced on their land, and instead would make their own arrangements for the sale of these commodities, and threatens the offenders with fines if they fail to comply. In June 1879 one monopoly holder, Sahu Ram Das, submitted a petition to the government in which he stated that:

> Wax and paper are being sold elsewhere in contravention of the monopoly regulations. Government offices too procure paper from other sources. How then can I operate these monopolies and pay the stipulated amounts to the government?

He went on to recommend a scale of fines against violators, and this recommendation was accepted by the government.

In the *Regmi Research Series* six monopolies are listed for 1901: 1. distilled alcohol, 2. (unknown); 3. wax; 4. paper; 5. hemp; and 6. buffalo horn (in the Kathmandu Valley). They are listed in descending order of revenue they generate, with alcohol the most lucrative at Rs 33,543, and buffalo horn the least at Rs 667; paper in the Marsyangdi-Dudhkosi region (i.e. the area around Manang) is fourth at Rs 3,771.

During the Second World War and afterwards a good many small industries were developed in Nepal. The Birganj Cotton Mills Limited was set up with local capital, while the Morang Cotton Mills Limited was the result of joint Nepalese and Indian resources under Indian management. Other industries that were set up between 1942 and 1944 were a factory manufacturing handmade Nepalese paper in Kathmandu, a ceramics and glass factory in Birganj, and a chemical factory in Biratnagar. After 1947 about 30 centres were opened around Kathmandu for training in cottage industries, mainly wool, hosiery, sericulture, leather, pottery, handloom weaving and paper industries. The products were exported to various parts of India.

The use of traditional paper in government offices declined drastically after the Interim Government of Nepal Act, 1951.[57] The people of Nepal continued to use handmade *lokta* paper and, until the Chinese occupation in 1959, traded in it with Tibet, where it was used in monasteries for writing religious texts. Remarks by M. C. Regmi concerning the situation in post-1950s Nepal suggest that Nepalese paper was at that time famous for its durability, as well as its resistance to tearing, humidity, insects and mildew, doubtless the reason this paper was traditionally the preferred choice for the recording official government records and sacred religious texts.

In the 1970s interest in rejuvenating *lokta* papermaking craft led to the majority of production now being dedicated to tourism and mundane purposes, such as wrapping incense, spices and medicine in order to retain their original smell and properties. An effective conservation programme was established in 1970 for the development of national parks and wildlife reserves in Nepal in order to provide raw materials for the development of forest-based industries such as the production of *lokta* paper. The methods of production are, however, wasteful, and the destruction of forests for materials and fuel wood constitutes a problem.

There are various factors which influenced the economic model in Nepal. The revival of papermaking has not been backed by a commercially viable support framework. It is supported by various NGOs. In the 1980s the United Nations Children's Fund (UNICEF) and the Agricultural Development Bank of Nepal/Small Farmer Development Program (ADBN/SFDP) launched the Community Development and Health Project (CDHP) to revive Nepal's indigenous papermaking processes. In the late 1980s and early 1990s, with the popularity of *lokta* paper on the rise, Nepalese social

[56] *Regmi Research Series*, 1981, Year 13, no. 1, p. 169.

[57] After the revolution of 1950–51 resulted in the overthrow of the Rana system, in 1951 King Tribhuvan Bir Bikram Shah set up an interim government and an interim constitution until a new Constituent Assembly could be elected. The interim constitution, based on principles in India's constitution and entitled the Interim Government of Nepal Act, 1951, ratified the end of the authority of the prime minister and the system attendant on that office.

and environmental entrepreneurs sought out and developed international trading partners. This is the time the export market for handmade *lokta* paper was established. Today the handmade paper industry in Nepal is growing at a rate of 15% per year. There remains, however, no significant international export trade that might bear comparison with economies of more developed countries.

A variety of goods are still made of Nepalese paper today. For example, important legal documents such as citizenship papers, land revenue certificates and registration forms continue to be made from this paper; greeting cards, notebooks, photo albums, photo frames, wrapping paper, writing sets, artists' paper and wallpaper are popular products suitable for export. It has also occasionally been used for painting and paper restoration.[58]

There is insufficient paper made in Tibet for major religious printing operations, so a significant amount still comes from Nepal for, among other things, the production of large religious scriptures (Kangyur and Tengyur). Handmade tourist paper items in Lhasa are often from Nepal. A significant proportion are brought in directly from Nepal by Chinese traders.[59]

Today raw *lokta* paper is produced in the following districts in Nepal: Sankhuwasabha, Panchthar, Illam, Terhathum, Solukhumbhu, Okhaldhunga, Bhojpur, Taplejung, Dolakha, Ramechhap, Sindhupalchok, Gorkha, Parbat, Myagdi, Baglung, Bajura, Rukum, Rolpa, Jajarkot, Dailekh and Accham. Finished *lokta* paper products, however, are produced mostly in the Kathmandu Valley and Janakpur, but there is a shortage of *lokta* on the market. As a result, low quality paper is being produced, and this has brought the prices of the final product down, and people are having difficulty exporting quality paper.

Papermaking plants of Nepal

The most important source materials for papermaking in the Himalayas were (and continue to be) the plants of the Thymelaeaceae botanical family, such as *Daphne*, *Wikstroemia*, *Edgeworthia* and *Stellera*.

Thymelaeaceae constitute a family of dicotyledonous flowering plants with 898 species in 50 genera. The phloem has a high hemicellulose content, which makes the bark of many species of this family eminently suitable for the manufacture of high-quality paper such as that used for bank notes and writing materials. These fibres are up to 4 mm long and narrow, and supportive cells provide a tensile strength without limiting flexibility. These characteristics render the bark a valuable material for papermaking. Most species are poisonous and some are important medicinally. The mouth should thus be suitably covered while collecting *lokta*. This poisonous quality makes them an especially good source material for paper production, since such paper is more resistant to insect infestation than paper made from other plants and is therefore more durable.

These paper plants are known by craftsmen in rural areas where they go by local names. In Tibetan these plants are generally called *shog gu me tog* ("paper flower"), *shog shing* ("paper tree"), and *shog ldum* ("paper plant").[60] These plants grow in most populated areas of Tibetan Plateau, and are easily collected, since they would have been readily available in the vicinity of papermaking workshops.

Handmade Nepalese paper is made largely from the fibrous inner bark of high elevation evergreen shrubs primarily from two species of *Daphne* plants: *Daphne bholua* and *Daphne papyracea*, known together and vernacularly as *lokta* bushes (Fig. 161).[61] *Lokta* proliferate in open clusters or colonies on the southern slopes of Nepal's Himalayan forests between 1600 m and 4000 m above sea level. These raw materials have different local names depending on region and the language spoken there. According to the *Nepali Lokta Quality Paper Production Manual 2065* these are black *baruwa*, white *baruwa*, *kāgate*, *kāgate pāt* and *shikre baruwa*.[62] *Lokta* is, however, the most commonly used. In 1940 Siva Narayana Sen mentioned the plant name *Kāgaj Pāt*.[63]

58 Suryawanshi and Agrawal 1996: 65–76.

59 Boulnois 2013, 457–76.

60 For information on Tibetan papermaking plants see: Boesi 2005: 33–48; Boesi 2014: 95–97; Boesi 2016.

61 Shrestha 1989; Storrs and Storrs 1998.

62 Sherpa et al. 2008: 6.

63 Sen 1940.

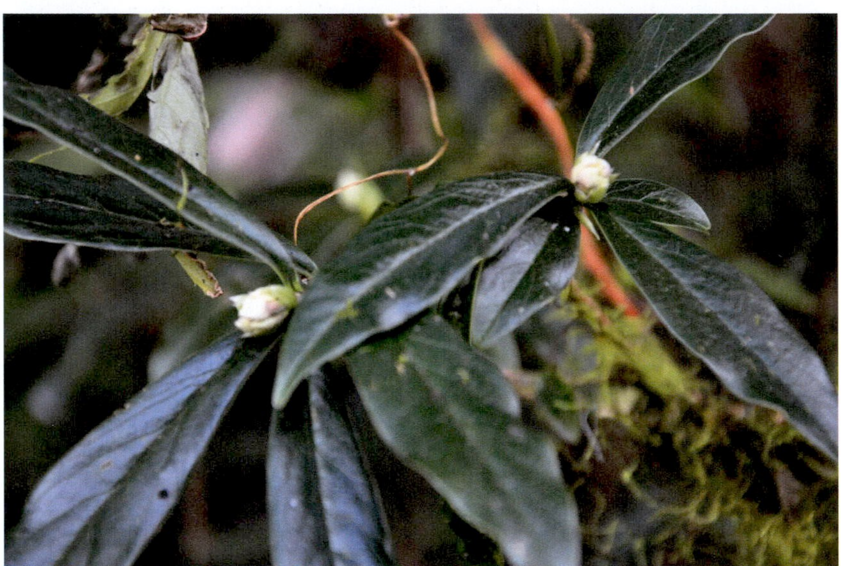

Figs 161 a–c. *Daphne bholua* plant found in the forest above Ghandruk. Photographs by Agnieszka Helman-Ważny.

According to Nepalese papermakers *lokta* is the best material for paper production, described as strong, with a strong smell, and usually harvested between June and October. It has longer leaves (with a leathery surface) than other plants of the Thymelaeaceae family. Its flowers are white with traces of purple. The fibres are very smooth, and this influences the texture of the paper.

According to Nepalese papermakers there are two types of *lokta*: black *lokta* and white *lokta*. Black *lokta* is evergreen and it has pinkish flowers. Its leaf is 5 cm to 10 cm long with a sharp or round tip. The plants flower in the months of Chaitra and Baishakh (between mid-March and mid-May in the Western calendar). During the flowering season dizziness may occur the first time someone goes near a *lokta* plant. Its poisonous properties deter other grasses from growing in the vicinity, and it is the reason cattle avoid eating it. The *lokta* is not widely used as firewood because it produces a great deal of smoke, a clear disadvantage. Paper made from this is more resistant to insects. White *lokta* may also be distinguished by the colour of its flowers, which are either white or greenish with an unpleasant smell. Its leaf is between 5 cm and 15 cm long and sharp. The leaf of the white *lokta* is darker than that of the black *lokta*. Its height is between 120 cm and 250 cm tall. According to "Nursery grandpa" interviewed in Nangi, white *lokta* bark peels off easily, but black *lokta* does not.

Since Nepal's borders were closed to foreigners until 1951, traditional plants were almost exclusively used. Some new raw materials were introduced when Nepal once more opened its borders to foreigners. After the Second World War trade with the West and an increasing demand for paper led papermakers to seek out new raw materials. The cheapness and abundance of paper from Western countries meant that it began to be imported. Craftsmen began to add other plants which were traditionally harvested to be sold as raw material for papermaking in India (such as sabai grass: Latin *Eulaliopsis binata*, or rice straw). According to Trier, these plants were used in the Kathmandu Valley paper mills. The introduction of larger paper factories, as in the Kathmandu Valley, led to the introduction of new species but in such cases they would also usually mix in pulp from traditional plants.[64]

As early as 1824 *Daphne bholua*, *Daphne papyracea*, *Daphne cannabina*, and *Edgeworthia gardneri* were described as the raw materials of Nepalese papermaking by Danish botanist, Nathaniel Wallich.[65] In 1972 Trier included *Daphne involucrate*, *Daphne sureil*, *Pollinidum augustifolium (Eulaliopsis binata* according to the current International Code of Botanical Nomenclature), and rice straw. He also mentions some experiments with *chiuli* fibres (possibly fibres of *Sterculia* sp.), and acknowledges the use of *Sterculia coccinea* in the Kathmandu Valley for making cardboard.[66]

From the 1970s *Daphne* plants have been overexploited, and therefore papermakers have had to seek out alternative raw materials. They have also begun to import wood pulp from western papermills. In the early 1980s Jean Paul Jeanrenaud explained that Japanese scholars and international organisations had decided to help the Nepalese to preserve their papermaking industry.[67] At that time new raw materials used originally in Japanese and Chinese papermaking were therefore introduced into Nepal. Nepalese paper was consequently cheaper to make and production became more profitable. This, however, led to the loss of an ancient craft. This type of raw material was fortunately mainly used in the Kathmandu Valley and in larger paper manufactories.

In late 1980s, N. P. Manandhar was the first to mention the use of *Wikstroemia canescens* in papermaking in Nepal. Julius Wiesner, however, talked of this plant's earlier use in Japan and Trier its use in Kumaon and Tibet (*Wikstroemia chamaejasme*).[68] It may nevertheless have been used in culturally Tibetan areas in Nepal.

These species grow wild, but many others from this genus have been cultivated, since species of *Daphne* have long been valued by gardeners for their fragrant flowers. *D. bholua* (*lokta*) grows well in the Himalayas and adjoining mountain ranges, from Nepal to Bhutan, Bangladesh, India, Myanmar and Vietnam, into Sichuan, Tibet, and north-western Yunnan. At lower altitudes it is found as an evergreen in thickets and forest margins; at higher altitudes it is deciduous and is found in pastures and grassy glades. It usually reaches a height of about 2.5 m, though some specimens reach 4 m or

[64] The Nepalese borders were closed to Westerners from 1850s to the 1950s. For the details on new fibres resources in Nepal see Trier 1972: 57, 88.

[65] Wallich 1824.

[66] Trier 1972: 57.

[67] Jeanrenaud 1984.

[68] Wiesner 1903.

Fig. 162. Regions in which *lokta* grows. Map by Dorota Helman.

more. This species has leathery leaves and deep pink flowers with a powerful fragrance, and a number of named cultivars have been bred and are grown as garden plants in Europe and North America.

According to a preliminary survey conducted by the *Lokta Forestry Survey and Research Centre* in 1984, the raw material for paper production (*lokta*) is found in 55 hill districts of Nepal (Fig. 162).[69]

Nepalese craftsmen sometimes used *E. gardneri* as a substitute for *lokta* (*Daphne* sp.). They knew it as *argeli*. This grows at lower altitudes than *Daphne* sp. and may be cultivated. Its flowers have a purple colour and its leaves are more rounded in shape with a silkier surface. The fibres of *argeli* are rougher, which influences the texture, and they require longer to cook. The genus *Edgeworthia*, first named around 1840, contains five species that grow in Asia, among which there are four species in China (three endemic). The species of *Edgeworthia* used for papermaking in the Himalayas is *E. gardneri*, which grows in moist parts of forests in Tibetan cultural areas (E Xizang, NW Yunnan), Bhutan, India, North Myanmar, and Nepal at an elevation of between 1000 m and 2500(/3500) m. Other species of this genus that may be used are *E. eriosolenoides*, which grows in SE Yunnan (Xichou), and *E. albiflora*, which grows in the forests and valleys at an elevation of between 1000 m and 1200 m in south-western Sichuan (Huili, Miyi). The one most commonly used for papermaking is *E. chrysantha* (synonymous with *E. papyrifera*), which grows in forests and on shrubby slopes between 300 m and 1600 m in its natural habitat in the Chinese provinces of Fujian, Guangdong, Guangxi, Guizhou, Henan, Hunan, Jiangxi, Yunnan, and Zhejiang. It grows wild, but has often also been cultivated in Nepal, China, Korea, Georgia, and Japan, where it is naturalised.

The genus *Wikstroemia* has about 70 species and is widely distributed in eastern Asia, Malesia, and the Pacific islands. In China, there are 49 species (43 endemic) found mainly in southern China, especially in the Hengduan Mountains. *Wikstroemia* is considered to be closely related to *Daphne* and also used for papermaking in Tibet. It grows between 1200 m and 2500 m.

It should be noted that *Stellera chamaejasme* thrives at high elevations, and in some regions of Tibet it has been used as the main raw material in papermaking. *Stellera* is a small genus of fewer than 10 species found growing in comparatively dry conditions in areas such as Central Asia

[69] Sherpa et al. 2008: 1.

and parts of China, Tibet, Bhutan, Mongolia, Nepal, and Russia. It is widely distributed along the Himalayan range, where it is found on dry, sunny slopes and in sandy places at elevations of between 2600 m and 4500 m. This plant was recorded first by Nikolai Przhevalsky in 1873, and subsequently by Hossie in 1910, along with some other "so-called plant hunters", botanists and geographers. It is a pest which successfully competes with other species and quickly colonises degraded pasturelands. From the 1960s onwards, over-exploitation of pasture has been a widespread phenomenon all over the Tibetan Plateau and *Stellera* has been increasingly significant. This implies that, considering the amount of source material for papermaking that was available in the past, we cannot rely on its current abundance and distribution. On the other hand, it is the only species used in papermaking that grows at altitudes greater than 3500 m above sea level. The production of paper from these *Stellera* roots is thus practised in the highest places in the world, where practically nothing else grows.

These root bast (phloem) fibres create a very specific soft type of paper that is considered to be of lower quality than bark paper made from *Daphne*, *Edgeworthia*, or *Wikstroemia* spp. The roots are especially difficult to harvest and this seriously limits the quantity of paper that may be produced. They also require longer to process. In general they are thus only used in papermaking when other sources are unavailable. On the other hand, the poisonous properties of these plants even more than *Daphne* sp. make the paper resistant to damage by insects, meaning that it may ultimately be more durable than other types of paper.

Chef of herbarium from the Godavari Botanical Garden in Kathmandu, when asked what plants are used to make paper in Nepal, replied that everything that has fibres is used. This at first glance dismissive answer describes the situation in Nepal well, where the papermakers are constantly searching for new raw materials to make production cheaper and more efficient in conserving traditional *lokta* resources. Many other plants were thus also used in Nepal in recent years, such as jute (*Corchorus* sp.); sunn hemp (*Crotalaria juncea*), roselle (*Hibiscus sabdariffa*), and ramie (*Boehmeria nivea*).[70] In north-western India (presumably in the first decade of the nineteenth century) under the Gorkha Administration in Garhwal, as well as in the eastern Himalayan region, the bark of the Satpura or Setbaruwa plant was used to manufacture whitish coloured paper, which was supplied to Srinagar and Almora, and also exported to Nepal, Tibet, and the plains.[71]

Methods of production

The great altitude of the Himalayas and the climatic extremes combine to distinguish the local conditions and vegetation from all other areas of Asia. The specific nature of papermaking there lies in the properties of the native plants, the living conditions of the people dwelling in the world's highest mountains, along with aspects of their culture that together create a distinctive craft. Nepalese papermaking, like Tibetan papermaking, has traditionally been rural and regional. It has made use of the abundant local plant and fibre resources. Papermakers developed methods that would reflect the unique qualities of their raw materials, and this resulted in paper products as well as writing accoutrements for books and documents with distinctive properties and features. A knowledge of the distribution of those plants crucial to papermaking in the Himalayas and Central Asia sometimes means that we may trace paper to its place of origin.

Nepalese paper is usually produced between December and March, a season unsuitable for farming in mountains regions.[72] Farmers therefore spend this time on other occupations in order to supplement their income. The production of paper has thus always played an important rôle in improving the lives of farmers in the mountains. The actual method of papermaking in Nepal, as in other Himalayan regions, seems to have changed very little over the centuries.[73]

The Nepalese perspective on the quality of paper is influenced by two factors: local opportunities and aesthetic sensitivities dictated by tradition. According to Nepalese craftsmen the criteria according to which the quality is evaluated are as follows:

70 Premchand 1995; Soteriou 1999.

71 The *Regmi Research Series*.

72 Kartik, Mangsir, Falgun and Chaitra according to the Nepalese calendar.

73 Gajurel and Vaidya 1984.

a. All sheets of paper should be of a consistent weight.

b. The paper should not vary in thickness.

c. The size of the paper should be constant, i.e. 20 × 30 inches (ca. 50 × 75 cm).

d. The edges of the paper should not be torn or cracked.

e. The colour of paper should be natural.

Collecting the raw material

The collection of raw material is usually carried out by plant gatherers rather than papermakers. It is important to select trees that are sufficiently large to have ample bark, as smaller specimens tend to require much more time and labour to retrieve the amount of raw material necessary. In such cases separating the inner bark from outer bark during the cleaning process is a lengthy process and the quality of paper produced then is poorer. The use of immature shorter fibres also produces weaker paper that is more easily torn, which significantly impoverishes the quality. Ideally, thick *lokta* trees between five and seven centimetres thick should be selected. A tree's branches are measured by a simple knot placed where the branch meets the trunk to ascertain whether it is ripe for cutting. Correct selection of the raw material helps the fellers to collect between one and three *dharni* (2.4 kg) of *lokta* per day. The fibres of *lokta* have a pungent smell, which may cause an allergic reaction, and this is the reason collectors cover their mouths and noses, as well as using protective boots and glasses. Improper collection usually increases the cost. Cutting small plants also involves exploiting more natural forest resources in order to collect the required amount of *lokta*. Extensive exploitation of *lokta* may cause erosion and possible landslides. Thus, proper *lokta* collection is important in environmental protection.

When papermakers realised the problem regarding the availability of *Daphne* plants, they developed a plan for the gathering of *lokta*, so as to avoid local overexploitation. The available plants in the forest are thus divided into five areas. The first area is cut in the first year, leaving the four other areas of the forest for subsequent years. After five years harvesting thus returns to the first area, where the plants should already have re-grown. Following this scheme would mean that *lokta* is continuously available in the forest, and that the economy of the production should be stable. The systematic use of the *lokta* forest resources therefore also secures continuity in business and ensures a constant income.

Extracting and processing the raw material

The best raw material for making paper is the inner bark; in botanical terminology, the phloem. The strips of phloem are separated from the wood, and the outer bark removed while the inner bark is still fresh, as the task becomes harder when the material has dried (Fig. 163). The paper quality depends on both the quality of the fibres and on the extent to which the phloem fibres are extracted and cleaned of impurities. The process is most effective if done just after cutting the *lokta* plant. Nepalese craftsmen use special knives to peel off the outer bark. What remains is left to dry in the sun. This is an important step, since if such fresh raw material is not properly dried, it will turn black and the paper will be of poor quality.

The floor on which the *lokta* is laid to dry should be properly covered. This helps to prevent the raw material from damage as a result of cold and moisture. The well-dried *lokta* should be properly covered, tied and kept separately when stored.

Lokta is traditionally soaked in water for 24 hours. This helps to soften the fibres and then accelerates the cooking process. The strips of bast should be completely immersed in water. The material may otherwise oxidise and turn black, and this would compromise the quality of the final product. The soaked *lokta* is usually cut into strips approximately 15 cm in length and between 3 and 4 cm in width. During the cutting of the *lokta*, the impurities in the bark, such as black particles of outer bark and unwanted woody parts, are removed.

Figs 163 a–b. Strips of phloem peeled off *lokta* trees in Ghandruk. Outer bark is being separated from the wood with knife. Photographs by Agnieszka Helman-Ważny.

Today, caustic soda is also added to boiling *lokta*. This helps to break up the raw material into separate fibres. Soaking the raw material in water and adding caustic soda speed up the cooking process, which in the end significantly reduces the need for firewood and the cost of production.

Preparing the paper pulp (*lugdhi*)

At this stage the raw material would have to be made into pulp. The two main processes involved in this are first cooking and then beating.

Cooking (Fig. 164 a–b):

1 kg of dry *lokta* is mixed with the appropriate amount of water. 100 grams of caustic soda is added during the cooking of the *lokta* (10 % of the total weight of the dry *lokta*). The water used to cook *lokta* may be re-used within a day. When this happens, after taking out the cooked *lokta*, the remaining water may be re-used; only 5 % of caustic soda may be added to this. The time required to cook *lokta* tends to be determined on the basis of the papermaker's experience and the stage of preparation, i.e. how loose the fibres are. The *lokta* may therefore be checked to ascertain whether the material is sufficiently processed. The common test for determining whether the *lokta* is sufficiently cooked is to put a small amount of bast (a strip) in cold water and then stretch it. If the strip of *lokta* splits perpendicular to the direction of pulling, then it is considered sufficiently cooked. If not, it should be cooked longer.

Traditionally ash was used in the place of caustic soda. It would come from the firewood used as the main source of fuel in the Himalayas. Each family would collect the ash every day. The *lokta* entrepreneur would periodically exchange goods such as soap and matches and the like for the ash from every household. Using ash increases the quality of the paper and is environmentally friendly, but less effective than adding caustic soda, which significantly accelerates the process.

Ash would often be mixed with water and left until it sank to the bottom of the vessel. This alkaline solution, *pasani*, would then need to be filtered. A single batch of ash could be used three or four times to obtain *pasani* before the ash needed to be changed. The *pasani* water obtained from the ash filtering would still need to be mixed with 5% of caustic soda for cooking. The water mixed with the ash may be disposed of in the ground with no destructive environmental consequences. Caustic soda water, however, pollutes the ground and damages growing plants.

The time required for cooking depends on the amount of *lokta*, the hearth and the way in which the cooking vessel is covered. In the end a good hearth may save on firewood and time, and optimise the quality.

Once the *lokta* is cooked with either ash water or caustic soda it needs to be thoroughly washed. During the cleaning process the raw material should be gently stirred while it is contained in small net. The *lokta* is once more dipped in water, and impurities such as black patches and other waste products are removed by hand.

The *lokta* should be cleaned near a water source and should have good sunlight. The sunlight helps to gently bleach the *lokta* so that the resultant paper is whiter. Sunlight bleaching will, however, never turn paper as white as when bleach is added. Today bleaching agents such as chlorine, hydrogen peroxide, or sodium peroxide are often used in papermaking industry. However, they require strongly acidic or alkaline environments to be effective, and then need to be properly neutralized. Whenever the process is not fully controlled the usage of these chemicals can easily make the bleached paper in time structurally weaker and less resistant to damage. Papermakers thus try to avoid using bleach, with the result that *lokta* paper can maintain its reputation for being acid-free.

Beating:

The pulp (*lugdhi*) is then prepared by beating the cooked *lokta* on a stone with a wooden mallet (*mungro*). A good wooden mallet should be made with good quality hardwood, so that no wood chips falls from the hammer during the threshing. The slab on which *lugdhi* is beaten needs to be clean, so no impurities from it find their way into the pulp. Modern slabs tend to be 120 cm wide and 180 cm long and are usually made from cement to avoid cracking during the threshing. Whenever electricity is available, a special beating machine is used to accelerate the process (Fig. 165).

Figs 164 a–b. Cooking *lokta* bast in Karimela. Photographs by Agnieszka Helman-Ważny.

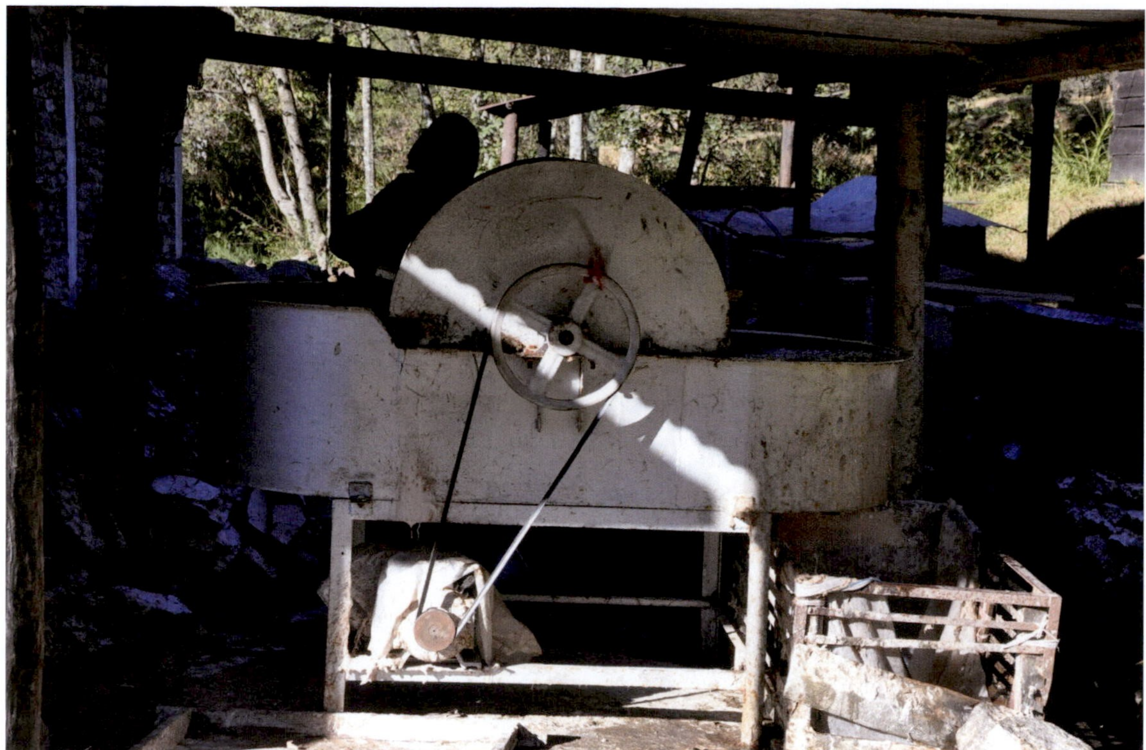

Fig. 165. Electric mixer for pulp processing. Photograph by Agnieszka Helman-Ważny.

Making the sheets of paper

At this stage, before the papermaker begins to make the sheets of paper, the following materials and tools need to be prepared: the pulp (*lugdhi*), a tank of water (*hauja*) and the papermaking mould (Fig. 166 a–b).

The pulp (*lugdhi*)

The beaten pulp should be mixed with water. The process of pulping and then the mixing of the pulp with the right amount of water is important for the quality of the paper. The water should be measured using the same vessel. The amount of pulp should also be carefully measured and kept at a constant consistency in order to maintain the correct weight for the paper, for example 5g, 10g or 15g. To prepare the correct amount of pulp, lumps of pulp are measured. The size of lump depends on the desired weight of the paper. In some places, instead of making lumps of pulp, they measure the mixture of pulp and water by using a jug. In such cases the weight of the paper may vary more and surplus pulp may then be wasted.

In order to make quality paper of a consistent weight the amount of water should first be measured and kept in a bucket. A proportionate amount of pulp should then be carefully added to the water in order to produce paper of a consistent weight. Before using a mug to add the pulp to the water, it should be mixed well by hand.

The water tank (*hauja*)

The water tank (*hauja*) is a sufficiently large vessel filled with water for the papermaking mould to float freely on it so that the paper can be levelled. The hauja may traditionally have been a natural reservoir of water such as a river, a pond, a lake or even a puddle on the surface of which a sheet of paper might be formed. Today it tends to be a large tank made of cement, smooth inside so that dust does not gather when levelling the paper. The tank should have a hole at the bottom, so that the water might easily be removed after the day's work, when the *hauja* may be thoroughly cleaned.

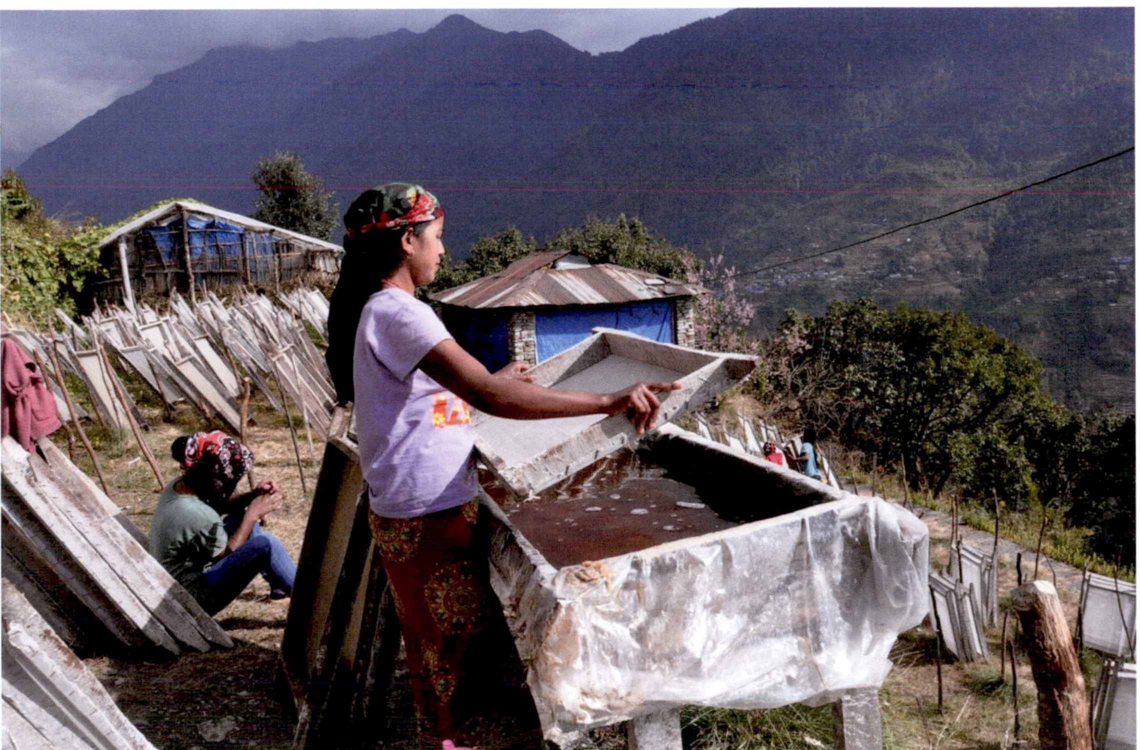

Figs 166 a–b. Making a sheet of paper in Ghandruk. Photographs by Agnieszka Helman-Ważny.

The papermaking mould

The sizes of the papermaking frames are determined by the size of paper needed. The wood used for the frame should be resistant to distortions, smooth, and of good quality. A good quality wooden-framed strainer of appropriate shape and size should also be used. It should be stretched tightly across the frame. A poor quality strainer may lead to tears and other flaws in the final product (Fig. 167).

Sal tree wood (*Shorea robusta*) is considered the best material for the frames for papermaking moulds.[74] The wood pieces should be well fixed so that the frame does not come loose with time and the shape of the paper does not deform. The use of iron nails would cause the frame to become loose with time and the paper shape would thus be skewed.

The mould type traditionally used in Nepal is called a floating mould because it is placed on the surface of a body of water, such as a lake, a pond, a river or a puddle. The other main type of papermaking mould is usually known as a dipping mould, and is thought to have developed after the floating mould. The dipping mould allows faster production of paper because it permits the removal of a wet sheet of paper directly from the sieve immediately after shaping. This means that papermakers need not wait until the paper has dried before using the mould to begin the next sheet. The main difference between the two types of mould is in their construction. The floating mould is made of a wooden frame with a woven textile attached to it. In the dipping mould, on the other hand, a movable sieve made from bamboo, reed or another kind of grass is attached to the wooden frame. Modifications to this technology have been reported, including a floating mould resembling a wooden box with a movable screen.

Independent of the techniques of the sheet formation, all papermaking sieves make an impression that is specific to the construction of the mould and sieve. This print is unaffected by most aging processes, and can be read centuries later. The print of a textile sieve made of cotton, hemp, or flax differs clearly from that of a movable sieve from a dipping mould made of bamboo, reed or other grasses. This information alone, however, cannot be used for the identification of the paper's provenance. According to Dard Hunter, in the south-western regions of China and the Himalayas the floating mould would often be used, whereas in the east the dipping mould with a bamboo sieve was developed.[75] Both types of mould would, however, have been used simultaneously from the early days of papermaking in Central Asia, and we have to take into consideration that the same papermaking workshop may have used both types of mould at the same time.[76]

As mentioned above, the modern Japanese papermaking mould is sometimes used, especially in the Kathmandu Valley (Fig. 168). While making paper in this way the *lugdhi* produced after beating is weighted according to need and then spread with help of *nuri* (mucilage) mixed with water. The quantity of *nuri* is increased in order to make thinner sheets of paper. To increase the weight of the paper the quantity of *nuri* is reduced and the quantity of *lugdhi* is increased. Such papermaking technology allows for a quicker drying process when sheets of paper (*tahu*) may be piled up while still wet and left on frames until totally dried. When a pile of between 200 and 300 sheets of paper is complete, it is put in the press and 70 percent of the water is removed and the sheets are then separated to dry in sunlight. The use of *nuri* means that the separate sheets of paper do not stick to one another during the pressing process.

[74] *Shorea robusta*, also known as sal, sakhua or the shala tree, is a species of tree belonging to the Dipterocarpaceae family.

[75] Hunter 1978: 84; Schaeffer 2009: 8.

[76] Helman-Ważny and van Schaik 2013.

Figs 167 a–b. Traditional papermaking moulds with cloth strainer on a wooden frame. Photographs by Agnieszka Helman-Ważny.

Figs 168 a–b. a) Japanese type of mould used in Kathmandu. b) Papermaking sieve made of bamboo doubled with textile. Photographs by Agnieszka Helman-Ważny.

The use of *nuri*

In the Japanese papermaking process, the use of *nuri* prevents flocculation and allows for a more even mix of the pulp (*lugdhi*) and water. The paper produced with *nuri* is therefore more even in thickness across the whole sheet. Naturally, the longer and more slender the papermaking fibres, the stronger their tendency to form relatively dense assemblies, or "flocs," in water suspension, and papermakers use the word "flocculation" to describe the phenomenon as it later manifests in the paper's uneven appearance when seen against light. This means that the most valuable papermaking fibres (longer fibres) are much more difficult to use in the papermaking, and require a special moulding technique.

This is the reason why mixing *nuri* with water before forming the sheets helps to spread the fibres evenly in the water tank *hauja*. One spoon of *nuri* is usually mixed in a separate bucket (*c.* 15 litres) of water and then left for 24 hours.[77] This solution is then added to the *hauja* and stirred thoroughly with the help of a wooden stick. The caustic soda should be washed carefully especially when *nuri* is used. Plant extracts may often be used instead of *nuri* in East Asia.

Before the sheet of paper is formed the pulp is mixed with water and poured onto the mould in measured quantities.

At this stage the papermaking mould is placed in a water tank, a *hauja*. The same vessel is used to measure the mixture of *lugdhi* and water which is poured into the strainer. The *lugdhi* kept in the strainer should be level so that the paper thickness is constant (Figs 169 a–b).

The papermaker then moves the frame in the water until the pulp covers the surface of the mould entirely and equally. He or she then tilts the frame gently to keep the sieve at the same level, until the water drains off. If the strainer is not lifted correctly, then there may be a chance of a bulge forming in the paper. The mould, with its newly-made sheet of paper, is then left undisturbed until the sheet is dry.

The drying process

At this stage the frames with new-made sheets of paper are left to dry in the sun. The drying frame should not be in a damp or muddy place.

The paper sheets are usually left to dry on the mountain slope, so that there is no stagnant water. Stands made from bamboo are used for drying. The frames should ideally face south in an inclined position while drying. There should be an appropriate distance between the stands, so that one frame casts no shade on another during the process. The place should be carefully selected and grass should be cut to avoid any dampness that might prolong the drying process. During the periods of time when papermaking moulds are unused on a daily basis, they should be cleaned, dried and stored in good condition, so they are neither distorted nor damaged.

The paper is removed from the frame only when it is completely dry. The condition of the paper is ascertained by looking at the bottom of the frame. If the sheet of paper is dry at the bottom, then the whole paper is dry. The paper should be removed carefully to avoid tearing it at the edges.

[77] The proportion should be 2 millilitres of *nuri* for 1 litre of water.

Figs 169 a–b. a) Levelling the pulp just poured on the papermaking sieve in Ghandruk; b) Forming the paper sheet and draining the water out. Photographs by Agnieszka Helman-Ważny.

Chapter 7
Mustang Paper:
A Glimpse into the Economic History of Paper Production in Western Nepal

"Mustang paper" – has anybody heard of it?

This chapter presents the first attempt at a reconstruction of the history of paper in Mustang after the eighteenth century, from two main mutually corroborative sources in the face of a complete lack of written sources on this subject. These are the documents themselves, accordingly dated – by looking at collections of the actual documents, identifying the paper and fibre components, and reconstructing the history of papermaking from the findings – and from the living tradition of papermaking that persists in various areas of Western Nepal, a tradition that could potentially be related to traditions in Mustang.

Considerable numbers of local manuscripts and documents preserved in village archives suggest that paper was relatively easily accessible in Western Nepal. Bearing in mind that the canyon of the Kali Gandaki River is one of the few corridors linking the world of the High Tibetan Plateau with the lower tropical lands of India, it is unsurprising that paper was a commodity traded on the nearby trade route. It also suggests that, in spite of the fact that no workshops have survived, paper had already been produced here, and it was known in Tibet as "Mustang paper." There are, however, no written records confirming this fact, but some senior Mustang inhabitants shared their memories of this during interviews conducted in 2015 and 2016.

Further, during travels in western Tibet in 2013, people mentioned the high quality paper they used to receive in trade from Mustang.[1] Later Rinchen Loden Lama from Humla also told us the story which is depicted in the *gompa* in Limi portraying the caravan of yaks that was sent to Mustang to bring paper for the interior of the large prayer mill. Our fieldwork in Mustang revealed neither active papermaking workshops nor people who had ever been directly involved in papermaking. We were, however, able to find people who clearly remembered those who produced paper or books there at least one generation ago. It should be noted here that it was difficult to discern the precise time referred to by these interviewees. They tended only to use expressions for "now" or "a long time ago". We were able to work out that "now" would mean up to about ten years ago, within living memory, and "a long time ago" meant two or three generations ago.

In the villages in Mustang we would ask village elders, medical doctors and older monks, and were able to confirm that in Mustang paper had been made in Dzar and Tiri, but that this had ceased at least fifteen years previously. In Dzar, we learned that the last person who had made paper and who could recall other families who shared the profession there had died fifteen years before. There was thus nobody with a detailed memory of this. In 2015 in Tiri, a small village twenty minutes' walk from Kagbeni along the upper Kali Gandaki River, we found an eighty-eight-year-old man named Samphel Dondrup, who shared with us his memories of books, trade of writing materials, papermaking and writing in the region (Fig. 170). He remembered that when he was a child, in about 1930, people made paper and books in his village. They collected raw material from the shrub forest above the village, possibly at about 3000m above sea level. The forest above Tiri was called Pangka Mutin. It was impossible to confirm whether this forest still exists, since nothing is visible from lower down the hill where we were. He did not know the name of the plant used to make the paper. Nor did he know *recakpa* (Tib. *re lcag pa*), *Stellera*. People in Tiri called a plant used to make paper a "paper tree," which suggests *Daphne* rather than *Stellera*, which is a herb rather

[1] Fieldwork in La stod area of Western Tibet conducted in collaboration with Hildegard Diemberger in June 2013.

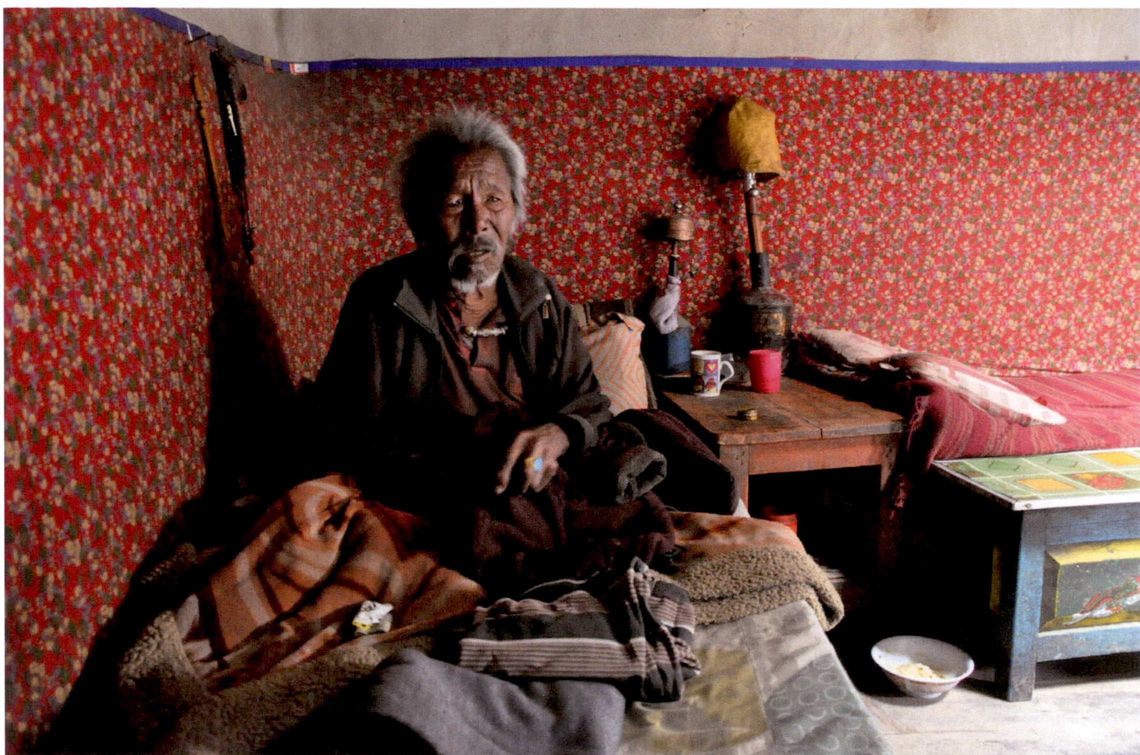

Fig. 170. Samphel Dondrup in his house in Tiri, interviewed in 2015. Photograph by Agnieszka Helman-Ważny.

than a tree. Sampel Dondup said that production in Tiri was very small-scale home production, as opposed to the large-scale operations in the area around Beni. He mentioned that, if people in Mustang needed paper for some important projects, they ordered it from Beni, the headquarters of Myagdi District. The places he mentioned where paper was made were the Ghar/Pakthar, area across the Kali Gandaki River. He also informed us that in the past *subbās* from Tukche took a great deal of paper to Lo Monthang, and from Lo Monthang they bought wool and brought it down to Butwal near the Indian border, where people had looms.

If people in the villages needed to have any legal document written, they would ask those who knew how to write. Those who knew how to write tended to be able to make ink and writing tools. According to what Sampel Dondup remembered they would mix soot and water to make ink. He also mentioned two types of paper, *dab shog* of better quality suitable for writing and *kyin shog* of inferior quality and used for making flags among other purposes. In response to enquiries regarding the places where people produced paper and books in the area, he first mentioned an area around Beni, a place named Rangok. He remembered from his childhood the paper drying on the moulds all around this area. He also mentioned Tichurong, in southern Dolpo, as a place associated with papermaking in the past.

Our colleague Nyima Drandul Gurung from Mustang remembered that his grandfather had made paper in Tshognam or Chongkhor. Considering the fact that his grandfather was seventy-seven when Nyima was 5, we may assume that paper production took place there in the early twentieth century, possibly around 1930. Nyima's grandfather learned his skills in Drakar Taso, near Kyirong in Tibet, and may have used *Stellera* roots to make his paper. Our sample of paper produced by Nyima's grandfather appeared after microscopic identification, however, to have been made of grass rather than *Stellera*. None of the papermakers interviewed mentioned the use of grass as an ingredient in Mustang. The presence of grass in some examples of Mustang paper therefore remains unexplained.

Interestingly, during interviews conducted in the area south of Mustang, when we asked papermakers whether they had heard of Mustang paper, nobody was able to provide any information. Some did not even know where Mustang was. Moti Raj Gautam from Darbang had not heard of Mustang paper, and he had never sold paper or raw material to Mustang. He had, however, heard that paper was brought to Tibet from Kathmandu. He also remembered that eleven or twelve years years before people would make paper in their homes. They would use simple tools, such as wooden hammers and wooden frames with cotton sieves on them. Such places produced paper solely for their own purposes.

When asked about what he knew about the history of Nepalese paper, Jagat Thing from Ghandruk said that he knew nothing about paper in the past. He had only heard from village elders that if one was injured, and placed *lokta* paper on the wound, it was extremely efficacious. His knowledge was therefore of more practical aspects of life. *Daphne* and *Stellera* both have medicinal properties and are a part of Tibetan pharmacopeia usually associated with Tibetan doctors.

Documents, papers and plants

Given that the papermaking and bookmaking tradition of Mustang died out at least 15 years ago, documentary materials found in remaining Himalayan archives, such as those from the villages of Geling, Lubrak, Dzar and Tshognam, are an extremely valuable source of knowledge about local paper and book production. The documents were locally produced and mostly dated to the year, and often to the day. The majority are from between the mid-nineteenth and the mid-twentieth centuries, but a few are from the early eighteenth century. The reconstruction of paper history therefore pertains to exactly the same period of time. Extant archival documents provide information essential not only to tracing the history and clarifying, among other things, the materials and technology employed, but also the pragmatic, social and economic factors involved in making paper. Apart from their textual content these local archives are evidence in their own material sphere, which can be retrieved by scientific examination of the materials composing them.

As reported in chapter 5, the raw material identified in our sample of 330 documents from Mustang was relatively homogenous, with the majority of the papers made from the Thymelaeaceae family of plants, including a variety of species such as *Daphne/Edgeworthia* and *Stellera*. Most documents were written on paper made from: 1) pure *Daphne/Edgeworthia* sp. fibres; 2) pure *Stellera* sp. fibres; 3) *Daphne/Edgeworthia* sp. mixed with *Stellera* sp. fibres; 4) paper based on previous compositions with the addition of singular recycled cotton or hemp fibres; 5) wood pulp; and 6) documents on paper made with a variety of grasses.

Fibre analyses failed to distinguish *Daphne* from *Edgeworthia*, and we must therefore consider the presence of both in our sample. From the interviews conducted, however, we learned that only *lokta* (*Daphne bholua*) was used for making paper in this region. Bearing this in mind, we may exclude *argeli* (*Edgeworthia* sp.). According to Poorna Bahadur Gurung, the owner of the papermaking workshop "Annapurna Lokta Paper & Handicraft" in Ghandruk, only wild-grown *lokta* is used in this region for making paper. He informed us, however, that today *argeli* is also widely used in other parts of Nepal and that it may be cultivated. According to Bal Krishna from Lekphat, *argeli*, also used for making paper in other regions, has a harder and stiffer bark and longer leaves. It is why it was also used for making robes. He thinks that the same plant may have different coloured flowers. Jagat Thing, a papermaker from the same factory in Ghandruk also said that everybody in the region gathered only *lokta*, but that he had heard about other plants used for papermaking in other places or abroad, such as banana, *alaichi* (black cardamom), *babiyo* (sabai, *Eulaliopsis binata*) and *khar* (grass). These must always, however, be mixed with *lokta*. He said that *lokta* grows at high altitudes and is not found at lower levels, so other plants were used at lower elevations.

Stellera was identified in almost half of our samples. In the literature it is usually mentioned in the context of Tibetan papermaking. Most of the papermakers we interviewed had not heard of this plant, which suggests that *Stellera* has never been used by Nepalese papermakers. This also suggests that some of the studied documents could have been written on paper produced in Tibet. However, it is not possible yet to identify the location more precisely.

We rarely found singular cotton or hemp fibres added to *Daphne* or *Stellera* paper. These examples may have originated from old cloth, robes or other textile waste recycled into new-made paper. Cotton could even have been from old, damaged papermaking sieves which through overuse had found its way into the pulp of new paper. Recycled cotton or hemp fibres were widely used in Central Asian paper, first found in the famous collection of Dunhuang and Turfan manuscripts.[2] Wood pulp points to modern industrial production, which never existed in Mustang or anywhere else in the vicinity. That type of paper was therefore probably imported, most likely from India or China. Grasses were commonly added in the Kathmandu Valley, but they were not used for making paper in Nepal alone. In our sample grass was found in a few documents from the Tshognam and Lubrak archives.

The questions that arise from the recorded raw materials concern the provenance of particular types of paper: what types of paper were locally produced in villages where archives were established, and what kinds were traded from farther afield. Bearing in mind that the villages under consideration here are located in the heart of the Kali Gandaki Valley corridor, which was a highway for travellers, traders and monks, as well as an obvious route for the dissemination of new ideas and technologies between Central Asia and India, we have two natural directions from which paper could be traded: north and south.

The villages whose archives we studied are all located at least 3000 m above sea level, which represents the upper range of *Daphne* sp. plants. This suggests that paper made of *Daphne* sp., used for the largest group of manuscripts, was probably brought to Mustang from more low-lying valleys, such as the Myagdi and Baglung Districts. The *Stellera* sp. plants present in a group of samples possibly originated from neighbouring villages, or elsewhere imported from the Tibetan Plateau, where the plant was often used. It was impossible to map the distribution of *Stellera* only on the basis of literature and botanical databases. During our fieldwork, therefore, besides looking at the distribution of papermaking plants in the Godavari Botanical Garden Herbarium in Kathmandu, during interviews with collectors of medicinal herbs we also took notes and GPS co-ordinates for places where papermaking plants are abundant today.

Stellera chamaejasme, known locally as *sibri mentok* (*sibri* means "smell of sweat"; *mentok* means "flower"), was very common around Muktinath, Dzar, Khingar and in the vicinity of Lo Monthang. Around Muktinath it begins at above 3300 m above sea level and grows up to 4000 m above sea level. It grows in abundance in the valleys and on the slopes. People there did not know, however, whether this plant had ever been used for papermaking in Tibet, or whether it may also have been used in Mustang for making paper.

Despite almost all our sample papers having been made in floating moulds with a textile sieve attached, when looking at sieve prints we observe some variety. The majority of the samples showed regular woven sieve prints with no pattern, which suggests that this paper was made with traditional cotton sieves. A significant amount of the paper in the sample, however, shows the clear pattern of a textile woven from coarse yarn, as seen in document MA/Geling/Tib/128 from the Geling archive in Chapter 5 (Fig. 131). Since none of the interviewees mentioned a sieve made from a coarsely woven textile, we may probably assume that this material was used in earlier times or only locally. Our interviewees informed us about nylon sieves that have been used in recent years, but the print of nylon sieve texture was undetected in our sample. Thus, results of paper examination tallied with information collected during the interviews with papermakers. Jagat Thing from Ghandruk presented us with modern papermaking moulds with nylon sieves, but told us that in the past only cotton sieves were used. According to him the cotton sieves needed to be replaced at least every two months, and a nylon sieve may be used for between seven and eight months. Dhala Bahadur Thing, a plant gatherer from Ghandruk also explained that in the past, there would be a *shore* (cloth strainer), which had very small holes. Strainers today are made from nylon. He added that with careful use nylon strainers last for between five and six months. Cloth strainers, on the other hand, are less durable, and with good care may last between two and three months.

[2] Helman-Ważny 2016c.

It is difficult to ascertain the size of papermaking moulds from extant documents, since they would have been cut to a desired format. Information collected from our interviewees shed some light on the typical sizes of papermaking moulds, and so on the sheets of paper produced. Bal Krishna from Lekphat informed us that the size of paper made in the past was four times the size we have today.[3] Moti Raj Gautam from Darbang informed us that the standard mould frame sizes are 20 × 30 inches (50.8 × 76.2 cm). According to Jagat Thing from Ghandruk the standard sizes of papermaking moulds in Ghandruk are 22 × 32 cm and 37 × 54 cm. Even from those few dimensions it is possible to see that there were no strict standards for the size of paper.

Lokta collectors and their job

Interviews suggest that the collection of raw material was not done by papermakers. Collecting papermaking plants was an established profession. However, there are probably very few people who are full-time gatherers of papermaking plants. People from villages in papermaking regions would usually take the job periodically to boost their income. One person would usually be able to collect up to 40 kg per day. The raw material tended to be collected within about a three-hour walk of the village and with the permission of the community forest office. For example, people from the village of Taman would collect *lokta* from the slopes of the hills above less than a two-hour walk from their village. In Darbang anyone from the village could collect *lokta*, but in 2015 the factory paid 100 rupees per kilo of *lokta*. Local people could thus take on an extra job. The factory paid taxes to the Forestry Department, since for the collection of *lokta* they use communal forests. They pay taxes of 5 rupees per kilo. Sometimes they buy or collect raw materials from other places and in such cases they pay royalties. The community forest would be divided into five or six blocks, and exploited one by one every year. However, they would always collect raw material from Myagdi District. Tul Bahadur Pun from Salija informed us that *lokta* plants were collected by about a hundred people from this ward alone. Collectors are paid at a rate of 35 rupees per kilo. The forest they gather *lokta* from belongs to the VDC, but only their ward has worked there so far. The neighbouring wards may, however, participate in the future. Bal Krishna from Lekphat told us that people used to collect *lokta* from the forest of Hampar, at an altitude between 3000 and 3500m above sea level, three hours on foot north of Lekphat. They would collect yearly branches. They would cut it one year and it would re-grow the next year.

People also tried to grow *lokta*, albeit without much success. There was, however, one exception: a man from Ramche Nangi known to locals as "nursery grandpa" was involved in protecting the forest and growing plants for papermaking and medicinal herbs for more than 40 years.[4] His name is Moti Bahadur Purja (Fig. 171). He is 72 years old and his face is full of wrinkles. He wears old clothes and worn shoes, and is more energetic than most young people in his village. He shared a snippet of his biography with us. When he was fifteen years old he fought on the British side in the Brunei revolt in 1962, for which he received permanent British citizenship. He did not, however, stay in the United Kingdom, but instead returned to his village and became involved in protecting the local forest. He registered a nursery for the purpose of planting commercial crops, including those used for food, medicine and papermaking. It has already been almost half a century since he created the nursery in Nangi. The plants first cultivated in the nursery are then planted in the forest. Moti Bahadur Purja believes that his work is beneficial to the villagers, but even more so to posterity. He focuses on the protection of endangered species. In 2017, when we visited him in Nangi, he had thirty endangered species of medicinal plants, seven species of rhododendrons, and various other rare species of plants, together in the region of twenty thousand different species.

[3] The sample we obtained is thick, used for covers and packing. For writing, thinner and better-quality paper was used. Samples were bought four years previously in Khania Ghat (produced in 2011).

[4] He was also mentioned in the national press: "Nursery grandfather of the forest conservation," *Kantipur*, Kathmandu, Feb. 14th, 2017.

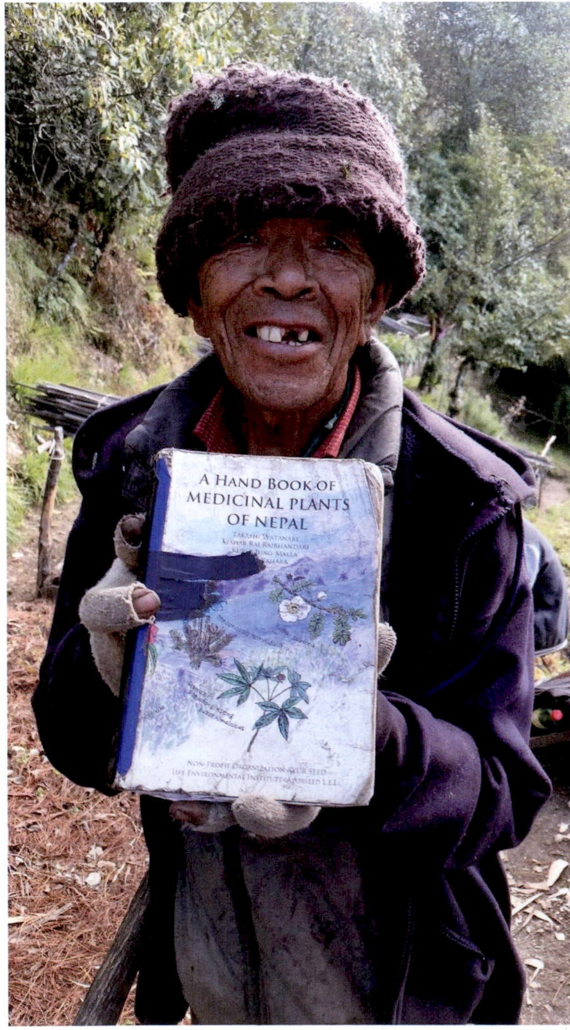

Figs 171 a–b. Moti Bahadur Purja, "nursery grandpa," showing us the book he follows to cultivate medicinal plants. Photographs by Agnieszka Helman-Ważny (above) and Rinchen Loden Lama (below).

Jagat Thing from Ghandruk said that they usually collect *lokta* during Bhadra, Ashoj, Kartik and Mangsir (mid-August to mid-December), as official permission (*purji*) has been granted to the community for those four months. The next collection period of time has been granted during the months of Falgun, Chaitra, Baishak and Jestha (mid-February to May). During that time they go to extract the *lokta* from the forest, carry it down the mountain and dry it. During the rainy season they refrain from collecting *lokta* due to mist, rain, and fog. It is extremely difficult to extract the bark at that time. He also explained that cutting *lokta* from a thick forest is beneficial to the forest, since it makes these trees expand and produce more. If the forest is not thinned the lifespan of a *lokta* tree is normally about ten years. After ten years the branches begin to dry and rot sets in. They therefore usually cut the thick branches and leave the thin ones.

We also had the good fortune to meet Dhala Bahadur Thing, a seventy-four-year-old plant collector from Ghandruk. He was more than happy to share his knowledge and told us about his work. He usually gathers *lokta* in local forest, then weighs it while raw, and spreads it out to dry. First, outer layer of the bark has to be peeled off, then the inner part is dried. He usually makes bundles of one *dharni* (2.5kg) each and weighs each bundle in a *tula* (beam balance) to prepare it for sale. This was the work that his grandfathers used to do in exactly the same way. We also learned that *lokta* bark may be collected at any time in the forest, but that it is best when extracted in summer. During the rainy season it is soft and tender, but during the winter months, Mangsir and Paush (December and January) it sticks stubbornly to wood. From Falgun (February) bark becomes increasingly easy to extract until Asar and Srawan (June and July), when bark may be peeled off with ease. During the monsoon, while peeling off bark, water splashes from it and hits one in the face. In winter the wood is not watery, so the bark must then be forcibly pulled off.

Bal Krishna, however, who used to be papermaker in Lekphat, considers the period from December to February as the best months to collect raw materials. He informed us that, because it was a long way to the gathering place, people might even prepare the raw material where it was collected in the forest. They would peel off the phloem; then strip off the outer bark and bring it to the village already in clean strips of inner bark. The plants would be collected at 2500 m above sea level.

After being peeled off, the bark strips would be wrapped tightly and moved to the factory. Dhala Bahadur Thing said that only trees of between two and three metres in height are cut roughly 30 cm from the ground in the forest, thus allowing the trees the chance to recover. They use the inner bark from both the trunk and the branches, so that nothing is wasted. They peel the inner bark in the forest and the rest they leave there until it has dried, when it is brought to the village and used for firewood.

Papermaking sites south of Mustang

The locations of papermaking workshops were not mentioned in any of the documents studied; nor can they be ascertained from an examination of the paper used to make the documents. Further ethnographic research is therefore necessary in order to shed some light on the existing paper factories, and this was done by Agnieszka Helman-Ważny with the help of Kemi Tsewang and Rinchen Loden Lama, who visited selected sites located in the districts of Myagdi, Baglung, Pharbat, and Kaski in Western Nepal, south of Mustang. The location of these places in Nepal today is difficult to determine. We obtained the list of small industries in Nepal with the kind help of Bal Ran Gautou from the Regional Service Centre of the Dhaulagiri Community Resource Development Centre (DCRDC), Baglung. On the long list we obtained, only four places claiming to produce paper were mentioned, as may be seen from the table below (Fig. 172). These were Taman, Tara khola, Ransinghkiteni and Darbang-Phulbari.

Research visit schedule:

Name of VDC	District	Remarks
Taman	Baglung	Handmade paper, 7 hrs from Baglung
Tara khola	Baglung	Handmade paper, 6 hrs from Baglung
Ransignhkiteni	Baglung	Using machine, 6 hrs from Baglung
Darbang-Phulbari	Myagdi	Herb gathering and papermaking, *Shole* herbs P. Ltd., 3 hrs from Baglung

Fig. 172. List of papermaking locations obtained from the Regional Service Centre of the Dhaulagiri Community Resource Development Centre (DCRDC), Baglung.

Any region known for papermaking would usually be characterised by workshops in close proximity to each other, often grouped along a river or in some other location favourable for papermaking. Indeed, on the map those places tended to be located relatively close to each other. The lack of roads, however, means that we usually needed between five and nine hours to reach the place. Out of four such places it was still possible to find only three. As we learned during our fieldwork, finding these places was quite an adventure; sometimes involving hours of trekking and a jeep drive on bumpy mountain passages; impossible to reach during the monsoon. They were also great fun and we felt great satisfaction when we found these locations.

It should be noted that the government record we obtained did not always reflect reality. The only way to verify whether those workshops still existed was thus to visit the places. The next important source of information was the Nepal Handmade Paper Association (HANDPASS) in Kathmandu, which we found and contacted in 2016. Their representatives kindly provided a list of their members, who are Nepal's registered papermakers.

These papermaking factories were located in the mountains, usually at the elevation at which *lokta* was found, and not always in close vicinity to larger villages or towns. In fact some of those factories are unregistered, and people living nearby hardly even know where to find them or how to get there. Some, however, are registered and lists of small industries may be found in district offices, such as the one that we obtained in Baglung. Such places usually exist for a couple of years, and only sometimes remain active for a longer period of time. Unlike larger factories in Kathmandu, these are usually small workshops producing paper on a small scale. In Kathmandu, most of these places are run by dealers rather than papermakers. They sometimes operate for only short periods during the year, and use recycled materials, or produce decorative products such as wrapping paper, notebooks, lamps or postcards. They also sell paper bought from smaller factories in the mountains including those we visited. More rarely, they buy raw material from collectors and make paper from scratch.

To ascertain whether local people know anything about the history of paper in Nepal, we asked them whether they knew of the existence of other papermaking factories in the region and in Nepal in general. In 2015, Bal Krishna from Lekphat informed us about the papermaking factory in Salija on the other side of the same mountain. Moti Raj Gautam, aged fifty-three, from the village of Darbang-Phulbari knew of four other papermaking factories in Myagdi District. These were Lulang, no longer in operation due to insufficient power; Pakhapani, no longer in operation due to insufficient water and power supply, as well as a lack of qualified workers resulting in their paper being of too poor a quality for commercial success because the workers received too little training; Nangi, still in operation; and Phulbari, in operation on a seasonal basis. Bal Krishna from Lekphat remembered another factory called Khania Ghat (Pharse), which was known for papermaking. He said that from there paper and rice were taken up to Tibet and traded for salt.

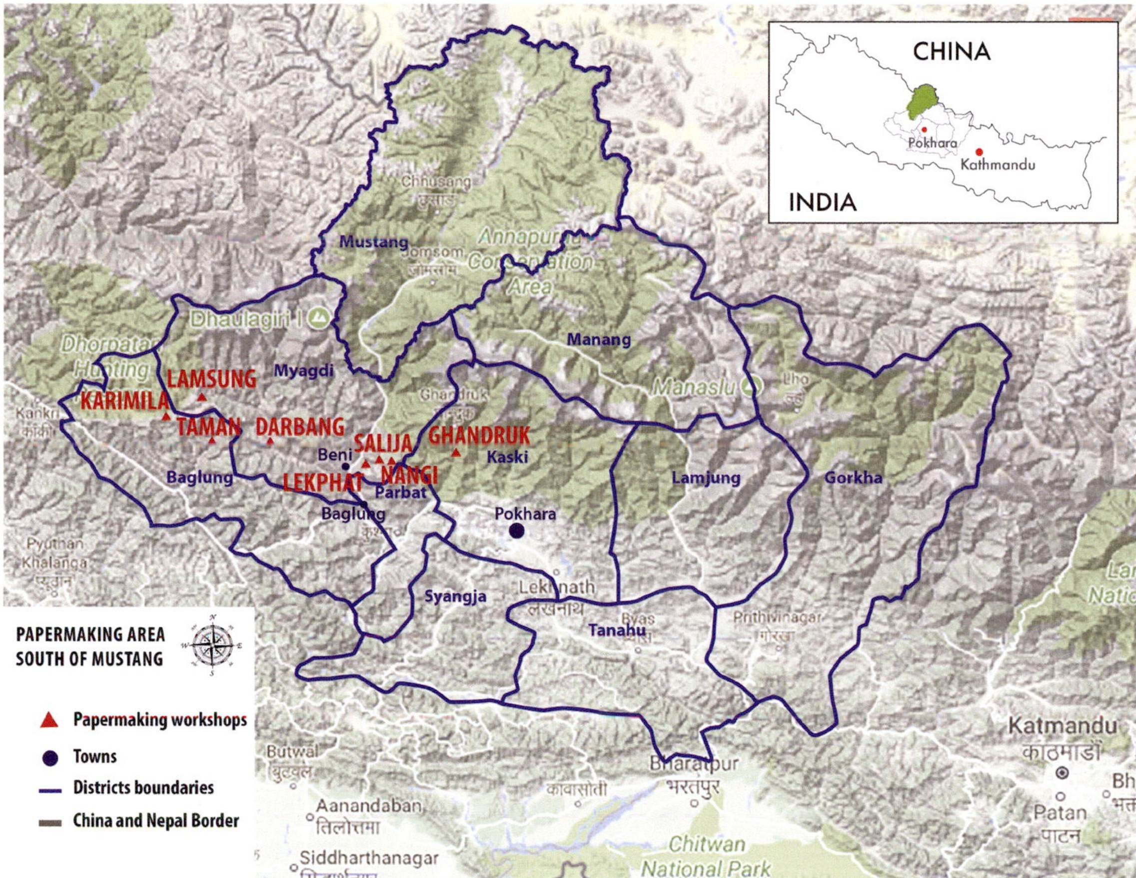

Fig. 173. Map of papermaking workshops located south of Mustang. Map by Dorota Helman.

Finally, we visited eight places south of Mustang: Lekphat, Salija, Ghandruk, Taman, Darbang-Phulbari, Lamsung, Karimila and Nangi (Fig. 173). These places were accessible with difficulty, usually requiring a drive of between seven and nine hours by jeep and a couple of hours' walk from main towns. This probably explains the reason why these places produce paper by traditional methods on a small scale. Their paper is of excellent quality, but it is difficult for them to sell their products due to insufficient paved roads and correspondingly expensive transportation.

Karimila, in Baglung District

This place was called Karimila in Tala Khola VDC (Village Development Committee), ward N° 7. It is now known as Rural Municipality Ward N° 5. The factory is known as the Julphe Handicraft workshop in Karimila, and is located in the valley near the river, at an elevation of 2088 m above sea level. It was established in 2013 (2070 BS) and in the last two or three years has been supported by the Baglung branch of the Federation of the Nepalese Chambers of Commerce and Industry. The workshop has been operating as a collective of between twenty and twenty-two workers for three years. Dhan Parsad Budha, aged fifty, whom we interviewed in 2017, informed us that this factory had ceased to operate as a village community. In the past, before the group was formed, it was operated by individual houses according to their capacity for buying *lokta* for the production. A group of private owners formed a union in order to obtain the help of an NGO (NGOs would not help individuals). This factory is thus now supported by the Samudayik Ban Pariyojana (the Community Forest Programme), an organisation known as Li-Bird which provided machinery, and the Udhyog Banijya Sangh (the Federation of the Nepalese Chamber of Commerce and Industry, Baglung) which takes care of market management and helps to sell Karimila paper.

There is an abundance of *lokta* in this area, and many people worked as plant gatherers. In time, people decided that instead of exporting the raw material they should learn to produce paper themselves. After the training, between 80 and 90 people began to produce paper.

Lamsung, in Myagdi District

This papermaking factory is located in Lamsung 5 in the district of Myagdi at an altitude of 2160 m above sea level, eight hours' trek from Darbang. We visited Lamsung on 7 November, 2017 and interviewed Kesar Bahadur Purja from Dolari, a recently elected member of the rural municipality N° 2. He used to manage a local team. Production had ceased in July 2016, when a monsoon landslide had cut off the road and destroyed the power station. A year later in July 2017 the monsoon caused further damage to the road. The power supply was cut off and thenceforth the factory ceased operating entirely.

The idea of establishing the factory arose from the abundance of *lokta* which had been exported to Khanyaghat. An NGO called "Sangam" then came to train about fifteen local people in papermaking. The paper they made was sold to the Bhaktapur Hastakala, then to Tibetan Handicraft in Kathmandu, for a higher price.

Taman, in Baglung District

At the time we visited Taman on 30 November and 1 December 2016 there were no active papermaking workshops, but there were people who had worked in paper production in recent years. The village is located at an elevation of 2048 m above sea level, and it is a long way from surfaced roads. Access is thus rather difficult and only possible by four-wheel-drive jeep. In the past, the transportation of goods was only possible thanks to porters or mules, and the journey took two or three days. Today, Taman-Baglung is six or seven hours away by car. This village is known for papermaking, and everybody there knew how to make paper. Many households still had traditional tools, such as mallets, papermaking frames, stones on which the *lokta* bast was beaten and wooden containers used as pools. Most people in the village were farmers, and papermaking has always been a sideline for them. They are no longer making paper. The labour-intensive nature of traditional paper production means that it is no longer profitable, bearing in mind the labour required with only simple, traditional tools. Traditional methods meant that they were unable to attain sufficient quality to sell their product for a reasonable price. It was sold at just 5 rupees per sheet. Another factor is that the village of Taman is a long way from surfaced roads, and access is difficult even in the dry season. It is therefore a long way from the tourist market. People also mention the strong scent of *lokta* as a reason for the production's demise, and the fact that some *lokta* collectors and papermakers suffer from skin problems and allergies.

Indra Kumari Buda, sixty-four years old, from the village of Lamala, Taman, whom we interviewed, could not remember exactly when she began papermaking, but she knew that she worked as a papermaker for around twenty years. There was an organisation called Bhaktapur Hastakala in Baglung that helped people in her village. According to her, the profits of papermaking were incompatible with the efforts of their labour. Some people made more profit from making alcohol. She remembered that there was an officer known as Gopal Hakim at Bhaktapur Hastakala. Taman people used to transport paper to Baglung while he was in charge. He sold Taman paper in Kathmandu, but at some point he stopped ordering their paper, and people could no longer sell their produce. They would get a *purji* (permit) document from him, and without this document they could not transport their paper, as the permit allowed them through various check posts. This is the way the Taman papermaking industry ended.

It is two years since she gave up making paper. While production continued, they would work all night without any real sleep. Due to the hard labour during the winter, the skin on their fingertips would crack, causing sores and bleeding. She emphasised many times that making paper is a hard job, but if they had a supportive partner organization, they would certainly make paper again. The village needs someone who will market or sell their paper. In the past the Hakim, the officer, of their partner organisation would provide the people of Taman with their *purji* permit. He used to pay the forest royalty and tell people which forest to go to collect *lokta*. As a large amount of *lokta* was required, they used to collect *lokta* from various places in different VDCs. For 1 *dharni* (2.5 kg) of *lokta*, the total cost including transportation was 200 rupees.

Darbang-Phulbari, in Myagdi District

This factory, in Darbang, has existed since 2008. There were, however, two years during which the factory was not in operation. The factory was first located in the village of Ruma (Ruma 5), but it moved to Ruma 9. The first name of the factory was Shole Herb Pvt. Ltd. (Ruma 5). When the factory moved to Ruma 9, the name changed to the Shole Public Nepalese Handmade Industry. Darbang, a village in the district of Myagdi at an altitude of 1100 m above sea level, is a six- or seven-hour trek from Beni.

The factory in Darbang has been producing paper for eleven or twelve years, but it does not operate all year long. It usually operates for three months per year (November, December and January), which is also usually the season for collecting *lokta* (the tree-felling season). They collect the *lokta* bast and bring it down to the factory for storage. They then make paper at any time with the exception of the monsoon, as long as they have the material. This usually means paper is produced for five months between January and May.

On 30 November 2016 we interviewed the former owner of the factory Moti Raj Gautam (age fifty-three) from the village of Darbang. He informed us that paper had been produced mostly in Baglung in the past, and only recently in Myagdi, where two or three places operate today; all were established at more or less the same time.

Recently he transferred ownership to the community in order to promote the papermaking industry. Two people from Dholka and two local people from Darbang were sent to Kathmandu for training. The idea to make paper in Darbang came from development organizations in the region. Twelve years or so ago the community of Darbang received help from development organization and the Forestry Department in order to encourage people to make paper, and it was suggested that they train people. A development organization for women in the community that works throughout Nepal encouraged women to seek training. While many have been trained, many have still never worked as papermakers.

The main aim of this factory was to promote *lokta* paper and create job opportunities for local people, as well as to induce the regeneration of *lokta* trees. Moti Raj Gautam said that the lifespan of the *lokta* tree is about twenty years, after which the tree will usually die. It was thought that recycling might help to maintain the *lokta* forests in the region, and therefore they seek to cut the trees every five or six years to help maintain the *lokta* trees in good condition.

Lekphat, in Myagdi District

This papermaking factory, which we visited on 16 April 2015, is located in the village of Lekphat in the district of Myagdi, not far from Baglung. Bal Krishna from Lekphat, whom we interviewed, informed us that the region he lives in is well-known for its papermaking, but at the moment production has been interrupted due to economic difficulties. He explained that there were many workshops in the area, but that they were all closed when the Maoists began to collect taxes from the owners. As a result no one produces paper there anymore because most of those who did so work abroad now, and they send money back to their families, so that they are no longer obliged to do such hard work as papermaking. About twelve years previously, however, in 2003, a good many local families were involved in the production of paper. All paper was produced from the same plant, which grows widely in the vicinity.

Salija, in Parbat District

This papermaking factory here is located in the village of Salija in ward N°6, Hampal, and it is supported by the Institute for Himalayan Conservation Japan. Tul Bahadur Pun, whom we interviewed, informed us that the factory was opened ten or twelve years ago, but began regular work only four or five years ago. He works as a volunteer and takes care of the running of the place. The workshop employs five women and the production capacity is on the increase. Our interviewee informed us that at the moment they have around 1,200 kilos of dried *lokta*. Since they opened the factory they have increased the quantity every year, from 600 kilos to 700 kilos to 800 kilos, and this year they harvested 1,500 kilos. Next year's target is 2,000 kilos. There are no restrictions on the amount they may harvest, but to be on the safe side they fell the trees in limited quantities; otherwise the plants might rot if they were to be stored too long in unfavourable weather conditions.

The main problem the owners of the factory face is that the land they have at their disposal is rather small. Since the factory is far from a river, they also experience a shortage of water, which is vital in the production of paper. Access to a large volume of fast-flowing water or at least a large reservoir would greatly accelerate and generally facilitate production. At the moment it takes two or three hours to wash the materials with the limited amount of water that can be carried by people at one time.

Tul Bahadur Pun from Salija also informed us that there was no longer anyone in the region who made paper according to the traditional method. He informed us that, were we go into the forest, we might still find areas where their ancestors used to make paper. They used to dig large pits in the ground, and it is still possible to see these, as well as the places they used to dry the paper.

He could not explain the reason the old tradition was discontinued. He believed that the older people who knew the old methods had died, and that the younger generation was not interested in learning the skills or maintaining the traditions. Only recently did people from Salija discover that Nepalese paper made from local materials is highly valued, and so they decided to produce the paper themselves.

Nangi, in Myagdi District

The papermaking factory in Nangi began to operate in 2062 BS (2006 CE) with a staff of nineteen. From interviews with Kumari Chuchangge Pun we learned that today, as men have travelled abroad to work and women have more to do in the household, the factory employs only eight people. Kumari Chuchangge Pun from the Annapurna Rural Municipality-8, Nangi is the chairperson of Himanchal Handmade Paper. She has been working in the factory since 2010. She explained that they are supported by Poverty Alleviation, while Small Scale Industry has helped them financially to buy machinery.

The Nangi factory is in a healthy state. When we asked where people from Nangi sell their paper, we learned that they do not; instead they sell diaries. Kumari Chuchangge Pun informed us that they sell diaries, bags and envelopes to Singapore, Japan, Australia and USA. The Poverty Alleviation Fund has also placed an order for an exhibition in Kathmandu. It is probably the only factory that is able to sell its products directly abroad without middlemen in Kathmandu.

Ghandruk, in Kaski District

The papermaking workshop we visited on 28 and 29 November 2016 is "Annapurna Lokta Paper & Handicrafts" in Ghandruk, owned by Poorna Bahadur Gurung. The address is Siddhartha Chowk, Ramkrisna Tole-4, Pokhara, Kaski, Nepal. Poorna Bahadur Gurung informed us that he began to work in the papermaking business 20 years ago, but Maoists made work and life progressively difficult, so he had to suspend production, re-opening the factory in

Ghandruk in 2013. He lives in Pokhara, where he has a shop, but the factory is in the village of Ghandruk in the district of Kaski. There we interviewed Dhala Bahadur Thing (aged 74), a plant collector, and Jagat Thing (aged 40), a papermaker.

"Annapurna Lokta Paper & Handicrafts" in Ghandruk makes raw paper of 5, 10, 20, 40 and 60 grams. They have made no paper heavier than that and have never produced dyed paper. Paper of 5g is used for the production of incense; paper of 10g is used as writing paper for Nepalese officials for administrative purposes; paper of 20, 40, and 60grams is exported.

The factory does not operate during the monsoon season because it rains a great deal and it is extremely wet. They work from Bhadra to Jestha (August to March), if the weather is good. If the weather is inclement and there is no sun, the paper will not dry until the following day.

The Ghandruk factory operates all year round with the exception of the three months of the rainy season. He estimates the production at a maximum of 3000 sheets per day in good sunlight. The factory employs ten people, eight papermakers and two *lokta* collectors. Of the factory's ten workers seven are female. Papermakers usually work between five and nine hours depending on the weather and the light, and *lokta* collectors work every morning in the forest between three and four hours' walk from the factory.

There are around 500 frames. If the weather is sunny, they can complete three *sara* in a day. One *sara* has 500 frames, so they can produce 1500 pieces of paper in one day if the weather is fine.

This is the only operational paper factory in the area. There may be other factories in other places. Jagat Thing has heard that there are paper factories in the Baglung area, but he has never been there.

A glimpse into old methods and the transmission of papermaking knowledge

The technology of paper production in Western Nepal has not changed significantly over the last couple of centuries during which time other parts of the modern world have established mechanised papermaking industries. Papermakers in Nepal, however, naturally see important differences in the papermaking process, which allow them to distinguish their methods from those used by their ancestors. This verifies that technological development has also occurred in paper production in the region, but on a much smaller scale.

According to people we interviewed the crucial changes in recent years are those connected with the use of electric machinery, which has replaced traditional tools, and the use of chemicals that accelerate production. In Taman traditional tools were, however, still in evidence. Indra Kumari Buda (aged sixty-four) from Lamala Village showed us the traditional papermaking mould with a cotton sieve stretched across a wooden frame, the stone slab and the wooden hammer which would be used to make paper in the past in the Taman area (Figs 174, 175 and 176). She assured us that she would still be able to use these tools were she to return to papermaking. She informed us that her ancestors made paper in the forest and that the only difference in their technique was that they would use ash-water to cook the *lokta*, whereas caustic soda is now commonly used. She could not imagine cooking *lokta* without caustic soda, without which, in her opinion, *lokta* cannot be cooked satisfactorily. She also explained that in the past nobody would use nylon sieves on the papermaking moulds. Papermakers would use *bhango* (cotton cloth) exclusively as strainers. It would be collected, thrashed and woven into thin cloth to make a strainer.

Fig. 174. The traditional papermaking mould with cotton sieve stretched across the wooden frame which would be used to shape the sheets of paper in Taman in the past. Photograph by Agnieszka Helman-Ważny.

Figs 175 a–b. The stone slab which would be used to beat the *lokta* bast in Taman in the past. Photographs by Agnieszka Helman-Ważny.

Fig. 176. The mallet would be used to beat the *lokta* bast by hand in Taman in the past. Photograph by Agnieszka Helman-Ważny.

Dhala Bahadur Thing, a plant collector from Ghandruk, who once owned a papermaking workshop in Sindhupalchok near Kathmandu, shared with us his observations on the differences between past and present practices (Fig. 177). The first difference he brought to our attention was that in the past, papermakers would use square iron boxes to cook the *lokta*, which could hold between 2 and 4 *dharni* (5 and 10 kg) of *lokta* per round of cooking. Three stones would usually serve as a fire stove below the iron box. He also confirmed that *lokta* would be cooked in strained ash water, which is today replaced by a solution of caustic soda. The ash water would be prepared in a container called a *chapani*, supported by four wooden spars. The upper part of the *chapani* would be wider than the lower part. Water would be poured into the *chapani*, mixed with ash and left to stand for couple of hours. Then the upper, clear part of the standing mixture would be poured into the iron cooking box in which the *lokta* would have been boiling. Today there is no need to prepare ash water or to filter out debris, because many papermakers use caustic soda, which makes pulping much quicker. There are, however, places where papermakers still choose to use ash-water and to follow the traditional way of production in order to avoid the use of chemicals. In the past *lokta* would also be beaten on a stone slab with a *mungro* (wooden mallet), before being kneaded into balls and dried, so that it might be kept for longer before the next stages of the papermaking process. In modern Ghandruk, however, machines are used for the more labour-intensive stages of the process, such as boiling or beating, and the only manual stages are sorting the raw material, cleaning the *lokta*-pulp and spreading the pulp on the frames. An electric beater is used to produce the pulp instead of wooden mallets, and an electric cooker for boiling *lokta* instead of iron boxes placed over an open fire.

Dhala Bahadur Thing also mentioned that during the time of their great-grandfathers, they would make a pit in the ground for soaking the paper frames. Similarly, the water pool where paper would be shaped would also be made in the ground in cases where a natural water source such as a river or lake was unavailable. He told us that even the drying process was now different from the way it had been in the past: formerly, a great deal of wood would have to be

Fig. 177. Dhala Bahadur Thing, a plant collector from Ghandruk sharing with us his memories of the way paper would be made in the past. Photograph by Agnieszka Helman-Ważny.

collected and burned to dry the paper: the bigger the fire, the faster the drying process. There were supposed to be between ten and twelve frames set up for drying. In a day efficient workers would be able to make between 3 *keri* (20 sheets = 1 *keri*) and 4 *keri* of paper using the heat of a fire. As the fire would die down, the paper would cool. In one whole day about 3 *keri* of paper could be made. This heating process is today no longer used, and papers are dried in the sun. Interestingly, we have not seen heated plates used very often in traditional papermaking workshops in China, South Korea and Japan since they require a stable supply of electricity.

Similarly to Dhala Bahadur Thing, Jagat Thing (age forty)[5] from the same factory in Ghandruk described the recent technological changes in the factory. We thus learned that today raw material is boiled in an electric heater with caustic soda (1 kg of caustic soda to 25 kg of *lokta*), which is considered new technology. Until 2015 they would cook *lokta* over a wood fire in an iron drum, but now they use an electric heater. After boiling, the *lokta* is washed in another container and then mixed in the electric beater for 10 minutes before it is ready to use. Until 2015 the beater would be pedal-powered. Two or three people would have to pedal as if on a bicycle, and before this, bast would be beaten with wooden mallets. Now they have electric machines for both cooking and beating. Jagat Thing explained that they had had electricity before, but insufficient to operate machines. It was therefore necessary to improve the electric power source before electric machines could be used. One member of a two-person team would do the beating, and the other would move and fold the beaten raw material. The bast would be washed, and then moved to the place it is poured into frames. Jagat Thing also explained the rôles of various pools we saw in the Ghandruk factory: one is for shaping paper, another is the freshwater reservoir, a third is for soaking *lokta*, and the last for washing. In the pool near the

[5] Jagat Thing is a senior papermaker with sixteen years' experience, who learned his skills just as Dhala Bahadur Thing in his village in Sindhupalchok. He learned from his father, grandfather and great-grandfather, beginning when he was twelve or thirteen years old, and he therefore represents the fourth generation of papermakers in his family.

washing stage *lokta* would first be soaked in water for 24 hours before boiling. *Lokta* would first be dried after being brought from the forest, sometimes soaked in water immediately while raw and removed from the water the following day, then boiled for three to four hours until softened into pulp.

In the past, paper would mostly be made in areas at higher altitudes, and the tools would be wooden. People would build a square concrete floor on the ground, and there the boiled *lokta* would be beaten with wooden mallets. People would then make a wooden container called a *phirke*, in which they would crush the raw material. Once the *lokta* had turned to pulp the papermakers would put it into the container, pour in water and stir the mixture vigorously. Today all this is done with an electric beater.

To level the sheet of paper on the mould, Jagat Thing uses *nuri*, which makes the water sticky and helps to give paper an even thickness. Using *nuri* is considered a new technique.

The freshly made sheets of paper are left to dry in the sun while still on their frames. Drying takes 20 minutes on a sunny day, but longer when there is little by way of sunlight. Dried sheets of paper are removed and the frames are collected. In one day in sunny weather it is possible to produce about 500 sheets in three shifts.

Jagat Thing manages the labour force in Ghandruk. He helps by teaching staff to mix the chemical *nuri* and answers any questions they might have. He decides whether the *lokta* paste is too thick or too thin, when to spread the *lokta* in the sun, and so on. When asked how many people in Ghandruk had learned this skill, he said that he had taught many people in the past. In Ghandruk he taught all the technical skills to female workers. In the past, he said, everyone in the village would be engaged in papermaking, but over time the older people left and those who had learned the skills left the community to make paper in other places, and the practice has consequently now been discontinued.

Note on paper quality

Paper is often viewed by those outside academia as a mundane object of daily use or of artistic expression selected for its texture, its appearance, or other property that might lend itself to artistic application. Artists may thus look at the quality of paper with the aim of achieving particular aesthetic effects. Scientists may view paper as an organic compound equipped with particular properties. Paper technologists may perceive it as a product that is the result of an economic chain connecting producers and buyers. Conservators may be most interested in what the processes of deterioration in paper might teach them about developing preservation techniques. Historians may attempt to date the paper, and connoisseurs may just cherish it in their own collections. Interestingly, each of these groups may define the quality of paper in very different ways depending on purpose and aesthetic value. The quality of Western paper is usually judged by the raw material,[6] paper texture (appearance),[7] opacity,[8] clarity,[9] transparency,[10]

[6] The quality of paper is largely determined by its raw material, as do both the appearance and the strength of paper. Raw materials also determine the type of paper.

[7] The paper texture is an important quality which exerts a considerable effect on subsequent performance characteristics. Each sheet of paper is double-sided. The bottom side, that in direct contact with the sieve during production, is called the sieve side or "natural verso". This side also bears the sieve mark (or wire mark in the case of European paper) and is slightly more uneven. The upper side is called the felt side or the "natural recto", as it is the first to come into contact with the felt. It is smoother and generally brighter, as fibres can be freely arranged on this side. It also contains more fillers. Surface smoothness, achieved both in the machine and during glazing, is also significant. Interestingly, in case of Nepalese paper the "natural verso" side is usually smoother than "natural recto" due to fact that the sheet of paper dries directly on the sieve and is not pressed.

[8] On the one hand, opacity is related to the thickness of the paper and, on the other, the content of filling agent has a direct effect on this characteristic.

[9] Clarity indicates whether the paper is coarsely or finely ground.

[10] Transparency is an undesirable characteristic for many types of paper, with the exception, however, of tracing paper or paper designed for detailed drawings.

sizing,[11] strength,[12] grammage (or thickness),[13] and resistance to ageing, determined primarily by the quality of raw materials.

The Nepalese people we interviewed have an eminently practical attitude to paper quality. To them good quality paper is paper that is not damaged, and the whiter and the thicker the better. Many of our interviewees, including Dhala Bahadur Thing (a *lokta* collector from Ghandruk), said that *lokta* is durable and is resistant to tearing, both of which point to the fact that it was *lokta* paper that was considered to be of the highest quality. Paper made from other materials, such as *gaipaad*, tears easily. If mixed with *lokta*, paper made from other materials is also flexible. Of the all types of paper, he said, the best is made from *lokta*.

Lokta gatherers reported that collecting the plant sometimes causes severe burning to the nose and eyes, as well as rashes. Some people suffer headaches from the smell of raw *lokta* plants. People become accustomed to it, however, so they can tolerate it. When the plant flowers, the effect intensifies. When the plant stem becomes watery, its flower begins to blossom. Peeling the bark from a plant that has flowered releases a good deal of water which burns. All papermaking plants from Thymelaeaceae family, however, including *Stellera chamaejasme*, have slightly poisonous properties and may cause allergic reactions in those in frequent contact with them. This toxic feature is nevertheless the reason the paper is more resistant to damage by insects, and therefore considered stronger and of better quality.

Indra Kumari Buda told us that there used to be two grades of paper. Taman papermakers would sell class "A" paper at 3 rupees and class "B" paper at 2.5 rupees, but she was unable to explain the difference between the two grades. Dhala Bahadur Thing emphasised that paper produced today is much better than in the past due to chemicals such as *nuri*, caustic soda and bleaching powder used during the production. He explained that the use of these chemicals gives the paper a shine and a whiteness; that ash-water mixed with *lokta* for cooking was less effective than caustic soda. He thus felt that mechanisation has increased efficiency in production and improved the quality of the final product.

Trade in paper and other commodities in the Kali Gandaki Valley

The Kali Gandaki Valley of Nepal was for centuries one of the main commercial highways between the Gangetic Plains and the Tibetan Plateau. In the period spanning the nineteenth and mid-twentieth centuries much of the paper that was used in the arid Annapurna region of Nepal was produced in the middle hills of the Myagdi and Baglung Districts, and subsequently transported north along the Kali Gandaki corridor (Fig. 178). The other link between Tibet and other Himalayan regions was through the Kyirong–Rasuwa corridor. Although the main commodities of this north-south trade were salt from Tibet in exchange for grain from the south, there were a great many other items of lesser importance. These two major corridors facilitated the development of the distinctive papermaking and bookmaking craftsmanship in the region.

On the basis of both interviews with papermakers and studies conducted on the paper used in the archival documents, our results suggest that paper was often traded along the Kali Gandaki corridor in both directions, while the raw material was usually collected in the vicinity of papermaking workshops. Since the majority of documents in our sample are from the late nineteenth and early twentieth centuries, we were able to link our results to the living tradition

[11] Sizing is especially important for writing and drawing paper, but also for other paper grades. The rôle of paper sizing is to bind the fibres and filling agents. It must be uniform and accurately measured so that, when ink is applied, the lines are clean and there is no bleed.

[12] Depending on the intended application of the paper, different testing methods are employed to determine its strength, such as its breaking strength, tensile strength, breaking length, elongation, tearing strength, folding resistance and stiffness.

[13] Grammage is defined as the weight per square metre and expressed as gsm. Grammages of up to 200 gsm are considered to be paper and from 200 gsm upwards they are referred to as paperboard or low-quality board. The thickness of paper, measured in microns, is significant when related to grammage. This parameter defines whether the paper is compact with a lot of fillers or high volume.

Fig. 178. The Kali Gandaki passage above Kagbeni. Photograph by Agnieszka Helman-Ważny.

of papermaking in Nepal (information collected from interviews), and to support all this with the picture obtained from the content of the Mustang archival documents.

Research carried out on the living tradition of papermaking in Nepal indicates that Myagdi and Baglung Districts, south of where most of the studied archives were located, are currently also the location of many small paper manufactories, and the region is known for paper production. *Daphne* and *Edgeworthia* plants are still the main materials for this purpose in the region. Information collected from craftsmen interviewed suggests that these manufactories do not usually exist for more than a couple of years: unlike European paper mills these workshops do not have a long continuous history. However, it seems that whenever one factory closed, another soon started to operate in the vicinity. The fact that the region is known for the production of good quality paper, and that tools, facilities, and skilled papermakers existed there, may also have contributed to the ease with which new workshops were established and the sale of products assured.

Today paper in Nepal is known as "Nepali Kagaz." The "Kagate"(or Kagatay) are an ethnic group related to the Yolmos who branched off from the original Yolmo inhabitants of the Helambu and Melamchi Valleys.[14] What distinguishes them is that the Kagate began migrating south-east from Helambu, and eventually, arrived in the Ramechhap District over 100 years ago; and that they practised the craft of papermaking during their wandering in order to make a living, thereby earning themselves the name "Kagate" (which is Nepali for "paper-maker"). They have since developed certain characteristics in their speech that are distinct from traditional Yolmo. The Yolmo-speaking groups in the Lamjung District and Ilam District have also historically been called "Kagate", although both groups claim a clear distinction between themselves and the Kagate of

[14] In the 1980s an increasing number of Yolmos began identifying themselves as the Helambu Sherpa, even using the appellation as a surname to associate themselves with the more prominent Sherpa people of the Solukhumbu District. Although this name is still used to refer to the Yolmo people and their language in certain instances, including the ISO 639–3 language codes, members of the Yolmo community are very unlikely to identify themselves as a subsection of the Sherpas at the present time.

Ramechhap. "Yolmo" and "Kagate", however, are often used interchangeably as terms for both the ethnic group and their dialect. The Yolmos may have migrated from the Kyirong Valleys of south-western Tibet between 200 and 300 years ago. They settled in the valleys of Helambu and gradually intermarriage between the male Yolmo lamas and the Tamang women local to the region became common. In the past the Tamang population, a branch of the Thakalis, of the Mustang area controlled by the Mangyul kings were by proud tradition papermakers.

The period for which we have the most documentation began in 1862 with the establishment of a monopoly on the collection of revenue from the goods exchange, and ended almost exactly a century later when the Chinese Government closed Nepal's northern border (see chapter 2). For much of the period under consideration trade was not free, but under the control of contractors who held a monopoly on the exchange of goods on the basis of government contracts. The smooth flow of trade required the co-operation of numerous groups: not only the government and the contractors, but also the different communities who lived along the route and who could, whenever disaffected, impose a blockade or random tariffs on traders passing through their territory. Paper was one of the dutiable commodities that was transported along this route, but documents concerning the volume of paper transported along the Kali Gandaki and the revenues involved are scant. Detailed records of goods that passed through the main customs offices and checkposts are preserved in a number of local trading houses, and these would constitute an extremely valuable basis for further investigation. It is likely that most of the documents in the families that controlled the trade deal with quantifiable aspects of the commerce, and there is no doubt much to be learned from this material. The one collection of such documents that is available to us contains an indication that the traffic of paper up the Kali Gandaki may have been substantial indeed.

The accounts of one of the main households of the salt-trade monopoly holders in the Kali Gandaki Valley for the years 1901– 1902 were obtained in 1995.[15] The house in question is situated in Tukche, southern Mustang. Monthly income and expenditure is meticulously recorded. There are at least eleven mentions of the purchase of paper, but in most cases the quantities involved are apparently rather small (a few rupees at most) and the paper is apparently intended for use by the purchaser (the office of the monopoly holder). In one case, however, there is reference to a purchase of paper to the value of 27 rupees. Whilst the quantity that this represents is not specified, from the prices of other commodities at this time it is reasonable to conclude that the quantity was very large, possibly several hundred kilogrammes. Unfortunately, the document does not make clear whether this paper was for onward transport to northern Mustang and possibly to Tibet. That this is likely is suggested by the sheer quantity involved, and the fact that paper was indeed one of the commodities that Nepal exported to Tibet at this time.

Broadly speaking, Tibetans would be permitted to bring salt down as far as Lo Monthang, the capital of Lo when it was still a kingdom. They would be permitted to travel no further south. The main northern market, however, was Tradum, well inside Tibet. This would have been the northern limit for traders from Nepal. Here the Nepalese would meet the Tibetan nomads who had brought salt from the Northern Plateau. How far south the Nepalese traders were allowed to transport the salt would depend on where in Mustang they lived. The Lopas would be permitted only as far south as Tukche, while the Baragaonles would be allowed to take their salt to the main customs office at Dana. The salt could be exchanged for grain at various points along the way, and the rate would be fixed by the authorities. The rate of exchange varied along the way, the highest rate being in Lo Monthang, and the lowest at Dana. In Tibet and northern Mustang goods would be carried by yaks. Dzos, yak-cow crossbreeds, have a greater tolerance for low altitudes and were used for stretches in the middle hills, but the best animals for the southerly routes were mules, which increasingly came to replace donkeys as beasts of burden in the villages of Mustang. A southbound trading expedition would take four days from Jomsom to Beni, and a further two days from Beni to Pokhara.

[15] We are indebted to Christian Seeber for making this material available to us. The general context of trading practices and trade relations along the Kali Gandaki during the nineteenth and twentieth centuries is presented in chapter 2.

As described in chapter 2, the point at which traders would pay revenues on the goods they carried would vary over the course of the decades, but was eventually fixed at Nyichung, just south of the Kore La pass that marks the border with Tibet.

Samphel Dondrub of Tiri used to be involved in the textile business. He would buy cotton and a variety of other raw textiles in the south of Nepal and sell them in Upper Mustang. The main market here, as for most traders from Mustang, was the town of Butwal, which Tibetan-speakers refer to as Batuli. He would use some of this material to make prayer flags and clothing for sale locally, and would also travel further to sell his merchandise in Dolpo or even further west still in Jumla. The cheapest and lowest-quality material would be used for making prayer flags, and probably also sieves for papermaking, while the superior cloth was reserved for garments. The trading cycle, from Tiri to Butwal, back to Mustang, on to Dolpo and Jumla before returning home, might take a full year.

Tansen, near Pokhara, was another much-frequented southern destination, though the motive for going there was as much legal as it was commercial, since the government court in the town was a venue where people would resolve disputes.

As early as the 1930s handmade paper production began to decline due to the import of paper from Tibet. By the 1960s the traditional Nepalese paper industry was virtually moribund due to competition from machine-made mass-produced paper from India.[16] In the 1970s, before the rejuvenation of the industry began, only a few families in Baglung in the neighbouring Parbat District retained the traditional knowledge of handmade *lokta* paper production. With the introduction of paper imports from Tibet in the 1930s, the production of handmade *lokta* paper began to decline.

Although most of the paper today is produced in the mountains in the *lokta* range, trade is centralised in Kathmandu. Most of the paper is sold in Kathmandu and used for making notebooks, calendars, dolls and other small commodities for tourists. Dhala Bahadur Thing told us that the owners take paper into market, but he did not know where this paper was sold. Most papermakers we talked to confirmed that paper produced in the mountains is transported and sold in Kathmandu. They know that some paper is sent to markets in foreign countries, such as the USA, Japan, and possibly others. As mentioned above, foreign exports were also organised from Nangi. Jagat Thing, however, mentioned that the owner of the Ghandruk factory has a shop in Pokhara, and would transport and sell the Ghandruk paper there. Moti Raj Gautam from Darbang has been selling most of his paper in Beni for the past two years. Prior to that, he would sell it in Kathmandu, Nangi, and Baglung. Today, when the factory is unoperational, they continue to sell the raw material (*lokta*) to other paper producers. In the past, however, paper was mainly used for writing legal documents such as loan contracts (*tamasuk*).

[16] Biggs and Messerschmidt 2005: 11.

Bibliography

Publications in print

Blezer, Henk, Kalsang Norbu Gurung and Saraju Rath. 2013. "Where to look for the origins of Zhang zhung-related scripts?" *Journal of the International Association for Bon Research*. Volume 1, 99–174.

Bhattarai, Bidur. 2020. *Dividing Texts*. Berlin, Boston: De Gruyter. DOI: https://doi.org/10.1515/9783110543087

Braarvig, Jens and Fredrik Liland. 2010. *Traces of Gandharan Buddhism: An Exhibition of Ancient Manuscripts in the Schøyen Collection*. Oslo: Hermes Pub.

Biggs, Stephen and Don Messerschmidt. 2005. "Social Responsibility in the Growing Handmade Paper Industry of Nepal." *World Development* 33 (November).

Bista, Dor Bahadur. 1971. "The political innovators of Upper Kali-Gandaki." *Man* (New Series), 6.1, 52–60.

Bista, H. H. Jigme S. P. and Susanne von der Heide. 1997. "An Account of Cultural Heritage and Nature Conservation in Mustang, Nepal." *International Journal of Heritage Studies* 3.3, 168–73. DOI: 10.1080/13527259708722203

Bloom, Jonathan M. 2001. *Paper before Print. The History and Impact of Paper in the Islamic World*. New Haven and London: Yale University Press.

Boesi, Alessandro. 2005. "Plant Knowledge among Tibetan Populations." In Alessandro Boesi and F. Cardi (eds), *Wildlife and plants in traditional and modern Tibet: conceptions, exploitation, and conservation*. Memorie della Società Italiana di Scienze Naturali e del Museuo Civico di Storia Naturale di Milano 33/1, 33–48.

Boesi, Alessandro. 2014. "Plants Used for Tibetan Paper-making." In Mark Elliot, Hildegard Diemberger and Michela Clemente (eds), *Buddha's Words. The Life of Books in Tibet and Beyond*. Cambridge: Museum of Archaeology and Anthropology, 95–97.

Boesi, Alessandro. 2016. "Paper Plants in the Tibetan World: A Preliminary Study." In Hildegard Diemberger, Franz-Karl Ehrhard and Peter Kornicki (eds), *Tibetan Printing: Comparison, Continuities and Change*, Leiden; Boston: Brill's Tibetan Studies library, vol. 39, pp. 501–31.

Boulnois, Luce. 2013. "Gold, Wool and Musk: Trade in Lhasa in the Seventeenth Century." In G. Tuttle and K. R. Schaeffer (eds), *The Tibetan History Reader*. New York, Columbia University Press, 457–76.

Cappelli, Raffaele, Matteo Ferrara and Davide Maltoni. 2010. "Minutia Cylinder-Code: A New Representation and Matching Technique for Fingerprint Recognition." *IEEE Transactions on Pattern Analysis and Machine Intelligence*, 32.12, 2128–41.

Cole, Simon A. 2001. *Suspect Identities: A History of Fingerprinting and Criminal Identification*. Cambridge: Harvard University. Press.

Cornu, Philippe. 1997. *Tibetan Astrology*. Boston: Shambhala.

Cüppers, Christoph. 1989. "On the Manufacture of Ink." *Ancient Nepal* 113, 1–7.

Dalton, Jacob, Tom Davis and Sam van Schaik. 2007. "Beyond Anonymity: Paleographic Analyses of the Dunhuang Manuscripts." *Journal of the International Association of Tibetan Studies* 3, 1–23.

Darnal, Prakash. 2001. "Cultural, Religious and Archaeological Heritage of Lo Manthang and Their Restoration." *Ancient Nepal* 148.

Darnal, Prakash. 2017. "Significant Heritages of Upper Mustang and Issue of Conservation." *Dhaulagiri Journal of Sociology and Anthropology* 11, 5–20.

Dhungel, Ramesh K. 2002. *The Kingdom of Lo: A Historical Study*. Kathmandu: Jigme S. P. Bista for Tashi Gephel Foundation.

Diringer, David. 1982. *The Book Before Printing: Ancient, Medieval and Oriental.* New York: Dover Publications.

Dotson, Brandon and Agnieszka Helman-Ważny. 2016. *Codicology, Paleography, and Orthography of Early Tibetan Documents: Methods and a Case Study.* Wiener Studien zur Tibetologie und Buddhismuskunde (Vienna: Arbeitskreis für Tibetische und Buddhistische Studien).

Duffy, Kate I. and Jacki A. Elgar. 1996. "An Investigation of Palette and Color Notations Used to Create a Set of Tibetan Thangkas". In Arie Wallert, Erma Hermens and Marja Peek (eds), *Historical Painting Techniques, Materials, and Studio Practice: Preprints of a Symposium, University of Leiden, the Netherlands, 26–29 June 1995.* Los Angeles: The Getty Conservation Institute, pp. 78–84.

Ernst, Richard R. 2001. "Arts and Sciences. A Personal Perspective of Tibetan Painting." *Chimia* 55 (11), 900–14.

Ernst, Richard R. 2010. "In Situ Raman Microscopy Applied to Large Central Asian Paintings." *Journal of Raman Spectroscopy* 41: 275–87. DOI: 10.1002/jrs.2443am.

Fieni, Luigi. 2011. "The Art of Mustang and Its Conservation." *Rivista Studi Orientali Supplemento* 1, 138–40.

Fisher, James F. 1987. *Trans-Himalayan Traders: Economy, Society, and Culture in Northwest Nepal.* Delhi: Motilal Banarsidass Publishers.

Formigatti, Camillo A. 2017. "Sanskrit Manuscripts in the Cambridge University Library: Three Centuries of History and Preservation." In Vincenzo Vergiani, Daniele Cuneo and Camillo A. Formigatti (eds), *Indic Manuscripts Cultures through the Ages: Material, Textual, and Historical Investigations.* Studies in Manuscript Cultures. Berlin: De Gruyter, pp. 3–45.

Foucault, Michel. 1972. *The Archaeology of Knowledge.* London: Tavistock Publications.

Fürer-Haimendorf, Christoph von. 1966. "Caste Concepts and Status Distinctions in Buddhist Communities of Western Nepal." In C. von Fürer-Haimendorf (ed.), *Caste and Kin in Nepal, India and Ceylon.* London: Asia Publishing House, pp. 140–160.

Fürer-Haimendorf, Christoph von. 1967. *Morals and Merit.* London: Weidenfeld and Nicholson.

Fürer-Haimendorf, Christoph von. 1975. *Himalayan Traders: Life in Highland Nepal.* London: J. Murray.

Gajurel, Chhabi Lal and Karuna Kar Vaidya. 1984. *Traditional Arts and Craft of Nepal.* New Dehli: S Chand & Co Ltd.

Gosavi, Prabhakar G. 1984. "Did India Invent Paper?" *Tappi Journal* 67.2, 42.

Gosavi, Prabhakar G. 2000. "Does Hand Made Paper (100% Cotton Rags) Need Acid Free Conditions?" *Paper History* 10.3, 54–56.

Graafen, Rainer. 2001. "The Importance of Trade for Kāgbeni." In Perdita Pohle and Willibald Haffner (eds), *Kāgbeni. Contributions to the village's history and geography.* Giessener Geographische Schriften 77. Giessen: Institut für Geographie, pp. 247–52.

Graafen, Rainer and Christian Seeber. 1993. "Important Trade Routes in Nepal and Their Importance to the Settlement Process." *Ancient Nepal* 133, 34–48.

Gutschow, N. 1994. "Kagbeni: Structural Analysis of Dendrochronological Data." *Ancient Nepal* 136, 23–50.

Harimoto, Kengo. 2011. "In Search of the Oldest Nepalese Manuscript." *Rivista Degli Studi Orientali* 84.1/4, nuova serie, 85–106.

Harimoto, Kengo. 2014. "Nepalese Manuscripts of the Suśrutasaṃhitā." *Journal of Indian and Buddhist Studies* 62.3, 1087–93.

Harimoto, Kengo. 2017. "The Dating of the Cambridge Bodhisattvabhūmi manuscript Add. 1702." Vincenzo Vergiani, Daniele Cuneo and Camillo A. Formigatti (eds), *Indic Manuscripts Cultures through the Ages: Material, Textual, and Historical Investigations.* Studies in Manuscript Cultures. Berlin: De Gruyter, pp. 355–76.

Harrison, John and Charles Ramble. 1998. "Houses and Households in Southern Mustang." *Ancient Nepal: Journal of the Department of Archeology* 140, 23–37.

Helman-Ważny, Agnieszka. 2001. "Traditional Papermaking in Mountains in Central Asia." *Conservator-Restorers' Bulletin* 12.2, 50–55.

Helman-Ważny, Agnieszka and Sam van Schaik. 2013. "Witnesses for Tibetan Craftsmanship: Bringing Together Paper Analysis, Palaeography and Codicology in the Examination of the Earliest Tibetan Manuscripts." *Archaeometry* 55.4, 707–41. DOI:10.1111/j.1475-4754.2012.00687.x

Helman-Ważny, Agnieszka. 2014. *The Archaeology of Tibetan Books.* Leiden; Boston: Brill's Tibetan Studies Library, vol. 36.

Helman-Ważny, Agnieszka. 2016a. "The Choice of Materials in Early Tibetan Printed Books." In Hildegard Diemberger, Franz-Karl Ehrhard, Peter Kornicki (eds), *Tibetan Printing: Comparison, Continuities and Change,* Leiden; Boston: Brill's Tibetan Studies Library, vol. 39, pp. 532–54.

Helman-Wazny, Agnieszka. 2016b. "Overview of Tibetan Paper and Papermaking: History, Raw Materials, Techniques and Fiber Analysis." In Orna Almogi (ed.), *Tibetan Manuscript and Xylograph Traditions, the Written Word and its Media within the Tibetan Culture Sphere.* Indian and Tibetan Studies 4. Hamburg: Department of Indian and Tibetan Studies, University of Hamburg, pp. 171–96.

Helman-Wazny, Agnieszka. 2016c. "More Than Meets the Eye: Fibre and Paper Analysis of the Chinese Manuscripts from the Silk Roads." *STAR: Science & Technology of Archaeological Research*, 2.2 (2016), 127–40, DOI: 10.1080/20548923.2016.1207971

Helman-Ważny, Agnieszka and Charles Ramble. 2017. "Tibetan Documents in the Archives of the Tantric Lamas of Tshognam in Mustang, Nepal: An Interdisciplinary Case Study." *Revue d'Études Tibétaines* 39. Paris: the UMR 8155 (CRCAO) of the CNRS, 266–341.

Herschel, Sir William J. 1916. *The Origin of Finger-Printing*. London: Oxford University Press.

Holmberg David, Kathryn March, Suryaman Tamang and Tamang elders. 1999. "Local Production/ Local Knowledge: Forced Labour from Below." *Studies in Nepali History and Society* 4.1, 5–64.

Hodgson, Brian H. 1832. "On the Native Method of Making Paper, Denominated in Hindustan, Nepalese." *Journal of the Royal Asiatic Society of Bengal* 1.1 (January), 11.

Hunter, Dard. 1978. *Papermaking. The History and Technique of an Ancient Craft*. New York: Dover Publications.

Hoernle, A. F. Rudolf. 1897. "The Bower Manuscript. Facsimile Leaves, Nagari Transcript, Romanised Transliteration and English Translation with Notes." *Archaeological Survey of India* 22. Calcutta: Office of Superintendent of Government Printing India.

Ilvessalo-Pfäffli, Marja-Sisko. 1995. *Fiber Atlas, Identification of Papermaking Fibers*. Berlin Heidelberg: Springer-Verlag.

Imaeda, Yoshiro. 1989. "Papermaking in Bhutan." *Acta Orientalia Academiae Scientiarum Hung* XLIII.2–3, 409–14.

Imaeda, Yoshiro and Tsuguhito Takeuchi (eds), 2007. *Tibetan Documents from Dunhuang Kept at the Bibliothèque Nationale de France and the British Library*. (Old Tibetan Documents Online Monograph Series, Vol. I.) Tokyo: Research Institute for Languages and Cultures of Asia and Africa, Tokyo University of Foreign Studies.

Jackson, David P. 1978. "Notes on the History of Se-rib, and Nearby Places in the Upper Kali Gandaki Valley." *Kailash* 6.3, 195–227.

Jackson, David P. 1984. *The Mollas of Mustang: Historical, Religious and Oratorical Traditions of the Nepalese-Tibetan Borderland*. Dharamsala: Library of Tibetan Works and Archives.

Jackson, David, and Janice Jackson. 1994. *Tibetan Thangka Painting. Methods and Materials*. London: Serindia Publications.

Jamgön Kongtrul Lodrö Tayé. 2012. *The Treasury of Knowledge, Book Six, Parts One and Two Indo-Tibetan Classical Learning and Buddhist Phenomenology*. Kalu Rinpoché Translation Group. Boston/ London: Snow Lion.

Jeanrenaud, Jean Paul. 1984. *Lokta (Daphne Spp.) and Craft Paper-making in Nepal: A Report on the Current Status, Based on a Literature Review and Preliminary Field Observations (May 1984–October 1984)*. Kathmandu: Forest Research and Information Centre, Forest Survey and Research Office, Department of Forest.

Jest, Corneille. 1975. *Dolpo: communautés de langue tibétaine au Népal*. Paris: Éditions du Centre national de la recherche scientifique.

Karmacharya, Madhab. 1996. *Mustang Documents in the Nepali Language (1667–1975 A.D.): Described and Edited in Facsimiles.* Bonn: VGH Wissenschaftsverlag.

Karmacharya, Madhab. 2001a. *Ten Documents from Mustang in the Nepali Language (1667–1975).* Bonn: VGH Wissenschaftsverlag.

Karmacharya, Madhab. 2001b. *Southern Mustang in Some Documents: Community Life and Regulations (1868–1957 A.D.).* Bonn: VGH Wissenschaftsverlag.

Konishi, Masatoshi A. 2013. *Hāth-Kāghaz, History of Handmade Paper in South Asia.* New Delhi: Aryan Book International.

Koretsky, Elaine. 1986. "Papermaking Today in Tibet and China." *Hand Papermaking* 1, 2–6.

Li, Zhimin, Lele Wang, Qinglin Ma and Jianjun Mei. 2014. "A Scientific Study of the Pigments in the Wall Paintings at Jokhang Monastery in Lhasa, Tibet, China." *Heritage Science* 2.21, 1–6. https://doi.org/10.1186/s40494–014-0021–2

Losty, Jeremiah. 1982. *The Art of the Book in India.* London: The British Library.

Macdonell, Arthur Anthony. 1900. *A History of Sanskrit Literature.* New York: D. Appleton and Company. Online version available at: https://archive.org/details/historyofsanskri00macduoft/page/n. 8 (accessed on 22/05/2019).

Manzardo, Andrew. 1978. *To be Kings of the North: Community, Adaptation and Impression Management in the Thakali of Western Nepal.* New Haven: Human Relations Area Files, Yale University.

Manzardo, Andrew. 1982. "Impression Management and Economic Growth: The Case of the Thakalis of Dhaulagiri Zone." *Kailash* 9.1, 45–60.

Mass, Jennifer, Jo-Fan Huang, Betty Fiske, Ann Shaftel, Xian Zhang, Richard Laursen, Courtney Shimoda, Catherine Matsen and Christina Bisulca. 2009. "Thangka Production in the 18th–21st Centuries: Documenting the Introduction of Non-Traditional Materials into Himalayan Painting Practice." In Mary Ballard and Carole Dignard (eds), *Proceedings of the Forum on the Conservation of Thangkas Special Session of the ICOM-CC 15th Triennial Conference, New Delhi, India, September 26, 2008, hosted by the Working Group on Ethnographic Collections, the Textiles Working Group and the Paintings Working.* Published by the International Council of Museums – Committee for Conservation (ICOM-CC), pp. 108–17.

Morris, Ron N. 2000. *Forensic Handwriting Identification: Fundamental Concepts and Principles.* London-San Diego, CA: Academic Press.

Moss, William W. 1996. "Tibetan Archives: A Report from China." *American Archivist* 59, 350–55.

Mohammed, Hussein, Volker Märgner and H. Siegfried Stiehl. 2018. "Writer Identification for Historical Manuscripts: Analysis and Optimisation of a Classifier as an Easy-to-Use Tool for Scholars from the Humanities." *2018 16th International Conference on Frontiers in Handwriting Recognition (ICFHR)*, Niagara Falls, NY, pp. 534–39.

Mullard, Saul. 2015. "Reading Ethnic Conflict in Sikkimese History: The Case of the Assassination of Chancellor Bho lod." In Hanna Havnevik and Charles Ramble (ed), *From Bhakti to Bon: Festschrift for Per Kvaerne*. Oslo: The Institute for Comparative Research in Human Culture/Novus Forlag, pp. 367–80.

Müller, Friedrich Max. 1968. *A History of Ancient Sanskrit Literature. The Chowkhamba Sanskrit Studies vol. XV*. Varanasi.

Neate, Sarah and David Howell. 2011. "Conservation Issues and Research Questions: the Role of Analysis in Book and Manuscript Conservation." In S. Neate, R. Ovenden, D. Howell and A. M. Pollard (eds), *The Technological Study of Books and Manuscripts as Artefacts*. BAR S2209, Archaeopress: Oxford, pp. 9–14.

"Nursery Grandfather of the Forest Conservation," *Kantipur*, Kathmandu, Feb. 14th, 2017.

Otsu, Nobuyuki. 1979. "A Threshold Selection Method from Gray-Level Histograms." *IEEE Transactions on Systems, Man, and Cybernetics*, 9.1, 62–66.

Pan, Jixing. 1981. "On the Origin of Papermaking in the Light of Newest Archeological Discoveries." *IPH Information* 15.2, 38–39.

Pandey, V. N. and Ayodhya Pandey. 1988. "A Study of the Nāvanītaka: The Bower Manuscript." *Bulletin of the Indian Institute of History of Medicine* 18.1, 1–46.

Pant, M. R. and P. H. Pierce. 1989. *Administrative Documents of the Shah Dynasty Concerning Mustang and Its Periphery (1789–1844 AD)*. Bonn: VGH Wissenschaftsverlag.

Pelliot, Paul. 1961. *Histoire ancienne du Tibet*. Paris: Adrien-Maisonneuve.

Petech, Luciano. 1984. *Medieval History of Nepal (c. 750–1482)*. Serie Orientale Roma LIV. Roma: Instituto Italliano per il Medio ed Estremo Orientale.

Plofker, Kim, Agathe Keller, Takao Hayashi, Clemency Montelle and Dominik Wujastyk. 2017. "The Bakhshālī Manuscript: A Response to the Bodleian Library's Radiocarbon Dating." *History of Science in South Asia* 5.1, 134–50. DOI: 10.18732/H2XT07. Online version available at: http:// hssa-journal.org

Premchand, Neeta. 1995. *Off the Deckle Edge. A Paper-Making Journey through India*. Bombay.

Purdy, Dan C. 2006. "Identification of Handwriting." In Jan Seaman Kelly and Brian S. Lindblom (eds), *Scientific Examination of Questioned Documents*. Boca, Raton, London, New York: Taylor & Francis Group, pp. 47–74.

Ramaseshan, Sita. 1989. "The History of Paper in India up to 1948." *Indian Journal of History of Science* 24.2, 103–21.

Regmi, Mahesh Chandra. 1980. *Regmi Research Series*. Kathmandu.

Regmi, Mahesh Chandra. 1982. *Regmi Research Series*. Kathmandu.

Rischel, Anna-Grethe. 1985. "Traditional Paper Making in the Far East." *Annual Newsletter of the Scandinavian Institute of Asian Studies* 19.

Rischel, Anna-Grethe. 2001. "Through the Microscope Lens: Classification of Oriental Paper Technology and Fibers." In John Slavin, Linda Sutherland, John O'Neill, Margaret Haupt and Janet Cowan (eds), *Looking at Paper: Evidence and Interpretation, symposium proceedings, Toronto 1999*. Ottawa: Canadian Institute of Conservation, pp. 179–88.

Salomon, Richard. 1999. *Ancient Buddhist Scrolls from Gandhara: The British Library Kharosthi Fragments.* University of Washington Press.

Salomon, Richard G. and Andrew Glass. 2000. *A Gandhari Version of the Rhinoceros Sutra: British Library Kharoṣṭhi Fragment 5B.* Seattle: University of Washington Press.

Sandermann, W. 1968. "Alte Techniken der Papierherstellung in Südostasien und den Himalaya Ländern." *Papiergeschichte* 18, 29–39.

Schaeffer, Kurtis R. 2009. *The Culture of the Book in Tibet.* New York: Columbia University Press.

Schafer, Edward H. 1963. *The Golden Peaches of Samarkand. A Study of T'ang Exotics.* Berkeley, Los Angeles, London: University of California Press.

van Schaik, Sam and Imre Galambos. 2012. *Manuscripts and Travellers: The Sino-Tibetan Documents of a Tenth-Century Buddhist Pilgrim.* Berlin, Boston: de Gruyter.

van Schaik, Sam. 2014. "Towards a Tibetan Paleography: A Preliminary Typology of Writing Styles in Early Tibet." In J.-U. Sobisch and J. B. Quenzer (eds), *Manuscript Cultures: Mapping the Field.* Berlin: de Gruyter.

Schneider, Hanna. 2002. "Tibetan Legal Documents of South-Western Tibet: Structure and Style." In Blezer, Henk and A. Zadoks (eds), *Tibet, Past and Present. Tibetan Studies I.* Leiden, 415–28.

Schneider, Hanna. 2012. *Tibetischsprachige Urkunden aus Südwesttibet (sPo-rong, Ding-ri und Shel-dkar),* 2 vols, Stuttgart: Franz Steiner Verlag.

Schomaker, Lambert and Sheng He. 2019. "DeepOtsu: Document Enhancement and Binarization Using Iterative Deep Learning." *Pattern Recognition* 91, 379–90.

Schuh, Dieter. 1973. *Untersuchungen zur Geschichte der tibetischen Kalenderrechnung.* Wiesbaden: Steiner Verlag.

Schuh, Dieter. 1981. *Grundlagen tibetischer Siegelkunde. Eine Untersuchung über tibetische Siegelaufschriften in 'Phags-pa-Schrift.* (Monumenta Tibetica Historica III/5.) Sankt Augustin: VGH Wissenschaftsverlag.

Schuh, Dieter. 1994. "Investigations in the History of the Muktinath Valley and Adjacent Areas. Pt. 1." *Ancient Nepal* 137, 9–91.

Schuh, Dieter. 1995. "Investigations in the History of the Muktinath Valley and Adjacent Areas. Pt. 2." *Ancient Nepal* 138, 5–54.

Scott, James. 1990. *Domination and the Arts of Resistance: Hidden Transcripts.* New Haven: Yale University Press.

Selter, Elke. 2007. *Upper Mustang, Cultural Heritage of Lo Tso Dhun.* Kathmandu: UNESCO Publications.

Sen, Siva Narayana. 1940. *Hand-made paper of Nepal.* Nepal Museum Publication Calcutta: Prabasi Press.

Sen, Jahar. 1971. "India's trade with Central Asia via Nepal." *Bulletin of Tibetology* 8, 21–40.

Sherpa, Sri Nima, Milan Dev Bhattarai, Sri Gopal Shrestha, Sri Iccha Bahadur Karki, Sri Benu Das Shrestha, Sri Parvat Gurung, Sri Divya Acharya, Sri Shishir Adhikari. 2008. *Nepali Lokta Quality Paper Production Manual 2065.* Kathmandu: Nepal Handmade Paper Association (HANDPASS).

Shrestha, Bharat P. 1989. *Forest Plants of Nepal.* Lalitpur: Educational Enterprise.

Soteriou, Alexandra. 1999. *Gift of Conquerors. Hand Papermaking in India.* New Delhi: Mappin Publ.

Spengen, Wim van. 2013. "The Geo-History of Long-Distance Trade in Tibet 1850–1950." In G. Tuttle and K. R. Schaeffer (eds), *The Tibetan History Reader.* New York, Columbia University Press, pp. 491–524.

Storrs, Adrian and Jimmie Storrs. 1998. *Trees and Shrubs of Nepal and the Himalayas.* New Delhi: Book Faith India.

Suryawanshi D. G. and Om Prakash Agrawal. 1996. "Evaluation of Hand-made Nepalese Paper for Lining Paintings." *Restaurator* 16.2, 65–76, DOI: https://doi.org/10.1515/rest.1995.16.2.65.

Takakusu, Junjirō. 1896. *An Introduction to I-tsing's Record of the Buddhist Religion as Practised in India and the Malay Archipelago (A.D. 671–95).* Oxford: Clarendon.

Takeuchi, Tsuguhito. 1995. *Old Tibetan Contracts From Central Asia.* Tokyo: Daizo Shuppan.

Takeuchi, Tsuguhito. 1998. *Old Tibetan Manuscripts from East Turkestan in the Stein Collection of the British Library.* Vol. 2. Descriptive catalogue. Tokyo and London: Toyo Bunko and the British Library.

Takeuchi, Tsuguhito. 2012. "Old Tibetan Buddhist Texts from the Post-Tibetan Imperial Period (mid-9 c. to late 10 c.)." In Christina Scherrer-Schaub (ed.), *Old Tibetan Studies: Proceedings of the 10th Seminar of the IATS 2003.* Leiden: Brill, pp. 205–16.

Trier, Jesper. 1972. *Ancient Paper of Nepal. Result of Ethno-Technological Field Work on its Manufacture, Uses and History – with Technical Analyses of Bast, Paper and Manuscripts.* Copenhagen: Jutland Archaeological Society Publications.

Tschudin, Walter Friedrich. 1958. "Älteste Papierbereitungsverfahren im Fernen Osten." *Textil-Rundschau* 13, 679–89.

Tschudin Peter F. 2002. *Grundzüge der Papiergeschichte.* Stuttgart: Hiersemann-Verlag.

Tschudin Peter F. 2004. "Non-destructive optical investigation of paper." In Rosella Graziaplena and Mark Livesey (eds), *Paper as medium of Cultural Heritage.* Roma: Istituto centrale di patologia del libro, pp. 135–41.

Tsien, Tsuen-Hsuin. 1985. *Paper and Printing.* Sciences and Civilization in China, ed. J.S Needham, vol. 5. Cambridge: Cambridge University Press.

Tsundru, Jampa. 2010. *Preserve and Development of the Manufacturing Technology of Traditional Tibetan Paper.* The Ethnic Publishing House.

Uebach, Helga. 2008. "From Red Tally to Yellow Paper: The Official Introduction of Paper in the Tibetan Administration in 744/45." *Revue d'Études Tibétaines* 14, 57–69.

Upreti, Manohar. 2004. "Lokta, King of Nepalese Paper." In Anne Westerhof (ed.), *Spirit of Paper.* Leiden: Performa Uitgeverij, pp. 238–39.

Uray, Géza. 1988. "New Contributions to Tibetan Documents from the post-Tibetan Tun-huang." In Helga Uebach and Jampa L. Panglung (eds), *Tibetan Studies: Proceedings of the Fourth Seminar of the International Association for Tibetan Studies*. Munich: Kommission für Zentralasiatische Studien, Bayerische Akademie der Wissenschaften, pp. 515–28.

Wallich, Nathaniel. 1824. *Tentamen florae nepalensis illustratae: Consisting of Botanical Description And Lithographic Figures of Select Nipal Plants.* Calcutta and Serampore.

Wang, Juhua. 1999. *Papermaking Raw Materials of China: An Atlas of Micrographs and the Characteristics of Fibres.* Beijing: China Light Industry Press.

Vinding, Michael. 1998. *The Thakali: A Himalayan Ethnography*. London: Serindia Publications.

Wiesner, Julius. 1903. *Die Rohstoffe des Pflanzenreiches*. Leipzig: Verlag von Wilhelm Engelmann.

Zhang, T. Y. and C. Y. Suen. 1984. "A Fast Parallel Algorithm for Thinning Digital Patterns." *Commun. ACM* 27.3 (March 1984), 236–39. DOI: https://doi.org/10.1145/357994.358023

Online resources

Bodleian Library. 2017. "Carbon Dating Finds Bakhshali Manuscript Contains Oldest Recorded Origins of the Symbol 'zero'". *Ancient Indian mathematical text at Oxford's Bodleian Libraries revealed to be centuries older than previously thought.* Available at: https://www.bodleian.ox.ac.uk/news/2017/sep-14 (accessed on 22/05/2019).

University of Cambridge Digital Library. *Sanskrit Manuscripts: Bodhisattvabhūmi (MS Add.1702).* Available at: https://cudl.lib.cam.ac.uk/view/MS-ADD-01702/6 (last accessed 27 December 2019).

Digitized Tibetan Archives Material at Bonn University. Available at: http://www.dtab.uni-bonn.de/ (last accessed 06 June 2017).

HAR (Himalayan Art Resources) website. Available at: http://www.himalayanart.org/ (last accessed 10 July 2017).

Janson, Svante. 2014. Tibetan calendar mathematics. *History and Overview* (math.HO), 2nd ed., 1–86. Available at: arXiv:1401.6285 [math.HO] (last accessed 07 October 2019).

Jaquin, Paul A. 2008. Analysis of historic rammed earth construction. Durham theses. Durham University. Available at Durham E-Theses Online: http://etheses.dur.ac.uk/2169/ (last accessed 03 April 2018).

Mansar, Youness. 2018. "Deep End-to-end Fingerprint Denoising and Inpainting." *ArXiv, abs/1807.11888*. Available at: https://arxiv.org/pdf/1807.11888.pdf (last accessed 30 December 2019).

Mini-Encyclopedia of Papermaking. Part Two: Definitions and Concepts. Fibrillation: https://projects.ncsu.edu/project/hubbepaperchem/Defnitns/Fibrilzn.htm (last accessed 27 December 2019).

Mohammed, Hussein. 2020. "Handwriting Analysis Tool (HAT)". 25-Feb-2020. DOI: 10.25592/uhhfdm.900. Available at: https://www.fdr.uni-hamburg.de/record/902#.XptAd8gzaUk#.XptAd8gzaUk (last accessed 05 April 2020).

Monumenta Tibetica Historica. Available at: http://www.tibetinstitut.de/monumenta-tibetica.html (last accessed 06 June 2017).Mulmi, Amish Raj. 2017. The Making of the Gorkha Empire: Part I – Land. *The Record Nepal*. Available at: https://www.recordnepal.com/wire/features/the-making-of-the-gorkha-empire-part-i-land-nepal-unification/ (last accessed 27 December 2019).

Old Tibetan Documents Online (OTDO). Available at: http://otdo.aa-ken.jp/ (last accessed 06 June 2017).

Regmi, M. C. 1969–1989. *Regmi Research Series.* Available at: http://www.digitalhimalaya.com/collections/journals/regmi/ (last accessed 27 December 2019).

The International Dunhuang Project: The Silk Road Online. Available at: http://idp.bl.uk/ (last accessed 02 June 2017).

Appendix 1: Visual documentation of the studied documents*

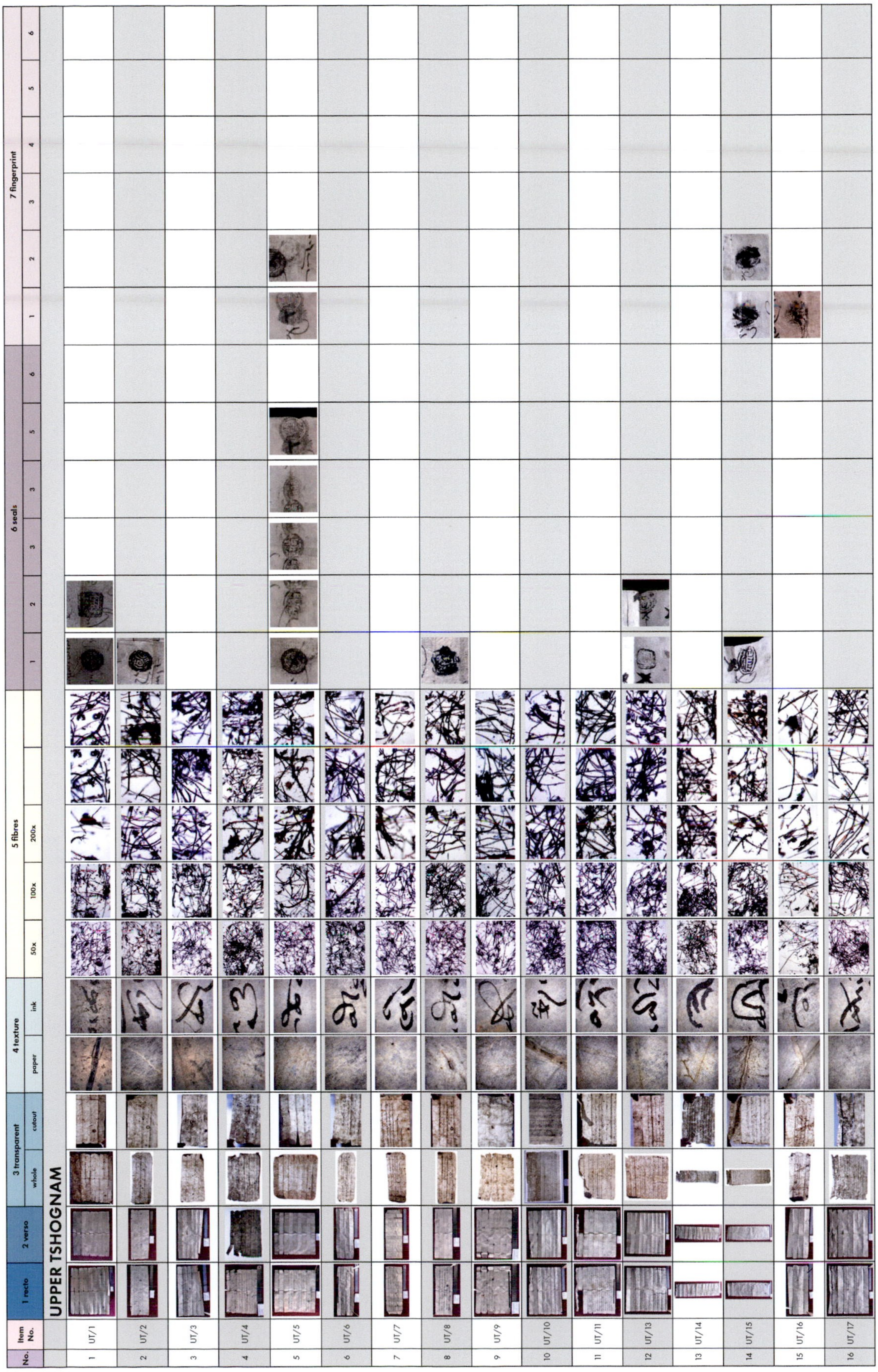

No.	Item No.	1 recto	2 verso	3 transparent whole	3 transparent cutout	4 texture paper	4 texture ink	5 fibres 50x	5 fibres 100x	5 fibres 200x	5 fibres	5 fibres	6 seals 1	6 seals 2	6 seals 3	6 seals 3	6 seals 5	6 seals 6	7 fingerprint 1	7 fingerprint 2	7 fingerprint 3	7 fingerprint 4	7 fingerprint 5	7 fingerprint 6
UPPER TSHOGNAM																								
1	UT/1																							
2	UT/2																							
3	UT/3																							
4	UT/4																							
5	UT/5																							
6	UT/6																							
7	UT/7																							
8	UT/8																							
9	UT/9																							
10	UT/10																							
11	UT/11																							
12	UT/13																							
13	UT/14																							
14	UT/15																							
15	UT/16																							
16	UT/17																							

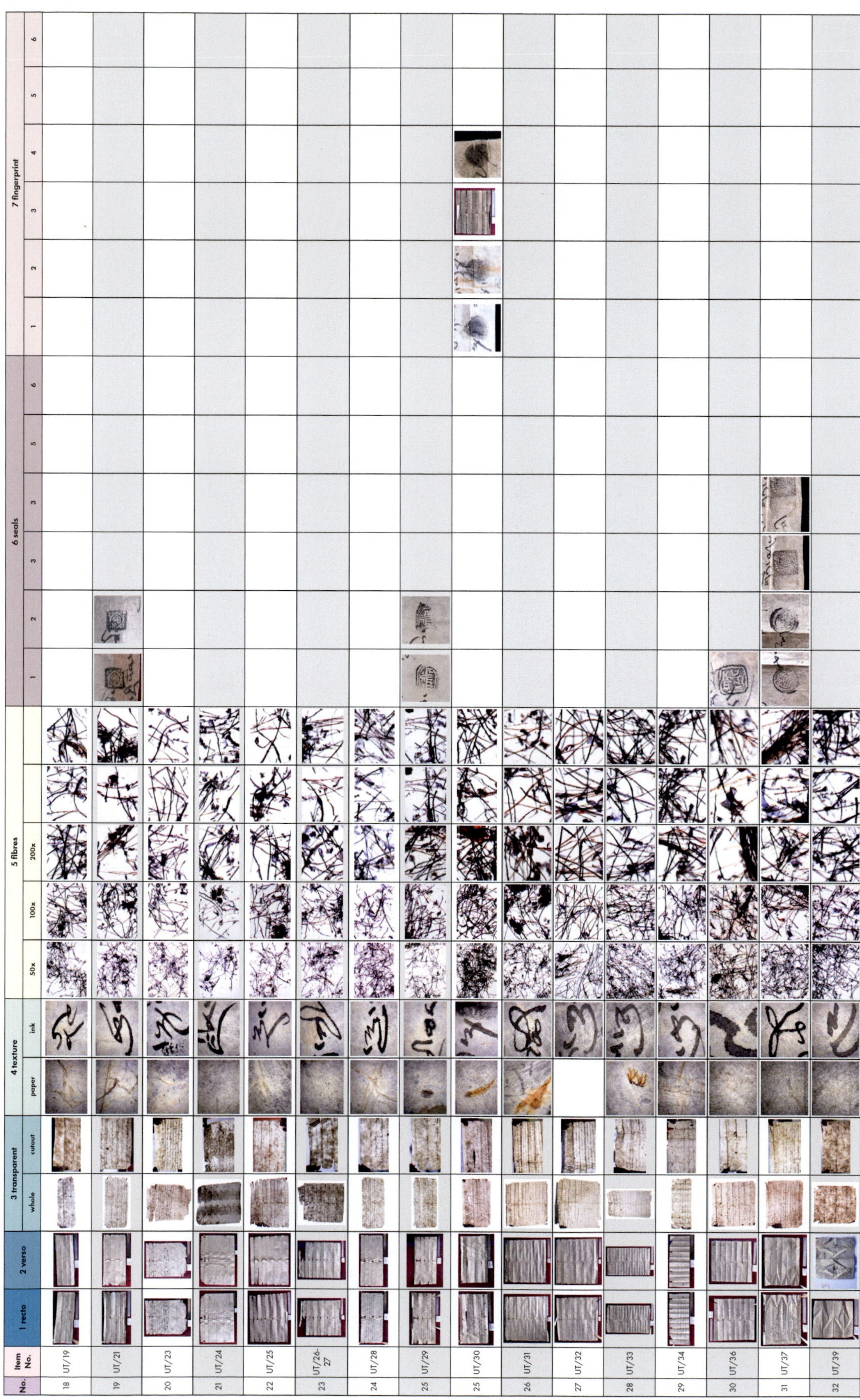
No.
Item No.
1 recto
2 verso
3 transparent
whole
cutout
4 texture
paper
ink
5 fibres
50x
100x
200x
6 seals
1
2
3
3
5
6
7 fingerprint
1
2
3
4
5
6
18 UT/19
19 UT/21
20 UT/23
21 UT/24
22 UT/25
23 UT/26-27
24 UT/28
25 UT/29
25 UT/30
26 UT/31
27 UT/32
28 UT/33
29 UT/34
30 UT/36
31 UT/37
32 UT/39

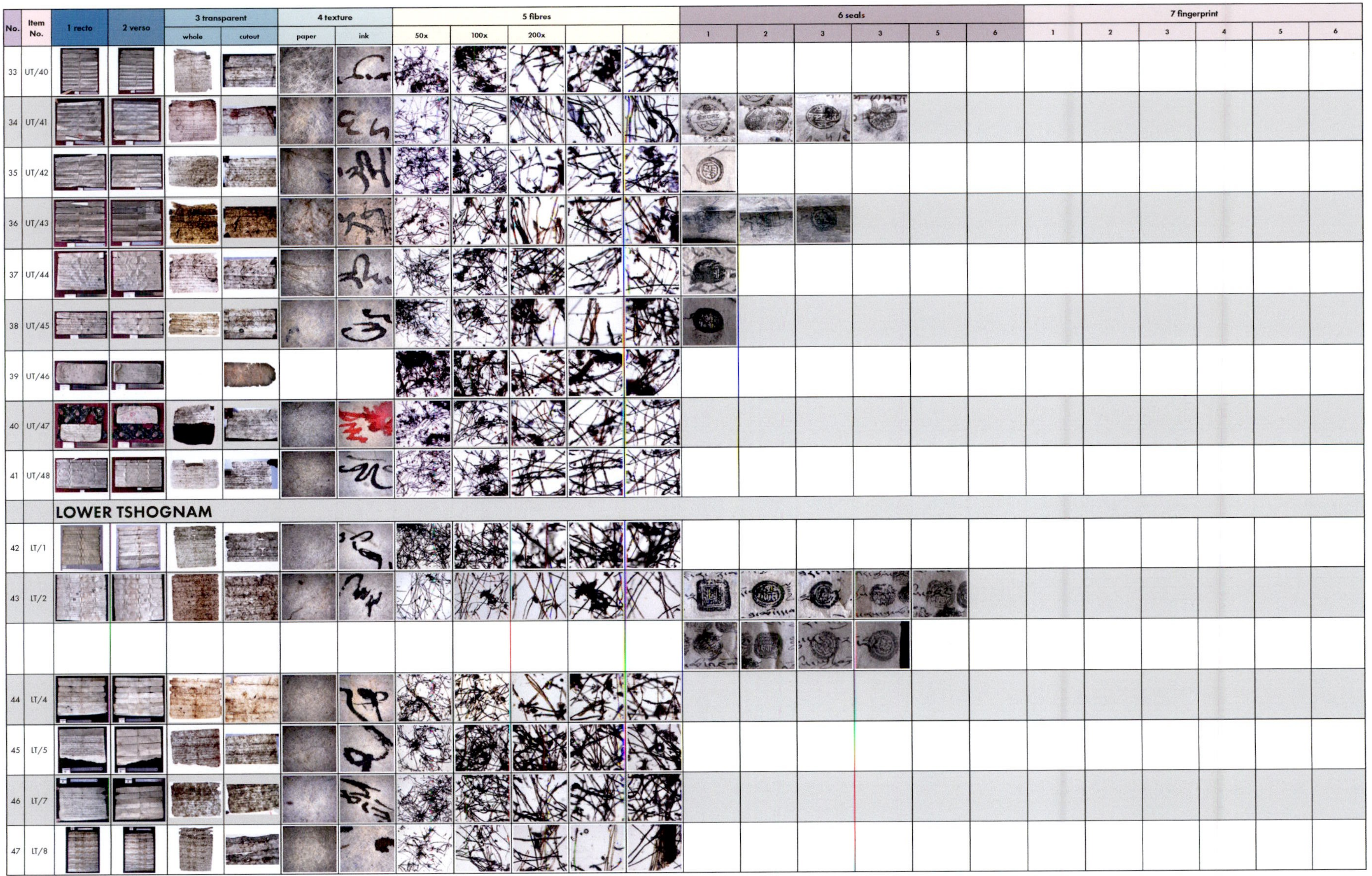
No.
Item No.
1 recto
2 verso
3 transparent
whole
cutout
4 texture
paper
ink
5 fibres
50x
100x
200x
6 seals
1
2
3
3
5
6
7 fingerprint
1
2
3
4
5
6
33 UT/40
34 UT/41
35 UT/42
36 UT/43
37 UT/44
38 UT/45
39 UT/46
40 UT/47
41 UT/48
LOWER TSHOGNAM
42 LT/1
43 LT/2
44 LT/4
45 LT/5
46 LT/7
47 LT/8

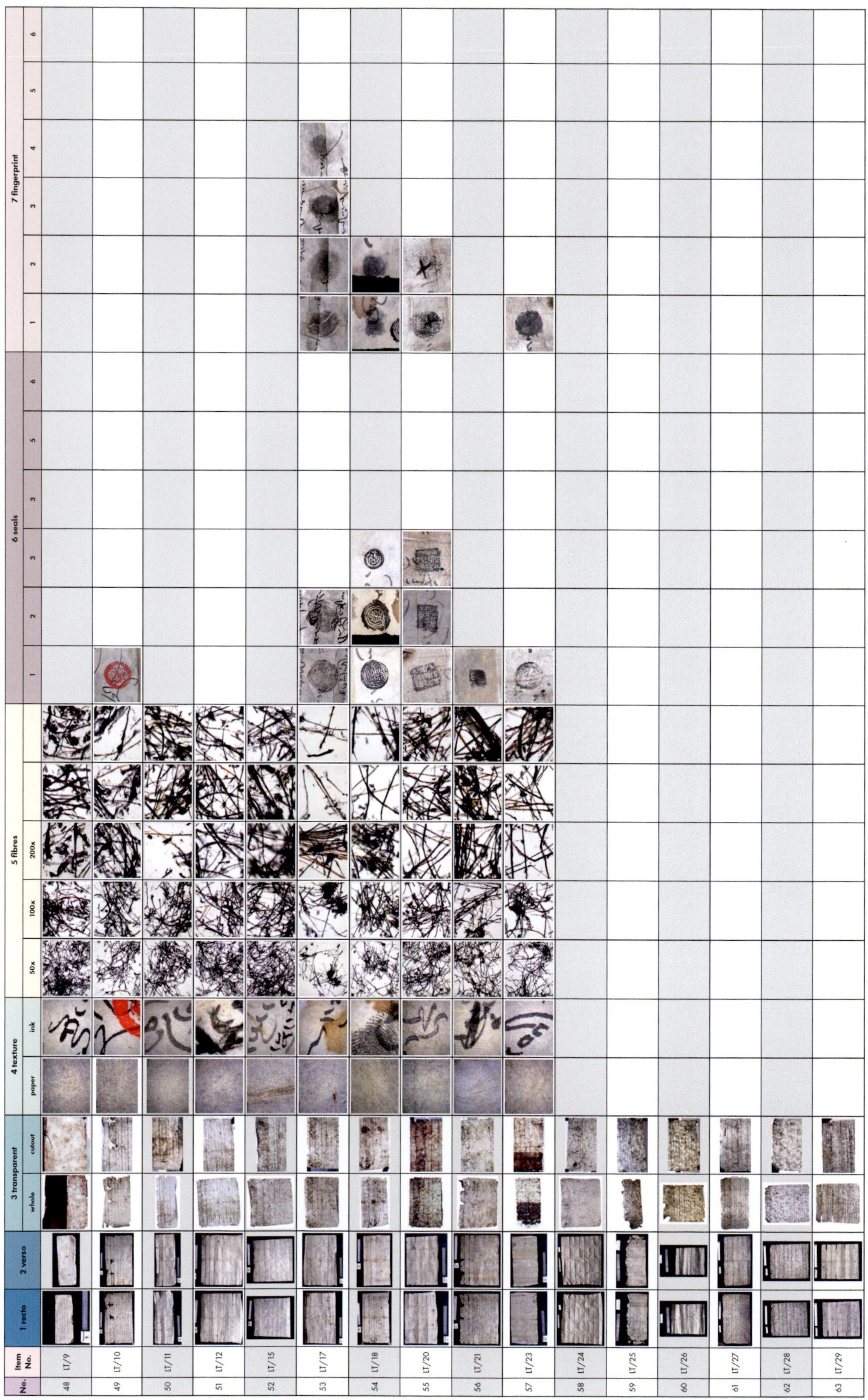
No.
Item No.
1 recto
2 verso
3 transparent
whole
cutout
4 texture
paper
ink
5 fibres
50x
100x
200x
6 seals
1
2
3
3
5
6
7 fingerprint
1
2
3
4
5
6
48 LT/9
49 LT/10
50 LT/11
51 LT/12
52 LT/15
53 LT/17
54 LT/18
55 LT/20
56 LT/21
57 LT/23
58 LT/24
59 LT/25
60 LT/26
61 LT/27
62 LT/28
63 LT/29

No.	Item No.	1 recto	2 verso	3 transparent		4 texture		5 fibres					6 seals						7 fingerprint					
				whole	cutout	paper	ink	50x	100x	200x			1	2	3	3	5	6	1	2	3	4	5	6
64	LT/30																							
65	LT/31																							
66	LT/36 to LT/32																		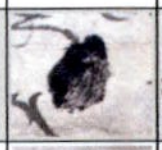		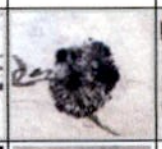		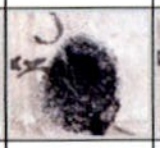	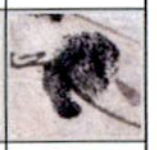
																				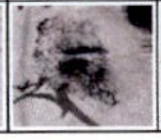	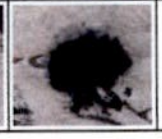			

No.
Item No.
1 recto
2 verso
3 transparent
whole
cutout
4 texture
paper
ink
5 fibres
50x
100x
200x
6 seals
1
2
3
3
5
6
7 fingerprint
1
2
3
4
5
6
DZAR
1 D/1
2 D/2
3 D/3
4 D/4
5 D/5
6 D/6
7 D/7
8 D/8
9 D/9
10 D/10
11 D/11
12 D/12

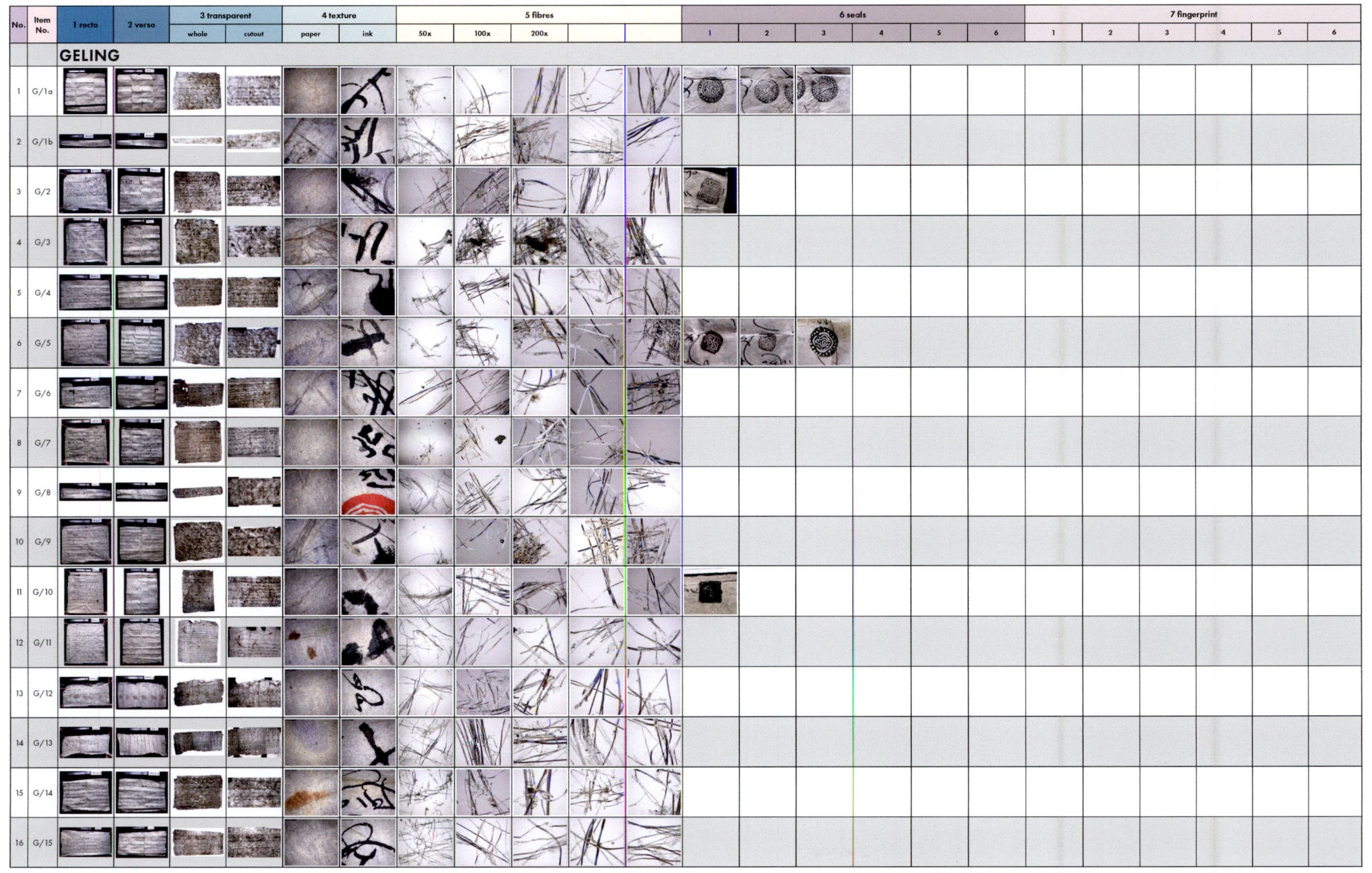
No.
Item No.
1 recto
2 verso
3 transparent
whole
cutout
4 texture
paper
ink
5 fibres
50x
100x
200x
6 seals
1
2
3
4
5
6
7 fingerprint
1
2
3
4
5
6
GELING
1 G/1a
2 G/1b
3 G/2
4 G/3
5 G/4
6 G/5
7 G/6
8 G/7
9 G/8
10 G/9
11 G/10
12 G/11
13 G/12
14 G/13
15 G/14
16 G/15

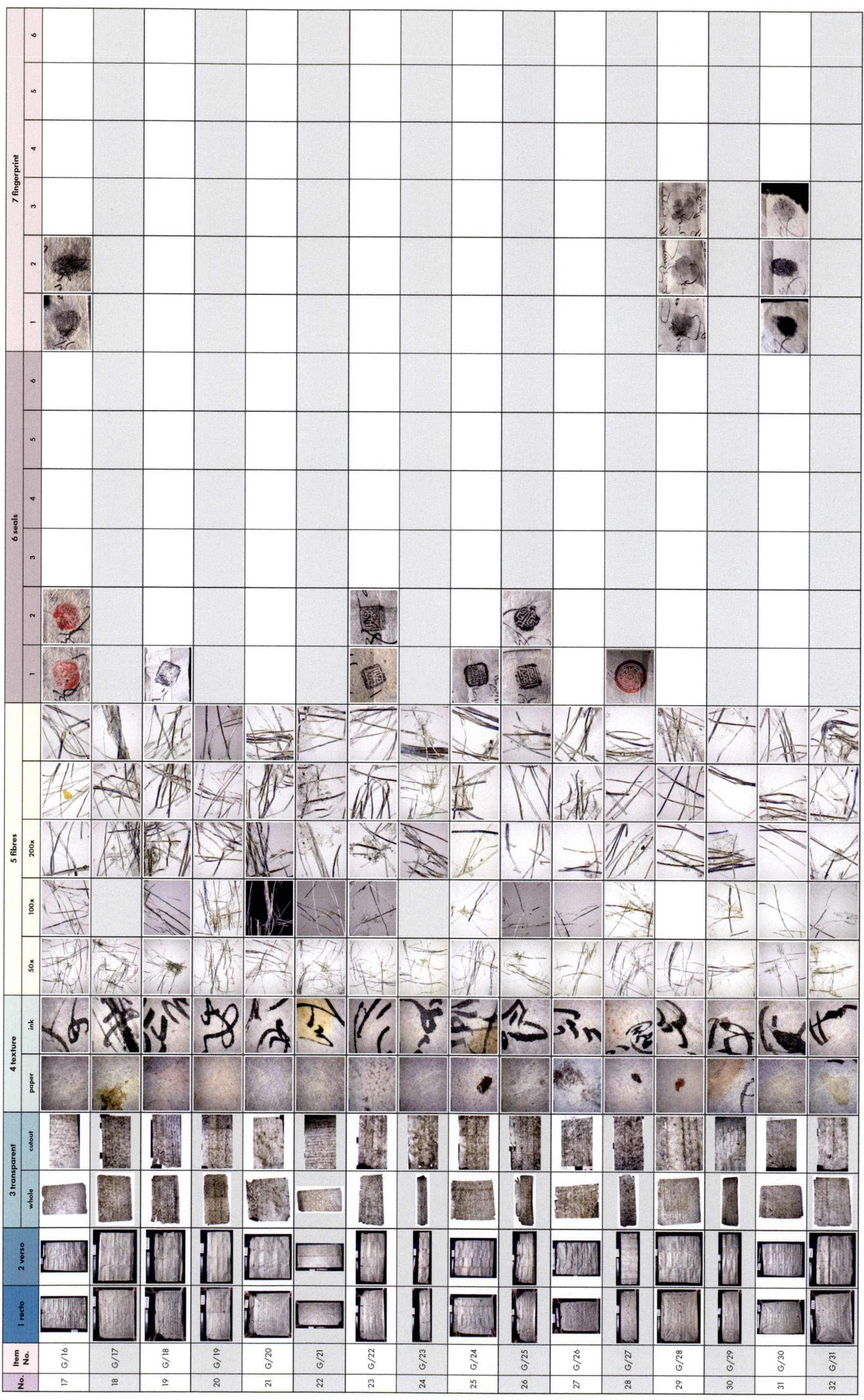

No.	Item No.	1 recto	2 verso	3 transparent		4 texture		5 fibres					6 seals						7 fingerprint					
				whole	cutout	paper	ink	50x	100x	200x			1	2	3	4	5	6	1	2	3	4	5	6
17	G/16																							
18	G/17																							
19	G/18																							
20	G/19																							
21	G/20																							
22	G/21																							
23	G/22																							
24	G/23																							
25	G/24																							
26	G/25																							
27	G/26																							
28	G/27																							
29	G/28																							
30	G/29																							
31	G/30																							
32	G/31																							

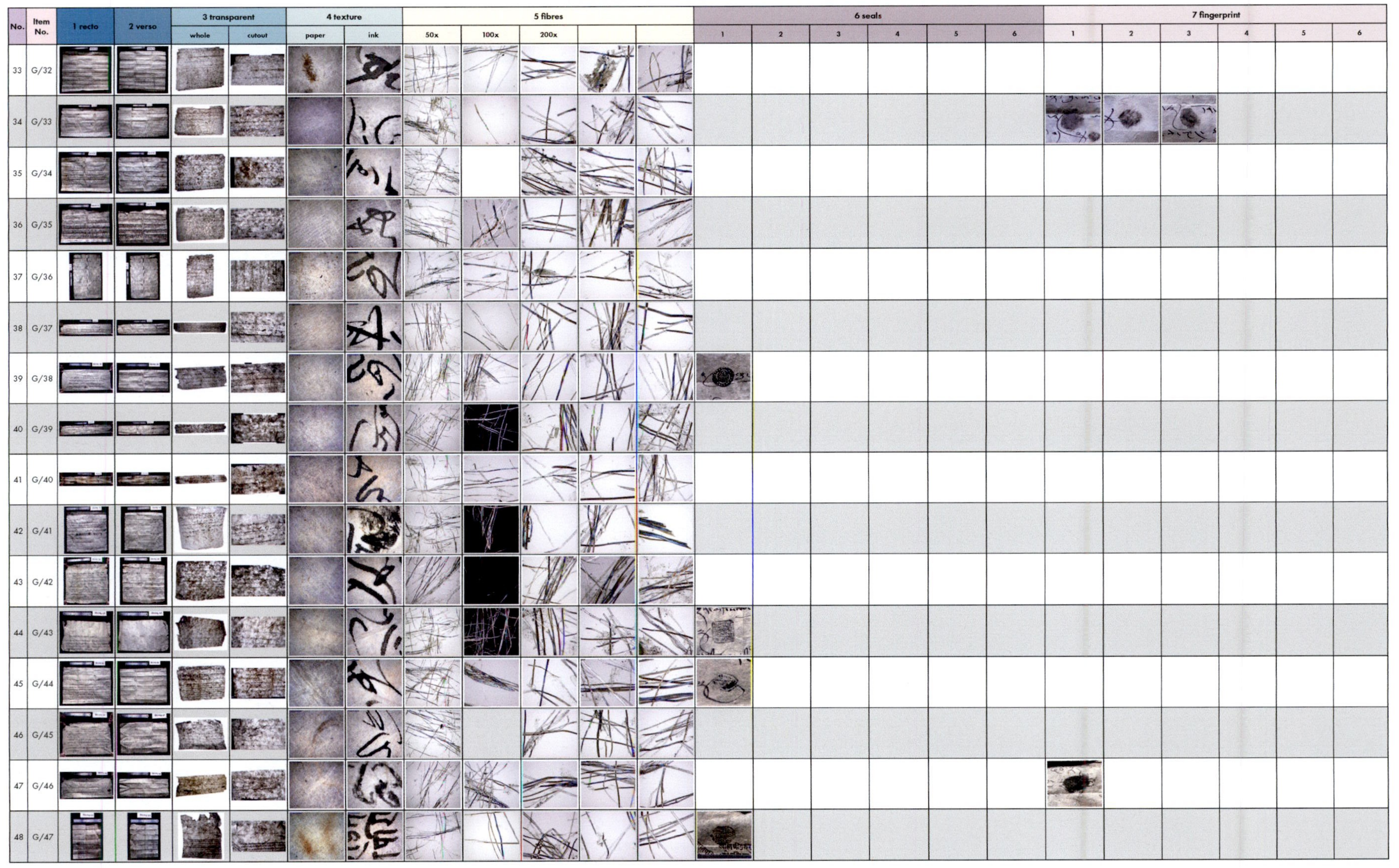

No.	Item No.	1 recto	2 verso	3 transparent		4 texture		5 fibres					6 seals						7 fingerprint					
				whole	cutout	paper	ink	50x	100x	200x			1	2	3	4	5	6	1	2	3	4	5	6
33	G/32																							
34	G/33																							
35	G/34																							
36	G/35																							
37	G/36																							
38	G/37																							
39	G/38																							
40	G/39																							
41	G/40																							
42	G/41																							
43	G/42																							
44	G/43																							
45	G/44																							
46	G/45																							
47	G/46																							
48	G/47																							

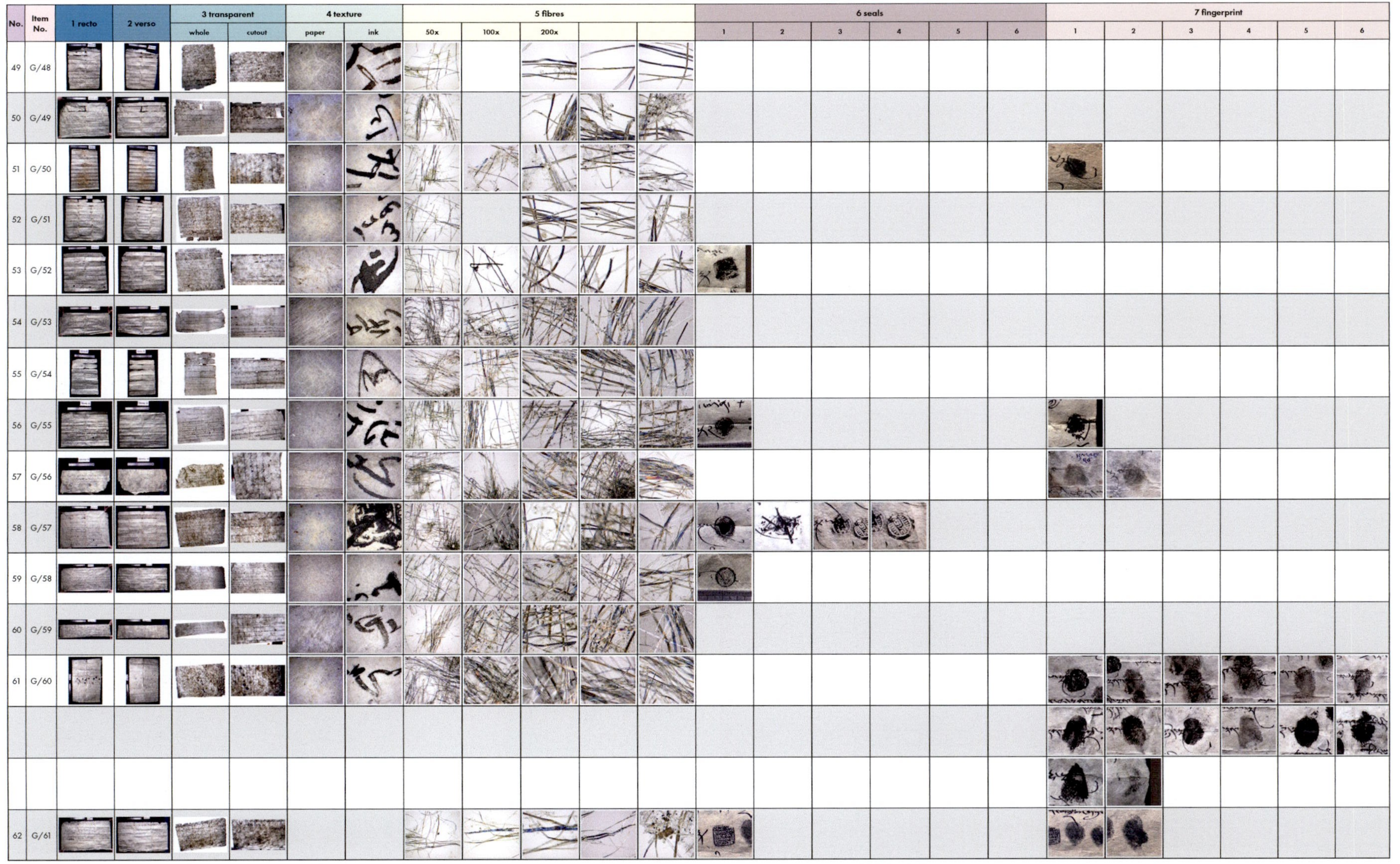

No.	Item No.	1 recto	2 verso	3 transparent		4 texture		5 fibres					6 seals						7 fingerprint					
				whole	cutout	paper	ink	50x	100x	200x			1	2	3	4	5	6	1	2	3	4	5	6
49	G/48																							
50	G/49																							
51	G/50																							
52	G/51																							
53	G/52																							
54	G/53																							
55	G/54																							
56	G/55																							
57	G/56																							
58	G/57																							
59	G/58																							
60	G/59																							
61	G/60																							
62	G/61																							

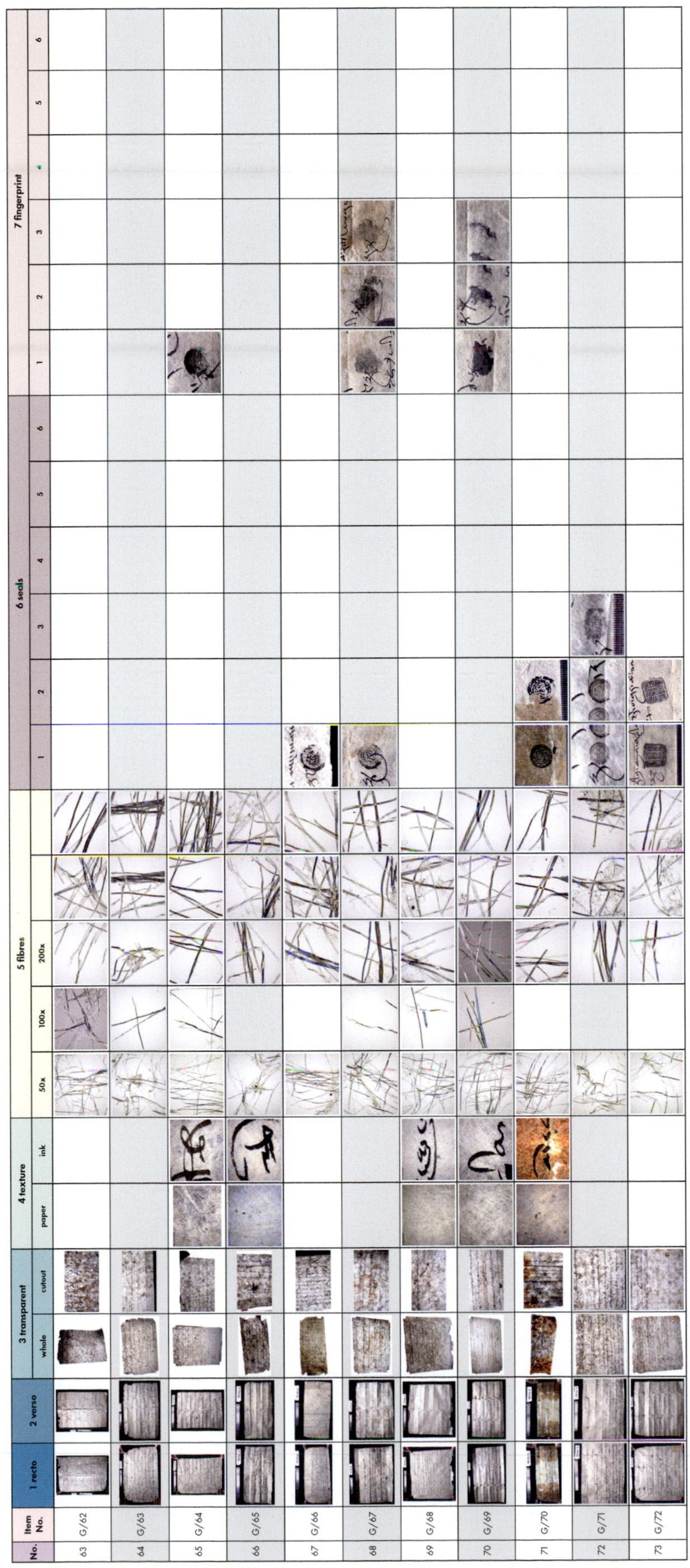
No.
Item No.
1 recto
2 verso
3 transparent
whole
cutout
4 texture
paper
ink
5 fibres
50x
100x
200x
6 seals
1
2
3
4
5
6
7 fingerprint
1
2
3
4
5
6
63 G/62
64 G/63
65 G/64
66 G/65
67 G/66
68 G/67
69 G/68
70 G/69
71 G/70
72 G/71
73 G/72

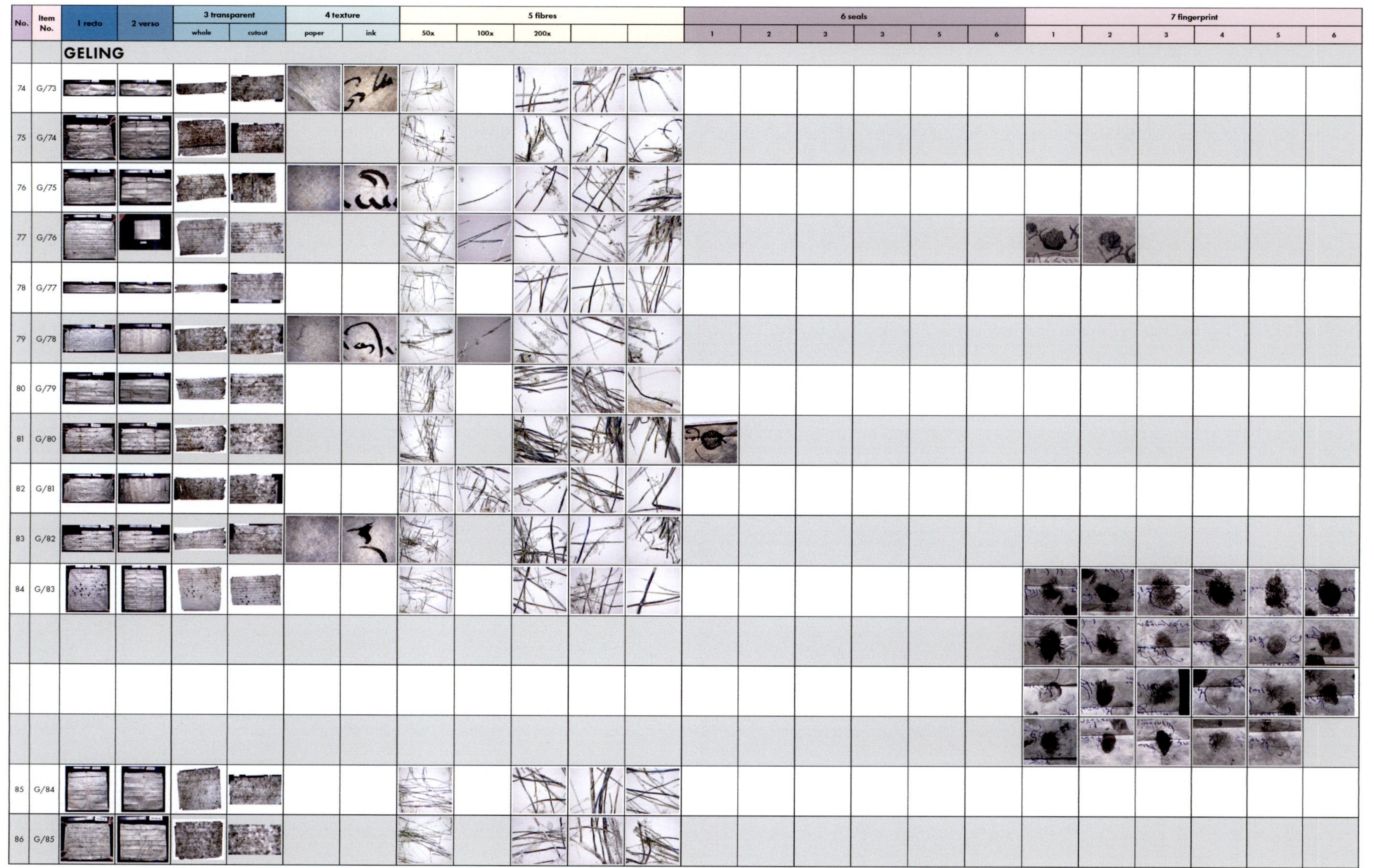

No.	Item No.	1 recto	2 verso	3 transparent		4 texture		5 fibres					6 seals						7 fingerprint					
				whole	cutout	paper	ink	50x	100x	200x			1	2	3	3	5	6	1	2	3	4	5	6
		GELING																						
74	G/73																							
75	G/74																							
76	G/75																							
77	G/76																							
78	G/77																							
79	G/78																							
80	G/79																							
81	G/80																							
82	G/81																							
83	G/82																							
84	G/83																							
85	G/84																							
86	G/85																							

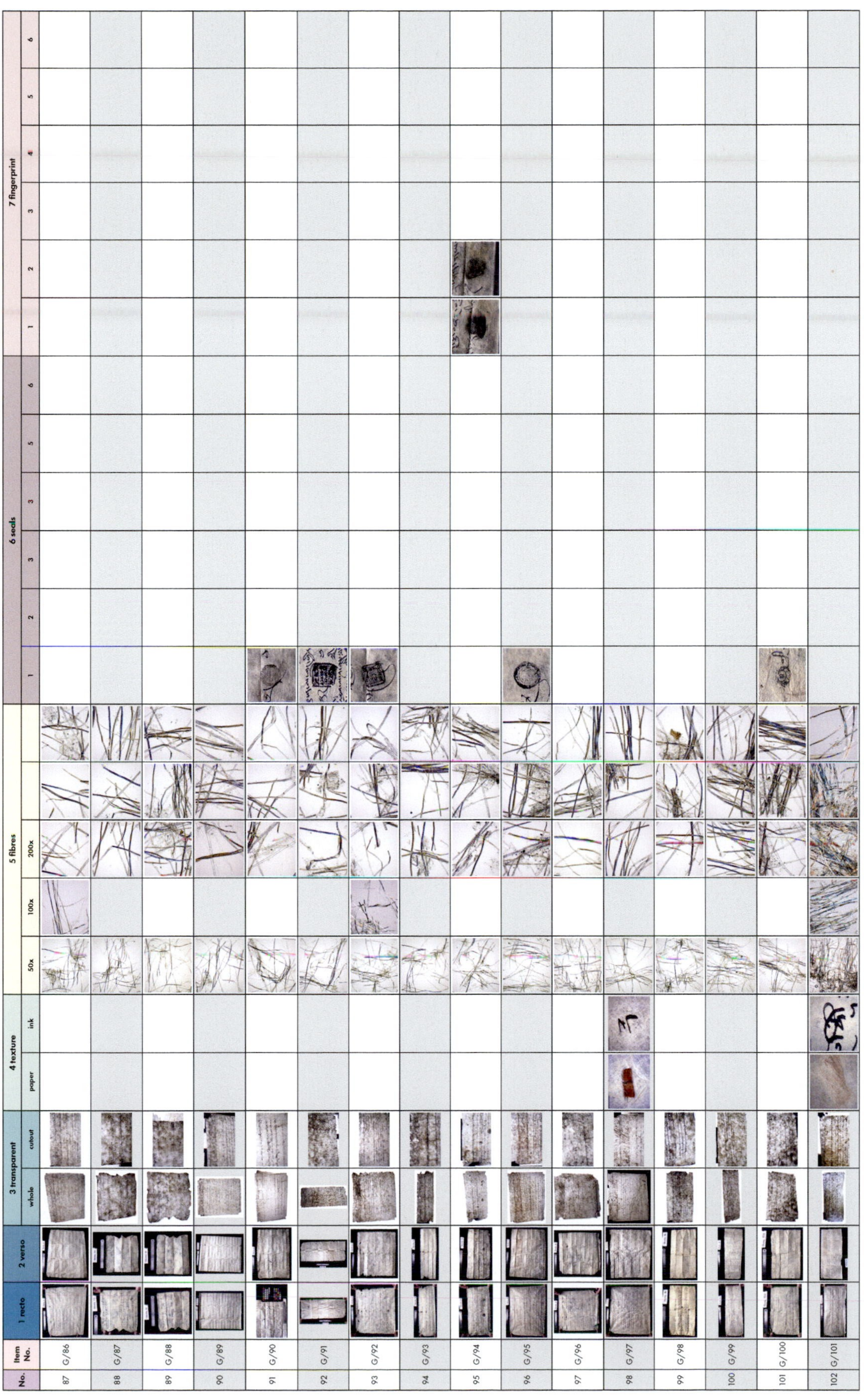
No.
Item No.
1 recto
2 verso
3 transparent
whole
cutout
4 texture
paper
ink
5 fibres
50x
100x
200x
6 seals
1
2
3
3
5
6
7 fingerprint
1
2
3
4
5
6
87 G/86
88 G/87
89 G/88
90 G/89
91 G/90
92 G/91
93 G/92
94 G/93
95 G/94
96 G/95
97 G/96
98 G/97
99 G/98
100 G/99
101 G/100
102 G/101

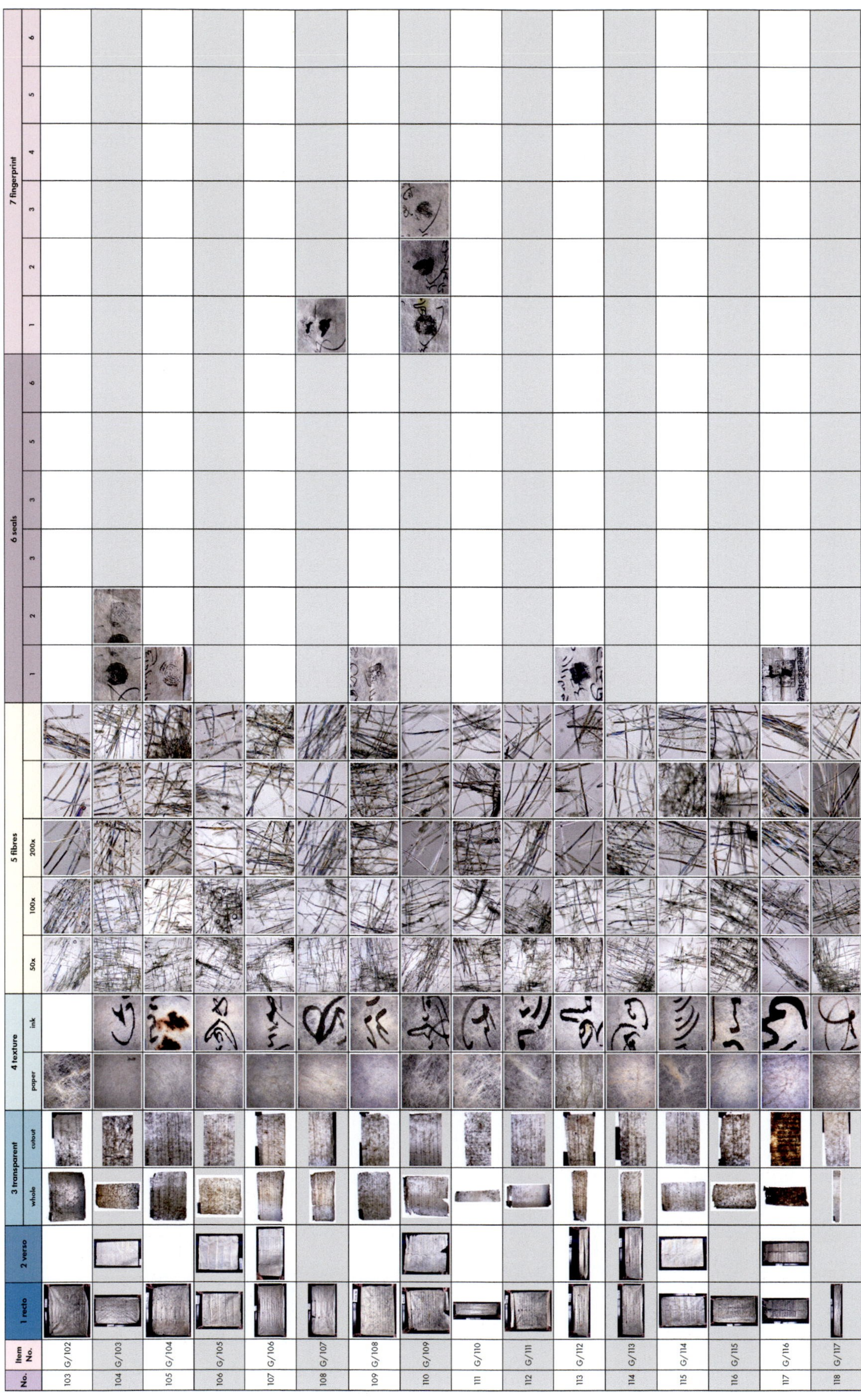
No.
Item No.
1 recto
2 verso
3 transparent
whole
cutout
4 texture
paper
ink
5 fibres
50x
100x
200x
6 seals
1
2
3
3
5
6
7 fingerprint
1
2
3
4
5
6
103 G/102
104 G/103
105 G/104
106 G/105
107 G/106
108 G/107
109 G/108
110 G/109
111 G/110
112 G/111
113 G/112
114 G/113
115 G/114
116 G/115
117 G/116
118 G/117

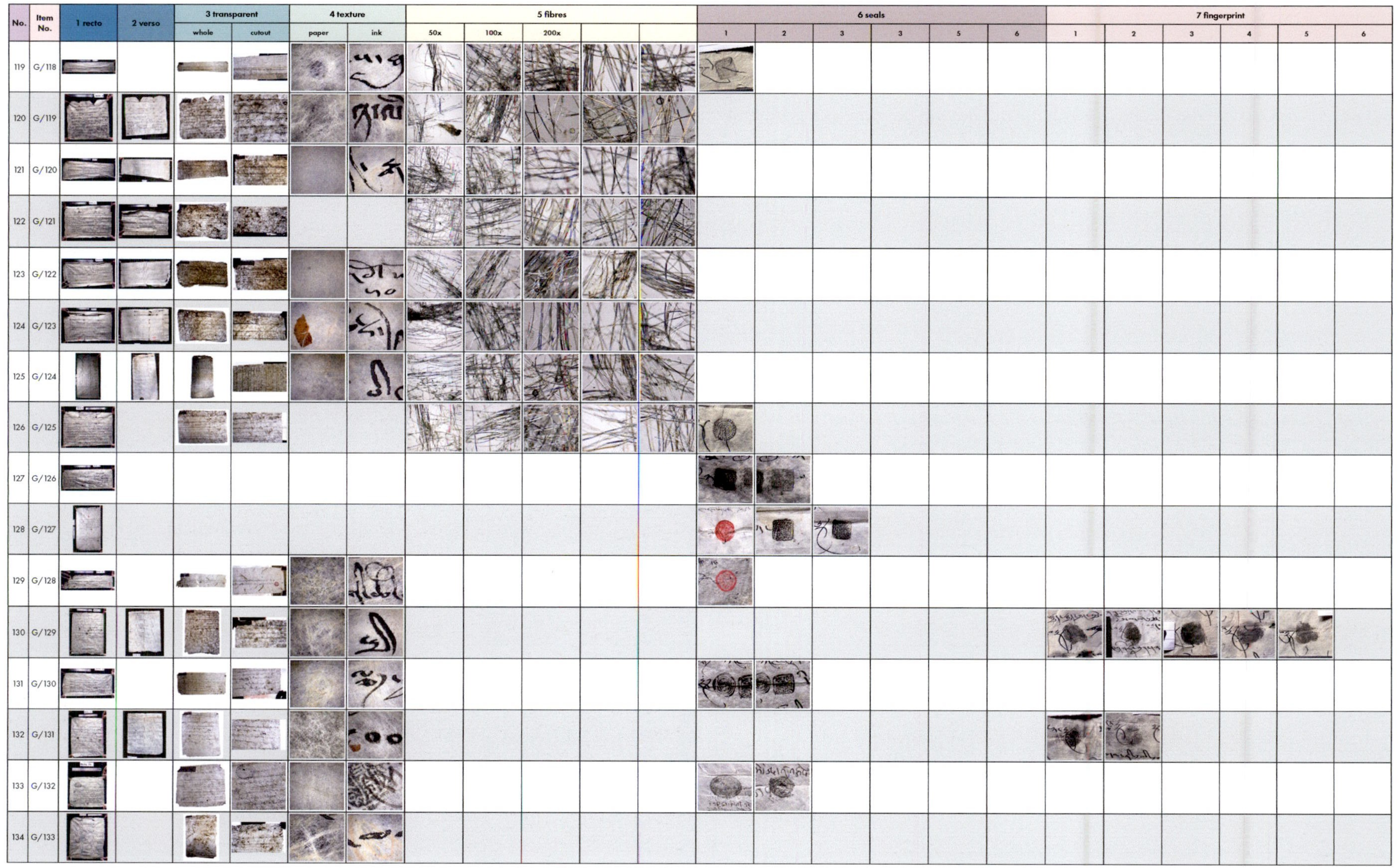

No.	Item No.	1 recto	2 verso	3 transparent: whole	3 transparent: cutout	4 texture: paper	4 texture: ink	5 fibres: 50x	5 fibres: 100x	5 fibres: 200x	5 fibres	5 fibres	6 seals: 1	6 seals: 2	6 seals: 3	6 seals: 3	6 seals: 5	6 seals: 6	7 fingerprint: 1	7 fingerprint: 2	7 fingerprint: 3	7 fingerprint: 4	7 fingerprint: 5	7 fingerprint: 6
119	G/118																							
120	G/119																							
121	G/120																							
122	G/121																							
123	G/122																							
124	G/123																							
125	G/124																							
126	G/125																							
127	G/126																							
128	G/127																							
129	G/128																							
130	G/129																							
131	G/130																							
132	G/131																							
133	G/132																							
134	G/133																							

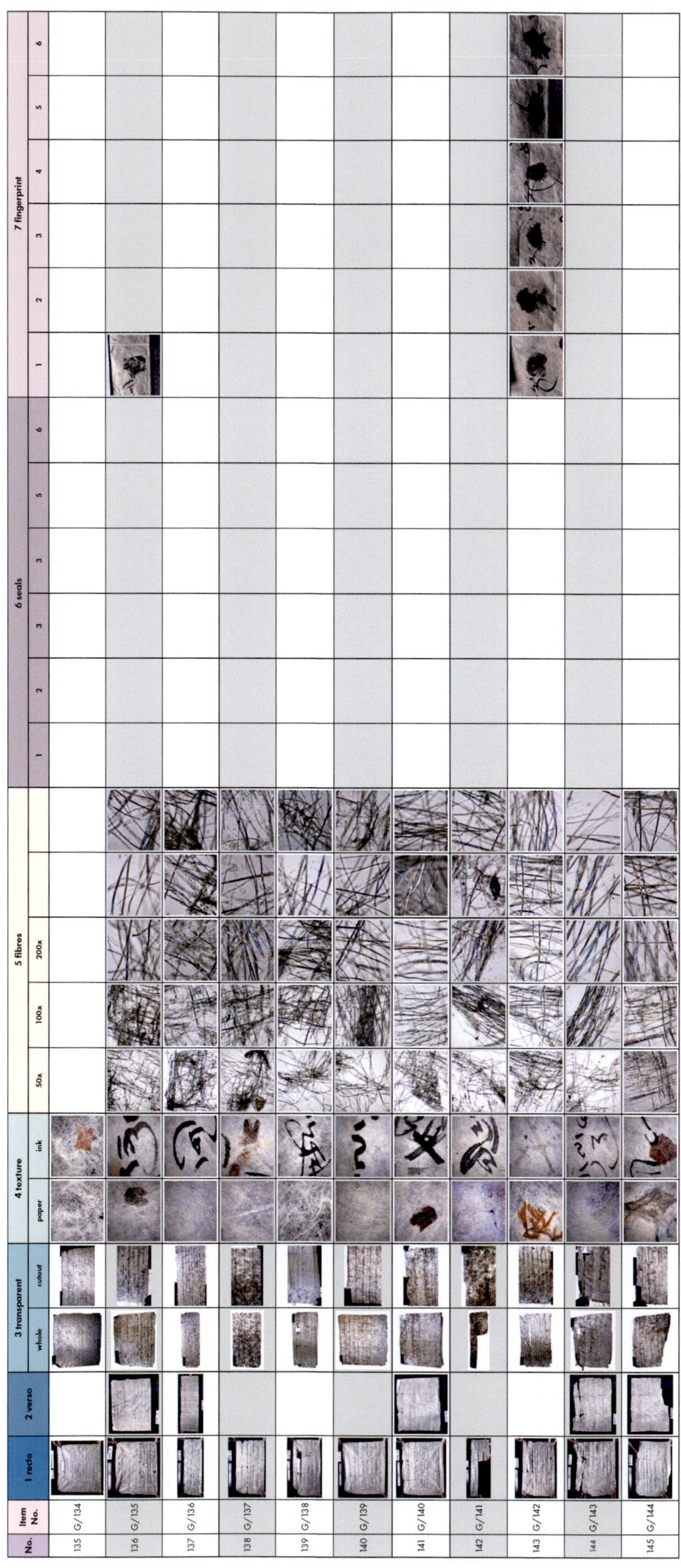
No.
Item No.
1 recto
2 verso
3 transparent
whole
cutout
4 texture
paper
ink
5 fibres
50x
100x
200x
6 seals
1
2
3
3
5
6
7 fingerprint
1
2
3
4
5
6
135 G/134
136 G/135
137 G/136
138 G/137
139 G/138
140 G/139
141 G/140
142 G/141
143 G/142
144 G/143
145 G/144

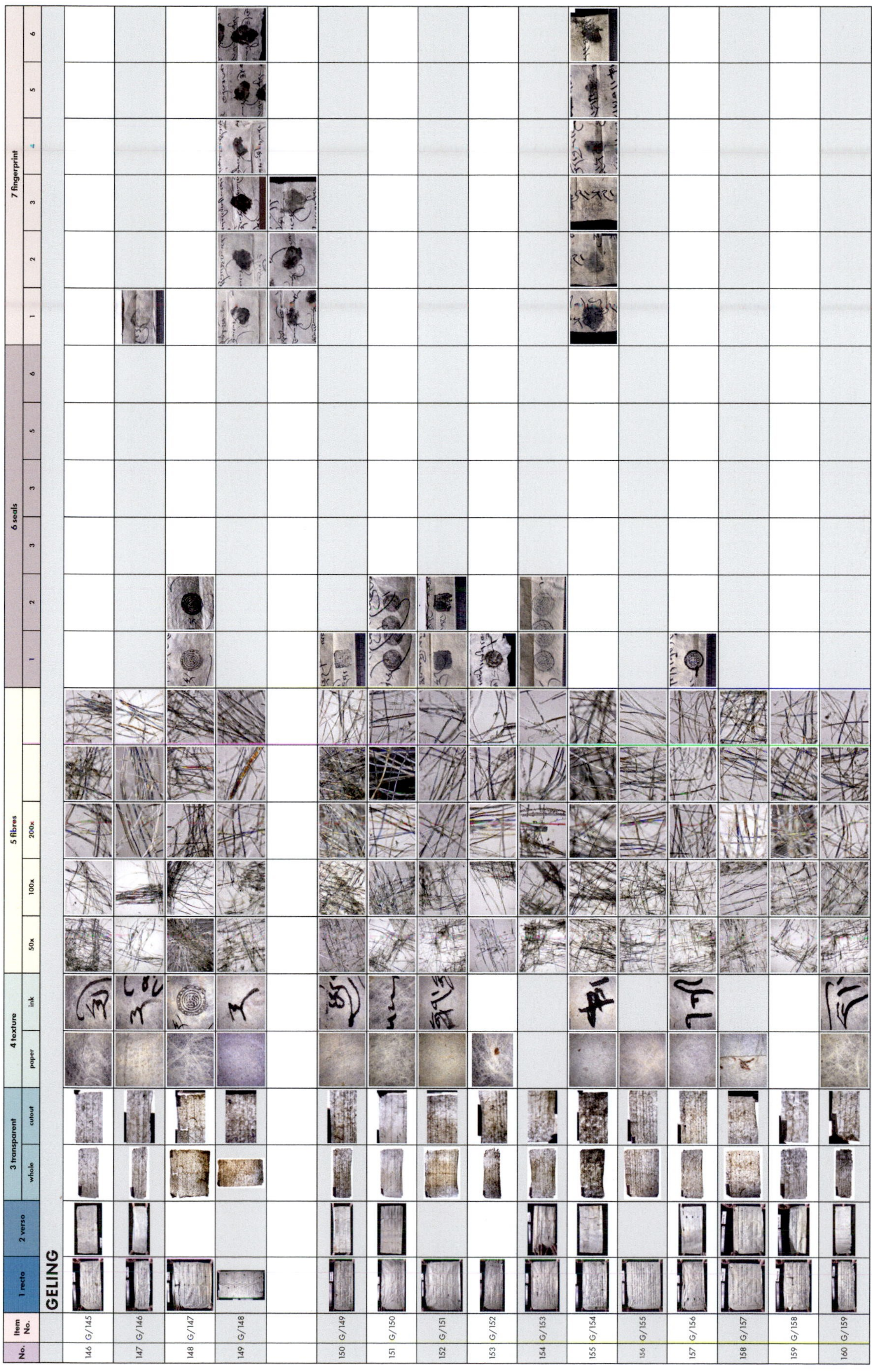
No.
Item No.
1 recto
2 verso
3 transparent
whole
cutout
4 texture
paper
ink
5 fibres
50x
100x
200x
6 seals
1
2
3
3
5
6
7 fingerprint
1
2
3
4
5
6
GELING
146 G/145
147 G/146
148 G/147
149 G/148
150 G/149
151 G/150
152 G/151
153 G/152
154 G/153
155 G/154
156 G/155
157 G/156
158 G/157
159 G/158
160 G/159

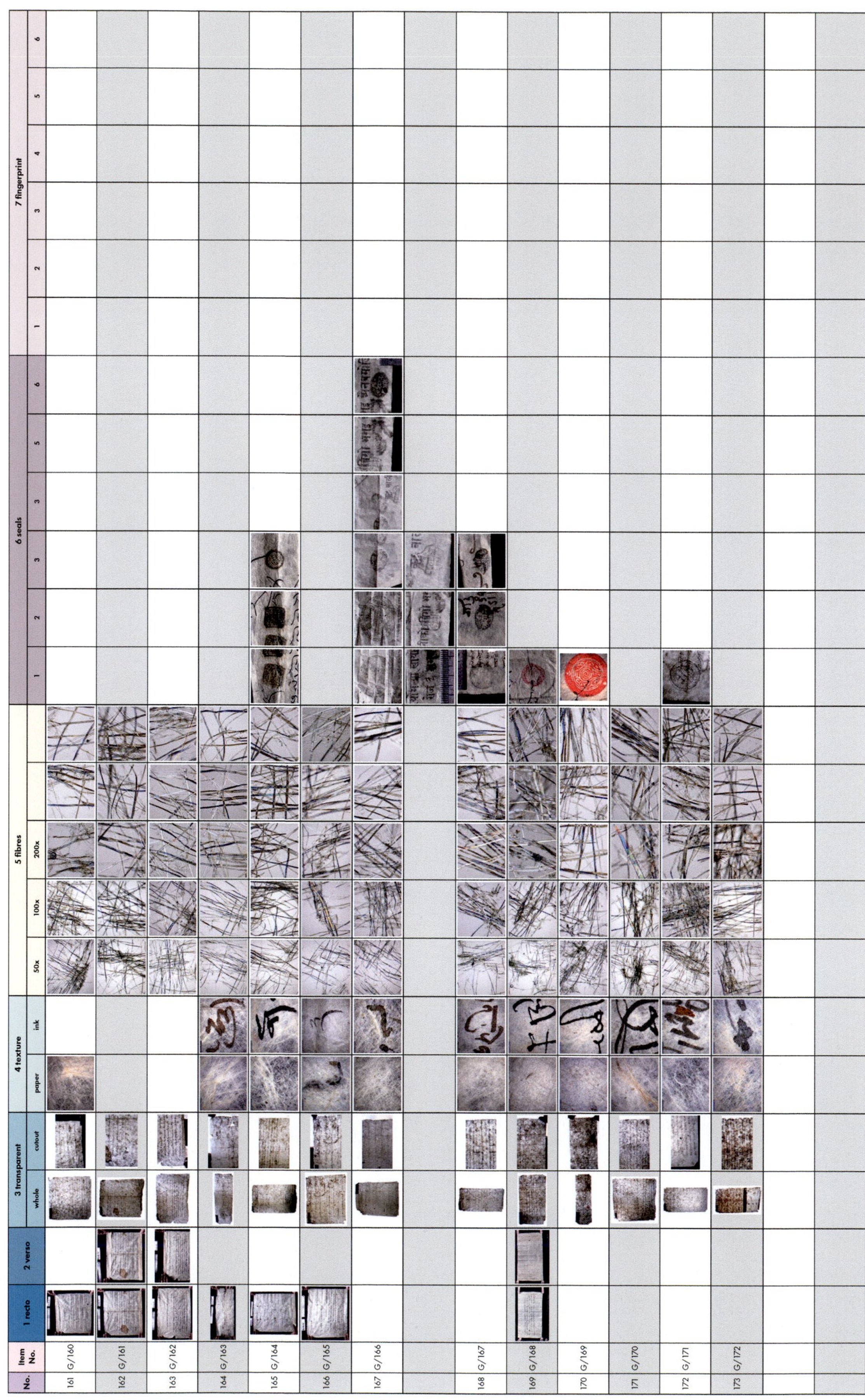

No.
Item No.
1 recto
2 verso
3 transparent
whole
cutout
4 texture
paper
ink
5 fibres
50x
100x
200x
6 seals
1
2
3
3
5
6
7 fingerprint
1
2
3
4
5
6
161 G/160
162 G/161
163 G/162
164 G/163
165 G/164
166 G/165
167 G/166
168 G/167
169 G/168
170 G/169
171 G/170
172 G/171
173 G/172

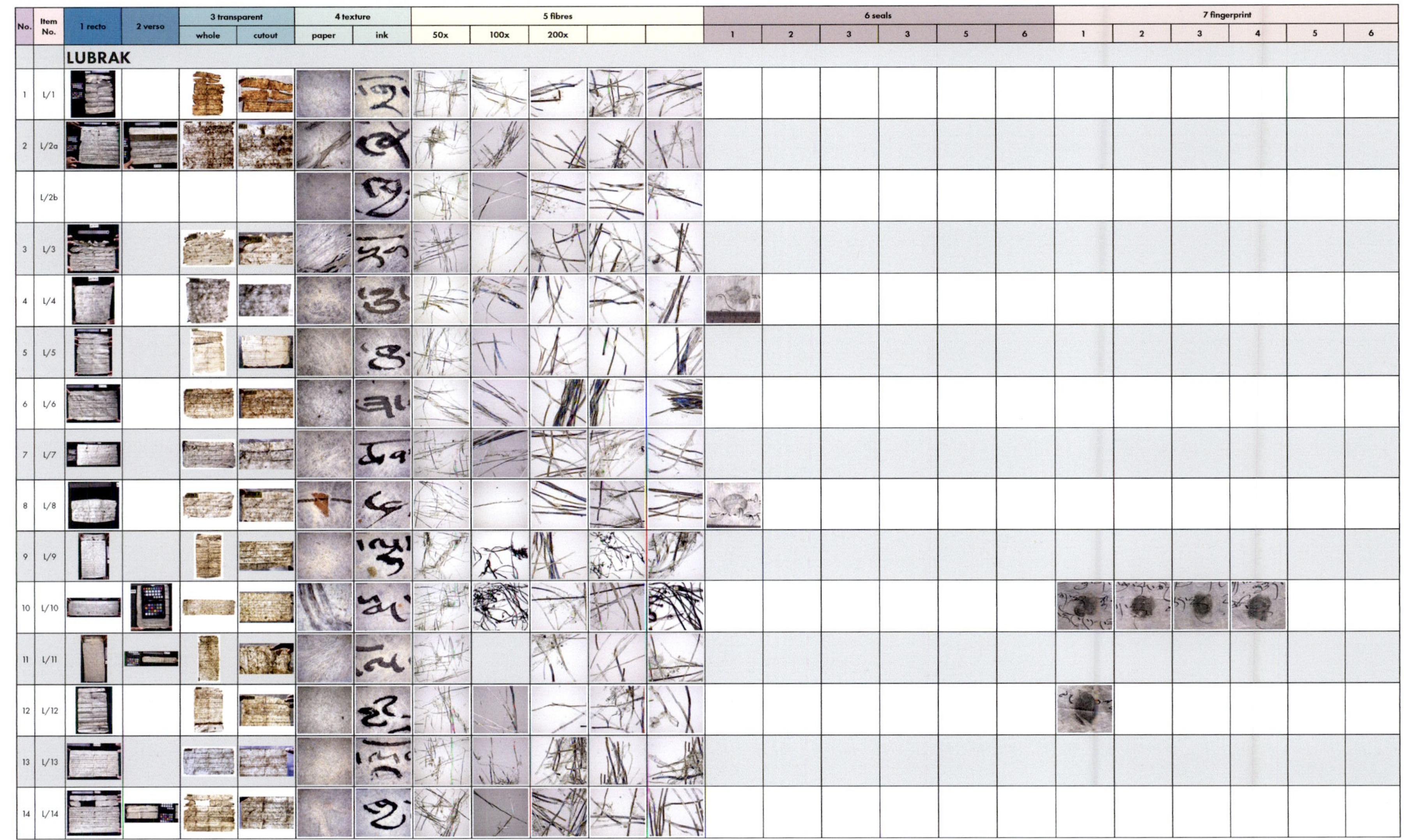
No.
Item No.
1 recto
2 verso
3 transparent
whole
cutout
4 texture
paper
ink
5 fibres
50x
100x
200x
6 seals
1
2
3
3
5
6
7 fingerprint
1
2
3
4
5
6
LUBRAK
1 L/1
2 L/2a
L/2b
3 L/3
4 L/4
5 L/5
6 L/6
7 L/7
8 L/8
9 L/9
10 L/10
11 L/11
12 L/12
13 L/13
14 L/14

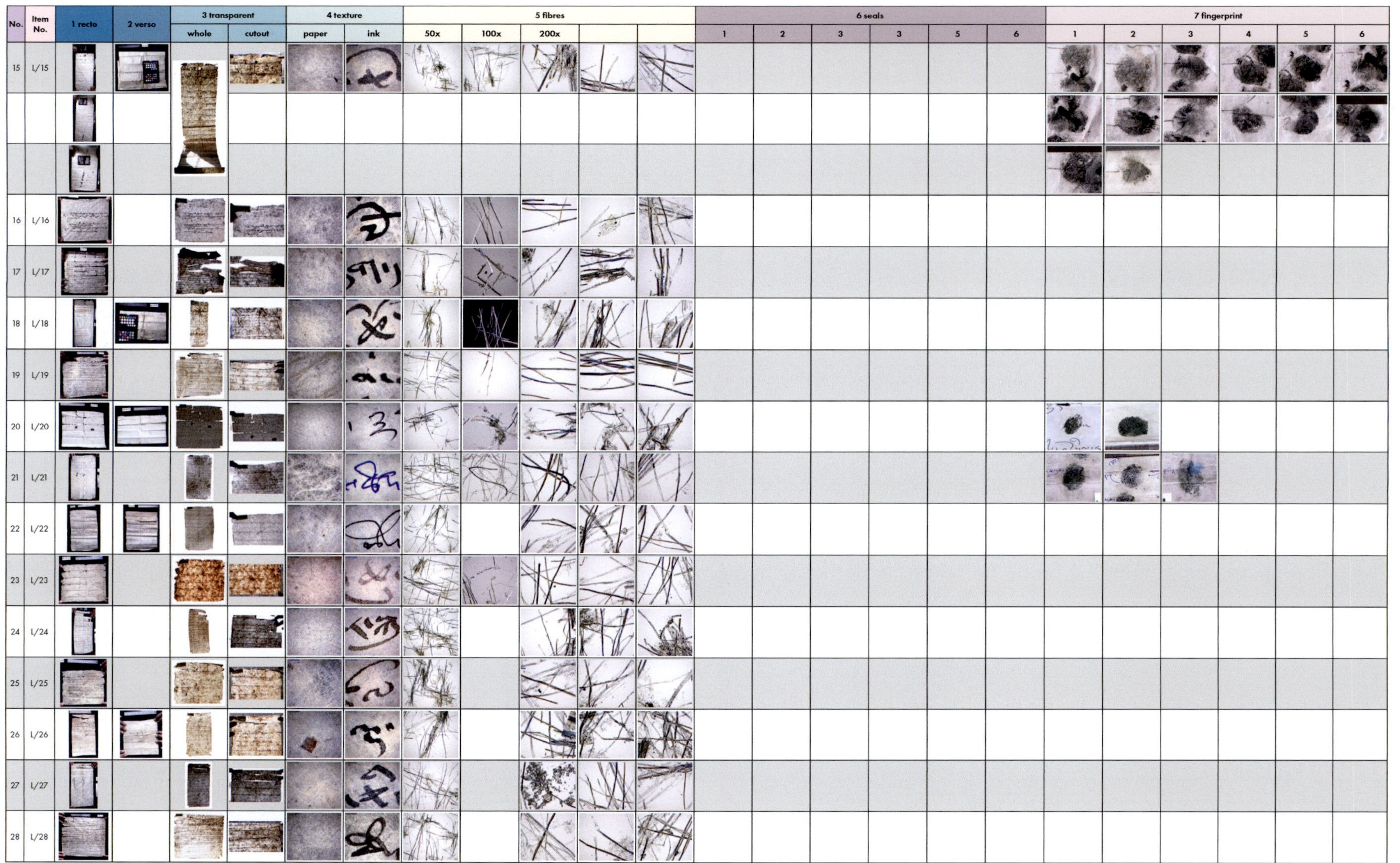

No.	Item No.	1 recto	2 verso	3 transparent		4 texture		5 fibres					6 seals						7 fingerprint					
				whole	cutout	paper	ink	50x	100x	200x			1	2	3	3	5	6	1	2	3	4	5	6
15	L/15																							
16	L/16																							
17	L/17																							
18	L/18																							
19	L/19																							
20	L/20																							
21	L/21																							
22	L/22																							
23	L/23																							
24	L/24																							
25	L/25																							
26	L/26																							
27	L/27																							
28	L/28																							

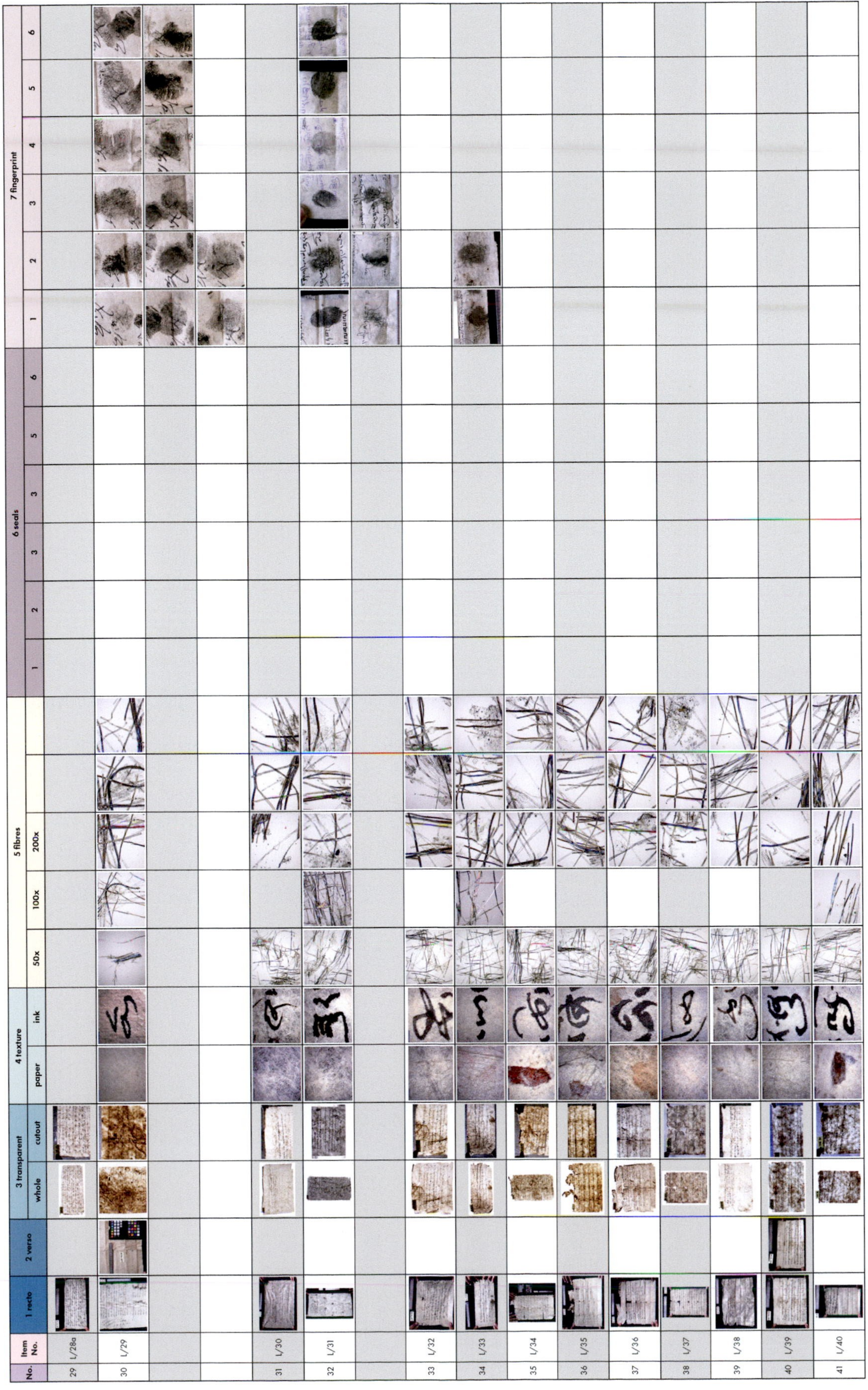
No.
Item No.
1 recto
2 verso
3 transparent
whole
cutout
4 texture
paper
ink
5 fibres
50x
100x
200x
6 seals
1
2
3
3
5
6
7 fingerprint
1
2
3
4
5
6
29 L/28a
30 L/29
31 L/30
32 L/31
33 L/32
34 L/33
35 L/34
36 L/35
37 L/36
38 L/37
39 L/38
40 L/39
41 L/40

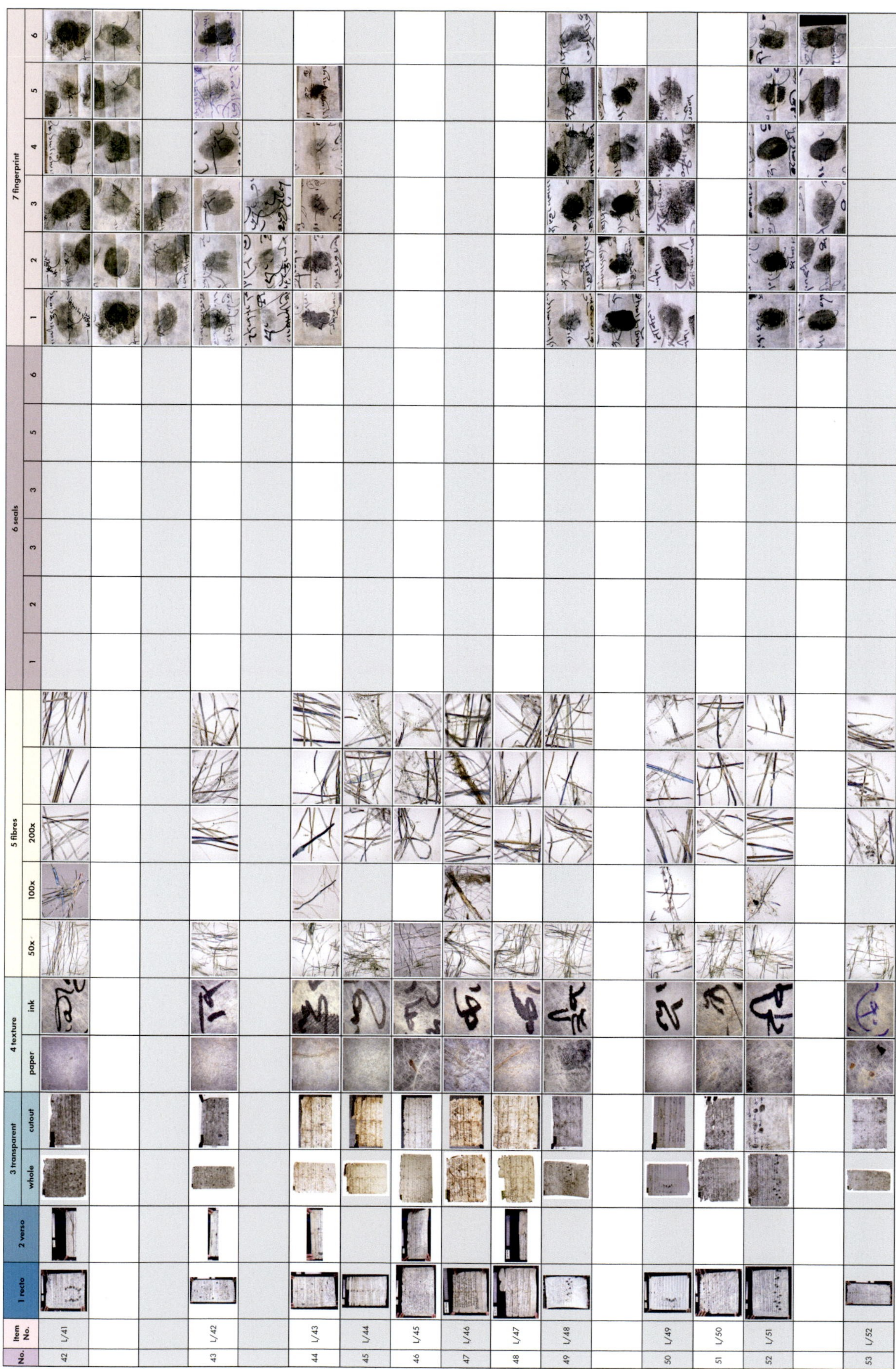
No.
Item No.
1 recto
2 verso
3 transparent
whole
cutout
4 texture
paper
ink
5 fibres
50x
100x
200x
6 seals
1
2
3
3
5
6
7 fingerprint
1
2
3
4
5
6
42 L/41
43 L/42
44 L/43
45 L/44
46 L/45
47 L/46
48 L/47
49 L/48
50 L/49
51 L/50
52 L/51
53 L/52

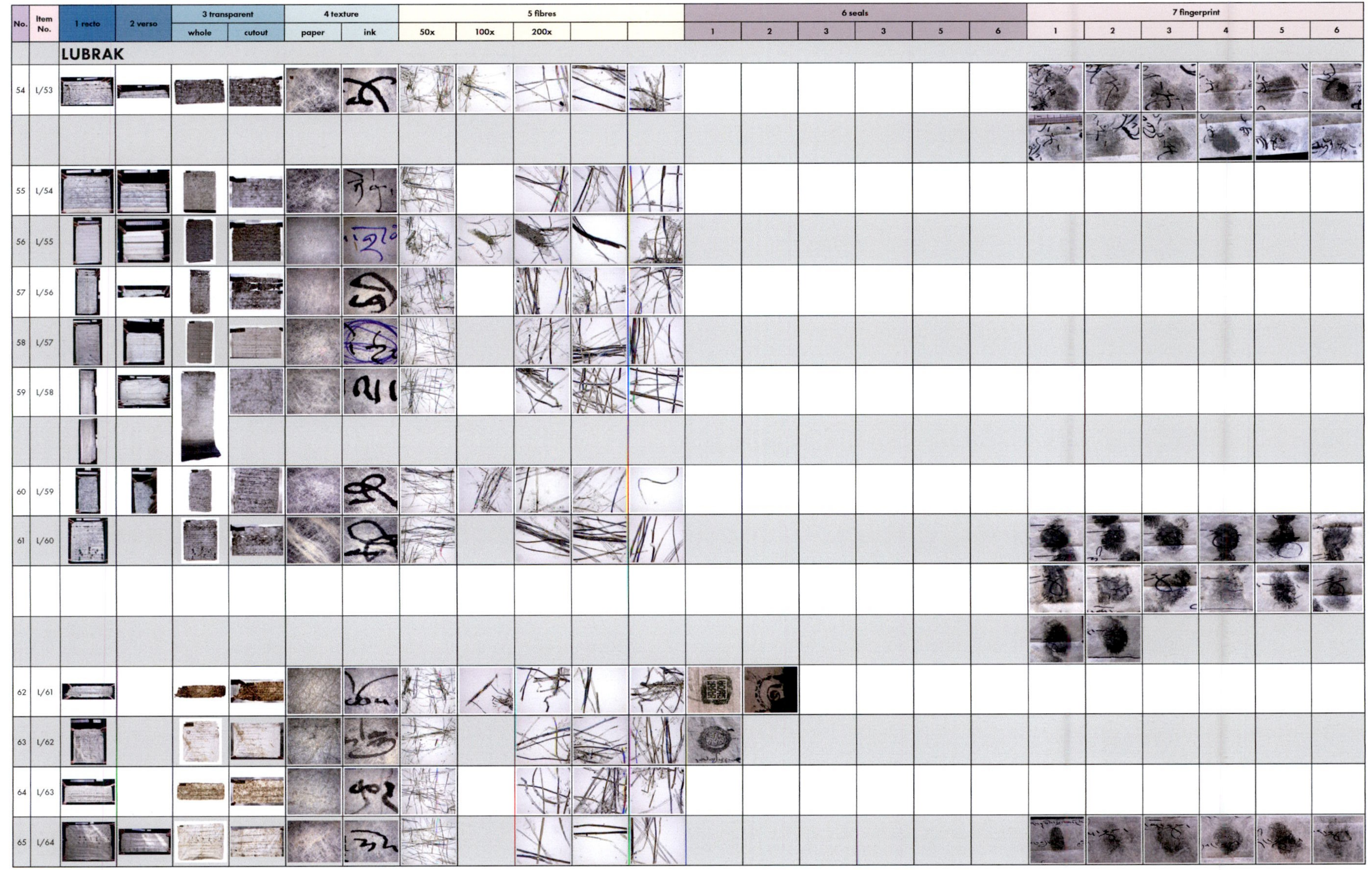

No.	Item No.	1 recto	2 verso	3 transparent		4 texture		5 fibres					6 seals						7 fingerprint					
				whole	cutout	paper	ink	50x	100x	200x			1	2	3	3	5	6	1	2	3	4	5	6
		LUBRAK																						
54	L/53																							
55	L/54																							
56	L/55																							
57	L/56																							
58	L/57																							
59	L/58																							
60	L/59																							
61	L/60																							
62	L/61																							
63	L/62																							
64	L/63																							
65	L/64																							

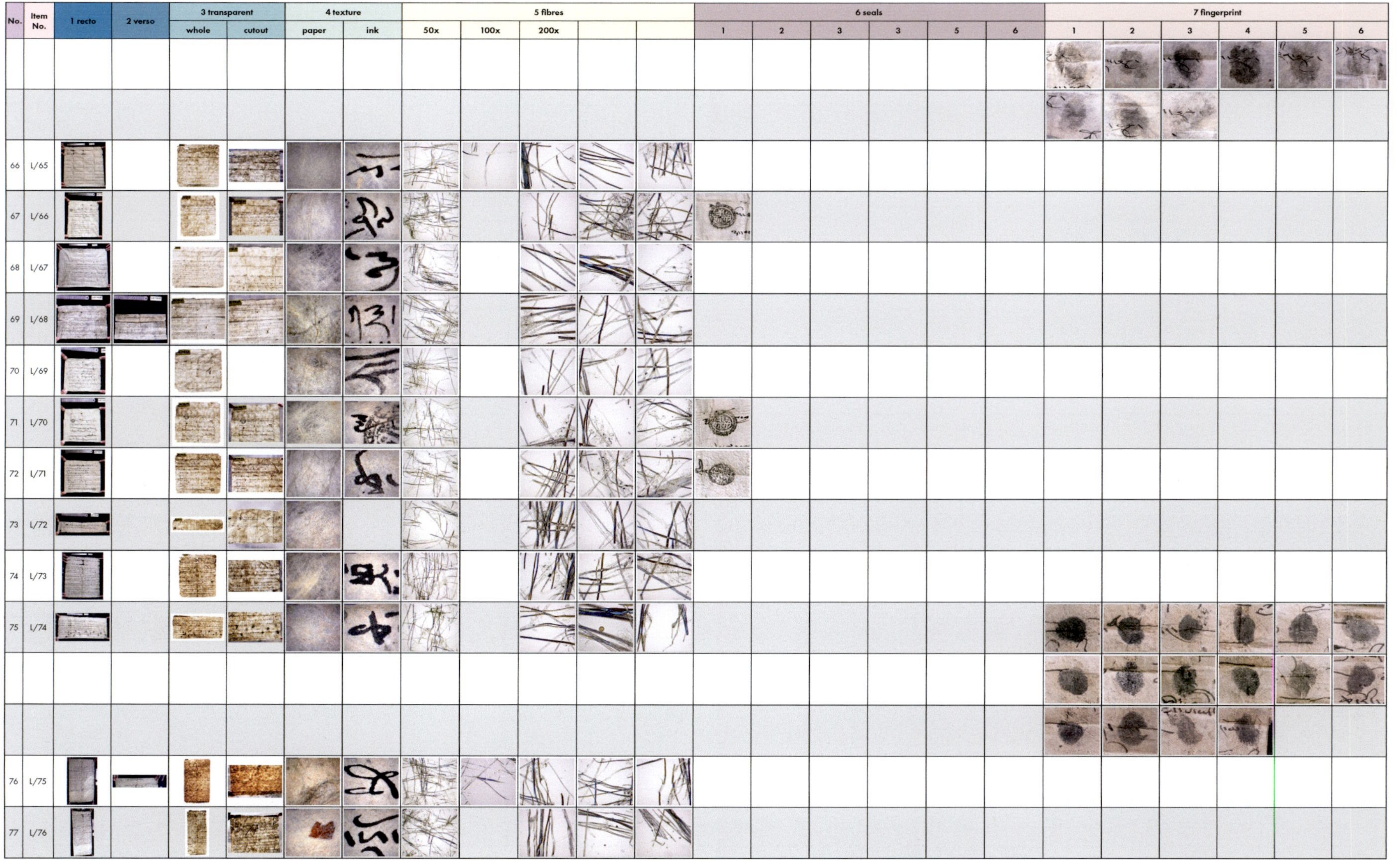

No.	Item No.	1 recto	2 verso	3 transparent		4 texture		5 fibres					6 seals						7 fingerprint					
				whole	cutout	paper	ink	50x	100x	200x			1	2	3	3	5	6	1	2	3	4	5	6
66	L/65																							
67	L/66																							
68	L/67																							
69	L/68																							
70	L/69																							
71	L/70																							
72	L/71																							
73	L/72																							
74	L/73																							
75	L/74																							
76	L/75																							
77	L/76																							

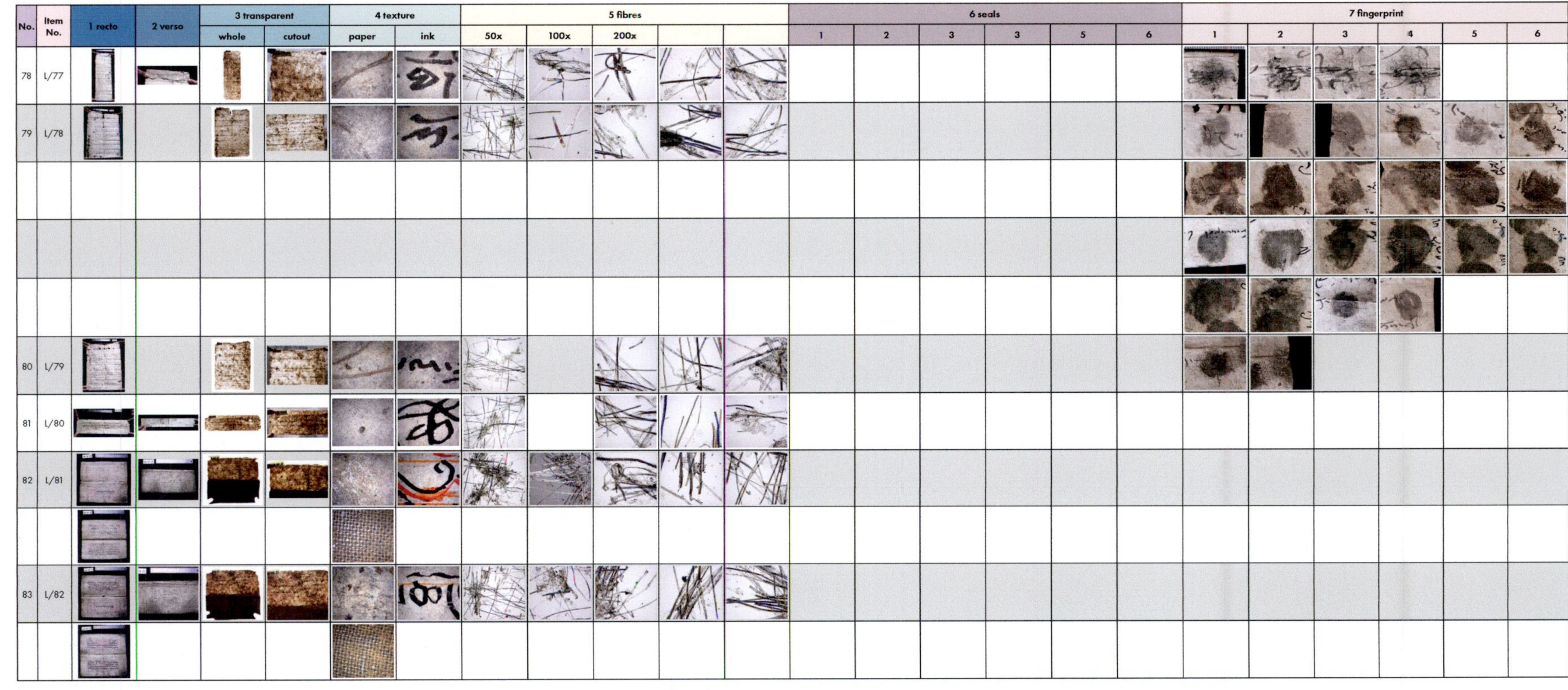

No.	Item No.	1 recto	2 verso	3 transparent		4 texture		5 fibres					6 seals						7 fingerprint					
				whole	cutout	paper	ink	50x	100x	200x			1	2	3	3	5	6	1	2	3	4	5	6
78	L/77																							
79	L/78																							
80	L/79																							
81	L/80																							
82	L/81																							
83	L/82																							

* The table presented here uses short versions of the catalogue numbers provided throughout the volume.

Appendix 2: Template for describing the studied documents

HMA Collection/Accession No.

Date of accession:
Archive location (village):

Category of text:
Title:
Date based on text:
Date based on ^{14}C:
Provenance:

Writing

Language:
Script:
Scribal hands:
Text execution:

Format and layout

Form:
Size (h × w) cm:
No of folds:
No of text lines:
No of folios:

Authentication marks

Seals:
Fingerprints:
Names of scribes:
Crosses:

Paper

Type of paper:
Fibre composition:
Sieve print:
Number of layers:
Thickness:
Texture:
Fibre distribution:
Fibre direction:
Notes:

Ink

Ink colour:
Ink composition:
Other colours:
Pigments:

Appendix 3: Summary of features of the studied archival documents

Acc. No.	Archive Location village	Date based on text	Category of text Title	Format and layout		Writing		Authen-tication marks	Paper							
				Size (h x w) cm No of folds	No of text lines	Type of script	Scribal hands Name of scribe if known	Seals, Crosses, and fingerprints	Fibre composition			Sieve print		Number of layers	Thickness	Fibre distribu-tion
									Daphne/ Edge-worthia/ Wikstro-emia	Stellera sp	Other	Woven	Laid			
MA/ Utshognam/ Tib/1	Upper Tshognam	1866	Draft of a petition prepared by Lama Rangdrol in an inheritance dispute with his brother Rigden.	Single sheet 31.5 × 38 9 folds	15	kmt		2 seals	++	++		+		1 Thick	0.1–0.26	Uneven with vis-ible fibre bundles
MA/ Utshognam/ Tib/2	Upper Tshognam	1869	Contract for sale of a field.	Single sheet 13 × 34.5 5 folds	6	kmt/ tshugs thung	Jamyang Wangdü	1 seal 2 crosses	+++	+		+		1	0.09–0.12	Even
MA/ Utshognam/ Tib/3	Upper Tshognam	1873	Contract for sale of a field.	Single sheet 15.5 × 29.5 6 folds	6	kmt		1 cross	+++	+		+		1	0.08–0.17	Even
MA/ Utshognam/ Tib/4	Upper Tshognam	1875	Contract for sale of four fields.	Single sheet 14.5 × 21 7 folds	10	kmt		3 crosses	+++	+		+		1	0.14–0.16	Even
MA/ Utshognam/ Tib/5	Upper Tshognam	1876	Resolution of dispute over ownership and use of a field.	Single sheet 29 × 31 9 folds	10	'khyug	Lama Thutob	6 seals 2 crosses (in the seals)	++	?	+ Singular recycled fibres	+		1	0.11–0.19	Even
MA/ Utshognam/ Tib/6	Upper Tshognam	1877	Contract for sale of a field.	Single sheet 10.5 × 29.5 4 folds	6	kmt		2 crosses	+++		+ epi-dermal cells	+		1	0.08–0.14	Even with slight irregulari-ties

MA/ Utshognam/ Tib/7	Upper Tshognam	1877	Contract for sale of a field.	Single sheet 11.5 × 33 12 folds	7	tshugs thung	Lama of Tshognam	1 or 2 crosses	+++	+		+		1	0.12–0.14	Even
MA/ Utshognam/ Tib/8	Upper Tshognam	1879	Contract for sale of a field.	Single sheet 9.5 × 26.3 4 folds	5	kmt		1 seal	+++	+?		+		1	0.10–0.14	Even
MA/ UTshognam/ Tib/9	Upper Tshognam	1880	Contract for sale of a field.	Single sheet 15.5 × 21 6 folds	5	kmt		1 cross	+	+++		+		1	0.09–0.12	Uneven
MA/ UTshognam/ Tib/10	Upper Tshognam	1881	Confirmation by a defaulting debtor that he will forfeit a field pledged as security on an loan.	Single sheet 22 × 31.5 8 folds	11	kmt	Lama Ösal Dorje	3 crosses	+	+++		+		1	0.09–0.18	Even with some irregularities
MA/ UTshognam/ Tib/11 a copy of MA/ UTshognam/ Tib/10	Upper Tshognam	1881	Copy of UT/10.	Single sheet 26 × 31 8 folds	14	kmt	Lama Ösal Dorje	3 crosses	++	++		+		1	0.08–0.20	Even with some irregularities
MA/ UTshognam/ Tib/12 missing	Upper Tshognam	1882	Contract for sale of a field to Lama Ösal Dorje.	Single sheet	7	'khyug		2 crosses								
MA/ UTshognam/ Tib/13	Upper Tshognam	1886	Public declaration by Baragaon of acceptance of apology from fraudulent leaders.	Single sheet 29.8 × 31.8 10 folds	21	kmt		1 seal 18 crosses	++ Fibrillated fibres	+	+ Singular cotton ? fibres	+		1	0.08–0.12	Even
MA/ UTshognam/ Tib/14	Upper Tshognam	1888	List of expenses incurred by Ösal Dorje in legal dispute over taxes to the community.	Single sheet 67.5 × 19.5 27 folds	49 (3 text lines in red ink)	tshugs thung (same hand, 2 different styli?)		-	++	++		+		1	0.08–0.38	Uneven

MA/ UTshognam/ Tib/15	Upper Tshognam	1888	Agreement on action to be taken over recurring theft of crops from a field.	Single sheet 58 × 19.5 23 folds	28	'khyug	Anchorite Sangye Tshecu of Purang	1 seal 2 sth ???	+	+++		+		1	0.09–0.15	Even with some irregularities
MA/ UTshognam/ Tib/16	Upper Tshognam	1889	Contract for loan of grain.	Single sheet 13.2 × 30 4 folds	7	kmt		2 crosses	+++	+		+		1	0.11–0.26	Uneven
MA/ UTshognam/ Tib/17	Upper Tshognam	1890	Transfer of responsibility for a house to Ösal Dorje from his mother.	Single sheet 25.7 × 32.5 8 folds	11	tshugs thung	Önpo Tshultrim of Te	-	++++			+		1	0.08–0.12	Uneven
MA/ UTshognam/ Tib/19	Upper Tshognam	1890	Receipt for loan of foodstuffs.	Single sheet 11.5 × 31.5 4 folds	5	check	Lama Ösal Dorje (signed 'I myself')	1 cross	++++			+		1	0.08–0.18	Uneven
MA/ UTshognam/ Tib/21	Upper Tshognam	1898	Contract for sale of a field.	Single sheet 15.8 × 34.5 6 folds	8	tshugs thung	Lama Ösal Dorje (signed 'I myself')	2 seals 5 crosses	++++			+		1	0.09–0.30	Even with some irregularities
MA/ UTshognam/ Tib/22 missing	Upper Tshognam	1904	Contract for loan of cash.	Single sheet	11	tshugs thung	Sonam Wangdü	3 fingerprints								
MA/ UTshognam/ Tib/23	Upper Tshognam	1906	Contract for loan of cash.	Single sheet 33 × 27 12 folds	13	kmt		10 crosses	++++	+?		+		1	Thin 0.06–0.10	Uneven
MA/ UTshognam/ Tib/24	Upper Tshognam	1906?	Contract for loan of grain.	Single sheet 63.5 × 58 15 folds	7	kmt		-	++++			+		1	0.08–0.25	Uneven
MA/ UTshognam/ Tib/25	Upper Tshognam	1907	Legal petition against Ösal Dorje et al. for various charges.	Single sheet 30 × 39.5 10 folds	25	kmt		-	++++		Singular fibres stained yellow/ orange	+		1	0.11–0.23	Uneven

MA/ UTshognam/ Tib/26–27	Upper Tshognam	1907	Formal response by Ösal Dorje et al. to petition in UT/25.	Single sheet 41.5 × 36.5 12 folds	24	kmt		-	++++			+		1	Thick 0.11–0.21	Uneven
MA/ UTshognam/ Tib/28	Upper Tshognam	1907	Contract for sale of a field.	Single sheet 16.5 × 38 6 folds	5	'khyug/ kmt	Lama Ösal Dorje's son, Tenpa Gyaltsen	2 crosses	++	++		+		1	0.10–0.18	Uneven ?
MA/ UTshognam/ Tib/29	Upper Tshognam	1909	Confirmation of previous sale of a field and assurance of lifelong maintenance for vendor.	Single sheet 17.5 × 38 6 folds	6	kmt		1 seal 1 cross	++++			+		1	0.13–0.17	Even with some irregularities
MA/ UTshognam/ Tib/30	Upper Tshognam	1910	Settlement of a dispute between Tenpai Gyaltsen and a blacksmith.	Single sheet 16 × 22.5 8 folds	9	kmt		4 fingerprints	++?		++?	+		1	0.11–0.16	Even
MA/ UTshognam/ Tib/31	Upper Tshognam	1912?	Legal petition in a dispute over property.	Single sheet 38 × 38 13 folds	24	kmt		-	++++ Fibrillation			+		1	0.07–0.43	Uneven
MA/ UTshognam/ Tib/32	Upper Tshognam	1912	Draft of UT/31	Single sheet 38.6 × 41 16 folds	23	kmt		-	+++	+ Singular fibres		+		1	0.07–0.15	Even
MA/ UTshognam/ Tib/33	Upper Tshognam	ca. 1912	Petition in a property dispute.	Single sheet 44.5 × 28.6 16 folds	35	kmt		-	++ Fibrillation	+	+ Recycled fibres	+		1	0.06–0.10	Even with some irregularities
MA/ UTshognam/ Tib/34	Upper Tshognam	1914	Contract for sale of a field.	Single sheet 13.5 × 34.7 10 folds	4	'khyug		1 cross	++	+	+ cotton?	+		1	0.11–0.18	Even with some irregularities
MA/ UTshognam/ Tib/35 (found in Lower Tshognam)	Upper Tshognam	1915	Agreement by nuns to take collective responsibility for theft from their convent.	Single sheet 19 × 33	8	kmt			++++			+		1	0.07–0.12	

MA/ UTshognam/ Tib/36	Upper Tshognam	1916	Agreement by community of Te to affiliate their nuns to Tshognam.	Single sheet 31 × 32 8 folds	12	’khyug		1 seal 13 crosses	+	+++		+		1	0.07–0.49	
MA/ UTshognam/ Tib/37	Upper Tshognam	1917	Agreement by community of Te to terms of a lama’s tenancy of an estate.	Single sheet 21.5 × 28.3 8 folds	12	’khyug/ kmt		3 seals	++++					1	0.08–0.11	
MA/ UTshognam/ Tib/39	Upper Tshognam	ca. 1920s	Letter to the lama of Te for advice on smallpox.	Single sheet 20.5 × 19.5 4 folds	11	kmt		-	++++					1	0.12–0.19	
MA/ UTshognam/ Tib/40	Upper Tshognam	ca. 1900	List of religious teachings received by a lama.	Single sheet 38.5 × 32.5 11 folds	35	kmt		-	++++					1	0.09–0.12	
MA/ UTshognam/ Tib/41	Upper Tshognam		Nepali document	Single sheet 22.5 × 26.7 9 folds	9			4 seals	++++					1	0.07–0.19	
MA/ UTshognam/ Tib/42	Upper Tshognam	none	Notes for ritual performance.	Single sheet 25 × 40.8 7 folds	25			1 seal	++	++	+?			1	0.08–0.14	
MA/ UTshognam/ Tib/43	Upper Tshognam	illegible	Illegible	Single sheet 23 × 28.5 7 folds	11			3 seals	++	++	+			1	0.14–0.29	
MA/ UTshognam/ Tib/44	Upper Tshognam	1884	Specification land taxes to be paid by a priestly house in Tshognam.	Single sheet 18.5 × 23 7 folds	9			1 seal	++++					1	0.09–0.54	
MA/ UTshognam/ Tib/45	Upper Tshognam	1871	Same as HMA/ LTshognam/ Tib/06.	Single sheet 13.5 × 31.5 4 folds	7			1 seal	++++					1	0.12–0.14	
MA/ UTshognam/ Tib/46	Upper Tshognam	none	Notes for ritual performance.	Book sewn at left side 20 pages 9.5 × 44	6-8 per page			-			++++ epidermal cells, vessels, parenchyma, fibres			1		

MA/ UTshognam/ Tib/47	Upper Tshognam		Text of songs of the Sixth Dalai Lama	Book sewn at the top 8.5 × 19 14 bi-folios 16 × 19	5-6 per page			-	++++					1	0.07–0.12	
MA/ UTshognam/ Tib/48	Upper Tshognam			Single sheet 27.5 × 47.5 10 folds	28			-	++++					1	0.10–0.15	
MA/ LTshognam/ Tib/1	Lower Tshognam	1816	Copy of covenant among the five Shöyul.	Single sheet 43.5 × 41.5 10 folds	15	kmt		-	++++					1	0.09–0.16	Even
MA/ LTshognam/ Tib/2	Lower Tshognam	1832	Covenant among the five Shöyul.	Single sheet 41 × 37	23	2 hands, kmt		9 seals 5 crosses	++++ Well preserved, clear fibres					1	0.12–0.25	Even (fibre bundles)
MA/ LTshognam/ Tib/4	Lower Tshognam	1860	Resolution of an inheritance dispute between two lama brothers.	Single sheet 26 × 34.5 8 folds	12		Kushog Trashi	2 seals	++++ many associated cells					1	0.1–0.23	Uneven
MA/ LTshognam/ Tib/5	Lower Tshognam	1871	Settlement of dispute over a debt.	Single sheet 19.5 × 24.5	10	kmt		2 crosses	++++					1	0.11–0.25	Even with rare fibre bundles
MA/ LTshognam/ Tib/6 missing	Lower Tshognam	1871	Confirmation of ownership of a house.	Single sheet	7	'khyug		1 seal								
MA/ LTshognam/ Tib/7	Lower Tshognam	1875	Will of a nun regarding inheritance of movable property from two estates.	Single sheet 20 × 29.5	14			-	++++					1	0.13–0.17	Uneven
MA/ LTshognam/ Tib/8	Lower Tshognam	1876, 1866	Copy (from 1876) of two settlements in dispute over field and house.	Single sheet 46 × 33.5	21	kmt	Nyilda Gyalpo and Thutob Lama	-	++	+	+?			1	0.06–0.09	Even with some fibre bundles spread regularly

MA/ LTshognam/ Tib/9	Lower Tshognam	1887	List of endowments and interest for an annual ritual.	Booklet (8 leaves) 6.5 × 17	5	kmt		-	+	++	+ Cotton Hemp			1	0.1–0.13	Uneven
MA/ LTshognam/ Tib/10	Lower Tshognam	1892	Letter from King of Lo two two lamas about trade tariffs.	Single sheet 30 × 53	8	'khyug		1 seal in red ink	++	++				1	0.05–0.11	Uneven
MA/ LTshognam/ Tib/11	Lower Tshognam	1897	Contract for loan of comestibles.	Single sheet 17 × 44	10		Drubpa Tshering Dorje	-	+++	+?	+ Synthetic fibers			1	0.05–0.13	Uneven
MA/ LTshognam/ Tib/12	Lower Tshognam	1897	Supplement to LT/11	Single sheet 30.5 × 36.5	11			-	++	+	+ Cotton Hemp			1	0.14–0.25	Uneven
MA/ LTshognam/ Tib/15	Lower Tshognam	1898	Description of a monastery in Tibet.	Single sheet 31 × 34	23	'khyug		-	+	+++				1	0.09–0.11	Uneven
MA/ LTshognam/ Tib/16 missing	Lower Tshognam	1904	Agreement between a Tshognam lama and nomads for resumption of butter payments by the latter.	Single sheet	6	'khyug										
MA/ LTshognam/ Tib/17	Lower Tshognam	1910	Confirmations of rights and privileges of the lamas of Tshognam	Single sheet 29 × 49	13	'khyug	Subba Bhagat Bahadur	2 seals 5 fingerprints	++++					1	0.06–0.2	Uneven
MA/ LTshognam/ Tib/18	Lower Tshognam	1910	Agreement to exchange fields for ten years.	Single sheet 20 × 37	7	'khyug	Lama Ogyan Rangdrol of Tshognam	3 seals 2 fingerprints	+++	+				1	0.08–0.17	Uneven

MA/ LTshognam/ Tib/19 missing	Lower Tshognam	1910	Formal response by Lama Ogyan Rangdrol to legal claim of property by his cousin.	Single sheet	13	'khyug										
MA/ LTshognam/ Tib/20	Lower Tshognam	1917	Contract for loan of cash.	Single sheet 19.5 × 30 8 folds	12		Gagyal	Finger prints; crosses, etc	++++					1	0.11–0.17	Uneven
MA/ LTshognam/ Tib/21	Lower Tshognam	1915	Agreement to provide lifelong maintenance to a divorced woman.	Single sheet 27.5 × 34.5	11		Bahadur of Marpha	-	+++		+?			1	0.03–0.06	Even
MA/ LTshognam/ Tib/22 missing	Lower Tshognam	1937	List of gifts presented at a lama's retirement ceremony.	Sincle sheet	21											
MA/ LTshognam/ Tib/23	Lower Tshognam	none	Settlement of an inheritance dispute.	Single sheet 18 × 37.5	9			1 seal	++++					1 (+ 1 fragment with secondary paper attached)	0.11–0.17	Uneven with many fibre bundles

Acc. No.	Archive Location village	Date based on text	Category of text Title	Format and layout		Writing		Authentication marks	Paper							
				Size (h x w) cm No of folds	No of text lines	Type of script	Scribal hands Name of scribe if known	Seals, Crosses, and fingerprints	Fibre composition			Sieve print		Number of layers	Thickness	Fibre distribution
									Daphne/ Edgeworthia/ Wikstroemia	Stellera sp	Other	Woven	Laid			
MA/ Dzar/ Tib/1	Dzar	1880	Rules for religious institutions	Single sheet 34 × 39.3 11 folds	17	dbu can	1	None	++++		+?	+		1	0.09–0.17	Uneven
MA/ Dzar/ Tib/2	Dzar	No date	Payments to monastery officials	48.4 × 32.2 15 folds	20	'khyug	1	None	+++	+		+		1	0.09–0.16	Even

MA/ Dzar/ Tib/3	Dzar	1844/1904	Management of village resources	23.6–25 × 32.8 7 folds	13	kmt	1	2 seals 2 thumbprints	++++			+		1	0.15–0.29	Uneven (fibre bundles)
MA/ Dzar/ Tib/4	Dzar	1878	Rules for ceremonies	Sewn book 10.3–11 × 28.6 Bifolio 22.4 × 28.6	18 pages, 6-7 lines per page	kmt, Devanagari	7?	1 thumbprint	++++			+		1	0.11–0.18	Even
MA/ Dzar/ Tib/5	Dzar	1878	Internal tax payments	Sewn book 18.2–13.6 × 30.2 Bifolio 27 × 30.2	6 pages, 6-7 lines per page	kmt	1	None	++++			+		1	0.10–0.46 (different sheets)	Even
MA/ Dzar/ Tib/6	Dzar	No date, ca. 1860	Rules for ceremonies	Sewn book (reminds whirlwind binding) 21.5 × 13.3	10 pages,	tshugs	8+?	None			++++	+ (felt print)		1	0.14–0.18	Even; machine made paper
MA/ Dzar/ Tib/7	Dzar	1874	Transfer of private property	Single sheet 17.2–18.1 × 33.2 7 folds ?	8	kmt	1	6-7? thumbprints	+++	+		+		1	0.15–0.37	Even
MA/ Dzar/ Tib/8	Dzar	1903	Transfer of a private house	Single sheet 13.5–15.4 × 30.1 14 folds	4	kmt	1	1 seal	+++	+		+		1	0.17–0.26	Uneven (fibre bundles)
MA/ Dzar/ Tib/9	Dzar	1866	Private loan contract	Single sheet 15.8 × 26.7 6 folds	4 recto 1 verso	kmt	1	3 thumbprints	++++			+		1	0.09–0.19	Even
MA/ Dzar/ Tib/10	Dzar	No date	Copy of Dzar Tib 6	Sewn book (reminds whirlwind binding but with the same size of each leaf) 30.2 × 17.5–19	6 pages, 7-21 lines	kmt	5-6?	None ?	++++			+		1	0.09–0.27	Even
MA/ Dzar/ Tib/11	Dzar	1870	Rules for annual dö (mdos) ceremony	Single sheet; Cloth backing on 4 outer folds 91 × 63 c.a. 27 folds	11 + 44+18	kmt	3?	None ?	++++			+		1	0.11–0.14; cloth 0.64–1.07	Even with many outer bark fragments
MA/ Dzar/ Tib/12	Dzar	1906	Loan contract between lender from Dzar and borrower from Gyaga	Single sheet 21–22.2 × 19 8 folds	11	kmt	1	4 thumbprints	++++			+		1	0.14–0.29	Uneven with surface processed

Acc. No.	Archive Location village	Date based on text	Category of text Title	Format and layout: Size (h x w) cm No of folds	Format and layout: No of text lines	Writing: Type of script	Writing: Scribal hands Name of scribe if known	Authentication marks: Seals, Crosses, and fingerprints	Paper: Fibre composition: Daphne/ Edgeworthia/ Wikstroemia	Paper: Fibre composition: Stellera sp	Paper: Fibre composition: Other	Paper: Sieve print: Woven	Paper: Sieve print: Laid	Paper: Number of layers	Paper: Thickness	Paper: Fibre distribution
MA/ Geling/ Tib/1a	Geling	Fire sheep 1907	Inheritance of a house and tax liability	Single sheet 32 × 42 7/3 folds	12	'khyug	1	3 seals, 5 crosses	+++	+		+		1	0.1–0.18	
MA/ Geling/ Tib/1b	Geling			Single sheet 5.5-4 × 40.8 2/3 folds 5.5 × 41	3	'khyug	1		+++	+		+		1	0.1–0.21 0.08-0.15	
MA/ Geling/ Tib/2	Geling	Wood bird 1885	Transfer of responsibility from old to new headman	Single sheet 21 × 35 11/4 folds 23.7 × 31.6 32.6 × 42.2	9	'khyug	1 Hand B	1 seal	++++			+		1	0.12–0.15 0.10-0.19 0.11-0.15	
MA/ Geling/ Tib/3	Geling	Earth horse 1918	List of grain contributions for building a guest house at the pilgrimage place of Cong gzhi	Single sheet 37 × 37 10/2 folds 37.3 × 37.8	7	'khyug	1		+++	+		+		1	0.11–0.25 0.08-0.28	Fibre bundles
MA/ Geling/ Tib/4	Geling	Fire sheep 1907	receipt of payments relating to a marriage?	Single sheet 20 × 35 5/4 folds 19.6 × 35.6	7	'khyug	1	3 crosses (witnesses)	++++			+		1	0.09–0.21 0.11-0.22	
MA/ Geling/ Tib/5	Geling	Fire sheep 1907	Promise by a couple never to steal again	Single sheet 33.5 × 36.5 10/3 folds 32.9 × 37.1	13	'khyug	1 Hand A?	2 seals, 2 crosses	++++			+		1	0.11–0.16 0.08-0.14	
MA/ Geling/ Tib/6	Geling	Earth ox 1889	Promise by the precentor of the monastery, who has failed with a woman, that he will observe his vows in future	Single sheet 22 × 42 8/4 folds 23.1 × 42.5	11	tshugs	1 Hand B	1 cross	+++	+		+		1	0.12–0.17 0.09-0.16	

MA/ Geling/ Tib/7	Geling	iron dragon 1880/1940	List of sheep entrusted to a herder	Single sheet 25.5 × 28.5 11/4 folds 25.7 × 28.4	11	’khyug, tshugs	2		++++			+		1	0.07–0.11	
MA/ Geling/ Tib/8	Geling	Hare (no element)	Payment to monks	Single sheet 9-11 × 51 5/6 folds 10 × 51.3	2	kmt	1	1 seal	++++			+		1	0.11–0.2 0.10-0.21	
MA/ Geling/ Tib/9	Geling	Earth bird 1909	Petition by a woman to the village on behalf of her son	Single sheet 28 × 36 13/4 folds 29.3 × 35.7	10	’khyug	1 Hand F	2 crosses	+++	+		+		1	0.11–0.13 0.08-0.13	
MA/ Geling/ Tib/10	Geling	Water ox 1913	Deed of transfer of a house and property	Single sheet 48.5 × 37.5 13/4 folds 48.6 × 38.3	14	kmt	1	1 seal	++++			+		1	0.11–0.21 0.10–0.14	Fibre bundles
MA/ Geling/ Tib/11	Geling	Water monkey 1872/1932	Testimony in a dispute	Single sheet 35 × 34.5 7/4 folds 35 × 34.4	16 + 2	kmt	1	No ?	++	++		+ Coarsely woven textile	+??	1	0.07–0.09 0.06–0.10	Water drops
MA/ Geling/ Tib/12	Geling	Fire horse 1906	Fine on several villagers for failing to attend a meeting	Single sheet 20 × 30 2/12 folds 20.5 × 40.8	3	’khyug	1	1 cross	+++	+		+		1	0.1–0.14 0.11–0.12	
MA/ Geling/ Tib/13	Geling	Fire sheep 1907	Failure of certain people to pay community and government taxes	Single sheet 45 × 19.5 2/14 folds 19 × 46.9	8	’khyug	1 rGyal mtshan	3 crosses	++++			+		1	0.09–0.11 0.05–0.15	Water drops
MA/ Geling/ Tib/14	Geling	Wood bird 1885	List of tax payments received	Single sheet 23.5 × 34 10/4 folds 23.3 × 33.5	15	kmt	2?	No	++++			+		1	0.06–0.1 0.04-0.13	
MA/ Geling/ Tib/15	Geling	Fire sheep 1907	List of debts inherited by a man from his deceased parents	Single sheet 27 × 57 8/6 folds 27.2 × 57.8	11			No	++++			+		1	0.07–0.14 0.05-0.18	Fibre bundles
MA/ Geling/ Tib/16	Geling	Fire hare 1867/ 1927	Acknowledgement of failure to repay a debt	Single sheet 68 × 38 13/4 folds 57.9 × 38.9	7	kmt, dbu can	1	2 red seals 3 thumbprints	+++	+		+		1	0.1–0.13 0.09-0.12	

MA/ Geling/ Tib/17	Geling	Earth monkey/ Iron dog 1908/ 1910	List of payments	Single sheet 28 × 38 9/3 folds 27.6 × 38.3	17	'khyug	1	No	++++			+		1	0.09–0.11	Cloudy structure
MA/ Geling/ Tib/18	Geling	Water monkey 1872/ 1932	List of payments	Single sheet 18 × 32 8/5 folds 18.6 × 32.6	8	kmt	1	1 seal	++++			+		1	0.1–0.18 0.08-0.17	
MA/ Geling/ Tib/19	Geling	No date	Part of a dispute between members of different communities	Single sheet 18.5 × 39 5/4 folds 19.4× 38.9	4	'khyug	1 rTsis pa bKra shis	1 cross	+++	+	Fibre A	+		1	0.11–0.20 0.09-0.17	
MA/ Geling/ Tib/20	Geling	Water hare 1903	Census of livestock	Single sheet 36 × 37 10/3 folds 36.5 × 38	13	'khyug	1	No	++++			+ Coarsely woven textile or nylon sieve?		1	0.07–0.09 0.06-0.26	Water drops
MA/ Geling/ Tib/21	Geling	Iron ox 1901	List of grain payments (yellow marks signify that payments have been made)	Single sheet 66 × 34 c.a. 32/2 folds 67.2 × 34.3	24 Yellow marking on some text lines	'khyug	1	No	+++	+		+		1	0.05–0.11 0.09-0.11	
MA/ Geling/ Tib/22	Geling	No date Subba Balbir mentioned	Permission for use of grassland?	Single sheet 27 × 55 8/6 folds 26.6 × 55.3	11	kmt	1	3 seals	+++	+		+ Coarsely woven textile or nylon sieve?		1	0.11–0.19 0.09-0.13	Cloudy structure
MA/ Geling/ Tib/23	Geling	Fire pig 1887	Order probibiting an external blacksmith from working on Geling's territory in competition with the local blacksmith.	Single sheet 12 × 60 3/6 folds 12.2 × 59.4	5	kmt	1	1 cross	+++	+		+		1	0.09–0.15 0.09-0.20	

MA/ Geling/ Tib/24	Geling	No date	Resolution of a complex dispute.	Single sheet 45 × 40.5 9/4 folds	16	kmt, tshugs ring	1 rGyal mtshan	1 seal	+++	+		+		1	0.1–0.12 0.08-0.13	
MA/ Geling/ Tib/25	Geling	No date	Dispute that occurred in a water mill about the quality of grain.	Single sheet 25 × 69 8/5 folds 26.1 × 82	8	kmt	1	2 seals	+++	+		+		1	0.16–0.25 0.07-0.13	Mixing mark
MA/ Geling/ Tib/26	Geling	Wood bird 1885	Prohibition on renting out horses and donkeys other than one's own; prohibition on cutting willow trees without supervision.	Single sheet 34 × 26 c.a. 14/2 folds 32.5 × 26	20	kmt	2? Hand B (sections 1 and 2) Hand C (section 3)	No	+++	+		+		1	0.08–0.14 0.07-0.12	Cloudy structure
MA/ Geling/ Tib/27	Geling	No date	Receipt from Ngor E wam monastery of payment for transfer of merit for a deceased person.	Single sheet 15.5 × 49.5 c.a. 5/12 folds 15.6 × 50.7	2	'khyug	1	1 red seal	+++	+		+		1	0.13–0.19 0.11-0.17	Woody fibre bundles
MA/ Geling/ Tib/28	Geling	Fire ox 1877	Arrangements for a nun giving up her vows.	Single sheet 49 × 53 12/5 folds 49.2 × 54.05	11	'khyug	1 or 2 Hand A (lines 1-4, 9-11)	3 thumbprints	+++	+		+		1	0.1–0.13 0.07-0.09	Cloudy structure
MA/ Geling/ Tib/29	Geling	Wood snake 1905	Arrangements for repayment of an overdue debt.	Single sheet 21 × 62.5 6/6 folds 20.8 × 63	6	kmt	1	No ?	+++	+		+ Coarsely woven textile or nylon sieve?		1	0.08–0.19 0.09-0.15	Woody fibre bundles
MA/ Geling/ Tib/30	Geling	No date	Fine on two men from Tshug for allowing their goats to enter Geling's fields.	Single sheet 50 × 38 15/3 folds 50.4 × 38.4	16	kmt	1 rtsi brung bkra shis	3 thumbprints	+++	+		+		1	0.07–0.11 0.07-0.16	Woody fibre bundles
MA/ Geling/ Tib/31	Geling	Earth monkey 1908	Village accounts.	Single sheet 30 × 41.5 11/3 folds 30.1 × 41.5	10?	kmt	1 Hand F	2 crosses	++++			+		1	0.06–0.12 0.07-0.12	Even, well cooked

MA/ Geling/ Tib/32	Geling	Earth sheep 1919	Statement by a party in a dispute.	Single sheet 40 × 46 10/3 folds 40.7 × 46.2	13	kmt	1	No ?	+++	+		+		1	0.09–0.12 0.07-0.12	Outer bark particles
MA/ Geling/ Tib/33	Geling	Fire sheep 1907	Legal case following theft from a temple.	Single sheet 40 × 69 10/4 folds 40.2 × 70.1	10	kmt	1	3 thumbprints 7 crosses	+++	+		+		1	0.1–0.17 0.08-0.10	Outer bark particles
MA/ Geling/ Tib/34	Geling	Earth hare 1879/1939	Letter from a monk in Ngor to his family.	Single sheet 34 × 47.5 .. folds 33.9× 47.9	9	'khyug	1 Ngag dbang bsam gtan	No	+++	+		+		1	0.1–0.17 0.10-0.17	Outer bark particle, cloudy structure
MA/ Geling/ Tib/35	Geling	Fire sheep 1907	Inventory of property of a deceased woman.	Single sheet 27 × 39.5 .. folds 26.1× 39.8	10	kmt	1	No	++	++	Fibre A	+		1	0.08–0.09 0.05-0.09	Cloudy structure, mixing marks
MA/ Geling/ Tib/36	Geling	Wood horse, wood dragon 1894, 1904	Dispute record.	Single sheet 56 × 35 .. folds 56.7 × 35.2	17	'khyug, kmt	1 Hand A	6 crosses	+++	+		+		1	0.08–0.13 0.07-0.14	Outer bark particles, woody fibre bundles
MA/ Geling/ Tib/37	Geling	Water rat 1912	Marriage regulation.	Single sheet 14 × 72.5 .. folds 13.8 × 72.5	3	'khyug	1	7 crosses	+++	+		+		1	0.08–0.12	Outer bark particles
MA/ Geling/ Tib/38	Geling	Iron monkey 1860	Financial arrangement.	Single sheet 16.5 × 38.5 .. folds 16.6 × 38.5	5	kmt	1	1 seal	+++	+		+		1	0.11–0.15	Woody fibre bundles
MA/ Geling/ Tib/39	Geling	Fire horse 1906	Agreement to pay overdue taxes.	Single sheet 11.5 × 66 .. folds 11.6 × 66.3	5	'khyug	1	2 crosses	++	++		+		1	0.08–0.28 0.08-0.12	Outer bark particles, woody fibre bundles, cloudy structure
MA/ Geling/ Tib/40	Geling	Earth rat 1888	Village expenditures.	Single sheet 9.5 × 59.5 .. folds	5	'khyug	1 Hand C	No	+++	+		+		1	0.09–0.12	

MA/ Geling/ Tib/41	Geling	Fire pig 1887	Agreement to adopt a child.	Single sheet 29 × 29.5 .. folds 28.7 × 29.6	7	’khyug	1	6 thumbprints, validated with Nep. sahi	++++			+		1	0.09–0.12 0.07–0.10	Outer bark particles, fibre bundles, well cooked
MA/ Geling/ Tib/42	Geling	Water monkey 1872	Concerning a legal case in a government court.	Single sheet 28 × 30.5 .. folds 28 × 30.7	12	’khyug	1 Hand A	No	+++	+		+		1	0.1–0.18 0.07–0.13	Cloudy structure, woody fibre bundles
MA/ Geling/ Tib/43	Geling	Earth dog 1898	Resolution of a dispute between two people.	Single sheet 17.5 × 29 .. folds 17.1 × 28.8	5	kmt	1 Hand A	1 seal	+++	+		+		1	0.08–0.13 0.09–0.13	
MA/ Geling/ Tib/44	Geling	Fire snake 1917	The terms of running an alehouse on the edge of Geling.	Single sheet 27 × 36 .. folds 26.1× 35.9	9	’khyug	1 Hand F Bu rGyal tshan	1 cross, 1 seal	++	++		+		1	0.2–0.5 0.16–0.24	Woody fibre bundles, mixing mark
MA/ Geling/ Tib/45	Geling	Water tiger 1902	Resolution of dispute over ownership of a turquoise.	Single sheet 17.5 × 27.5 .. folds 17.6 × 27.6	8	kmt	1 bKra shis	2 crosses	++++			+		1	0.1–0.14 0.07–0.19	Woody fibre bundles
MA/ Geling/ Tib/46	Geling	Iron bird 1921	Loan agreement.	Single sheet 14 × 37 .. folds 13.9 × 37	7	kmt	1 So nam ?	1 thumbprint, 2? crosses	++++			+		1	0.1–0.23 0.12–0.20	Woody fibre bundles
MA/ Geling/ Tib/47	Geling	check ms	Nepali	Single sheet 21 × 17.5 .. folds 21.1 × 17.4	17	kmt	1	No	+++	+		+ Coarsely woven textile		1	0.07–0.1 0.06–0.16	Woody fibre bundles
MA/ Geling/ Tib/48	Geling	Earth monkey 1848/ 1908	Dispute over the sale of a 15-year old girl as a slave.	Single sheet 39 × 31.5 .. folds 39 × 30.9	12	kmt	2	No	+++	+		+		1	0.08–0.24 0.07–0.17	Woody fibre bundles
MA/ Geling/ Tib/49	Geling	Wood tiger 1914	Part of a case in a dispute.	Single sheet 28.5 × 42 .. folds 28.9 × 42.2	13	’khyug	2	No	+++	+		+		1	0.08–0.1 0.05–0.27	

MA/ Geling/ Tib/50	Geling	No date	Dispute arising from elopement of a nun with a layman.	Single sheet 40 × 26.5 .. folds 39.7 × 26.5	17	'khyug	1 rGyal mtshan	2 thumbprints	+++	+		+		1	0.08–0.16 0.07-0.11	Few woody fibre bundles
MA/ Geling/ Tib/51	Geling	Fire dog 1886	Letter from a monk in Ngor to his family.	Single sheet 51 × 48 .. folds 50.1 × 48.1	26	kmt	1 Blo ldan	No	+++	+		+		1	0.15–0.19 0.08–0.11	Woody fibre bundles, cloudy structure
MA/ Geling/ Tib/52	Geling	Iron snake 1881/ 1941	Promise by two thieves from Chötsong, who have stolen images from Geling temple, that they will never offend again.	Single sheet 34.5 × .. .. folds 34.7 × 39.1	17	'khyug	1	1 seal, 3 crosses	+++	+	Fibre A, fibre B	+		1	0.09–0.13 0.06–0.10	Good quality, even, well cooked
MA/ Geling/ Tib/53	Geling	Fire pig 1887	Petition by two disputing parties that Geling council judge their case.	Single sheet 19 × 45 .. folds 19.4 × 45.3	6	tshugs	1 Hand B	1 cross	+++	+		+ Coarsely woven textile		1	0.04–0.08 0.03–0.08	Good quality, even, well cooked
MA/ Geling/ Tib/54	Geling	Wood dragon 1904	Resolution of an inheritance dispute.	Single sheet 29 × 21 .. folds 28.7 × 20.9	13	kmt	1 Hand D	1 cross	++++			+ Coarsely woven textile		1	0.1–0.14 0.09–0.22	
MA/ Geling/ Tib/55	Geling	Wood rat 1924	Contract for sale of field and other property.	Single sheet 23.5 × 32.5 .. folds 24 × 32.7	10	kmt	1 Zin dpon Phun tshogs	2 seals	+++	+		+ Coarsely woven textile		1	0.05–0.08 0.06–0.11	
MA/ Geling/ Tib/56	Geling	Fire horse 1906	Loan agreement.	Single sheet 14 × 32 .. folds 16 × 31.8	5	'khyug	2 [pran] Mi gyur	2 thumbprints	+	+++		+		1	0.12–0.23 0.07-0.35	Woody fibre bundles
MA/ Geling/ Tib/57	Geling	No date	Loan agreement.	Single sheet 37 × 50.5 .. folds 37.3 × 50.7	13	tshugs ring, kmt	2	3 seals, 2 crosses	+++	+		+		1	0.15–0.24 0.10-0.13	Fibre bundles

MA/ Geling/ Tib/58	Geling	No date	Letter from a monk in Ngor to his family.	Single sheet 29 × 64 .. folds 29.3 × 64.6	14	'khyug	1 Shes mong blo gros cen	No	+++	+		+		1	0.05–0.16 0.06–0.09	Cloudy structure, good quality, even
MA/ Geling/ Tib/59	Geling	Iron sheep 1871/1931	Letter from 3 Geling people in Kathmandu to the village.	Single sheet 12.5 × 49 .. folds 12.2 × 48.5	7	kmt	1	No	++	++		+ Coarsely woven textile		1	0.06–0.09 0.05–0.11	
MA/ Geling/ Tib/60	Geling	Earth pig 1899	Clarification of a person's identity?	Single sheet 57.5 × 39 .. folds 57.5 × 38.5	10	'khyug	1	14 thumbprints	+++	+		+		1	0.24–0.31 0.17–0.29	Cloudy structure, mixing mark, woody fibre bundles
MA/ Geling/ Tib/61	Geling	Earth bird 1909/1969		32.9 × 56	8	'khyug		1 seal, 2 dig. prints	++	++	Hardwood, fibre C	+		1	0.13–0.26	Woody fibre bundles, mixing mark
MA/ Geling/ Tib/62	Geling			58.7 × 41.6		'khyug		No	+++	+	Fibre D	+		1	0.10–0.33	Woody fibre bundles, mixing mark, outer bark particles
MA/ Geling/ Tib/63	Geling	No date		34 × 55.2	8	'khyug		15 crosses	++++			+		1	0.05–0.09	Woody fibre bundles, outer bark particles
MA/ Geling/ Tib/64	Geling	Water dragon 1892/1952		35.1 × 28.2	7	'khyug		2 dig. prints , 1 cross	+++	+	Fibre A	+		1	0.06–0.07	

MA/ Geling/ Tib/65	Geling	Iron monkey 1920	List of grain payments for unspecified purposes. Note that each person specifies that it was his 'bo measure that was used.	13.7 × 28	5	kmt		No	+	+++		+		1	0.10-0.15	Woody fibre bundles
MA/ Geling/ Tib/66	Geling	Fire dog 1886 Earth mouse 1888	Inventory of contents of a household of someone who has diasppeared	14.1 × 30.8	11	tshugs thung		1 seal	+++	+		+		1	0.09-0.14	Woody fibre bundles, outer bark particles
MA/ Geling/ Tib/67	Geling	Water tiger 1902	The headman Norbu has two wives and wishes to take another. He agrees to give his house to his junior wife and her son.	27.2 × 41.1	8	'khyug	brTsis bdrung Ka mi	9 dig. prints, 1 seal	+++	+		+		1	0.10-0.21	
MA/ Geling/ Tib/68	Geling	Iron dragon Iron snake Water horse Water sheep 1940-1944	List of expenditures - mainly repayment of debts to Laliman and Sheti subbas.	32.3 × 36.8	8	'khyug		No	+	+++		+		1	0.07-0.21	Woody fibre bundles, outer bark particles

MA/ Geling/ Tib/69	Geling	Earth horse 1918	Document of reconciliation (mi-laipatra) between Watermill Gyatso and Ogyan Butri	30.9 × 55.3	8	'khyug		4 crosses, 2 dig. prints	+	+++		+ Coarsely woven textile		1	0.04-0.06	
MA/ Geling/ Tib/70	Geling	Fire pig 1887	A list of guarantors for a number of individuals who have not paid their taxes in full.	11.1 × 28	7	kmt		1 seal	+++	+		+		1	0.11-023	Few woody fibre bundles
MA/ Geling/ Tib/71	Geling	Fire sheep 1907	Transfer of ownership of a household.	23.5 × 41.4	8	kmt		3 seals	+++	+		+		1	0.06-0.11	Few woody fibre bundles
MA/ Geling/ Tib/72	Geling	Water tiger 1902/1962	Memorandum of three agreements by the village council.	37.4 × 42	13	'khyug		2 seals	+++	+		+		1	0.08-0.12	Cloudy structure, good quality
MA/ Geling/ Tib/73	Geling	Fire dog 1886/1946	Receipt for a loan of grain to a no-mad named Pema by Gelung Norbu.	Single sheet 12 × 55 .. folds 12.5 × 55.1	2	'khyug		3 red dig. prints	++	++		+		1	0.12–0.26 0.12-0.20	Woody fibre bundles, outer bark particles
MA/ Geling/ Tib/74	Geling	Wood horse 1894/1954	Record of a dispute between two people, one of whom accuses the other of having insulted him/her.	28 × 36.9	13	'khyug		3-4 crosses	+++	+		+		1	0.07-0.12	Woody fibre bundles, outer bark particles, mixing mark
MA/ Geling/ Tib/75	Geling	No date	Letter from the former ruler of Geling declaring that he hopes one day to regain his position.	17.3 × 32.4	6	kmt	Karma De?	No	+++	+		+		1	0.08-0.18	Mixing mark
MA/ Geling/ Tib/76	Geling	Iron mon-key 1920	Settlement of a theft.	16.5 × 35.6	10	'khyug		3 crosses, 2 dig. prints	++	++		+		1	0.11-0.13	

MA/ Geling/ Tib/77	Geling	Water ox 1913	Memorandum of various domestic items loaned to neighbours	11.7 × 68.7	2	'khyug		No	+++	+		+		1	0.07-0.13	Good quality
MA/ Geling/ Tib/78	Geling	Fire sheep 1907	Regulations for management and irrigation of an area of fields.	19.3 × 43.3	6	'khyug		1 crosses	+++	+	Fibre D	+		1	0.11-0.22	Woody fibre bundles, outer bark particles
MA/ Geling/ Tib/79	Geling	Water rabbit 1903	An old woman with no friends or sons receives permission from the sDe ba and from the village to relinquish her estate and will not oppose anyone who wishes to take it over.	17.6 × 38.8	7	kmt	Hand B?	2 crosses, 1 dig. print	++++		Fibre A	+		1	0.11-0.22	Woody fibre bundles, outer bark particles
MA/ Geling/ Tib/80	Geling	Fire horse 1906	Resolution not to pay certain categories of taxes.	20.9 × 42.4	6	'khyug		1 seal, 1 cross	+++	+		+		1	0.09-0.15	Woody fibre bundles
MA/ Geling/ Tib/81	Geling	No date	Part of a dispute concerning two people who are accused of having sexual relations.	22.8 × 47.7	10	'khyug		1 cross	+++	+		+		1	0.10-0.25	Woody fibre bundles, outer bark particles
MA/ Geling/ Tib/82	Geling	Fire mon- key 1896/1956	List of debts.	17.1 × 42.8	6	kmt		3 crosses, 1 dig. cross	+++	+		+		1	0.06-0.11	Even, good quality
MA/ Geling/ Tib/83	Geling	Iron dog 1970	Agreement to restore the community house	43 × 42	13	'khyug		24 dig. prints	+++	+	Fibre D	+		1	0.05-0.09	Mixing mark

MA/ Geling/ Tib/84	Geling	Fire sheep 1907 Wood Tiger 1914	One of three documents in a case in which a thief's stepdaughter is given to the village as a slave as the price for avoiding punishment by amputation.	37.9 × 38.8	8	kmt		1 dig. cross	+++	+		+		1	0.11-0.42	Woody fibre bundles, outer bark particles
MA/ Geling/ Tib/85	Geling	Wood monkey 1884/1944	Receipt of lead, sulphur and saltpe-ter to make gun-powder	22.9 × 30	8	kmt		No	+++	+		+		1	0.09-0.12	Cloudy structure, mixing mark
MA/ Geling/ Tib/86	Geling	Wood snake 1905	Testimony by a witness that a woman who had added three turquoises to someone else's zhule (ceremonial headdress) removed them before he took it away	33.6 × 41.4	7	kmt		No	+++	+		+		1	0.07-0.11	Few woody fibre bundles, outer bark particles, good quality
MA/ Geling/ Tib/87	Geling	Water horse 1942	Payment of wages in grain and cash to various people by the subb⊠ Lalit-man.	18.8 × 21.6	6	kmt		1 dig. print	+++	+		+		1	0.06-0.13	Few impurities
MA/ Geling/ Tib/88	Geling	Iron snake 1941	List of kids and money	19 × 21.8	5	'khyug		?	+++	+	Fibre D	+		1	0.06-0.14	Few impurities

MA/ Geling/ Tib/89	Geling	Earth monkey 1908	Someone from Marpha has stolen and killed a goat from Geling. He is let off but told that he will have to pay a 50 Rs fine if he does it again.	48.3 × 41.9	8	'khyug	Hand E	4 crosses	+++	+	Fibre B	+		1	0.09–0.13	Outer bark particles
MA/ Geling/ Tib/90	Geling	Earth horse 1918	Partial repayment of a debt of 50 rupees, with interest.	30.6 × 48.4	5	kmt	sGan Mig dmar	1 seal	++	++		+ Coarsely woven textile		1	0.06–0.10	Few woody fibre bundles
MA/ Geling/ Tib/91	Geling	Fire pig 1887/1947	Regulations for managing the roster for taking care of donkeys.	60.8 × 26.3	21	kmt		1 seal, 14 crosses	+++	+		+		1	0.09–0.13	Cloudy structure, mixing mark, outer bark particles
MA/ Geling/ Tib/92	Geling	Iron dog 1910	Rules for handing over livestock to the designated herder, and fines for allowing animals to enter the fields.	34.9 × 40.8	13	kmt	Hand G	2 seals	++	++		+		1	0.11–0.13	Woody fibre bundles, mixing mark, outer bark particles
MA/ Geling/ Tib/93	Geling	Water tiger 1902/1962	Rules for planting a group of fields	13.7 × 41.6	13	kmt		No	+++	+		+		1	0.11–0.35	
MA/ Geling/ Tib/94	Geling	Earth rabbit 1879/1939	Compensation for someone wrongly accused of theft	16.4 × 35.1	6	kmt	'Gra 'dul	2 dig. prints	+++	+		+		1	0.05–0.12	Few woody fibre bundles
MA/ Geling/ Tib/95	Geling	Earth ox 1889/1949	Reconciliation between a couple who had separated.	36.5 × 51.3	12	kmt		1 seal, 1 cross	+++	+		+		1	0.06–0.09	Woody fibre bundles, outer bark particles

MA/ Geling/ Tib/96	Geling	Wood rabbit 1915	Irrigation regulations	35.1 × 36.1	12	kmt		No	+++	+		+		1	0.06.-012	Woody fibre bundles, outer bark particles, mixing mark
MA/ Geling/ Tib/97	Geling	Wood sheep 1895/1955	Letter home from a monk in Ewam Chöden monastery in Tibet	43.4 × 51.2	13	kmt	1 ban rgan ngag bsaM pa	?	+++	+		+		1	0.08-0.10	Woody fibre bundles, outer bark particles
MA/ Geling/ Tib/98	Geling	Fire pig 1887/1947	The goatherd Phuntshog admits to having stolen a goat from the nobleman dPal 'byor, but denies stealing any other goats.	16 × 30.7	8	kmt		1 dig. print, 2 dig. crosses	+++	+		+		1	0.10-0.17	Cloudy structure, few woody fibre bundles, outer bark particles
MA/ Geling/ Tib/99	Geling		A headman and his descendants are accorded lifelong tax exemption for outstanding service to the community.	16.5 × 47.3		kmt		No	+++	+	Fibre A	+		1	0.09-0.14	Cloudy structure, few woody fibre bundles, outer bark particles
MA/ Geling/ Tib/100	Geling	No date	Letter from Subba Candra Singh to send him 2 'bo khal of grain from Geling	15.8 × 25.7	5	kmt		1 seal	+++	+		+		1	0.08-0.34	Mixing mark, woody fibre bundles, outer bark particles
MA/ Geling/ Tib/101	Geling	No ele-ment/ snake year	Agreement about grain trade among Baragaon, Manang, Thak and adjacent enclaves	22.6 × 51.6	7	kmt		1 cross	+++	+		+		1	0.09-0.21	Woody fibre bundles, outer bark particles

MA/ Geling/ Tib/102	Geling	Earth horse 1918	Agreement among three people: Dondrub and Tenzin Wangmo agree to stop having an affair, and Tenzin Wangmo's husband, Trashi, agrees that he will no longer beat her and smash her jewelry. She agrees to stay with him if he abides by his undertaking.	42.2 × 52.5	8	'khyug	Bu rGyal mtshan	4 dig. prints	+	+++		+ Coarsely woven textile		1	0.04-0.08	Woody fibre bundles, outer bark particles
MA/ Geling/ Tib/103	Geling	Wood bird 1885/1945	Agreement to purchase tea from the subba	61.5 × 35	20	kmt		1 seal, 1 cross	+++	+		+		1	0.15-0.26	Woody fibre bundles, outer bark particles
MA/ Geling/ Tib/104	Geling	Fire dog 1886/1946	A letter from two monks in Tibet about goods to be sent up from Geling	32 × 40.3	12	kmt	Ngawang Loden and Ngawang Rabsel	3 dig. marks	++	++		+		1	0.05-0.32	Cloudy structure, outer bark particles
MA/ Geling/ Tib/105	Geling	Fire Pig 1887/1947	Regulations for the use of irrigation water from different sources; regulations for the roster for taking care of cows.	32.3 × 26.7	21	kmt		15 crosses, 1 dig. cross	+	+++		+		1	0.09-0.13	Woody fibre bundles, outer bark particles
MA/ Geling/ Tib/106	Geling	Wood rabbit 1915	Determination of the paternity of a child that is being carried by a young woman of Geling.	36.9 × 70.8	8	kmt	Hand H	8 crosses	++++			+		1	0.08-0.13	Woody fibre bundles, outer bark particles

MA/ Geling/ Tib/107	Geling	Earth monkey 1908	Dispute over an unpaid debt that is resolved by mediators	31.2 × 69.8	8	'khyug	Hand E sTag lha	3 crosses, 1 dig. cross	++++			+		1	0.11-0.14	
MA/ Geling/ Tib/108	Geling	No date	Rule that legal disputes must be settled within the community without recourse to any external authority.	21.8 × 32.9	9	'khyug		1 seal	++	++		+		1	0.07-0.11	Few outer bark particles
MA/ Geling/ Tib/109	Geling	Fire dog 1886/1946	List of interest to be paid on grain loans from people of Gemi.	40.4 × 35.9	12	'khyug		4 dig. prints	+++	+		+		1	0.06-0.09	
MA/ Geling/ Tib/110	Geling	Wood tiger 1914	List of debts in cash, grain and other commodities collected by the subb☒ Mohanman Serchan.	73.7 × 18.8	17	'khyug		1 cross	+++	+		+		1	0.07-0.12	Mixing mark, woody fibre bundles, outer bark particles
MA/ Geling/ Tib/111	Geling	Wood dragon 1904	A monk takes responsibility for holding his family estate intact	57.7 × 31.8	8	'khyug		1 cross	+++	+		+		1	0.04-0.12	Few woody fibre bundles, outer bark particles
MA/ Geling/ Tib/112	Geling	Fire sheep 1907	Agreement that an elderly woman may occupy a dependency and use a field and threshing yard, as well as domestic property, until her death.	12.9 × 41.8	4	'khyug		1 dig. cross	+	+++		+		1	0.07-0.17	Few woody fibre bundles

MA/ Geling/ Tib/113	Geling	Water tiger 1902	A servant whose son has stolen two goats from Headman Taglha, because he has no money to pay the rkun 'jal, must forefeit his house to the village as public property.	17.3 × 42.5	7	'khyug		3 crosses	++++			+		1	0.07-0.14	
MA/ Geling/ Tib/114	Geling	Water 0x 1913 Wood tiger 1914 Iron mon-key 1920	List of grain debts owed to a lender from Te.	48.1 × 32.9	20	'khyug	Bu Nyi ma bsam sgru	?	+++	+		+		1	0.06-0.24	Woody fibre bundles, outer bark particles
MA/ Geling/ Tib/115	Geling	Water monkey 1932	Letter home from the representatives of Geling who are fighting a legal case for the village in Kathmandu.	47.8 × 28.1	23	'khyug		No	++	++		+		1	0.08-0.23	Woody fibre bundles, outer bark particles
MA/ Geling/ Nep/ 116	Geling	No date	Establishment of certain rotating duties.	Single sheet 51 × 21.5 .. folds	11	devanagari, kmt	Ma' lde ba ju (Mahadeva Ju?)	2 dig. prints		++++		+		2	0.18-0.26	Woody fibre bundles, mixing mark, cloudy structure

MA/ Geling/ Tib/117	Geling	Earth tiger 1938	Someone from Thak has lost a turquoise and two corals in Tamagang, and receives partial compensation, possibly from the owner of the lodge.	7.9 × 60.7	2	kmt		2 crosses	++++			+		1	0.05–0.09	
MA/ Geling/ Tib/118	Geling	Fire horse 1906	Letter from the community of Geling to a father and son who did not come back from winter trading. If they do not return, they will forefeit their estate.	12.8 × 62.6	3	'khyug		1 seal	++++			+ Coarsely woven textile sieve		1	0.11–0.12	Water drops
MA/ Geling/ Tib/119	Geling	Wood monkey 1884/1944	Norbu Drandul entusts some of his goats to the care of the nomads of Chödzong.	27.6 × 29.7	10	'khyug, tshugs		1 dig. print	++++			+		1	0.07–0.28	Woody fibre bundles, outer bark particles
MA/ Geling/ Tib/120	Geling	Fire sheep 1907	A young house-owner has died before he had heirs, and the estate is given to the younger son of the headman	29.5 × 70.2	8	'khyug	Hand A	5 crosses, 1 dig. cross	++++			+		1	0.08–0.30	Outer bark particles

MA/ Geling/ Tib/121	Geling	Earth monkey 1908	Agreement that one man of Mar-pha may pasture his yaks in Geling for 10 rupees per year. No other outsiders may pasture their yaks here.	28.1 × 42	11	kmt		3-4 crosses	+++	+		+		1	0.11-0.33	Cloudy structure, woody fibre bundles, mixing mark, recycled materials possible
MA/ Geling/ Tib/122	Geling	Fire pig 1887/1947	List of items probably purchased for the community	21.7 × 43	6			1 dig. print	++++			+		1	0.11-0.17	Outer bark particles
MA/ Geling/ Tib/123	Geling	Water tiger 1902	Rules for use of a new field perimeter wall; rules for daily care of the village cows	39.8 × 62	14	kmt		1 red dig. print	++++			+		1	0.11-0.26	Woody fibre bundles, outer bark particles
MA/ Geling/ Tib/124	Geling	No date	Letter home from a monk in Ewam Choden, Tibet	Single sheet 106.4 × 51.7 29 folds	8	'khyug		2 seals	+++	+		+		1	0.10-0.13	Woody fibre bundles, outer bark particles
MA/ Geling/ Tib/125	Geling	Water ox 1913	Two people of Geling lease an area of fields to a Marphali for a period of eight years	28.1 × 41.8	56	'khyug		1 seal, 2 crosses	++++			+		1	0.08-0.11	Woody fibre bundles, outer bark particles
MA/ Geling/ Tib/126	Geling	Fire tiger 1926	Permission for the headman to tether his horses in the village fields		5	'khyug		2 seals				+		1		
MA/ Geling/ Tib/127	Geling	Iron dragon 1880/1940	Tax concessions for a new royal chaplain who is marrying into Geling		10	'khyug		3 seals				+		1		

MA/ Geling/ Tib/128	Geling	No date	Recipt from Ngor Ewam Choden that the gift of offer-ings of tea and cash etc. has resulted in purification of the donor's sins.	11.1 × 45.6	2	'khyug		1 seal				+ Coarsely woven textile sieve		1	0.09-0.23	Woody fibre bundles, outer bark particles, water drops
MA/ Geling/ Tib/129	Geling	Fire ox 1937	Settlement of a dispute in which the offended party claimed that he had been partly paid in inferior quality tea.	44.4 × 34.8	11	'khyug		6 dig. prints, 2 crosses				+		1	0.09-0.13	Outer bark particles
MA/ Geling/ Tib/130	Geling	Iron mouse 1921	Financial affairs of the community	17.5 × 38.9	7	kmt	Bu Ka mis	2 seals				+		1	0.03-0.10	
MA/ Geling/ Tib/131	Geling	Earth bird 1909	Contract for the sale of a house	33.4 × 28.9	7	kmt		3 dig. prints				+		1	0.06-0.11	Even, good quality
MA/ Geling/ Tib/132	Geling		Nepali document	17.2 × 20.05								+		1	0.07-0.08	Even, good quality, long fibres
MA/ Geling/ Tib/133	Geling	Wood dragon 1904	Tibetan translation of a Nepali document concerning taxes	55.2 × 40.1	20	'khyug	Hand D?	No				+		1	0.10-0.15	Woody fibre bundles, outer bark particles
MA/ Geling/ Tib/134	Geling	Water mouse 1852/1912	Reconciliation between an estranged son and his family	38.4 × 42.9	10	'khyug		4 crosses				+		1	0.04-0.06	Mixing mark, outer bark particles
MA/ Geling/ Tib/135	Geling	Fire ox 1877/1937	Loan contract, with fields as security.	24.6 × 31.3	5	kmt	Bu Rin grags	1 dig. print				+		1	0.06-0.11	Few woody fibre bundles
MA/ Geling/ Tib/136	Geling	No date	Memorandum concerning non-payment of taxes	13.4 × 41.2	7	kmt		1 cross				+		1	0.08-0.12	Good quality, even

MA/ Geling/ Tib/137	Geling	Fire sheep 1907	Payments of yield for use of the common fields	20 × 38.6	4	'khyug, tshugs		No				+		1	0.10-0.17	Mixing mark, woody fibre bundles, outer bark particles
MA/ Geling/ Tib/138	Geling	No date	Undertaking by a thief never to steal again	22.4 × 47.1	4	kmt	bKra shis don grubs	2 crosses, 1 dig. cross				+		1	0.04-0.08	
MA/ Geling/ Tib/139	Geling	Water ox 1853/1913	Copy of G 10	36.7 × 40.3	11	kmt		No				+		1	0.09-0.25	Few woody fibre bundles, outer bark particles
MA/ Geling/ Tib/140	Geling	Wood dragon 1904	Agreement by monastery to pay the village's taxes	31.4 × 36.8	6	'khyug		4 crosses	+++	+		+		1	0.05-0.10	Woody fibre bundles, outer bark particles
MA/ Geling/ Tib/141	Geling	Fire dog 1886/1946	Sums of money received following the death of an unnamed individual.	20.8 × 64.4	9	'khyug		1 cross	++++			+		1	0.17-0.35	Woody fibre bundles, outer bark particles
MA/ Geling/ Tib/142	Geling	Earth mouse 1888/1948	Regulations for the use of Geling's grasslands by Tangkya.	24 × 40.8	9	tshugs	mChod gnas lha rgyal	4 dig. prints, 2 dig. crosses	++++			+		1	0.10-0.14	Woody fibre bundles, outer bark particles
MA/ Geling/ Tib/143	Geling	Wood dragon 1904	Order that an area of fields must henceforth be planted	30.5 × 39.7	11	kmt		5 crosses	++++			+		1	0.05-0.09	Few woody fibre bundles
MA/ Geling/ Tib/144	Geling	No date	List of salary payments in kind.	27.4 × 38.4	6	'khyug		1 dig. print	++	++		+		1	0.09-0.27	
MA/ Geling/ Tib/145	Geling	Earth horse 1858/1918	Loan contract	14.9 × 35	4	'khyug		1 dig. print	++++			+		1	0.04-0.08	

MA/ Geling/ Tib/146	Geling	Fire ox 1877/1937	Document for loan of bitter buck-wheat, with a field as security	10.6 × 32.5	3	'khyug		1 dig. print	++++			+		1	0.10-0.11	
MA/ Geling/ Tib/147	Geling	Fire horse 1906	Document in two parts: 1. Payment of Great Government Tax, and 2. Rules for the Dachang festival	33.7 × 40.4	7	kmt		2 seals	++++			+ Coarsely woven textile sieve		1	0.09-0.79	Woody fibre bundles, outer bark particles
MA/ Geling/ Tib/148	Geling	Fire dog 1886/1946 Fire pig 1887/1947	Loan contracts for several people who are travelling to Kathmandu	61 × 36.7	25	'khyug	sBu Ka mi	11 dig. prints	++	++		+		1	0.11-0.21	Woody fibre bundles, outer bark particles
MA/ Geling/ Tib/149	Geling	Water tiger 1902	Receipt for sev-eral small sums of money	13.5 × 35.5	6	tshugs		1 seal, 1 cross	++++			+		1	0.07-0.12	Woody fibre bundles
MA/ Geling/ Tib/150	Geling	Water horse 1882/1942	Two brothers have one wife, and agree that they will not take another on pain of paying a fine of 4 rupees	24.5 × 54.7	6	'khyug	Bu rGyal mtshan	2 seals, 3 crosses	++	++		+ Coarsely woven textile sieve		1	0.04-0.07	Few woody fibre bundles
MA/ Geling/ Tib/151	Geling	Fire pig 1887/1947	Authorisation for the village to assume legal autonomy for three years	38.5 × 55.1	Part 1: 14 Part 2: 7	tshugs		37 crosses, 2 seals	++++			+		1	0.05-0.09	Cloudy structure, woody fibre bundles, mixing mark

MA/ Geling/ Tib/152	Geling	No date	A woman publicly denies an accusation that she slept with a man from Gemi while she was in Butwal for winter trading with a group of others from Geling	19.4 × 54.2	10	tshugs		1 seal, 1 cross	++++			+ Coarsely woven textile sieve		1	0.04-0.18	Woody fibre bundles
MA/ Geling/ Tib/153	Geling	No date	Agreement by the village that authority should be with the headman and community, not the hereditary ruler	22.8 × 41.5	7	kmt		3 seals	+++	+		+		1	0.07-0.17	Woody fibre bundles
MA/ Geling/ Tib/154	Geling	Water sheep 1883/1943	Resolution of a dispute between a woman and her daughter-in-law	18.5 × 37.8	9	kmt	Pad dbang (Possibly Padma dbang 'dus of Lubrak?)	5 dig. prints	+	+++		+		1	0.12-0.28	Woody fibre bundles, cloudy structure
MA/ Geling/ Tib/155	Geling	Iron bird 1921	Complaint by a nomad that someone has stolen the tails of eight of his yaks	26.3 × 37.5	10	'khyug		1 cross, 1 dig. cross	+++	+		+		1	0.12-0.25	Woody fibre bundles
MA/ Geling/ Tib/156	Geling	No date	Letter from a monk in Ngor to his family, expressing his relief and gratitude that he has survived a bout of smallpox	24.6 × 50.2	11	'khyug	Ngag dbang bstan 'dzin	1 seal, 2 dig. prints (?)		++++		+		1	0.07–0.18	Woody fibre bundles, outer bark particles

MA/ Geling/ Tib/157	Geling	Wood rabbit 1915 Iron Pig 1911	Declaration by a man that he spent only one night with a young woman at a villager's house four years earlier	22.6 × 31.4	5	kmt		2 crosses	+++	+		+		1	0.09-0.13	Few woody fibre bundles
MA/ Geling/ Tib/158	Geling	Wood snake 1905	A woman swears that the father of the daughter she has just borne is her husband, the father of her elder daughter.	16.8 × 30.8	8	kmt	Hand D	1 cross	+++	+		+		1	0.06-0.09	Cloudy structure, even, well cooked, good quality
MA/ Geling/ Tib/159	Geling	Water ox 1913	Letter to several people from Geling who have abandoned the village because of their inability to pay debts	13.8 × 38.9	7	kmt		No	++	++		+		1	0.07-021	Woody fibre bundles
MA/ Geling/ Tib/160	Geling	Wood Rabbit 1915	Declaration by a thieving monk that he will never steal again	31.6 × 31.8	10	kmt	Hand H	1 dig. print	++	++		+		1	0.09-0.11	Few woody fibre bundles, outer bark particles
MA/ Geling/ Tib/161	Geling	Water dog 1862/1922	Document related to the theft of the tails of a visiting nomad's yaks	40.3 × 34.7	10	kmt		1 seal	+	+++		+		1	0.06-015	Few woody fibre bundles, outer bark particles
MA/ Geling/ Tib/162	Geling	No year 5th month	Letter from a monk in Tibet about financial affairs	30 × 45.4	9	kmt	lHa dgos / byin chags (?)	No	++	++		+		1	0.07-0.11	Few woody fibre bundles, water drops

MA/ Geling/ Tib/163	Geling	Water mouse 1912	Letter from the subba demanding the return of 8 tax fugitives from Geling who have fled to Manang	18 × 50.8	7	’khyug		1 seal	++++			+		1	0.04-0.11	Woody fibre bundles
MA/ Geling/ Tib/164	Geling	Fire horse 1906	In two parts. First, the village offers the lama a field that will be worked by the nuns, who will also pay taxes on it. Second, a certain Gyatso is marrying one of the nuns and pays a fine to the village and the religious community in the form of a pregnant cow worth 15 rupees	66.2 × 43.4	10	’khyug		3 seals	++	++		+		1	0.10-0.17	Woody fibre bundles, outer bark particles
MA/ Geling/ Tib/165	Geling	Water dog 1862/1922	A headman is losing his sight and wishes to retire, but the village have begged him to continue to act as headman	29.9 × 38.5	10	kmt		16 crosses	+++	+		+		1	0.11-0.19	Woody fibre bundles, outer bark particles
MA/ Geling/ Tib/166	Geling		Nepali document	33.7 × 26.6	5				++	++		+ Coarsely woven textile sieve		1	0.05-0.12	
MA/ Geling/ Tib/167	Geling		Nepali document	44.7 × 23.8					++++			+		1	0.10-0.18	

MA/ Geling/ Tib/168	Geling	No date	Order from the king of Lo to the people of Nye-shang that they should not come to bring down the new salt from the border of Lo and Tibet	17.3 × 32.6	5	'khyug		1 seal	+++	+		+		1	0.08-0.13	Few woody fibre bundles
MA/ Geling/ Tib/169	Geling	No year 9th month	Receipt for the return of a borrowed gun	10 × 33.5	3	kmt		1 seal	+	+++		+		1	0.06-0.17	Woody fibre bundles, outer bark particles
MA/ Geling/ Tib/170	Geling	Earth dog 1898/1958	The complicated consequences of a nun who has had sexual relations	42 × 42.2	10	kmt	Hand A	3 crosses	++	++		+		1	0.08-0.15	Woody fibre bundles, outer bark particles
MA/ Geling/ Tib/171	Geling		Nepali document	41.7 × 23.9					++	++		+		1	0.05-0.13	Cloudy structure, good quality
MA/ Geling/ Tib/172	Geling	No date		45.4 × 25.2	Part 1: 30 Part 2: 5			No	+++	+		+		1	0.06-0.11	Woody fibre bundles, outer bark particles

Acc. No.	Archive Location village	Date based on text	Category of text Title	Format and layout		Writing		Authentication marks	Paper							
				Size (h x w) cm No of folds	No of text lines	Type of script	Scribal hands Name of scribe if known	Seals, Crosses, and fingerprints	Fibre composition			Sieve print		Number of layers	Thickness	Fibre distribution
									Daphne/ Edgeworthia/ Wikstroemia	Stellera sp	Other	Woven	Laid			
MA/ Lubrak/ Tib/1	Lubrak	No date	Land tax document	37.2 × 26.3	26	tshugs		-	++++						0.20–0.35	
MA/ Lubrak/ Tib/2A	Lubrak	No date	Land tax document	38.3 × 39.2	17	tshugs			+++	+					0.09–0.98	
MA/ Lubrak/ Tib/2B	Lubrak	No date	Land tax document	32.8 × 37.3	17	tshugs		-	++++						0.07–0.21	
MA/ Lubrak/ Tib/3	Lubrak	Water ox 1853/1913	Prohibition on selling beer in the village	16 × 24.5	6	'khyug			+++	+					0.07–0.25	
MA/ Lubrak/ Tib/4	Lubrak	Fire pig 1887/1947 No date	Receipt for government tax payment by village	18.2 × 18	13	'khyug, with Nepali numerals		1 seal	++	++					0.08–0.16	
MA/ Lubrak/ Tib/5	Lubrak	No date	Resolution by Baragaon	30.1 × 24.3	Part 1: 1-11; Part 2: 12-15 (in two columns)	'khyug		30 crosses	+++	+					0.07–0.15	
MA/ Lubrak/ Tib/6	Lubrak	Iron Hare 1951	Land tax document	18.8 × 31.4	7	kmt		7 crosses	+++	+					0.12–0.18	
MA/ Lubrak/ Tib/7	Lubrak	No date	Complaint that a new stupa interferes with a willow tree	30.5 × 61.6	6	kmt		-	++	++					0.07–0.10	

MA/ Lubrak/ Tib/8	Lubrak	No date	Receipt for payment of government taxes by village	9.5 × 17.7	4	'khyug, with Nepali numerals		1 seal	+++	+					0.07–0.08	
MA/ Lubrak/ Tib/9	Lubrak	Earth tiger 1878	Endowments for ceremonies	60.1 × 34.1	29	kmt		-	++	++	Fibre A				0.14–0.18	
MA/ Lubrak/ Tib/10	Lubrak	Earth ox 1889/1949	Settlement between two halves of a shared estate	17 × 62	8	kmt		4 dig. prints	+++	+	Grass				0.12–0.31	
MA/ Lubrak/ Tib/11	Lubrak	No date	Investments for temple ceremonies	66 × 29.7	40	kmt		-	+++	+					0.12–0.55	
MA/ Lubrak/ Tib/12	Lubrak	Wood rat 1924	Resumption of an estate by a couple who had left the village	36.2 × 23.8	18	kmt		1 dig. print	++	++					0.06–0.18	
MA/ Lubrak/ Tib/13	Lubrak	Fire rat 1936	Settlement concerning an estate in Lubrak belonging to a Chongkhor couple	17 × 33	11	kmt		1 dig. cross	++++						0.10–0.19	
MA/ Lubrak/ Tib/14	Lubrak	Fire sheep 1907	Rules for the conduct of the summer horse-racing festival	29 × 40.5	10	kmt		-	++++						0.09–0.17	
MA/ Lubrak/ Tib/15	Lubrak	Iron snake year 1881/1941	Rules for conduct during temple ceremonies	130.2 × 36.4	13	kmt		11 dig. prints	++	++					0.15–0.27	
MA/ Lubrak/ Tib/16	Lubrak	No date	A financial matter relating to Kag	20.8 × 23.2	7	'khyug		-	+++	+	Fibre D				0.06–0.07	
MA/ Lubrak/ Tib/17	Lubrak	No date	Land tax document	Single sheet with textile attached 33.5 × 32	16	kmt, several hands		-	++++						0.06–0.25	

MA/ Lubrak/ Tib/18	Lubrak	Iron dog 1910	Endowments for ceremonies	70 ×29.5		kmt			+++	+					0.10–0.45	
MA/ Lubrak/ Tib/19	Lubrak	Water pig 1923	Payments for villagers who travel to Kathmandu on official business	34.2 × 37	14	kmt		8 crosses	++	++					0.06–0.11	
MA/ Lubrak/ Tib/20	Lubrak	Wood dog 1994	Receipt for loan of grain from village fund	26.5 × 28.6	10	kmt; modern industrial paper		2 dig. prints			Grass, softwood, hardwood, sunn, fibre E				0.06–0.07	
MA/ Lubrak/ Tib/21	Lubrak	Water bird 1993	Regulations for forest use	59.3 × 33	11	kmt; signatures in Roman and devanagari		3 dig. prints	+++	+	Fibre D				0.08–0.20	
MA/ Lubrak/ Tib/22	Lubrak	Iron sheep 1931	Land tax documents	38.7 × 25.6	14	'khyug		-	+++	+					0.06–0.16	
MA/ Lubrak/ Tib/23	Lubrak	No date	Irrigation management	22.3 × 27.8	15	kmt		12 crosses	+++	+					0.09–0.20	
MA/ Lubrak/ Tib/24	Lubrak	Water bird 1933	Endowments for ceremonies	73.2 × 32.6	7	tshugs		-	++	++					0.06–0.16	
MA/ Lubrak/ Tib/25	Lubrak	No date	Receipt for government tax payment by village	18.8 × 23	10	kmt		-	+++	+					0.05–0.09	
MA/ Lubrak/ Tib/26	Lubrak	No date	Rules for the management of the spring archery festival	31 × 18	9	kmt		-	+++	+					0.07–0.10	
MA/ Lubrak/ Tib/27	Lubrak	Wood pig 1935	Rules for the establishment of the spring archery festival	52.6 × 27.8	29	kmt		-	+++	+					0.06–0.21	

MA/ Lubrak/ Tib/28	Lubrak	No date	Land tax document	13.7 × 31.5	11	kmt		-	+++	+					0.04–0.06	
MA/ Lubrak/ Tib/29	Lubrak	Fire monkey 1959	Settlement of dispute between two people during the archery festival	52.5 × 31.7	25	'khyug	Khing ka Tshe dbang hri thar ZAYIG	14 dig. prints	++	++	Fibre D				0.11–0.26	
MA/ Lubrak/ Tib/30	Lubrak	Fire Horse 1906	Endowments for a ceremony	29.4 × 45.7	6	tshugs, kmt, (several hands)		-	+++	+	Fibre A				0.04–0.07	
MA/ Lubrak/ Tib/31	Lubrak	Water Pig year, Fire tiger year (1986), Earth snake year (1989), Part 4: Water monkey year (1992)	Creation of an endowment to fund government tax	52.4 × 28.1	Part 1: 7 Part 2: 6 Part 3: 6 Part 4: 3	tshugs, 'khyug, several hands		7 dig. prints	++	++					0.04–0.08	
MA/ Lubrak/ Tib/32	Lubrak	No date	Regulations for forest use	20.1 × 24.5	8	'khyug		-	++	++					0.03–0.22	
MA/ Lubrak/ Tib/33	Lubrak	No date, ca. 1960	Covering letter for gifts to all religious people in Baragaon from a Dangkardzong patron	32.3 × 13.6	5	'khyug		2 dig. prints	+++	+	Fibre A				0.04–0.10	
MA/ Lubrak/ Tib/34	Lubrak	Fire monkey 1956	Land tax document	48.7 × 27.7	20	tshugs		-	++	++					0.07–0.14	
MA/ Lubrak/ Tib/35	Lubrak	Water hare 1903, Earth sheep 1919	Rules for food and tormas in rituals	30.1 × 40	Part 1: 9 Part 2: 5	tshugs		-	++++						0.09–0.20	
MA/ Lubrak/ Tib/36	Lubrak	Fire pig year 1887/1947	Investment fund to pay government tax	29.4 × 35.1	9	kmt		-	+++	+					0.07–0.46	

MA/ Lubrak/ Tib/37	Lubrak	No date	Lubrak and Chongkhor refuse to call a meeting of Baragaon	25.2 × 17.5	17	kmt		13 crosses	+++	+					0.08–0.14	
MA/ Lubrak/ Tib/38	Lubrak	Fire horse 1966, Earth horse 1978	Responsibilities of village headmen	21.3 × 31.1		'khyug		-	+++	+					0.04–0.17	
MA/ Lubrak/ Tib/39	Lubrak	Earth dragon 1928	Rule for fixing the intercalary month in the calendar	17.4 × 25.3	9	kmt		-	++	++					0.10–0.36	
MA/ Lubrak/ Tib/40	Lubrak	Fire sheep 1907/1967	List of endowments in a ritual	20.9 × 15.7	5	tshugs		4 crosses	+++	+					0.10–0.24	
MA/ Lubrak/ Tib/41	Lubrak	Wood ox 1985	Regulations for cutting trees around fields	34.9 × 31.5	13	kmt		15 dig. prints	++	++					0.05–0.10	
MA/ Lubrak/ Tib/42	Lubrak	Earth monkey (1968), Iron pig (1971), Fire snake (1977), Iron monkey (1980)	Record of successive investments of an endowment for the payment of government tax	58.2 × 30.7	Part 1: 6 Part 2: 7 Part 3: 5 Part 4: 8	khyug, kmt, several hands		9–10 dig. prints	+	+++					0.05–0.06	
MA/ Lubrak/ Tib/43	Lubrak	Iron dog 1910/1970, Water ox 1913/ 1973	Record of local grain taxes	44 × 32.1	22	khyug, kmt, several hands		5 dig. prints	+++	+	Fibre D				0.03–0.08	
MA/ Lubrak/ Tib/44	Lubrak	Water ox 1853/1913	Rules against animals entering fields	38.9 × 27	13	kmt		-	++	++					0.03–0.12	
MA/ Lubrak/ Tib/45	Lubrak	Earth bird 1909/1969	Investments and funds for tea drinking in temple	31.6 × 48.5	8	'khyug		-	+++	+	Fibre A				0.02–0.06	

MA/ Lubrak/ Tib/46	Lubrak	No date	Partial list of documents contained in the archive	16.1 × 19.6		kmt			++++						0.08–0.44	
MA/ Lubrak/ Tib/47	Lubrak	Earth bird year 1909/1969	Prohibition on selling beer in the village	20.5 × 27.1	10	'khyug		-	++	++					0.07–0.22	
MA/ Lubrak/ Tib/48	Lubrak	Wood tiger 1974	Tax liability of a villager who has two estates	60 × 44.4	13	'khyug		10 dig. prints	+++	+					0.05–0.12	
MA/ Lubrak/ Tib/49	Lubrak	Water pig 1983	Agreement to establish a school in the village	39.2 × 29.2	18	kmt		5 dig. prints			Grass, softwood, hardwood, fibre C				0.06	
MA/ Lubrak/ Tib/50	Lubrak	No date	List of temple property	35.1 × 37		kmt		-	+++	+	Fibre D				0.05–0.18	
MA/ Lubrak/ Tib/51	Lubrak	Wood hare 1975	Procedures to be adopted in the event of dispute with neighbours	32.5 × 42.2	11	kmt		13 dig. prints	++	++					0.06–0.09	
MA/ Lubrak/ Tib/52	Lubrak	No date	List of property in Samtenling temple	58.3 × 27.5	3	'khyug		-	++	++					0.07–0.08	
MA/ Lubrak/ Tib/53	Lubrak	Water snake 1952	Prohibition on fighting in the village	27.8 × 57.2	13	kmt			++	++					0.06–0.13	
MA/ Lubrak/ Tib/54	Lubrak	Water Pig 1983	Beer allocations during a ceremony	56.4 × 32	11	kmt		-	+	+++					0.05–0.06	
MA/ Lubrak/ Tib/55	Lubrak	Wood ox 1985	Beer making regulations for clearing of the reservoir irrigation canal	28.9 × 18.6	6	kmt		-			Grass, sunn, fibre A, fibre E				0.07	
MA/ Lubrak/ Tib/56	Lubrak	No date	Rules for the use of community-owned fermentation jars	60.6 × 28.1	Part 1: 18 ; Part 3: 3	kmt		17 crosses	+++	+					0.09–0.13	

MA/ Lubrak/ Tib/57	Lubrak	Iron horse 1990	Grain taxes for an area of fields	39.5 × 23.6	21	'khyug		1 dig. print	+++	+					0.05–0.06	
MA/ Lubrak/ Tib/58	Lubrak	No date	Temple property list	136 × 49		tshugs, kmt (several hands)		-	+++	+					0.04–0.11	
MA/ Lubrak/ Tib/59	Lubrak	Earth bird 1969	Village grain taxes	28.6 × 15.3		kmt			+++	+					0.04–0.07	
MA/ Lubrak/ Tib/60	Lubrak	Iron rat 1960	Management of first use of reservoir water	37.3 × 31.7	15	'khyug		14 dig. prints	+++	+					0.09–0.11	
MA/ Lubrak/ Tib/61	Lubrak	Horse [element missing]	Tax payments to Manang	10.3 × 42.5	5	tshugs		2 seals	+++	+					0.09–0.14	
MA/ Lubrak/ Tib/62	Lubrak	Fire horse 1906/1966	Tax payments to Kag	20.9 × 19.1	13	'khyug, with Nepali numerals		1 seal	+++	+					0.03–0.08	
MA/ Lubrak/ Tib/63	Lubrak	Earth rat 1948	Rules for use of the water mill	12.1 × 34.3	4	kmt		-	+++	+					0.11–0.13	
MA/ Lubrak/ Tib/64	Lubrak	Water tiger 1962	Irrigation regulations	45.6 × 60.1	8	kmt		15-16 dig. prints	++	++					0.04–0.07	
MA/ Lubrak/ Tib/65	Lubrak	Earth horse 1918/1978	Rules for use of the water mill	36.6 × 35.7	9	kmt		8 crosses	+++	+					0.07–0.18	
MA/ Lubrak/ Tib/66	Lubrak	Fire horse 1906	Receipt for tax payment by village to Dzar	22.3 × 19.4		'khyug			+++	+					0.06–0.11	
MA/ Lubrak/ Tib/67	Lubrak	Earth bird 1909/1969	Document concerning suspected theft from a village temple	33.4 × 43	3	'khyug		-	++	++					0.05–0.07	
MA/ Lubrak/ Tib/68	Lubrak	no date	Endowments for a ceremony	15.3 × 22.8	20	'khyug		-	++	++					0.05–0.06	

MA/ Lubrak/ Tib/69	Lubrak	no date	Miscellaneous payments for animals and grain	14.2 × 15.6	8	'khyug		-	+	+++					0.08–0.13	
MA/ Lubrak/ Tib/70	Lubrak	Earth bird 1909/1969	Receipt for payment of village taxes	16.4 × 13.5	7	'khyug		1 seal	+++	+					0.08–0.09	
MA/ Lubrak/ Tib/71	Lubrak	Wood dragon 1904/1964	Receipt for payment of village taxes	19.3 × 21.8	10	'khyug		1 seal	+++	+					0.09–0.15	
MA/ Lubrak/ Tib/72	Lubrak	Water monkey 1932/1992	Receipt for payment to someone from Khyinga	6.4 × 30.7	2	tshugs		?	++	++					0.07–0.16	
MA/ Lubrak/ Tib/73	Lubrak	No date	Endowments for a ceremony	41.9 × 36.1	15	kmt		-	+++	+					0.06–0.19	
MA/ Lubrak/ Tib/74	Lubrak	Wood bird 1945	Irrigation regulations	23.9 × 53.5	10	kmt		16 dig. prints	+++	+					0.11–0.14	
MA/ Lubrak/ Tib/75	Lubrak	Fire sheep 1967	Payments of government tax	62.7 × 37.1	20	kmt		-	+++	+					0.11–0.33	
MA/ Lubrak/ Tib/76	Lubrak	No date	Endowements for ceremonies and regulations	69.8 × 30.1	18	tshugs		-	+++	+					0.11–0.24	
MA/ Lubrak/ Tib/77	Lubrak	Wood bird 1945	Agreement to pay a guard to supervise irrigation system	47.7 × 16.8	19	kmt		3 dig. prints	+++	+	Fibre A, fibre D				0.09–0.54	
MA/ Lubrak/ Tib/78	Lubrak	Earth hare 1939	Legal case against a villager who became drunk and violent	49.6 × 34.4	25	kmt	Bla [ma] dbang [rgyal]	20 dig. prints	+++	+					0.11–0.20	
MA/ Lubrak/ Tib/79	Lubrak	Iron sheep 1871/1931	Rules for management of an abandoned estate	41.5 × 30.7	14	kmt		1 dig. print	+	+++					0.05–0.17	
MA/ Lubrak/ Tib/80	Lubrak	Earth dog 1958	Summons by the widow of a former subba in South Mustang	9.8 × 36.2	5	kmt		-	+++	+					0.11–0.38	

MA/ Lubrak/ Tib/81	Lubrak	No date	Booklet of temple endowments	11 × 24		'bru tsha, 'khyug, kmt			+++	+					0.23–0.65	
MA/ Lubrak/ Tib/82	Lubrak	No date	Booklet of temple endowments	11 × 24		'bru tsha, 'khyug, kmt		-	+++	+					0.24–0.29	

APPENDIX 4: SEALS IN THE MUSTANG ARCHIVES

No.	Seal image	Document no.	Owner or user	Seal description
	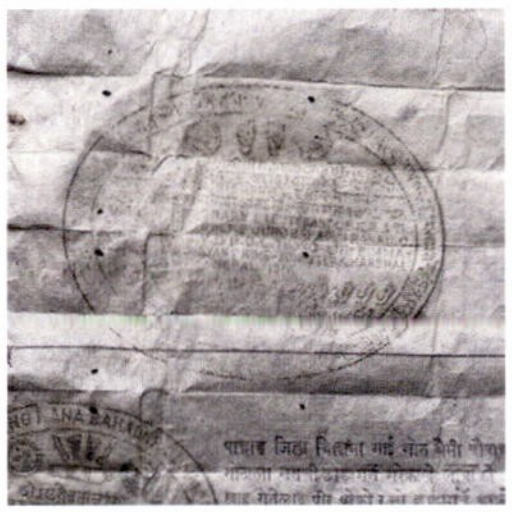	MA/Geling/Tib/166	Chandra Shamshere Jung Bahadur Rana, Prime Minister of Nepal	Elliptical, black; central spaces has three horizontally-arranged blocks of lettering, Devanāgarī, Roman, Arabic; Roman text reads: MAHARAJA HONORARY LIEUTENANT GENERAL SIR/ CHANDRA SHUMSHERE JUNG BAHADUR RANA C.C./ ...PRIME MINISTER... MARSHAL/ NEPAL 1916 perimeter band contains Tibatan text, partly legible: SHAM SHER JANG+GA BHA DUR RĀ ṆA
		MA/Geling/Tib/166	General Bhim Shumshere Jung Rana Bahadur, Commander-in-Chief of Nepal Army	Elliptical, black; central area contains two horizontally arranged blocks of text, in Devanāgarī and in Arabic. Border contains Roman script: GENERAL BHIM SHUM SHERE JUNG RANA BAHADUR COMMANDER-IN-CHIEF NEPAL 1901
		MA/Geling/Nep/116	Ruler of Jumla, possibly King Surath Shah	Horizontally rectangular, black, black Devanāgarī lettering on white background around perimeter. In centre is a horizontal conch.
	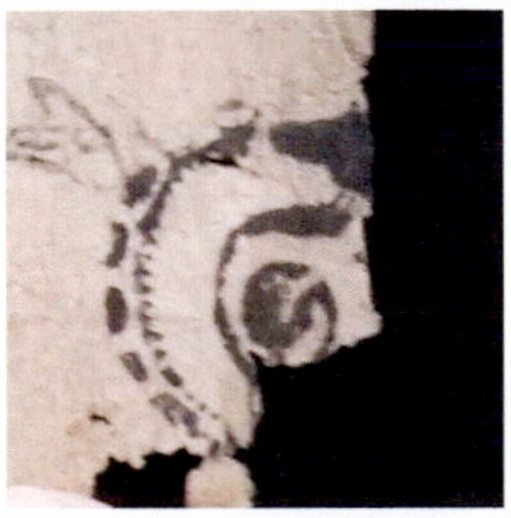	MA/Lubrak/Tib/61	Manang A	Complex spiral motif and other features, damaged
		MA/Lubrak/Tib/61	Manang B	Square, black, centre contains black geometric motifs on square plain background, in two vertical columns, resembling Hor yig but not recognisable as script

	 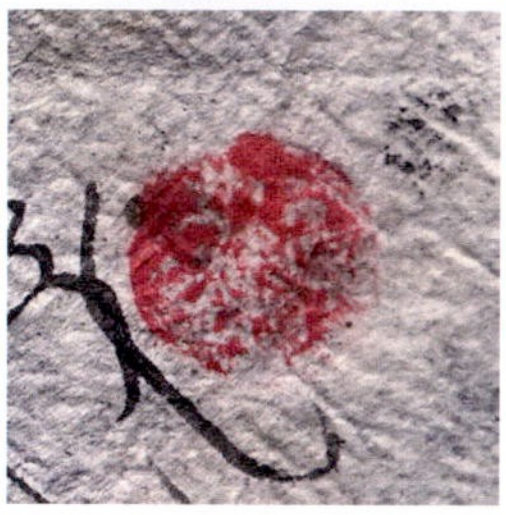   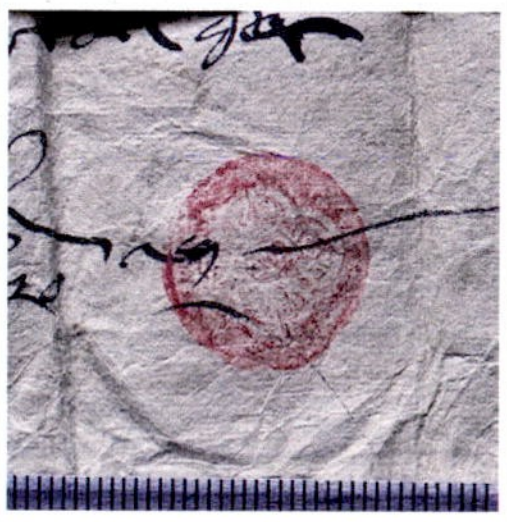 	MA/Geling/Tib/16, MA/Geling/Tib/127, MA/Geling/Tib/128, MA/Geling/Tib/168, MA/LTshognam/Tib/10	King of Lo	Round, red, crossed vajra

NEPAL GOVERNMENT OFFICES				
		MA/Lubrak/Nep/1	Kagbeni customs office	Elliptical, black, three lines of Devanāgarī SRĪ/ KĀGBENI BHAN/ SĀR AḌḌA
		MA/Lubrak/Tib/8		Elliptical, black, three lines of Devanāgarī SRĪ/ KĀGBENI BHAN/ SĀR AḌḌĀ
		MA/Lubrak/Nep/2	Nepali, govt office	
		MA/Lubrak/Nep/2	Nepali, govt office	
		MA/Lubrak/Nep/2	Nepali, govt office	
		MA/Lubrak/Nep/2	Nepali, govt office	

	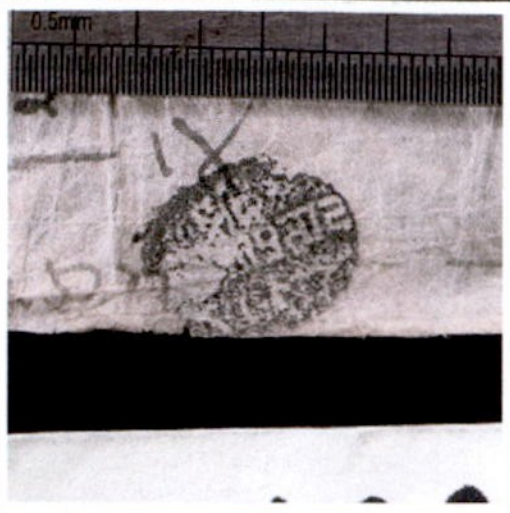	MA/Lubrak/Nep/2	Nepali, govt office	
	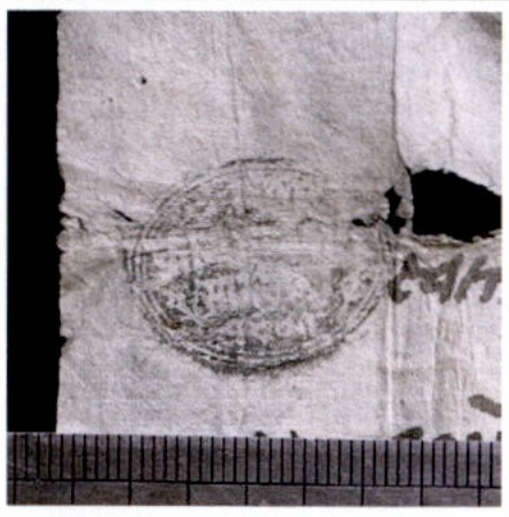	MA/Lubrak/Nep/4	Nepali, govt office	
		MA/Lubrak/Nep/5	Nepali, govt office	
		MA/Lubrak/Nep/6	Nepali, govt office	
		MA/Lubrak/Nep/7	Nepali, govt office	Black, elliptical, indistinct
	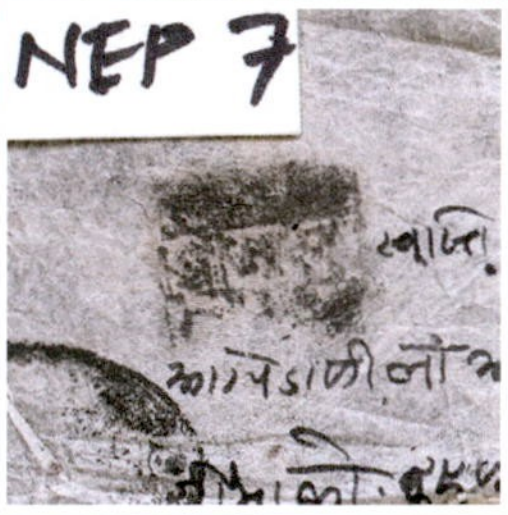 NEP 7	MA/Lubrak/Nep/7	Possibly the government land revenue (*mālpot*) office	Horizontally rectangular, 3 rows, central row contains Devanāgarī text, positive on white background, SRĪ MĀL

		MA/Lubrak/Nep/7	Nepali, govt office	Round, black, indistinct
		MA/Lubrak/Nep/8	Nepali, govt office	Black, four-lobed on cruciform axis, possibly with smaller lobes on an X axis, indistinct.
		MA/Lubrak/Nep/8	Nepali, govt office	Black, elliptical, indistinct
		MA/Lubrak/Nep/8	Possibly the government land revenue (*mālpot*) office	Horizontally rectangular, 3 rows, central row contains Devanāgarī text, positive on white background, SRĪ MĀL
	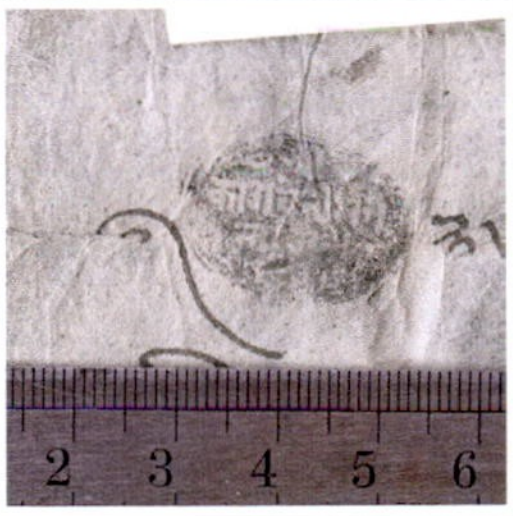	MA/Lubrak/Tib/4	Kagbeni customs office	Elliptical, black, three lines of Devanāgarī SRĪ/ KĀGBENI BHAN/ SĀR AḌ[Ḍ]A
		MA/Lubrak/Tib/8	Kagbeni customs office	Elliptical, black, three lines of Devanāgarī SRĪ/ KĀGBENI BHAN/ SĀR AḌ[Ḍ]A

		MA/Geling/Tib/132	Nepali; Thak Court	Elliptical, black three lines of Devanāgarī; line 1: SRĪ; line 2: THAK ADĀLAT; ornamented upper and lower borders that follow the rims to the left and right extremities.
		MA/Geling/Tib/171	Nepali. Same as G167_NEP0894_2	Round, black, Devanāgarī lettering in centre, decorated outer rim.
		MA/Geling/Tib/47	Nepali	Black, elliptical, 3 lines of Devanāgarī. First line may read ŚRĪ GURURṄ
		MA/UTshognam/Tib/41	Nepali, govt office	Elliptical, black, small, Devanāgarī SRI MANA===
	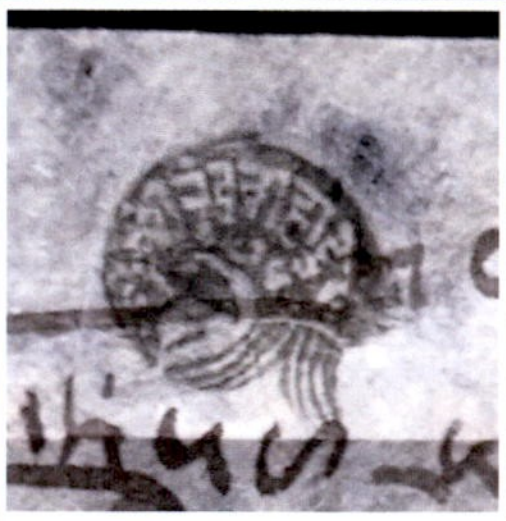	MA/UTshognam/Tib/41	Nepali, govt office	Round, small, with decorative motifs, Devanāgarī ===BAHADUR
		MA/UTshognam/Tib/41	Nepali, govt court	Round, black, large, "positive"; horizontal inside panel contains Devanāgarī SRI ADĀLAT, imposed on crossed khukuris, cutting edge upwards, topped by elaborate sun-and-moon motif, inside two concentric black circles, outer perimeter consists of black cog-like triangles.

			Nepali	Horizontally elongated octagonal, black, Devanāgarī
			Nepali	Horizontally rectangular, black, very ornate; unsure if this is a seal or some other motif. Official printed government document.
INSTITUTIONS IN TIBET				
		MA/Geling/Tib/27	Ngor Ewam Khangsar (monastic college)	Round, red, crossed vajra, letter E in centre
	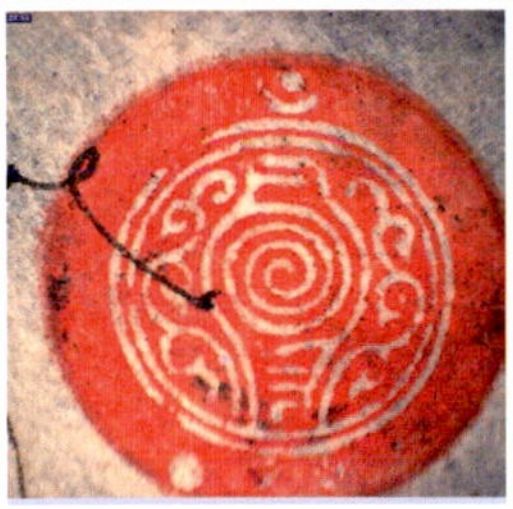	MA/Geling/Tib/169	Garpön (local governor) of Trarik, in Tibet	Round, red, conch in centre, sun-and-moon motif in outer rim
BARAGAON NOBILITY				
		MA/Dzar/Tib/8	Trithok Trashi Thokgyal, Lord of Baragaon	Round, black, conch at centre, middle ring of lotus petals
		MA/Dzar/Nep/11	Lord of Baragaon?	Elliptical, 3 lines of lettering; top: moon symbol, Devanāgarī SRI, sun symbol; line 2: Devanāgarī, possibly CANDRABAHADUR? Line 3: decorative motifs, perhaps with Tibetan letter JA, or name DZAR?

		MA/Dzar/Nep/11	Lord of Baragaon?	As above
	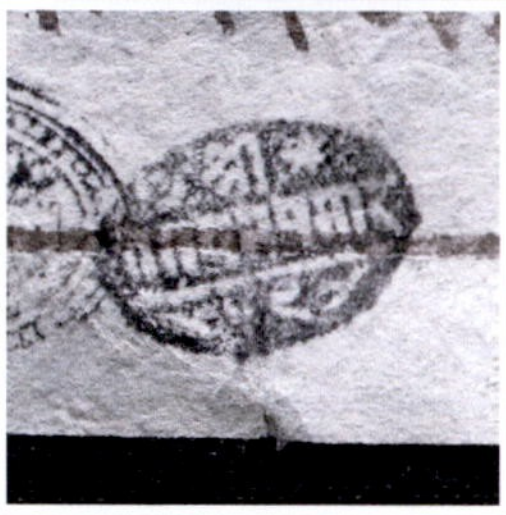	MA/Dzar/Nep/16	Local dignitary?	Elliptical, 3 lines of lettering. Top: moon symbol, Devanāgarī SRI, sun symbol; line 2: Devanāgarī, possibly ending in -PAMAR; Line 3: decorative motifs, indistinct.
	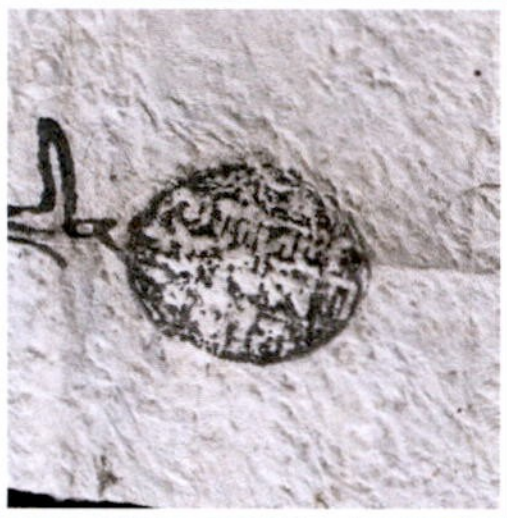	MA/Lubrak/Tib/71	Dzar Dekyi Phodrang (Noble house)	Elliptical, black, Devanāgarī lettering
	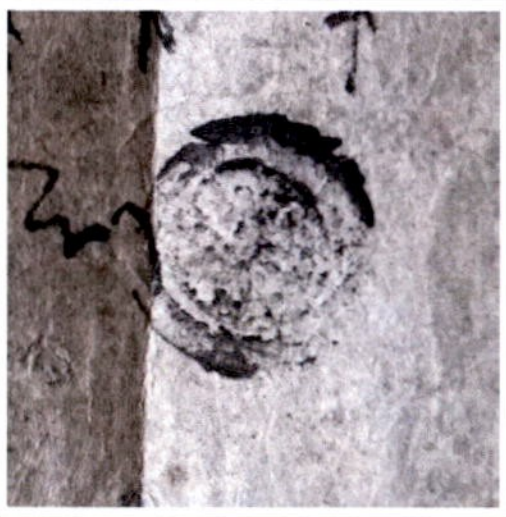	MA/UTshognam/Tib/37	Zangpo Dorje, the Lord of Baragaon	Round, black, central motif unclear due to smudging
		MA/UTshognam/Tib/45	Candra Bir, a nobleman of Dzar.	Elliptical, black, Devanāgarī ŚRĪ PṚTHVĪ
		MA/Dzar/Nep/22	Unknown; probably a nobleman	Round, red

VILLAGE COMMUNITIES				
	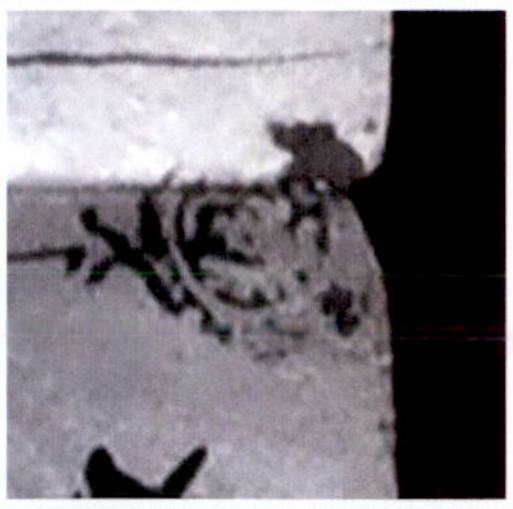	MA/UTshognam/Tib/13	Gyaga community	Round, black, centre contains letters or geometrical motif, indistinct
	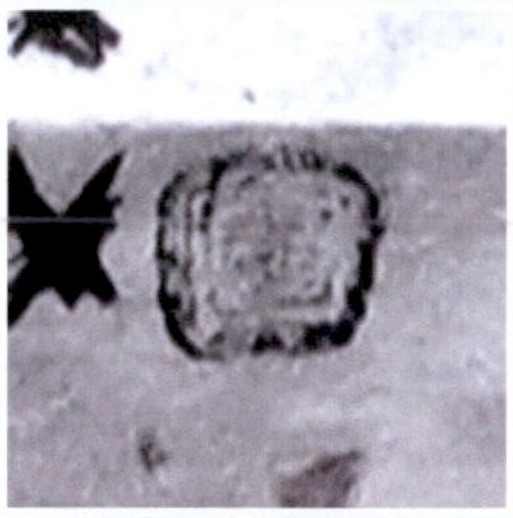	MA/UTshognam/Tib/13	Tshug community, predates the village's teardrop-shaped seal (below)	Square, black, possibly applied twice, indistinct
		MA/LTshognam/Tib/2	Taye community	Round, black, indistinct
		MA/LTshognam/Tib/2	Te community	Round, black, indistinct
	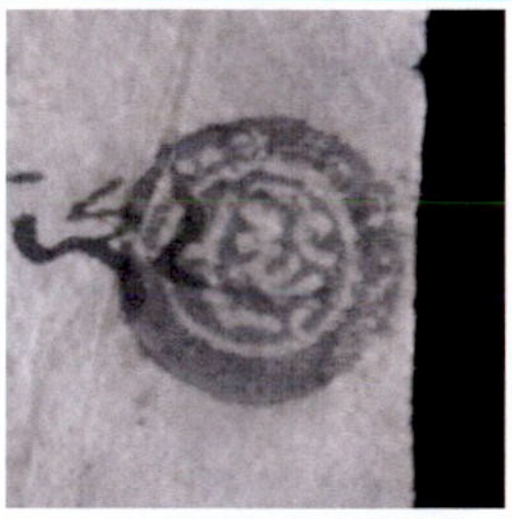	MA/LTshognam/Tib/2	Gyaga community	Round, black, Tibetan syllables in centre RDO RJE, surrounded by a circle; outer ring of dots
		MA/LTshognam/Tib/2	Tsele community	Ellipitical; black; Devanāgarī lettering in centre, possibly GANES; Surrounded by elliptical circle; outer ring of white dots, outer ring.

		MA/LTshognam/Tib/2	Tshug community	Two seal imprints, unclear whether they are the same. Square with rounded corners, lettering in centre, surrounded by concentric squares with rounded corners.
		MA/Geling/Tib/2	Geling community	Square, black, 3 double columns or rows of indistinct lettering, possibly pseudo-Zhangzhung script.
		MA/Geling/Tib/24	Geling community	Square, black, 3 double columns or rows of indistinct lettering, possibly pseudo-Zhangzhung script.
		MA/Geling/Tib/43	Geling community	Square, black, 3 double columns or rows of indistinct lettering, possibly pseudo-Zhangzhung script.
		MA/UTshognam/Tib/37	Te community, different from LT_2	Square, black; diagonal conch, surrounded by a square border of dots and floral decoration
	 	MA/Geling/Tib/147, applied twice	Geling village assembly, but probably belonging to a village official	Round, black, Tibetan letters in centre (RTAM?); two solid concentric circles, outer circle of dots.

		MA/Geling/Tib/80	Community (lung pa) of Geling, but probably belonging to an individual	Round, black, Tibetan letters in centre (RTAM?); two solid concentric circles, outer circle of dots.
		MA/Geling/Tib/10	Community of Geling	Square, black, unclear due to smudging
	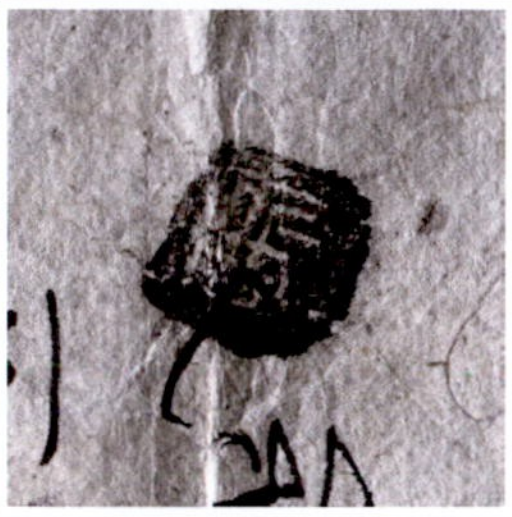	MA/Dzar/Tib/3	Possibly the seal of the community of Dzar, or of the thümi (thud mi, recte thus mi), a category of local official	Square, black, with geometric design, possibly lettering (unclear)
		MA/Geling/Tib/151	"the whole community" (lung pa dkun [sic]) of Geling	Square, black, indistinct due to smudging
		MA/Geling/Tib/151	"All members of the community" (yul pa thun mong)	Square, black, indistinct due to smudging
	 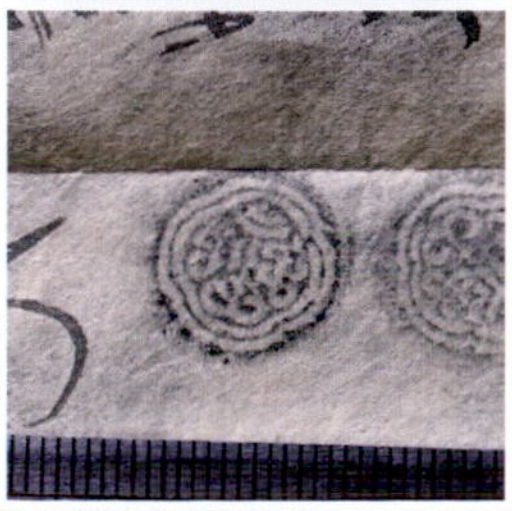	MA/Geling/Tib/153	"The war party as a whole" (dmag mkhu thun mong) Same seal applied three times. Same as G 130_KMI4943	Round, black, sun-and-moon motif atop a vertical axis; rest of centre indistinct; surrounded by two four-lobed concentric rings.

		MA/LTshognam/Tib/17	Community of Tshug 1910	Teardrop-shaped, black, Tibetan lettering TSHUG YUL SPYI=
		MA/LTshognam/Tib/17	Community of Tshug 1910	Teardrop-shaped, black, Tibetan lettering TSHUG YUL SPYI=
		MA/UTshognam/Tib/36	Community of Te, 1916	Square, centre contains Tibetan on two lines GTER/ LUNG (Te Community), framed by square surround.
	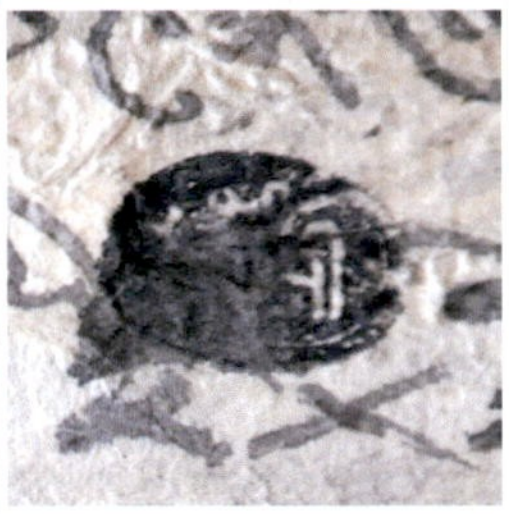	MA/UTshognam/Tib/44	Community of Tshug, 1884	Elliptical, black, Devanāgarī lettering, indistinct
RELIGIOUS FIGURES				
	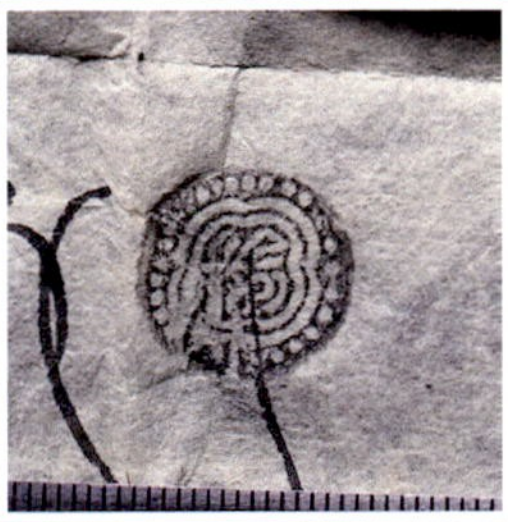	MA/Geling/Tib/125	Monk or lama from Marpha	Round, black, Tibetan letters in centre, CHOS. Two four-lobed concentric rings; round outer circle of dots

	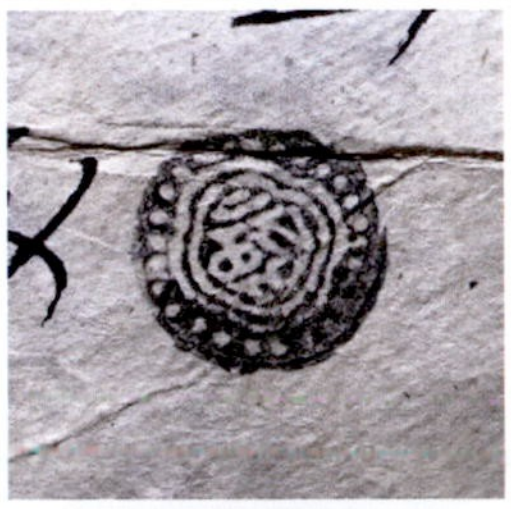  	MA/Geling/Tib/1, applied three times to represent three different people	"The seal was borrowed from Gatru" (Name of Marpha monk?).	Round, black, Tibetan letters in centre, CHOS. Two four-lobed concentric rings; round outer circle of dots
		MA/Geling/Tib/104	Ngawang Rabsal and Ngawang Loden (two monks)	Round, black, Tibetan letters in centre, CHOS. Two four-lobed concentric rings; round outer circle of dots
	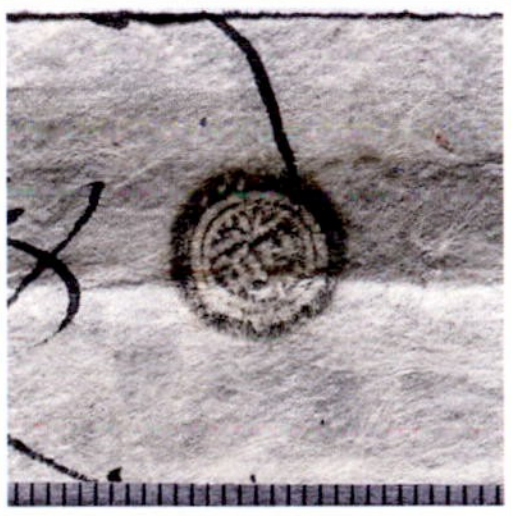	MA/Geling/Tib/164	The community of nuns	Round, black, Tibetan letters in centre (MOS? LOS?); two solid concentric circles, outer circle of dots.
		MA/Geling/Tib/156	Monk Ngawang Tenzin	Round, black, Tibetan lettering in centre, between parallel lines: TSHE/ RING; surrounded by two concentric rings.
	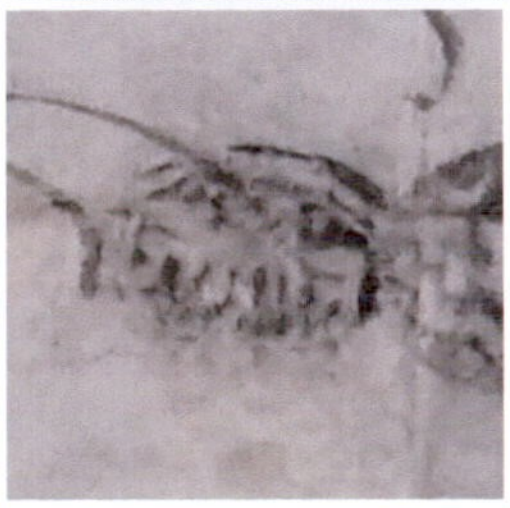	MA/UTshognam/Tib/5	Thita Adam, Lama Thuthob, Lama Dawa Gyalpo (Impossible to attribute any of the and the following two seals to any one of the three individuals; Thita Adam is a layman from Marpha)	Elliptical, black, Devanāgarī lettering in centre encircled by elliptical ring

	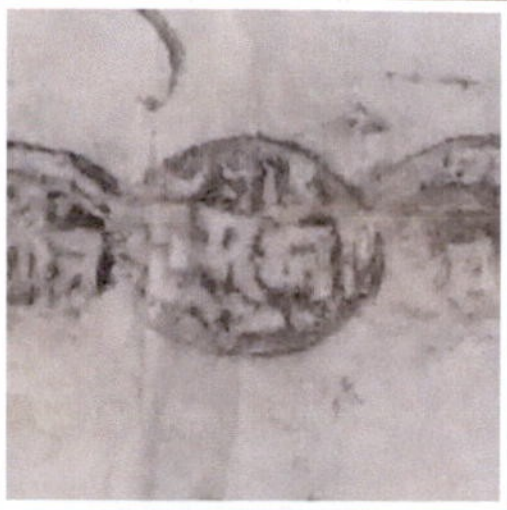	MA/UTshognam/Tib/5	Thita Adam, Lama Thuthob, Lama Dawa Gyalpo	Elliptical, black, Devanāgarī lettering in centre, indistinct
	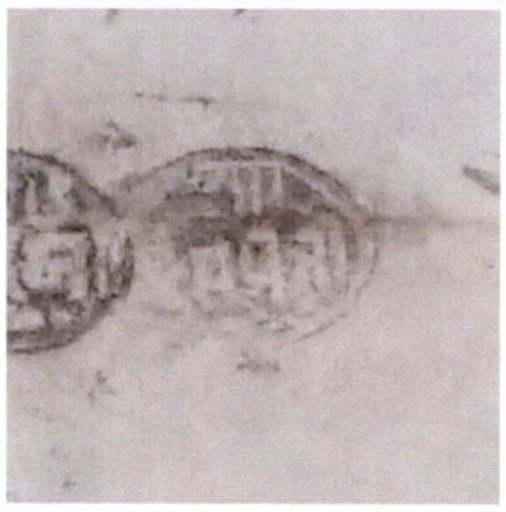	MA/UTshognam/Tib/5	Thita Adam, Lama Thuthob, Lama Dawa Gyalpo	Black, elliptical, Devanāgarī lettering in centre encircled by elliptical ring
		MA/UTshognam/Tib/15	Tshampa Sangye Tshecu of Purang	Elliptical, black, Devanāgarī lettering in centre, possibly ŚRĪ GAṆES, encircled by an elliptical ring
		MA/UTshognam/Tib/43	"The son [lama] Rigden"	Square, black, two concentric white squares visible.
		MA/UTshognam/Tib/43	Rangdrol, same seal as 43_1	Square, black, faint impression, indistinct
		MA/UTshognam/Tib/1	Lama Rangdrol, probably same as above	Square, black, centre apparently contains two columns with lettering or geometrical motifs, framed by two concentric square borders
		MA/UTshognam/Tib/43	Phurba Angmo (woman from priestly family; sister of Lamas Rigden and Randrol)	Round, black, indistinct motif at centre, encirled by two concentric rings.

		MA/UTshognam/Tib/42	Lama Tenpai Gyaltsen	Round, black, centre contains Tibetan PA ZA/ NG, possibly for [D]PA[L B]ZANG, encircled by one ring
	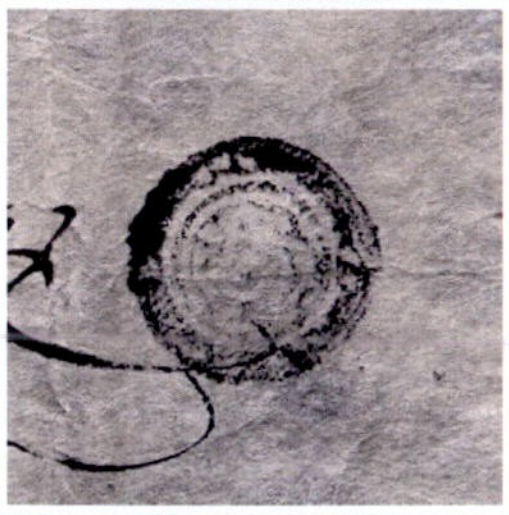	MA/Geling/Tib/95	Drangsong Dargye	Round, black, indistinct
		MA/LTshognam/Tib/2	Lama Jamyang Wangdü	Square, black, indistinct lettering in centre; surrounded by two concentric squares
		MA/Geling/Tib/52	Dzogchen Lama	Square, black, geometric motifs or lettering in centre, indistinct due to smudging
	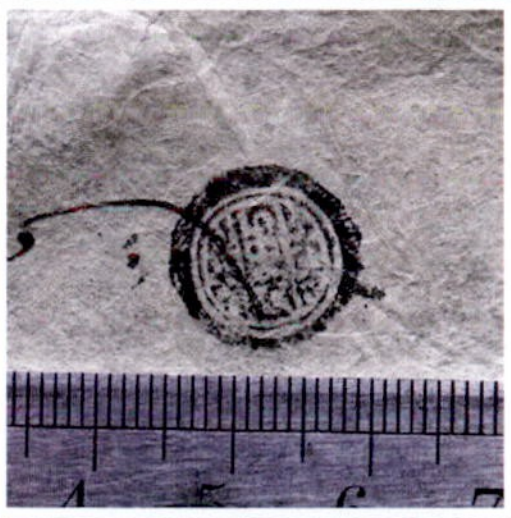	MA/Geling/Tib/58	Applied on verso; same as G156_NEP0976, therefore probably Monk Ngawang Tenzin	Round, black, Tibetan lettering in centre, between parallel lines: TSHE RING; surrounded by two concentric rings.
		MA/Geling/Tib/71	The monk Cangdruk from Marpha	Round, black, possibly containing Tibetan lettering
		MA/Geling/Tib/130	Gelong (ordained monk) Palden Chöphel or Gelong Ngawang Rabsal	Square, black, indistinct motifs in centre, surrounded by square border.

		MA/Geling/Tib/130	Gelong (ordained monk) Palden Chöphel or Gelong Ngawang Rabsal	Round, black, sun-and-moon motif atop a vertical axis; rest of centre indistinct; surrounded by two four-lobed concentric rings.
		MA/UTshognam/Tib/1	Lama Tshewang Bumpa	Black, round, geometric motifs in centre encircled by two concentric rings.
	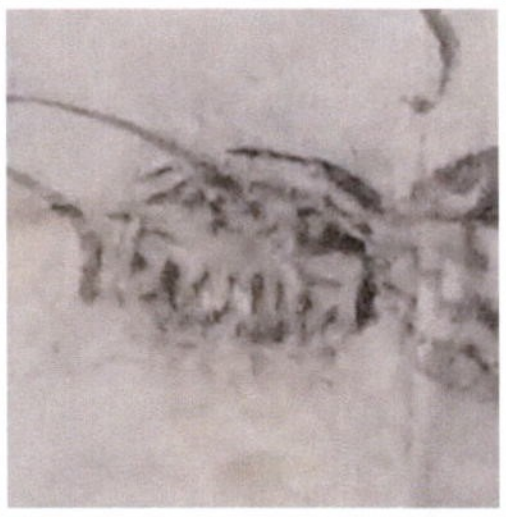	MA/UTshognam/Tib/5	Ösal Dorje (with thumbprint and cross)	Black, round, geometric motifs in centre, encircled by ring with four lobes
	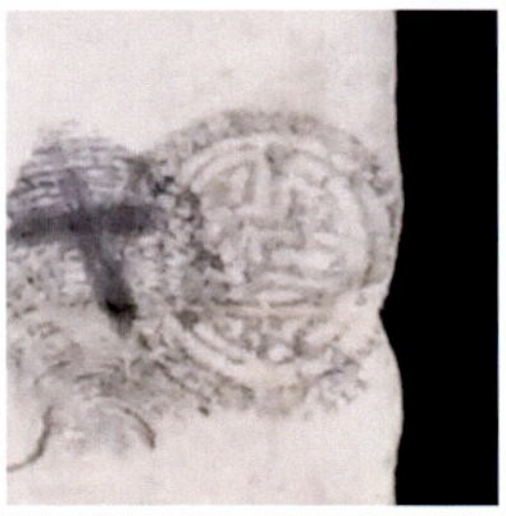	MA/UTshognam/Tib/5	Lama Tshewang Bumpa (with thumbprint and cross) Same as MA/UTshognam/Tib/1	Round, black, geometric motifs in centre encircled by two concentric rings.
		COMMONERS		
		MA/Geling/Tib/38	Tobgye	Round, black; conch at centre, surrounded by four-lobed ring; outer ring of dots
		MA/Geling/Tib/70	Unknown	Round, black, central motif unclear; surrounded by two concentric rings; outer ring of dots
		IMG_20190903_105130	Unknown	Round, black; conch at centre, surrounded by four-lobed ring; outer ring of dots

		MA/LTshognam/Tib/2	Unknown	Round, black, indistinct
		MA/UTshognam/Tib/37	Probably the headman of Te, named Chökyab Phuntshog	(Left seal) Round, black, Tibetan letters centre: CHO/ PHU RGYA, probably representing the owner's name.
	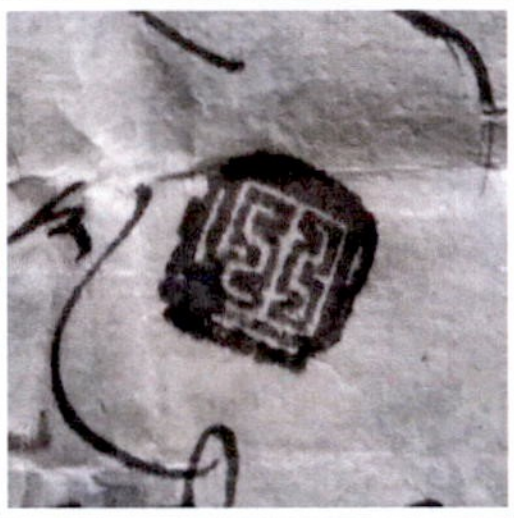	MA/Geling/Tib/5	Könchok	Square, back; mirror-image figure "3"-like motif in centre (possibly Tibetan letter A?); surrounded by square border
		MA/Geling/Tib/5	Könchok's wife, (za mi), Hrangnye	same seal
		MA/Geling/Tib/25	Könchok	Square, back; Mirror-image figure "3"-like motif in centre (possibly Tibetan letter A?); surrounded by square border
		MA/Geling/Tib/25	Hrangnye (almost certainly Könchok's wife)	Round, black, unidentified geometric motifs
		MA/Dzar/Nep/22	Unknown	Round, red, centre contains Tibetan letter A, surrounded by a ring of petal-shaped motifs, encircled by two concentric rings

11		MA/UTshognam/Tib/21	Gara Dondrub of Tshug	Square, black; centre contains Tibetan CHA or TSHA, surrounded by a square set perpendicularly to the outer border; three dots in each of the outer corners.
		MA/UTshognam/Tib/21	Phurpa Palmo (wife of Gara Dondrub)	As above
		MA/Dzar/Tib/3	Possibly the seal of the gopön (go spon, recte 'go dpon, a local official)	Round, black, geometric designs or letter in centre (unclear), surrounded by circle
		MA/Geling/Tib/22	Headman Samdrub Chöphel	Square, black, geometric motifs or lettering in centre, surrounded by two concentric squares
		MA/Geling/Tib/22	Jamyang	Square, black, geometric motifs or lettering in centre, surrounded by two concentric squares
		MA/Geling/Tib/25	Hrangnye (Könchok's wife)	Round, black, geometric designs round, centre
	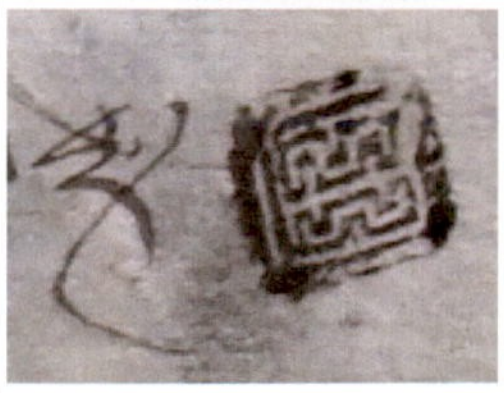	MA/Geling/Tib/25	"Konchok and his wife"	Square, back; Mirror-image figure "3"-like motif in centre (possibly Tibetan letter A?); surrounded by square border

	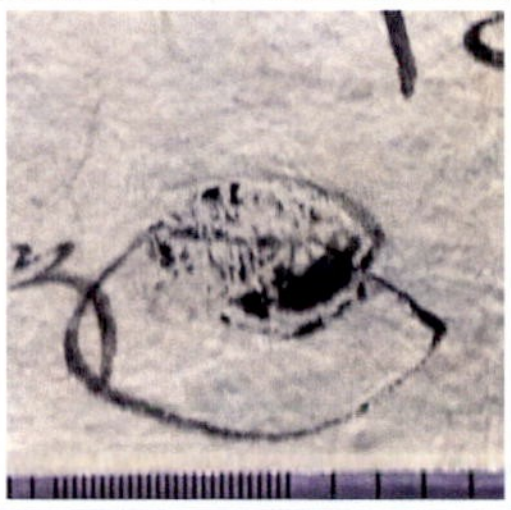	MA/Geling/Tib/44	Kunzang Trashi	Elliptical, black, indistinct
	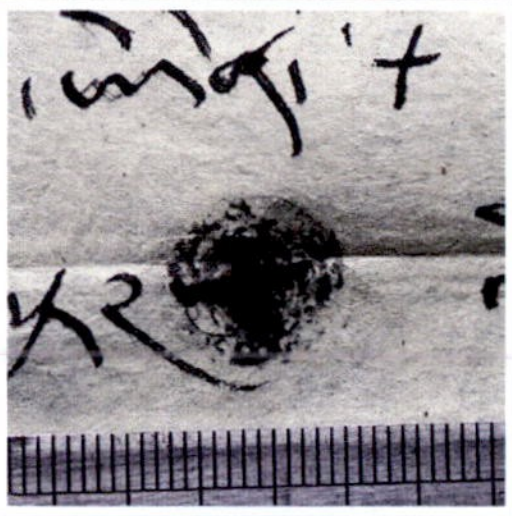	MA/Geling/Tib/55	Zangpo Lugkal and his wife	Round, black, geometric motifs in centre, imposed on a cross
		MA/Geling/Tib/57	Phurbu	Round, black, centre invisible due to a large hole in the paper.
	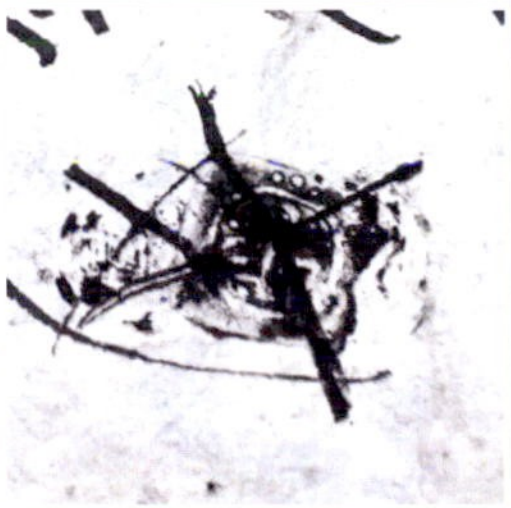	MA/Geling/Tib/57	Tshering Hrithar and his wife	Two seals: one round, one square, both black, both indistinct and each with a superimposed cross.
		MA/Geling/Tib/57	Unidentified couple; seal is applied twice	Round, black, Tibetan syllable in centre, RGYAL; the L is subscribed beneath stacked RGYA. To either side are vertical lines each with 6 short perpendicular lines towards exterior. Surrounded by a circle.
		MA/Geling/Tib/57	Copy of above	
		MA/Geling/Tib/66	Household of Tobgyal, who has disappeared	Round, black, possible Tibetan lettering in centre in rectangular box; surrounded by two concentric rings.

		MA/Geling/Tib/67	Headman Norbu	Round, black, Tibetan lettering in centre, probably NOR BU; surrounded by two concentric circles; perimeter circle of dots
	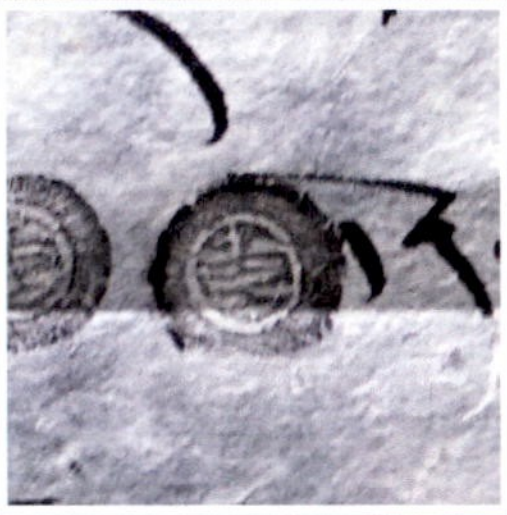	MA/Geling/Tib/71	Pemba Hridar and his son (applied twice)	Round, black, horizontal striations in centre across a vertical axis; surrounded by a circle.
		MA/Geling/Tib/71	Nyima Tshering; same as G 71_NEP0861_2	Round, black, vertical rectangular box in centre, surmounted by sun-and-moon motif; box may contain Tibetan lettering; to either side are half-circles with double perimeters. Inside may be letters or geometric motifs.
		MA/Geling/Tib/90	Nyima Tshering	Round, black, vertical rectangular box in centre, surmounted by sun-and-moon motif; box may contain Tibetan lettering; to either side are half-circles with double perimeters. Inside may be letters or geometric motifs.
	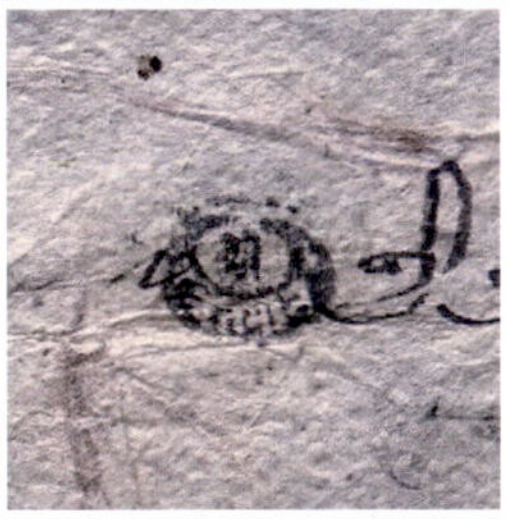	MA/Geling/Tib/100	Probably Subbā Candra Singh, the issuer of the document	Elliptical, black, elliptical space at top contains black letters, possibly ŚRĪ. Below, in negative lettering, is name or word in Devanāgarī.
		MA/Geling/Tib/103	Karzang of Tshug	Round, black, indistinct due to smudging.
	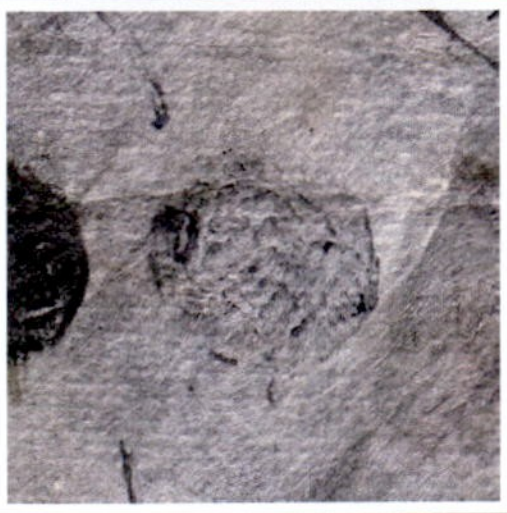	MA/Geling/Tib/103	Unknown, possibly previous seal applied a second time.	Round, black, indistinct

	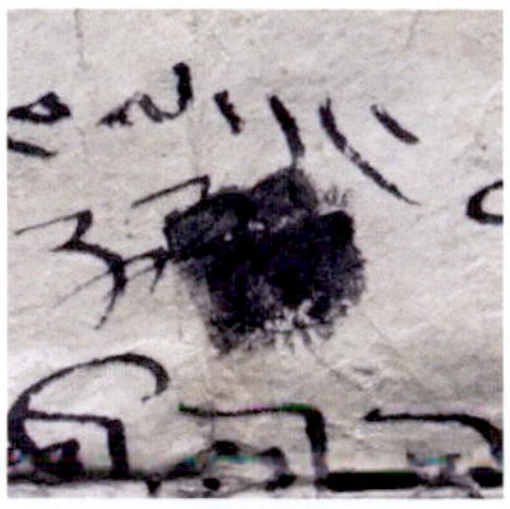	MA/Geling/Tib/112	Possibly Pemba Tshomo (an elderly woman)	Square, black, indistinct due to smudging.
		MA/Geling/Tib/132	Nepali	Slightly elliptical, black, three lines of indistinct Devanāgarī, surrounded by a circle.
	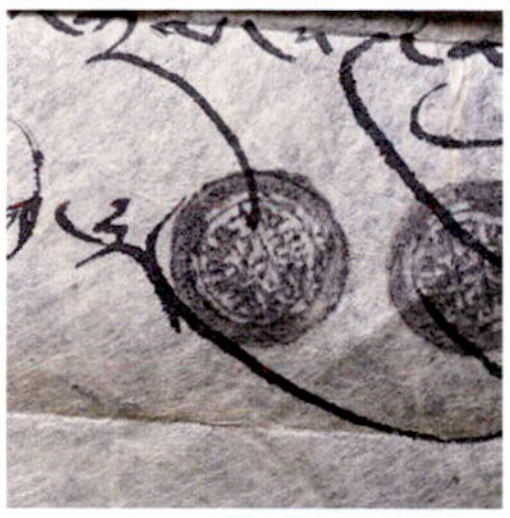 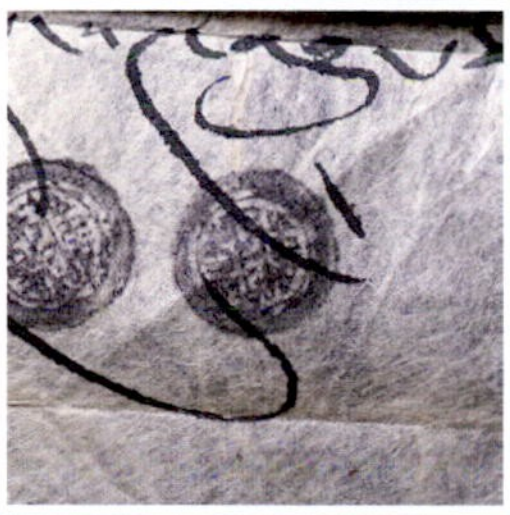	MA/Geling/Tib/150	Tshewang Namgyal and his son Trashi Dondrub; same seal applied twice	Round, black
	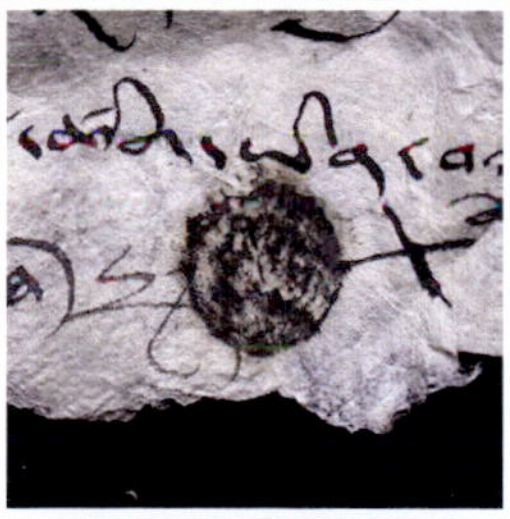	MA/Geling/Tib/152	The woman Dechen	Round, black, indistinct due to smudging
	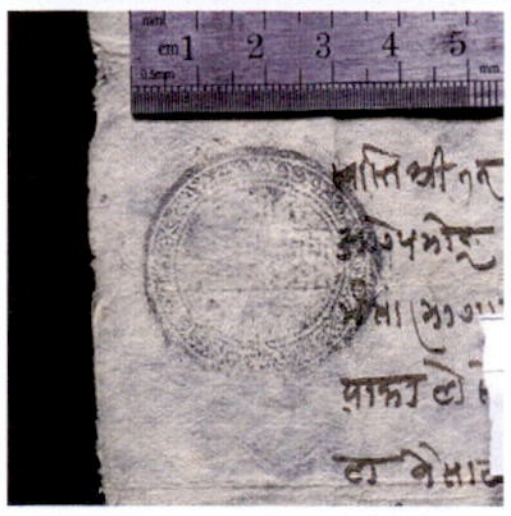	MA/Geling/Tib/167	Nepali	Round, black, Devanāgarī in centre with ornate perimeter band.
	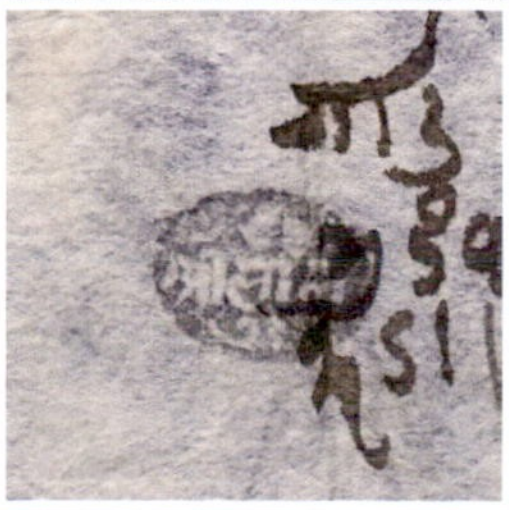	MA/Geling/Tib/167	Nepali	Elliptical, black, three lines, first and third lines probably decorative motifs. Middle line, Devanāgarī ŚRI LAKSHMI

		MA/Geling/Tib/167	Nepali	Black, elliptical, three lines, first and third lines probably decorative motifs. Middle line, Devanāgarī, not legible due to superimposed writing.
		MA/LTshognam/Tib/18	Tshering Trashi	Round, black, three lines of Tibetan: PAD/ MA/ KHA'GRO
		MA/LTshognam/Tib/23	"four witnesses"	Slightly elliptical, black, indistinct
		MA/UTshognam/Tib/29	Hrithar Tshering	Horizontally elongated octagonal, centre contains angular Devanāgarī on two lines, SRĪI¯ …? Framed by two concentric octagonal surrounds
		MA/UTshognam/Tib/2	Phurba Dorje	Round, black, centre contains geometrical motif, possibly conch
		MA/UTshognam/Tib/8	Chökyab Dorje	Apparently square with rounded corners, black, indistinct

Appendix 5: Radiocarbon analytical report

The following analytical report contains ^{14}C analysis from the University of Arizona AMS Laboratory.

Data Qualifiers: Fraction Modern Carbon and Radiocarbon Age were calculated as weighted averages of combined machine runs to reduce overall error. A small sample correction is applied to samples with a carbon mass less than 0.50 mg.

Report generated by: Richard Cruz Report Generation Date: 8/1/2017

Reviewer: Greg Hodgins Date: 8/1/2017

Lower Tshognam 1

Results

δ13C (± 0.1‰):	-26.4 ‰
Fraction of modern carbon:	0.9802 +- 0.0024
Uncalibrated ^{14}C Age:	161 +- 20 years BP
Calibration Program / Dataset:	OxCal 4.2 / IntCal13 atmospheric
Calendar Age Range (68%):	1674 calCE to 1942 calCE
Calendar Age Range (95%):	1666 calCE to present

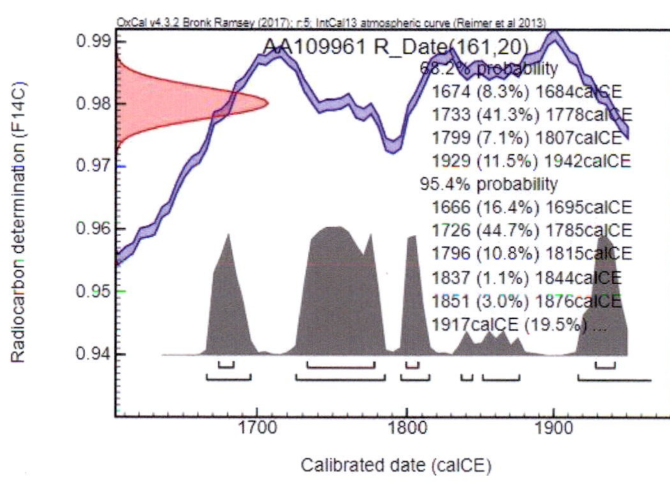

Lower Tshognam 15

Results

δ13C (± 0.1‰):	-27.3 ‰
Fraction of modern carbon:	0.9872 +- 0.0026
Uncalibrated ^{14}C Age:	103 +- 21 years BP
Calibration Program / Dataset:	OxCal 4.2 / IntCal13 atmospheric
Calendar Age Range (68%):	1695 calCE to 1917 calCE
Calendar Age Range (95%):	1689 calCE to 1926 calCE

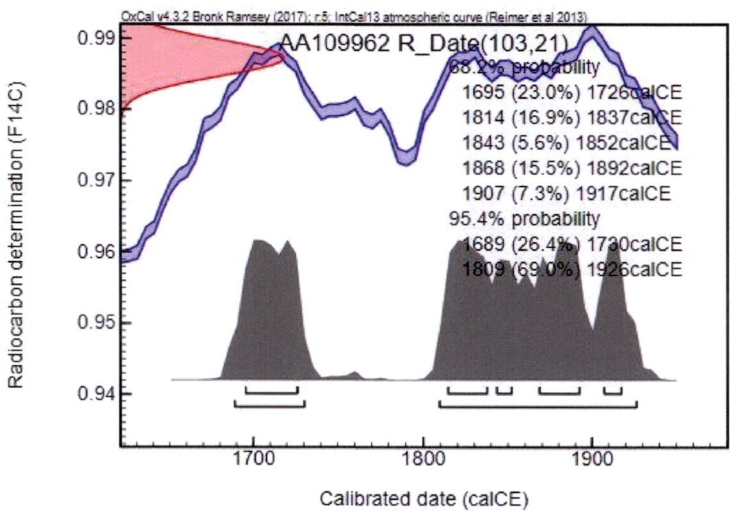

Geling 116

Results

δ13C (± 0.1‰):	-26.8 ‰
Fraction of modern carbon:	0.9900 +- 0.0025
Uncalibrated ^{14}C Age:	81 +- 20 years BP
Calibration Program / Dataset:	OxCal 4.2 / IntCal13 atmospheric
Calendar Age Range (68%):	1700 calCE to 1915 calCE
Calendar Age Range (95%):	1694 calCE to 1919 calCE

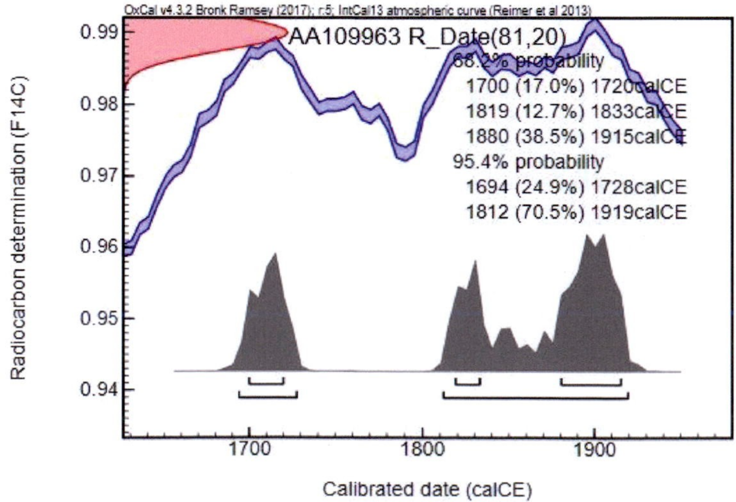

Lubrak Tib. 1

Results

δ13C (± 0.1‰):	-25.8 ‰
Fraction of modern carbon:	0.9777 +- 0.0024
Uncalibrated ^{14}C Age:	181 +- 20 years BP
Calibration Program / Dataset:	OxCal 4.2 / IntCal13 atmospheric
Calendar Age Range (68%):	1668 calCE to 1950 calCE
Calendar Age Range (95%):	1663 calCE to present

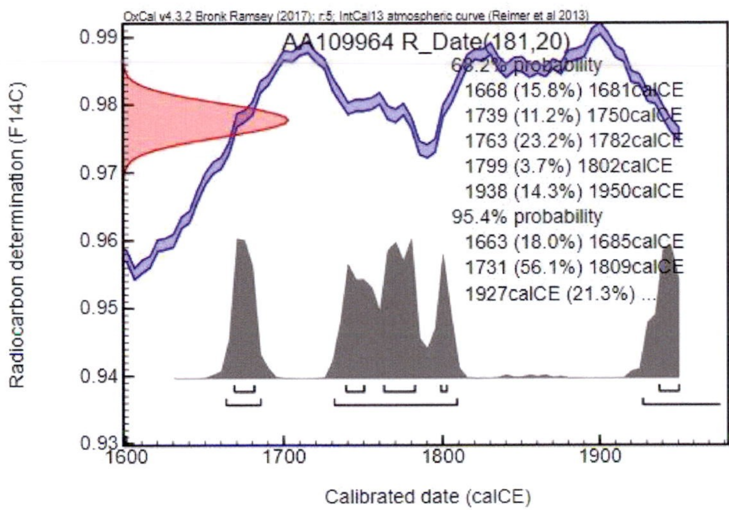

Lubrak Tib. 6

Results

δ13C (± 0.1‰):	-26.7 ‰
Fraction of modern carbon:	0.9805 +- 0.0024
Uncalibrated ^{14}C Age:	158 +- 20 years BP
Calibration Program / Dataset:	OxCal 4.2 / IntCal13 atmospheric
Calendar Age Range (68%):	1675 calCE to 1942 calCE
Calendar Age Range (95%):	1666 calCE to present

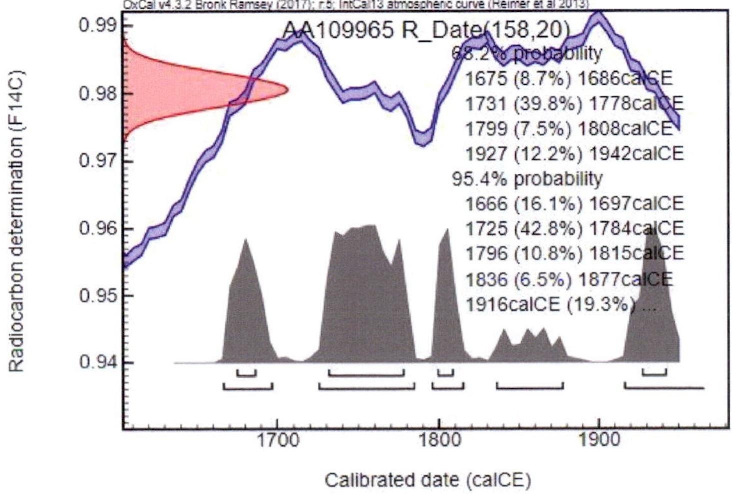

Index